Wall Art

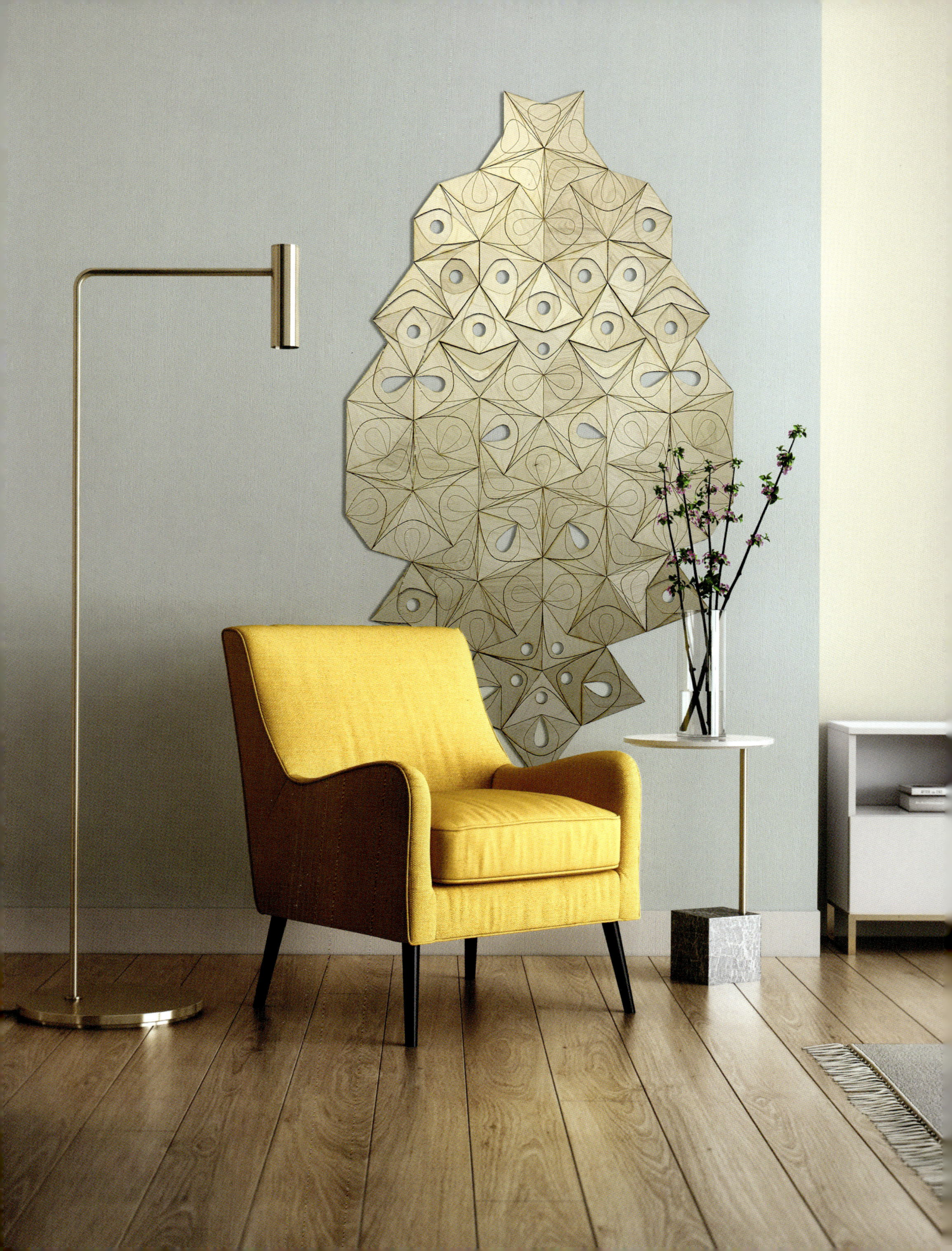

Wall Art

14 STUNNING FEATURE WALL PROJECTS TO TRANSFORM YOUR HOME

PATRICIA MOFFETT
& CLARE BAGGALEY

SCHIFFER PUBLISHING
4880 Lower Valley Road • Atglen, PA 19310

Authored by: Patricia Moffett and Clare Baggaley

Library of Congress Control Number: 2020952429

Produced by BlueRed Press Ltd., 2021
Designed by Clare Baggaley, *www.clarebaggaley.graphics* and Patricia Moffett, *www.patriciamoffett.com*

Type set in Larosa and Capital Gothic

ISBN: 978-0-7643-6210-1
Printed in India

Published by Schiffer Publishing, Ltd.
4880 Lower Valley Road
Atglen, PA 19310
Phone: (610) 593-1777; fax: (610) 593-2002
Email: Info@schifferbooks.com
Web: www.schifferbooks.com

For our complete selection of fine books on this and related subjects, please visit our website at *www.schifferbooks.com*. You may also write for a free catalog.

Schiffer Publishing's titles are available at special discounts for bulk purchase for sales promotions or premiums. Special editions, including personalized covers, corporate imprints, and excerpts, can be created in large quantities for special needs. For more information, contact the publisher.

We are always looking for people to write books on new and related subjects. If you have an idea for a book, please contact us at *proposals@schifferbooks.com*.

Cover picture credits: *Front cover, top left,* Adobe Stock Library; *top right,* Patricia Moffett; *bottom pictures,* Design Cuts. *Back cover, top,* Adobe Stock Library; *bottom,* Alex Mockups.

CONTENTS

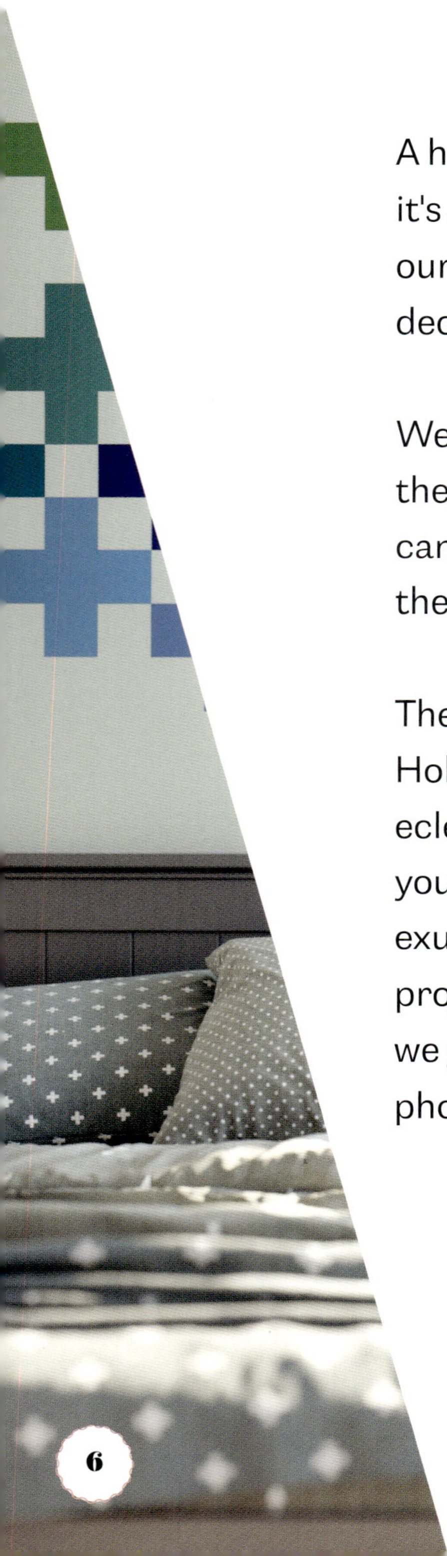

INTRODUCTION

A home isn't just a roof over your head, or a commodity, it's a reflection of the people who live in it. We all express our personality through the objects, style details, and decorations that dress our rooms.

We have designed fourteen projects for you to create—they also have lots of variations and extra-fun ideas. You can either follow the steps exactly, or go off-piste and use the methods as a guide for your own visions.

There are projects to suit lots of room styles, from Hollywood glamour, through midcentury cool, to BoHo eclectic. Let the wit of Grand Stag Trophy delight your visitors or entertain them with the sheer fun and exuberance of our interactive Marble Run. All of the projects are suitable for a range of skill levels, since we guide beginners with comprehensive step-by-step photographs and descriptions.

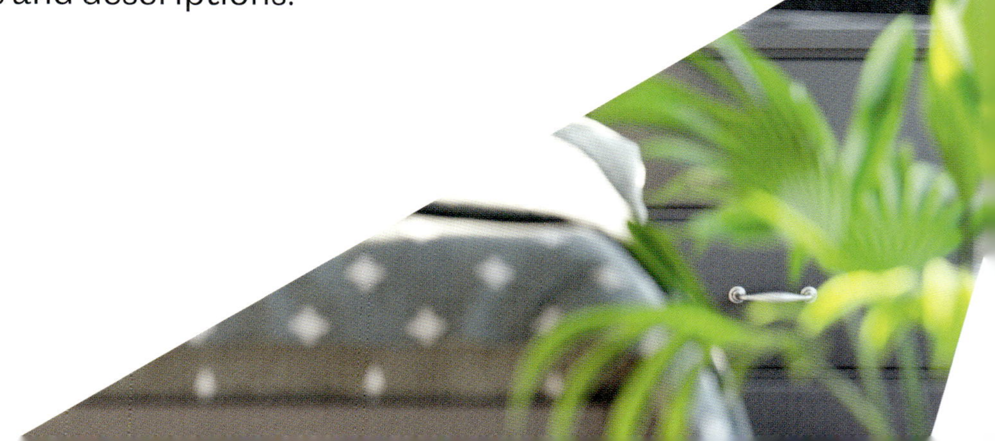

Where will you start first? Do you have a piece of furniture, or a cushion, that you love and want to use as a key piece to unite the room? Or is it more of a feeling you'd like to conjure—contemplative and restful, invigorating, playful, or light and airy? There's advice on how to use color to achieve this in your space.

Quite a few of the projects use recycled materials: Do you have lots of cardboard boxes? Try the stag on page 20. About to throw away plastic soda pop bottles? Turn to page 70 and cast flowers from them (yes, really!). Have your little ones grown big? Have some old clothes? Go to page 44 and tear material into strips and create some string art.

Use your imagination to get creative!

We hope you enjoy transforming your walls as much as we have!

Patricia and Clare

TOOLS & EQUIPMENT

Every project has its own tailored list of tools at the beginning, but there are some general pieces of equipment needed for many of the projects. If you don't have a particular tool, and you'll use it only once, then why not rent or borrow it?

IMPORTANT NOTE

Be extremely careful with the following products and keep out of reach of children. Craft and heavy-duty knives, glue gun and sticks, paints, and solvents. Wear eye protection when needed.

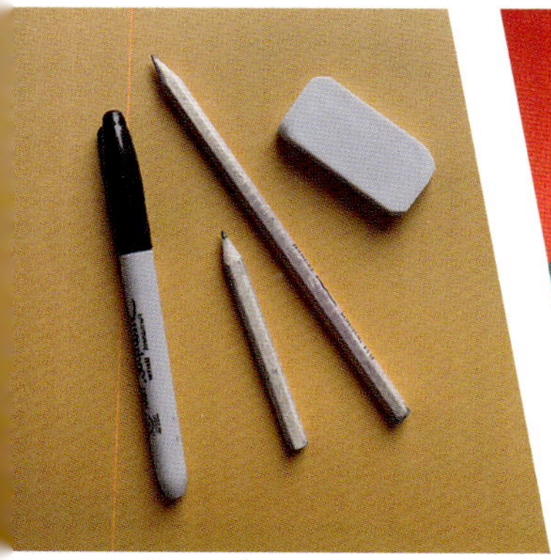

Pencil, eraser, and marker pen

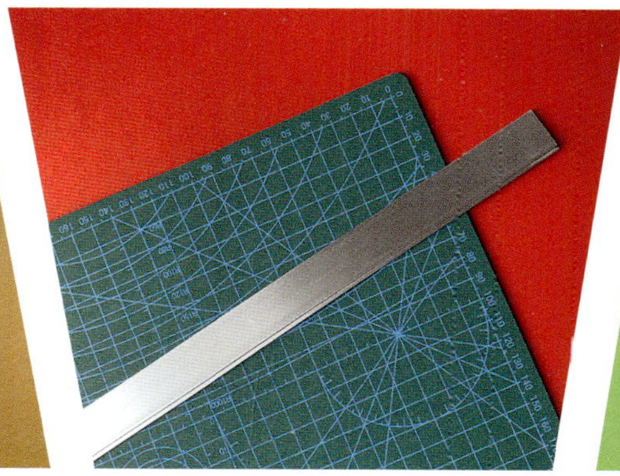

Cutting mat and metal ruler

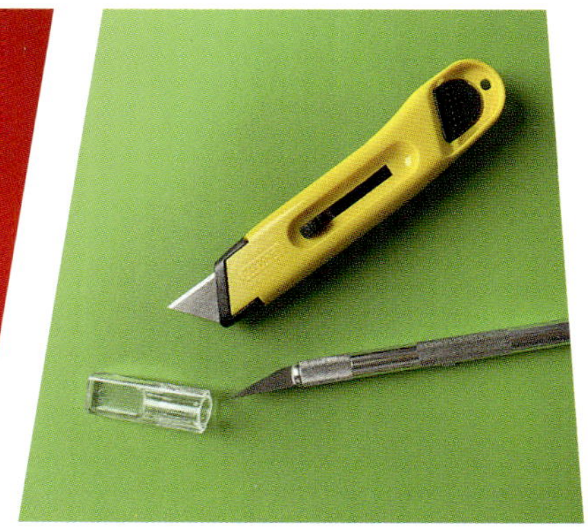

Heavy-duty and craft knife

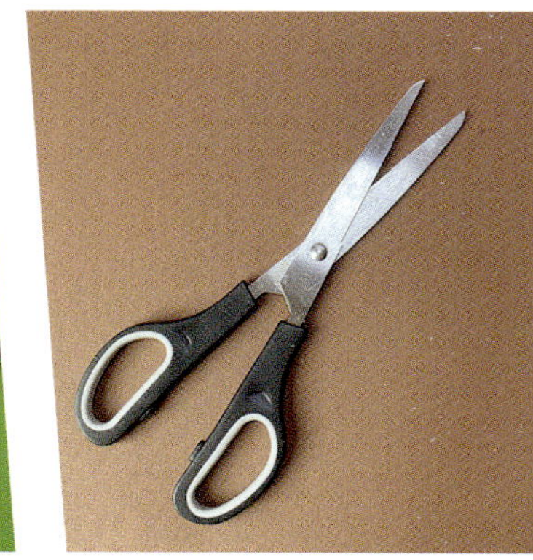

Scissors

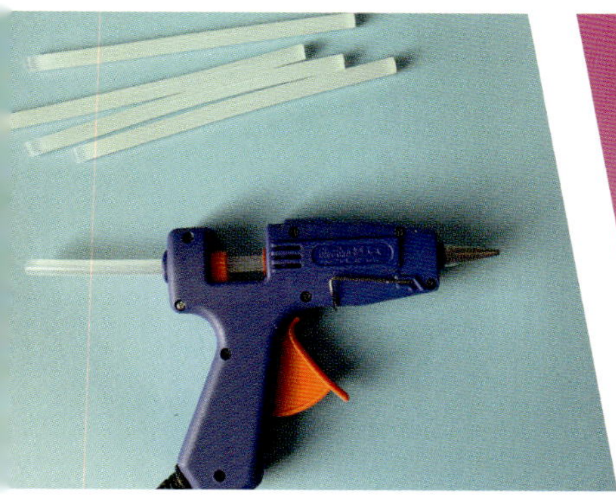

Glue gun and glue sticks

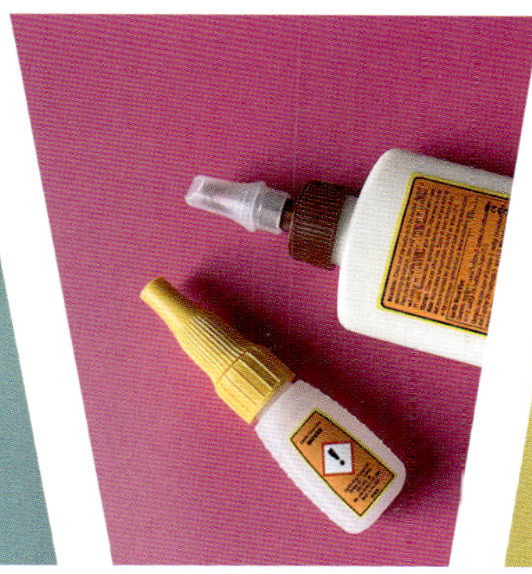

Glues

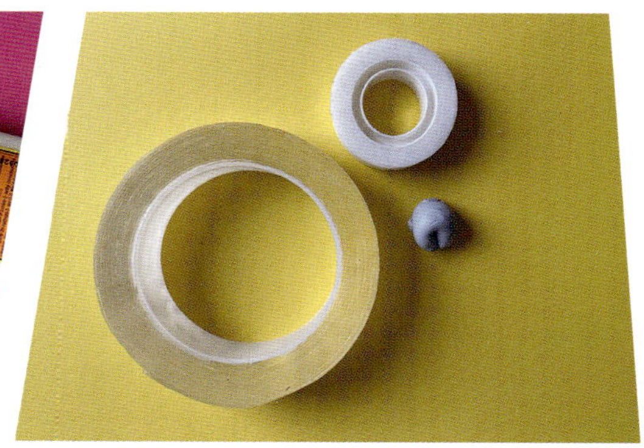

Tapes and reusable adhesive putty

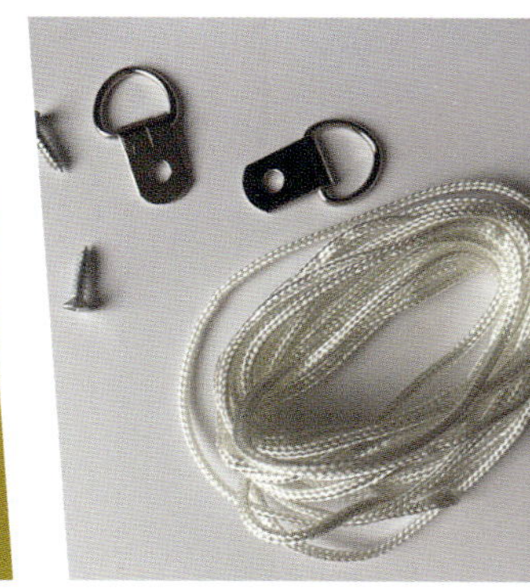

Fixings

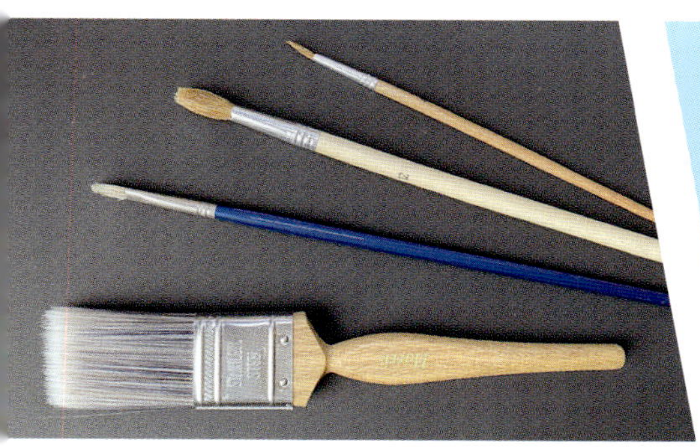

Paintbrushes

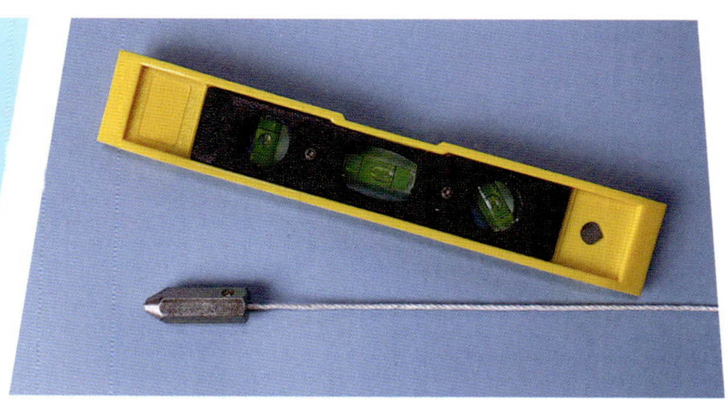

Spirit level and plumb line

UNDERSTANDING COLORS

The projects in this book give you flexibility to choose colors and color schemes that suit your taste and the location where you'll be creating your wall art. So it is particularly useful for you to understand a little bit about how colors actually work.

THE COLOR WHEEL

The color wheel is based on three main colors, plus the other colors that are created from them when they are mixed together.

PRIMARY COLORS There are three primary colors—yellow, red, and blue.

SECONDARY COLORS Mixing two primary colors together makes secondary colors—orange, purple, and green.

TERTIARY COLORS Mixing a primary and secondary color together makes tertiary colors—pinks, jades, and orange-yellows.

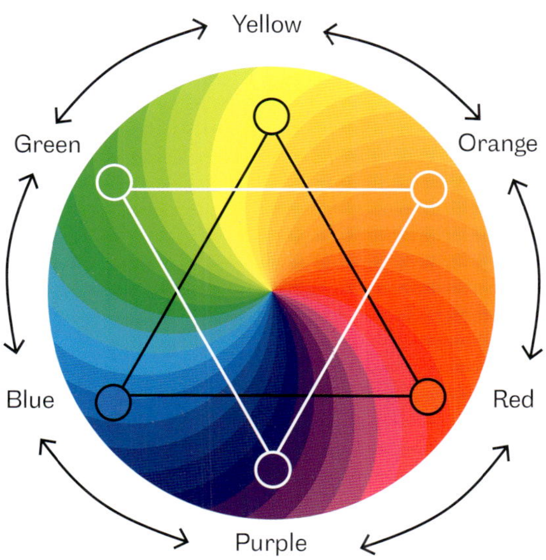

Yellow, red, and blue are primary colors (black triangle). If you mix two primary colors, you get secondary colors (white triangle). For example, yellow and red mix to form orange.

MIXING COLORS AND TONES

Using the color wheel can help you come up with some interesting color combinations.

Do you want a zingy bright scheme? Try using complementary colors. These are chosen from opposite sides of the color wheel—complementary colors!

If you mix black and white into any color on the wheel, you can make tonal changes to the hues.

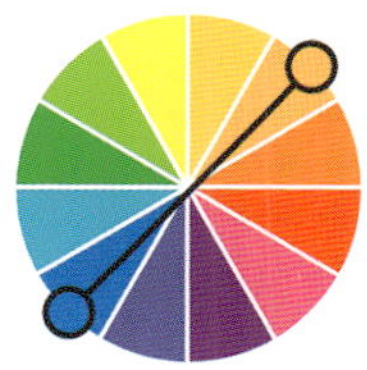

Orange and blue are opposite sides of the wheel

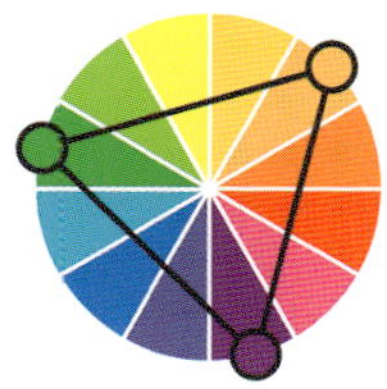

Orange, blue, and purple are at three equal points on the wheel

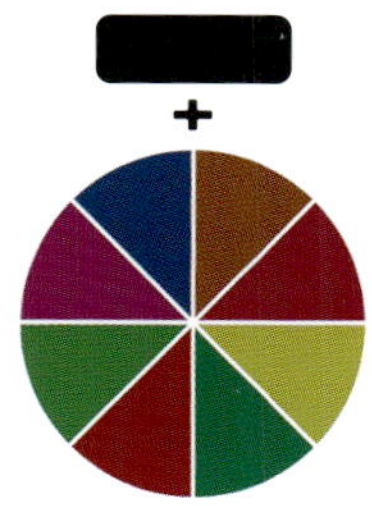

Mixing black makes the color darker and muted

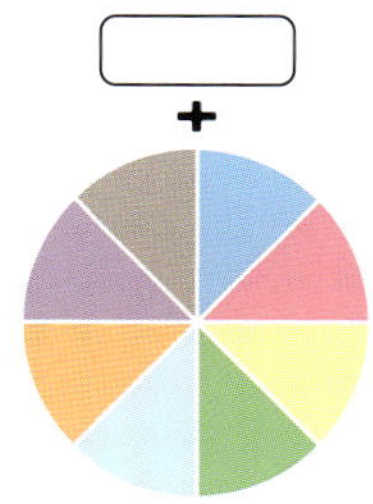

Mixing white makes the color lighter and paler

Every color has a range of tones depending on how much white or black you add in.

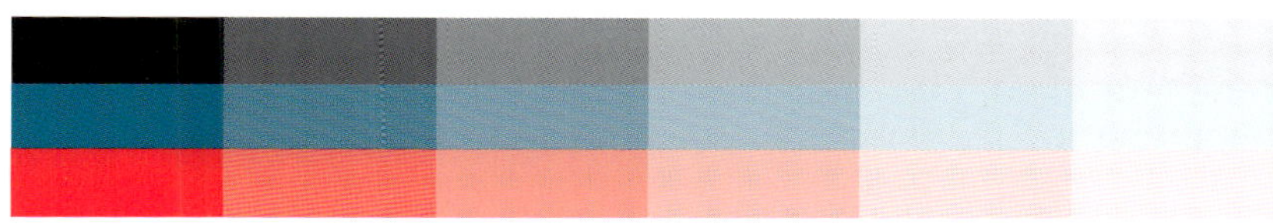

COLOR MEANING

Colors can change the way we feel, especially in our homes. They can make us feel calm, invigorated, or creative—so choosing the right scheme for your room can make a difference in how you feel living in that room.

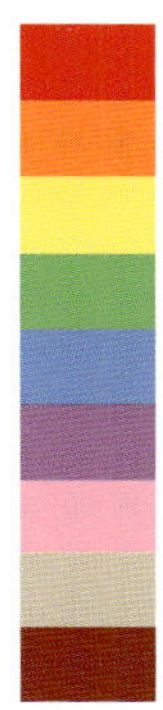

Red: love, passion, energy
Orange: vitality, happiness, optimism
Yellow: optimism, cheerful, intellect
Green: balance, nature, positivity
Blue: calm, peace, restfulness
Purple: creative, imaginative
Pink: love, caring, romance
Beige/ivory: quiet, simplicity, calm
Brown: earth, comfort, hearth

USING TEMPLATES

For some of the projects in the book we have given you templates to use. When choosing how to size your templates, take a look at the space you want to use and think about how large or small you want to reproduce your wall art.

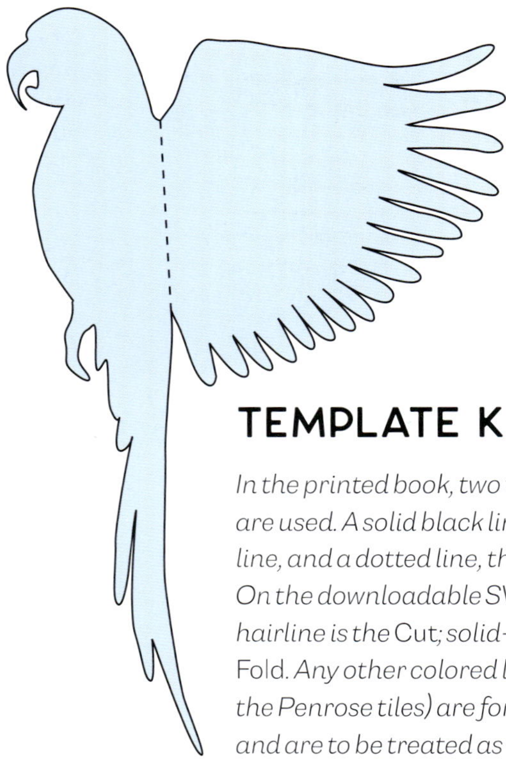

TEMPLATE KEY

In the printed book, two types of line are used. A solid black line is the Cut *line, and a dotted line, the* Fold. *On the downloadable SVG files, a black hairline is the* Cut*; solid-pink lines are* Fold. *Any other colored lines (such as in the Penrose tiles) are for laser cutting and are to be treated as engraved rather than cut.*

--------------- Fold lines

——————— Cut lines

Some templates also need glue points; these are indicated using a crosshatched area.

Glue points

SIZING THE TEMPLATES

You can size the templates to any dimension you like. We just give you the final size of the projects that we have made, but you are free to size the templates up or down to fit the space you want to fill. The equation for resizing is this: what you want in mm / what you have in mm x 100.

On Grand Stag Trophy (page 20) we tell you a size to enlarge the templates and the final size this will give you.

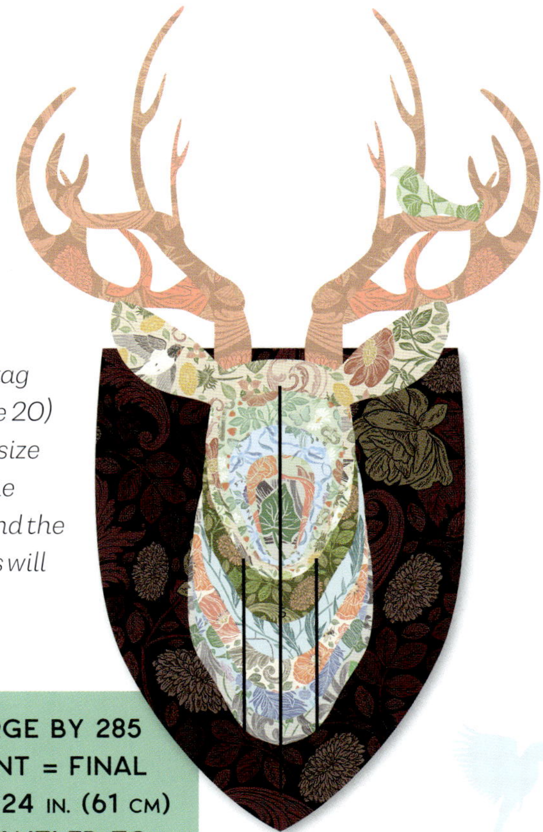

ENLARGE BY 285 PERCENT = FINAL SIZE OF 24 IN. (61 CM) FROM ANTLER TO BOTTOM OF SHIELD, AND 14.5 IN. (37 CM) FROM WALL TO NOSE

USE SIZE

To make more variety in your art (for projects such as The Flying Parrots on page 14), you can flip the templates and size them differently. For the parrots this will give you some depth since the smaller parrots will appear to be farther away from you. It's a simple visual trick.

FOLDING AND SCORING

Often, making a tiny nick at either end of the fold line will facilitate a crisp fold without scoring. If you are downloading files to use on your electronic cutter, set the pink lines to "score."

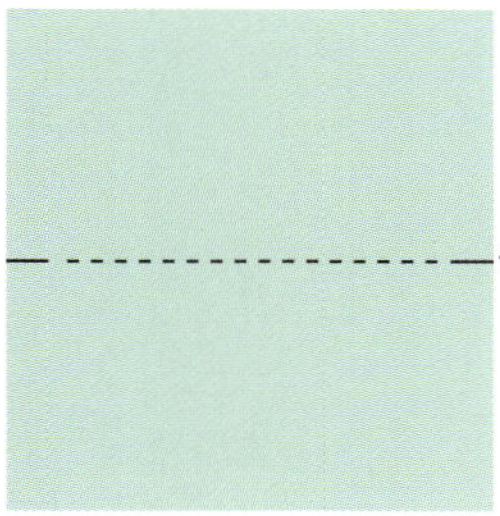

Tiny nick on either side

Fold and crease gently with your thumb

If the nick on either side doesn't give you a clean fold, use the blunt side of a pair of scissors and a metal ruler, and score gently along the line.

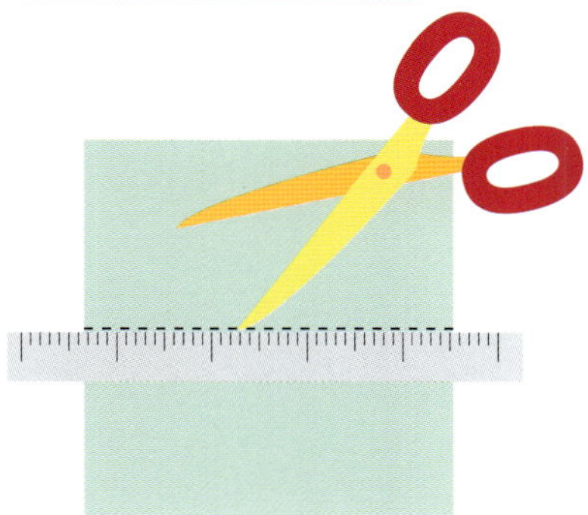

TRACING FROM TEMPLATES

It's possible to buy transfer paper (graphite paper) in very large sheets. It's available in both dark and light versions, depending on the color of the material you'll be tracing onto. It's a wise purchase for large-scale projects such as the Ghost Sign (page 106). For smaller projects, it's possible to make your own quite easily: sharpen a graphite stick over some tracing paper. Use a tissue to rub the sharpenings well into the tracing paper before using.

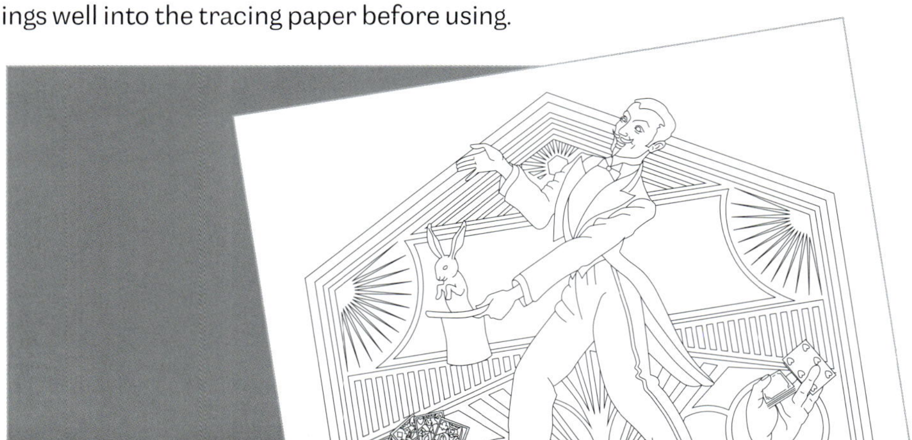

HOW TO PRINT WHEN ENLARGING MASSIVELY

Many home printers have the ability to print tiles of a file that can be stuck together to make a large image. Sometimes this is called "poster format."

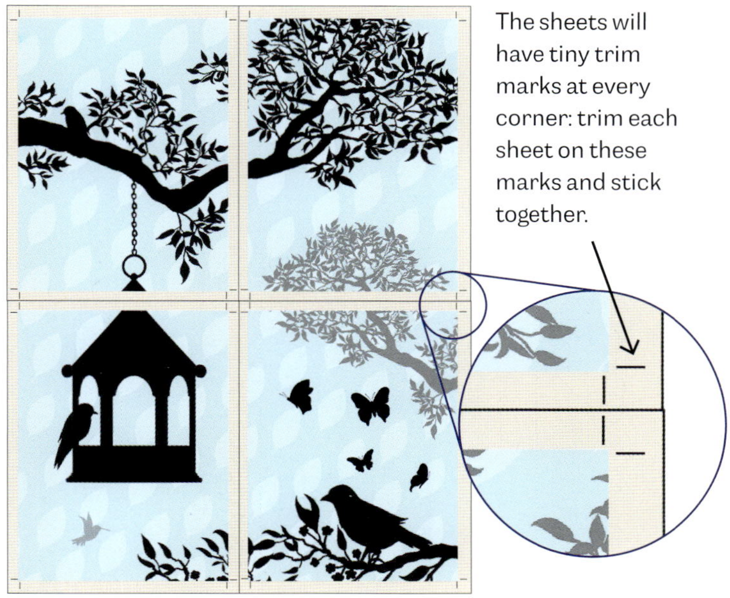

The sheets will have tiny trim marks at every corner: trim each sheet on these marks and stick together.

If your printer doesn't support that, then software such as Microsoft Picture Window can be used. Place your template into a document at the finished size and use the software to generate tiles of the image to print. If this doesn't work, it's possible to draw your image in position, using a squared grid (as in the illustration).

HOW TO ACCESS THE DIGITAL FILES

Find and download the templates here:
https://www.schifferbooks.com/wallarttemplates

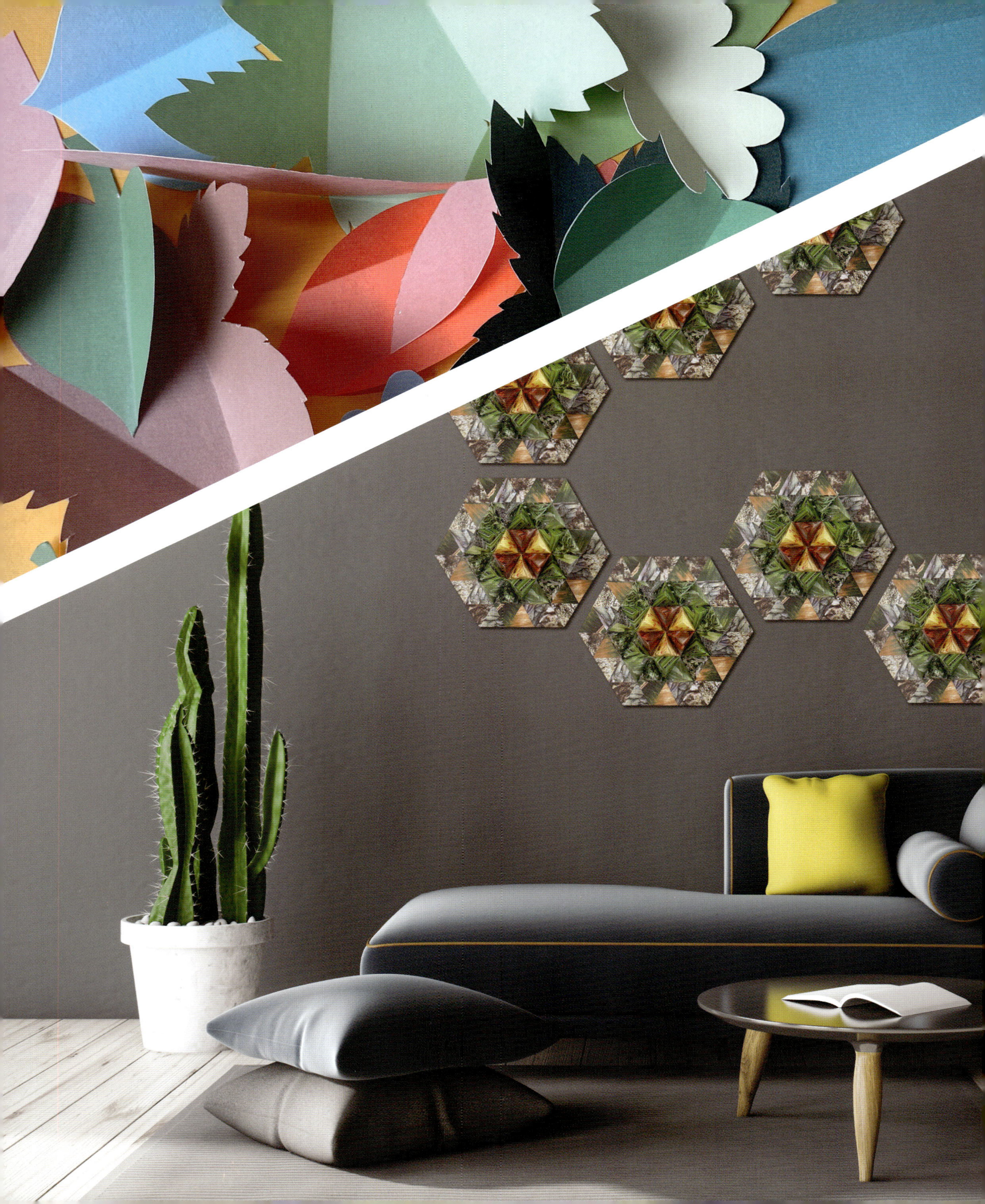

FOLD & CUT IT!

Paper and card are some of the most versatile and easy materials you can get hold of. The projects here can make use of the recycled papers and cardboard boxes that we all have strewn around our homes. Save your patterned wrapping paper, take off the sticky tape, iron, and store it flat. Collecting various recycled paper and card will give you unique and bespoke art pieces.

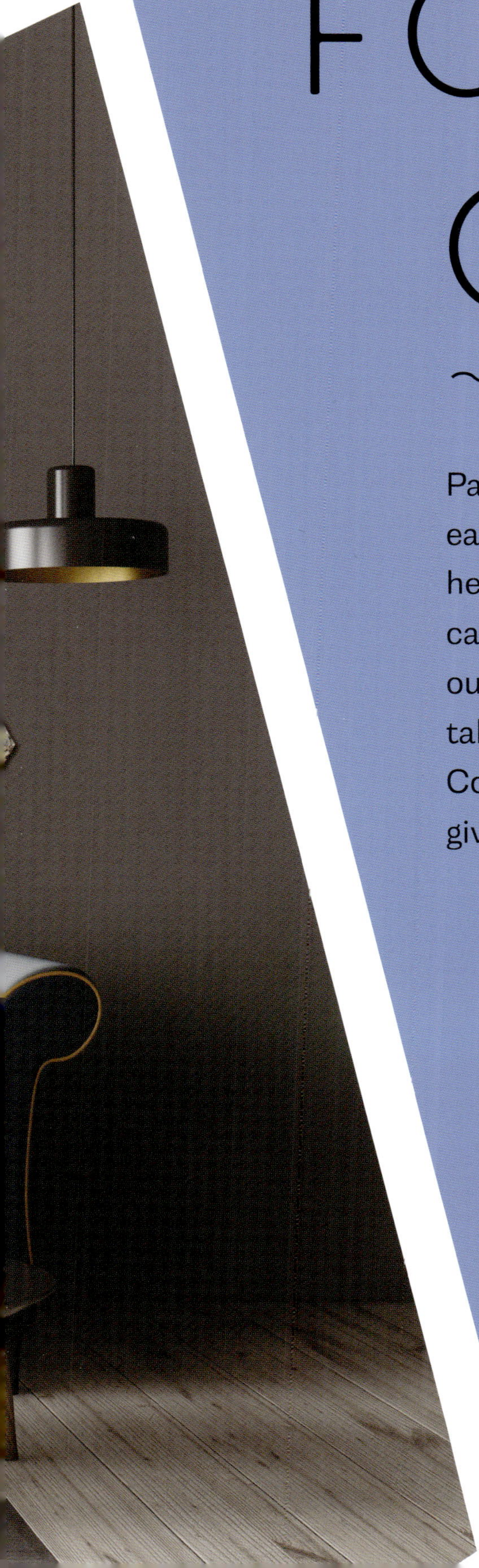

1

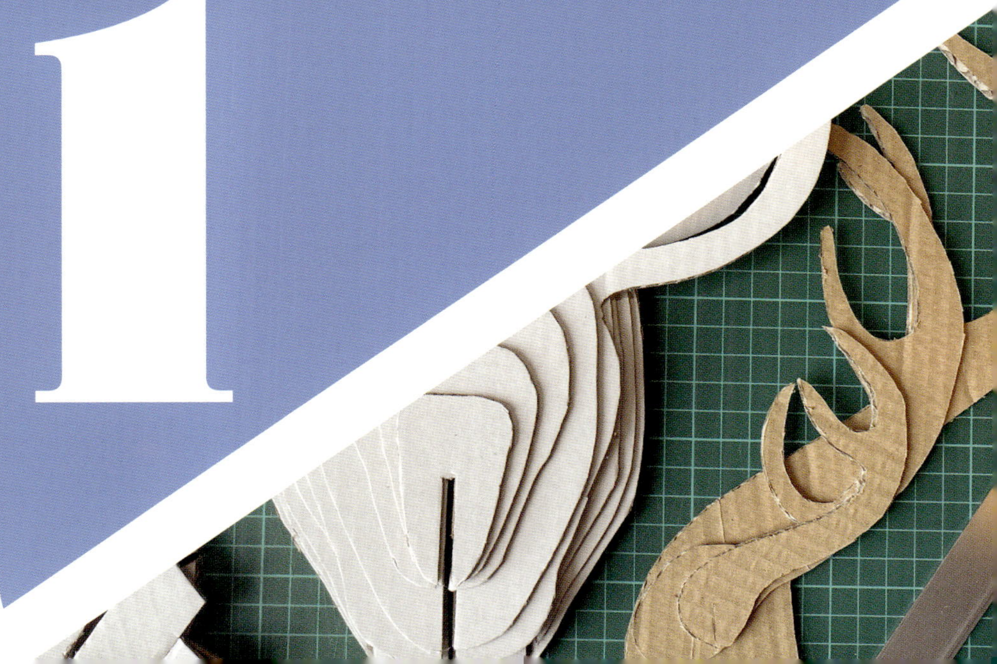

THE FLYING PARROTS

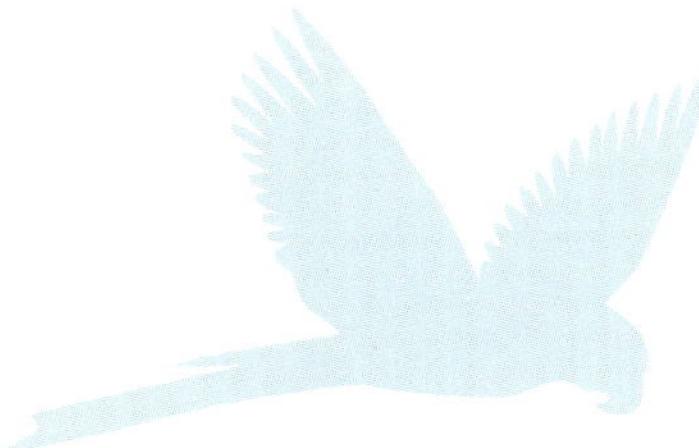

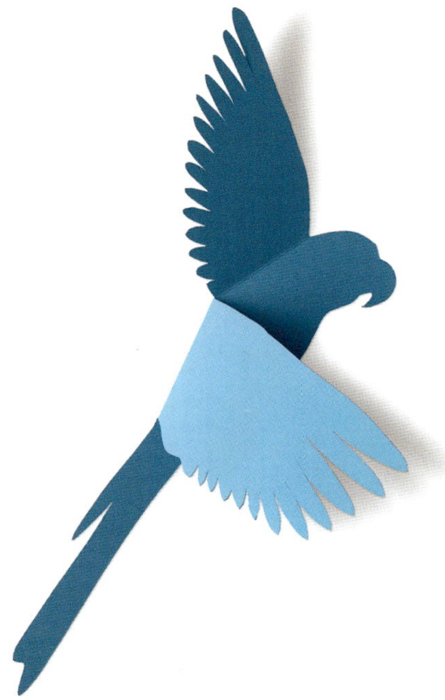

We have kept the first project simple: all you do is make a template, then cut and fold colored paper. It will refresh and liven up a blank wall, giving you maximum effect with minimum effort.

To get the best impact, use color cleverly, choosing either complementary colors or lightening the tone of the parrots to completely change how the art makes you feel. For this project we chose to take our strong-blue wall color and use a lighter blue that also matched the color of the blue chair.

Simple folded parrots make beautiful artworks. Additionally, their wings gently move in the breeze!

You might think about a whole new color scheme and paint the wall a punchy color that will show off your paper shapes. Choosing a very strong color and using it only on a feature wall will automatically draw the eye to that wall, as our blue on the right proves.

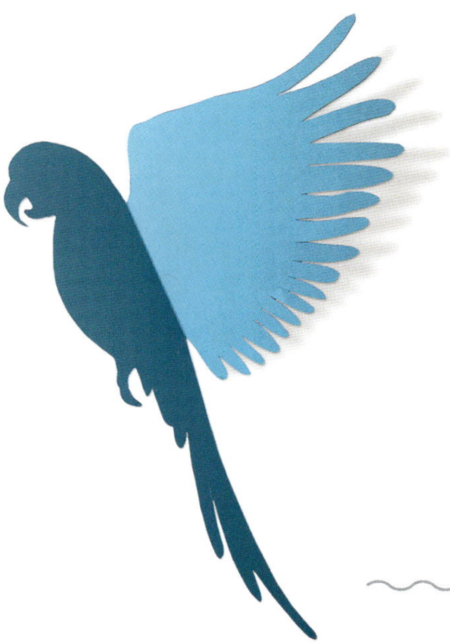

The brave use of strong, vibrant colors is a statement. The parrots give the room movement and life—and if you want to change your wall seasonally, it's an excellent opportunity to keep creative and refresh your wall.

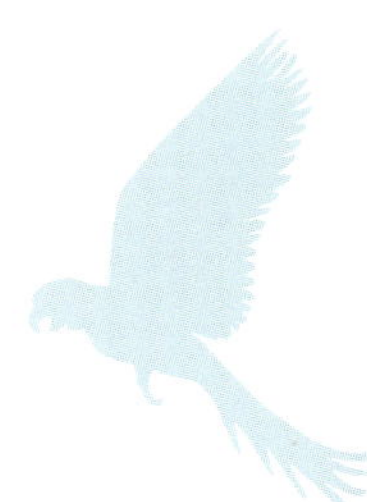

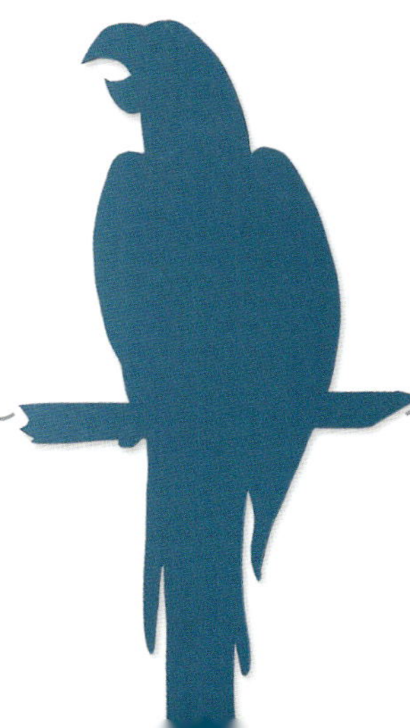

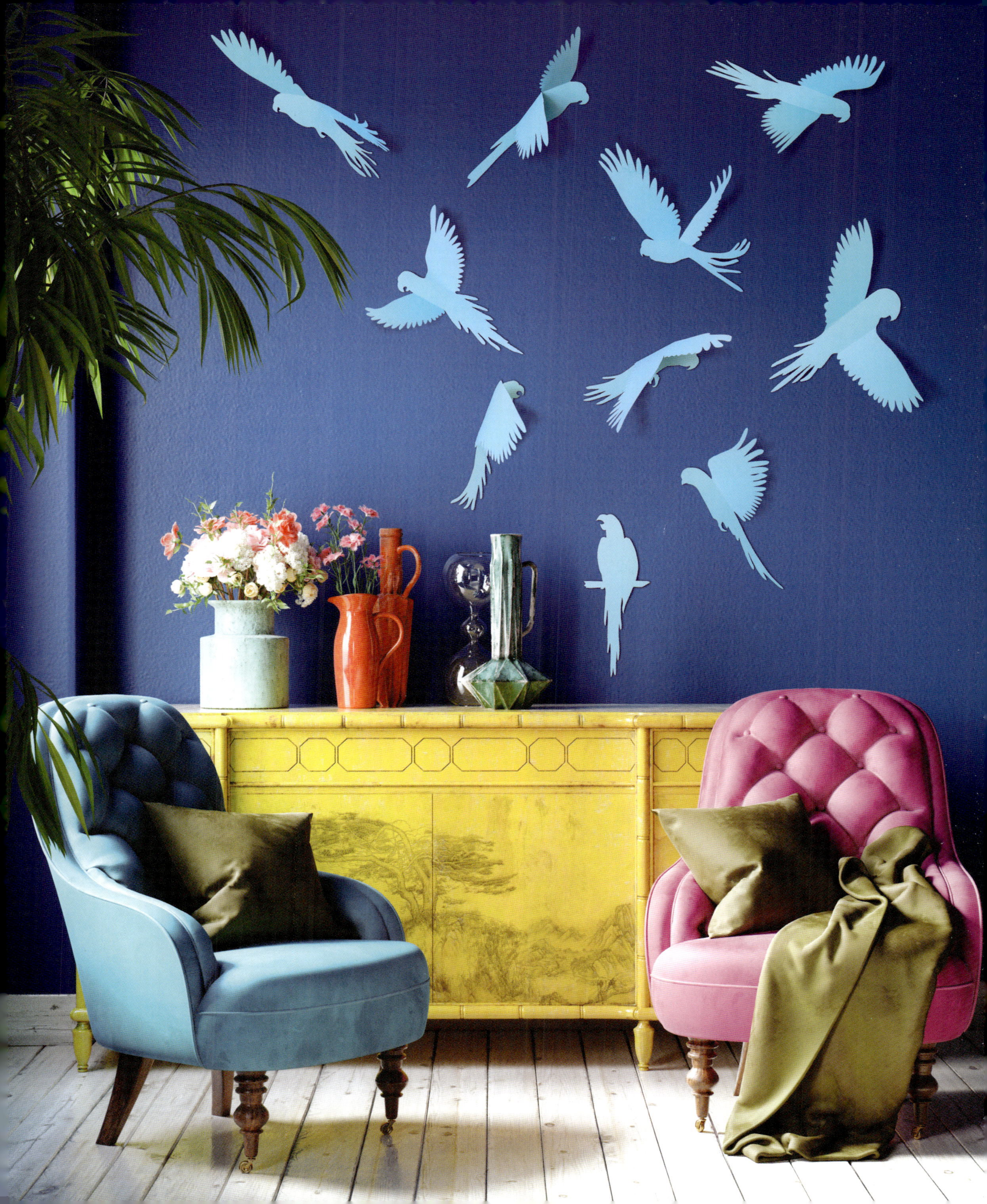

STEP-BY-STEP INSTRUCTIONS

YOU WILL NEED

- *10 x sheets of colored 185 gsm A3 (11.75 x 16.5 in. / 29.7 x 42 cm) colored card*
- *Pencil and ruler*
- *Reusable adhesive putty or grip tape for fixing*
- *Scissors*

STEP 1

COLOR SCHEME

Once you have chosen a location for your parrots to live, take a look at the colors you could use. We used turquoise because it will stand out from the blue background, without being too dominant.

If you're stuck, have a look at page 9 about choosing colors and color combinations.

STEP 2

TEMPLATES

Use the templates on pages 17–18. There are ten, but you don't need to use all of them. It can be just as effective to use three or four and repeat them. Scan, size, and print out the templates as described on pages 10-11.

We increased them by 280 percent so the result was a parrot 11.5 in. (29 cm) tall.

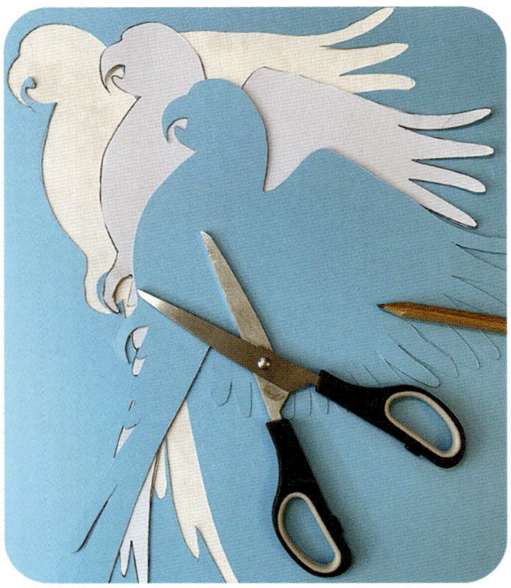

STEP 3

CUT

Cut out the parrot from the template, lightly tape it to your card, and draw around it. Then use scissors to cut out your bird.

Repeat for as many parrots as you need to make your wall art. We used all ten parrots for our wall.

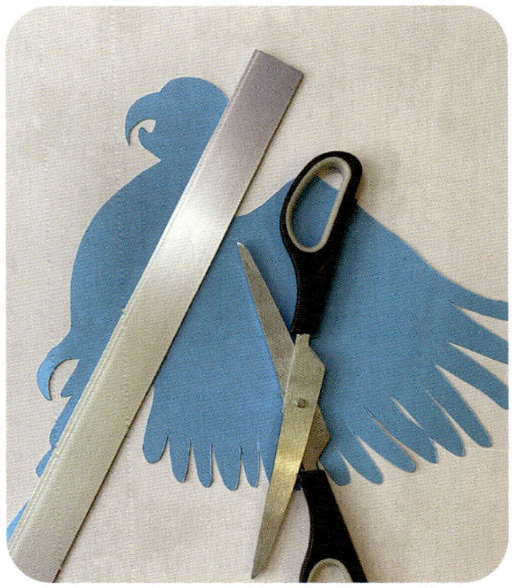

STEP 4

FOLD

Following the fold marks on the template, lightly score the fold line, using the scissors and a metal ruler. Fold carefully.

TIP

If you find scissors hard to get around the intricate edges, try a craft knife and cutting mat, or what about decoupage scissors for an interesting edge?

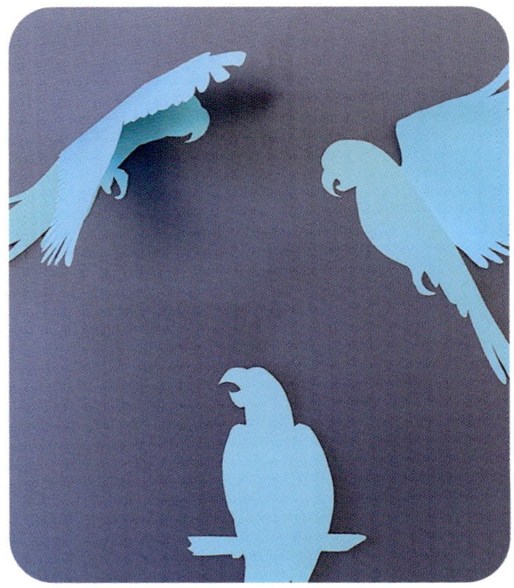

STEP 5

MOUNT

Position and arrange your parrots with low-tack tape until you are happy with your composition. If you want to keep your art for a lengthy period of time, fix them to your wall with grip tape. If you think you might want to change them around, or create new art in a few months, then low-tack tape will hold them for a reasonable amount of time. But beware: low-tack can still leave a mark on your wall.

TEMPLATES

Use as many shapes as you like: you could create your wall art with three, four, or more parrots.

For our wall space we printed our templates at 280 percent. See page 10 on how to size these templates up.

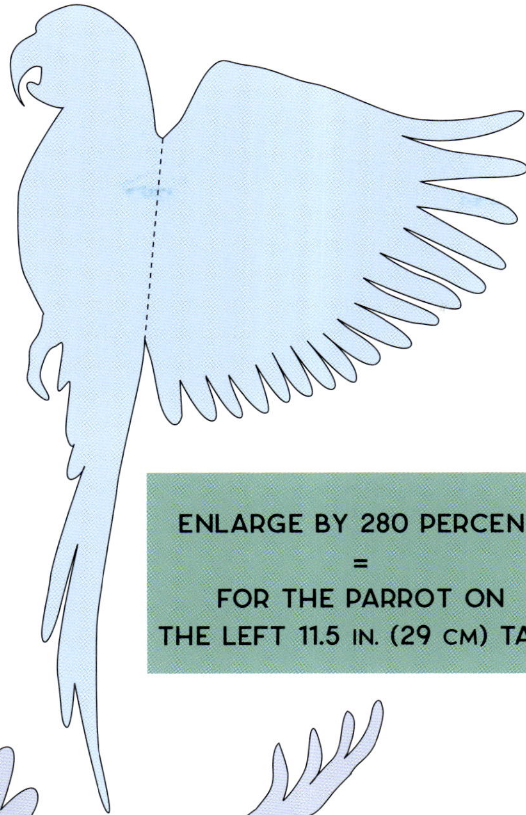

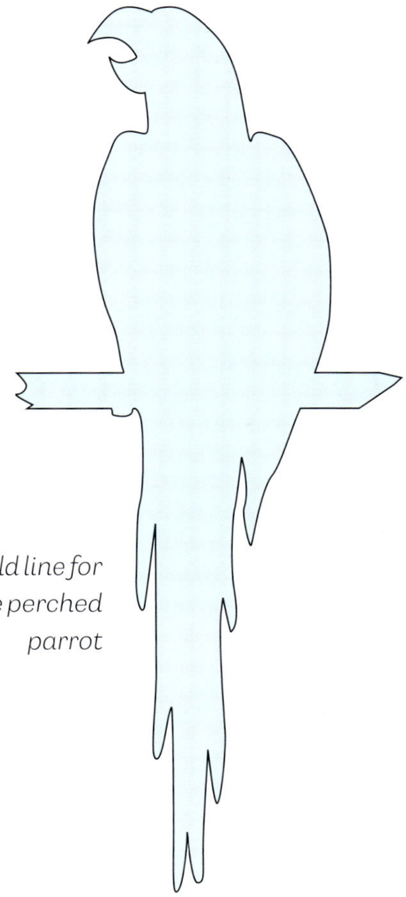

ENLARGE BY 280 PERCENT
=
FOR THE PARROT ON THE LEFT 11.5 IN. (29 CM) TALL

No fold line for the perched parrot

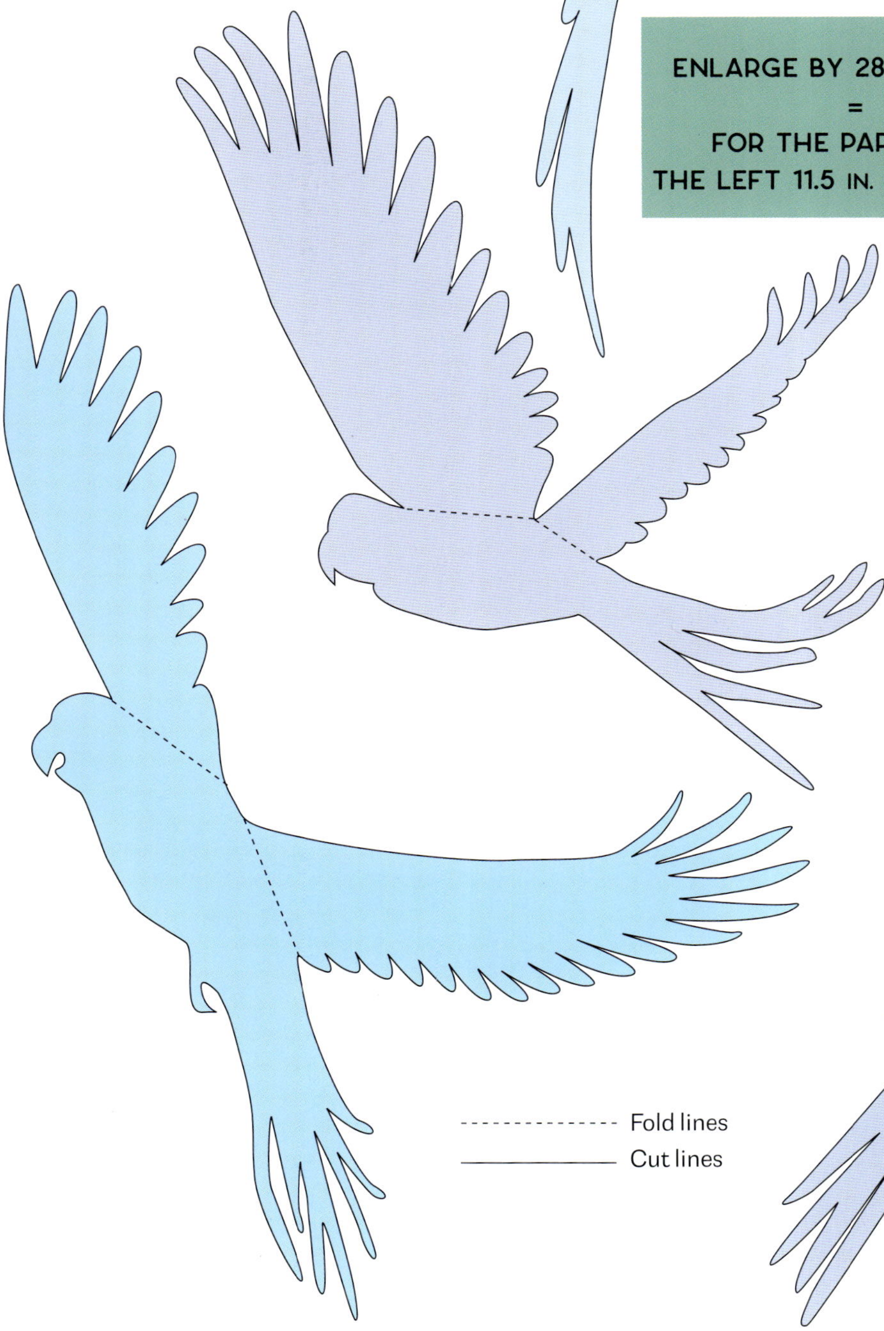

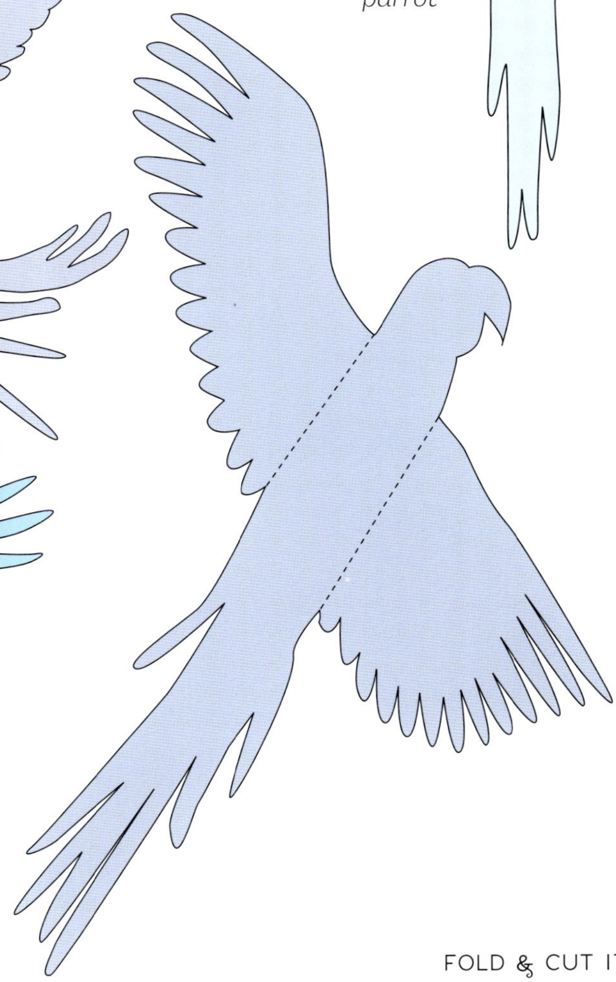

- - - - - - - Fold lines

——— Cut lines

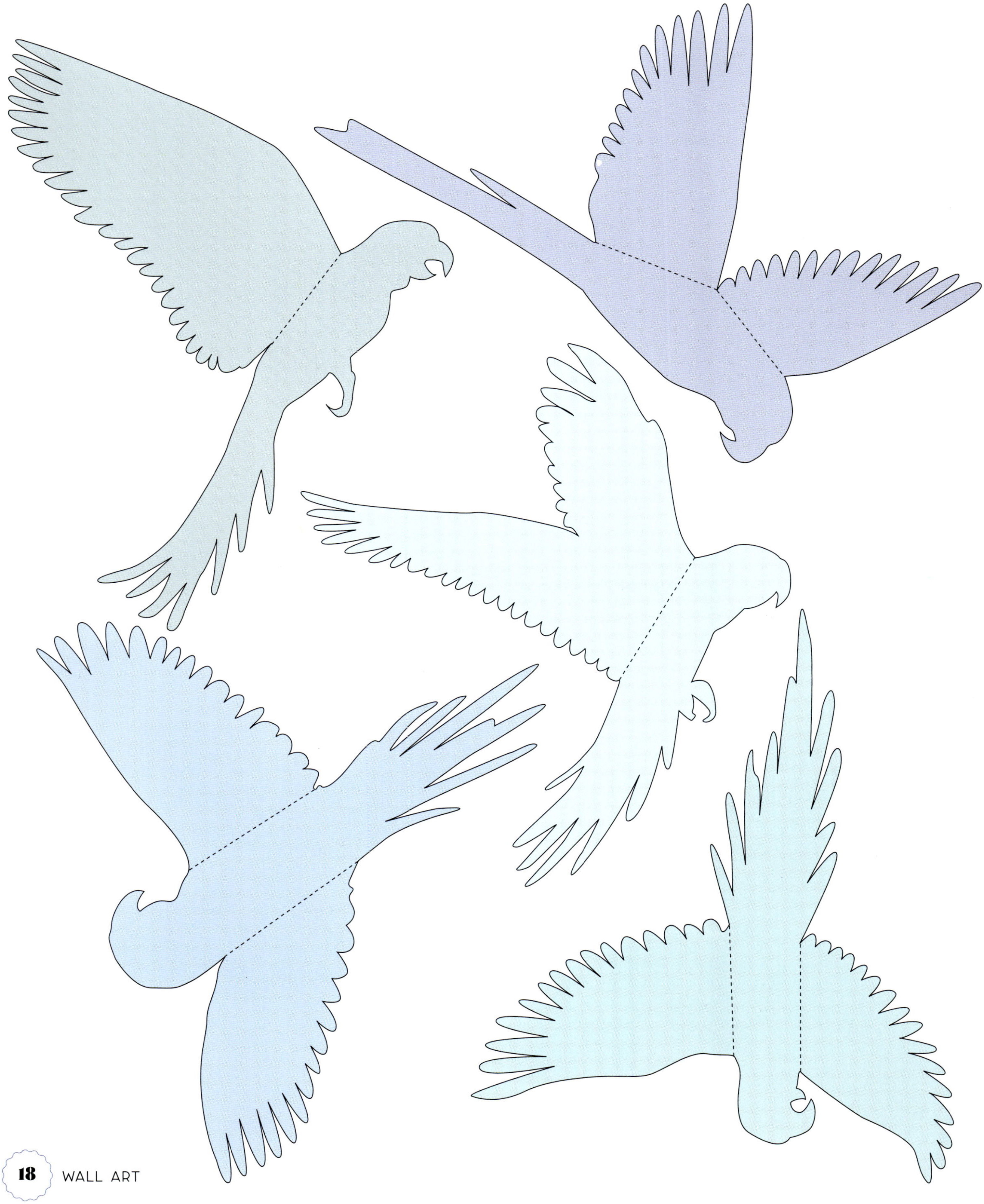

VARIATIONS

What about creating a fall-themed room? Cut and fold at the edges of the leaves to make them 3-D.

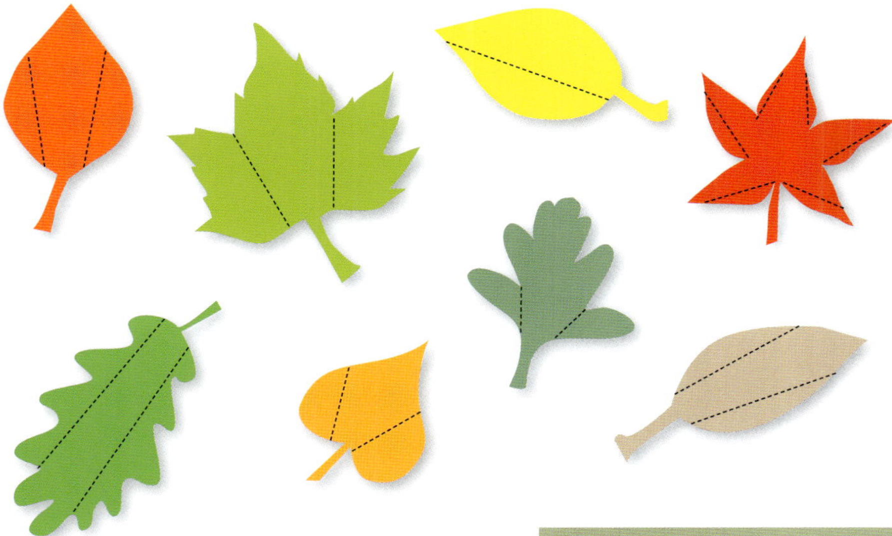

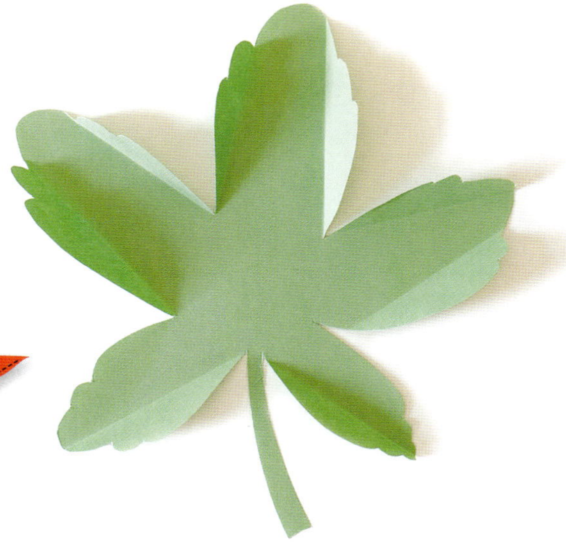

Below: *Using a variety of shapes, sizes, angles, and shades, we arranged these leaves as though a wind had blown and swirled them around.*

Below: *Go out in fall and collect differently shaped leaves. Bring them home, dry them, and use them as templates. Use lots of different-colored papers to make your final wall richer and more visually interesting.*

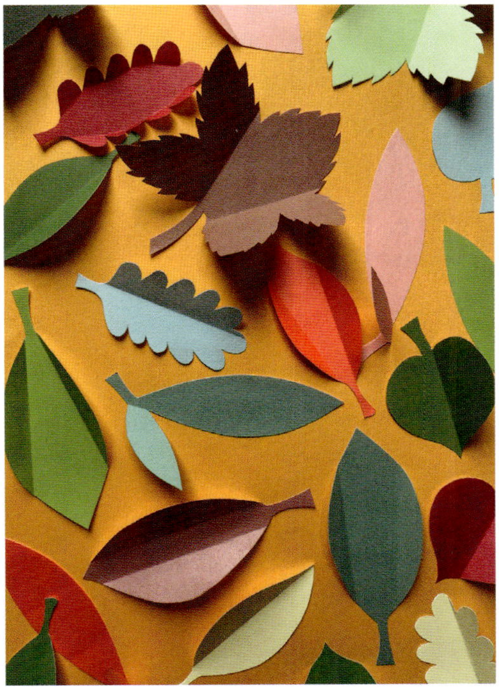

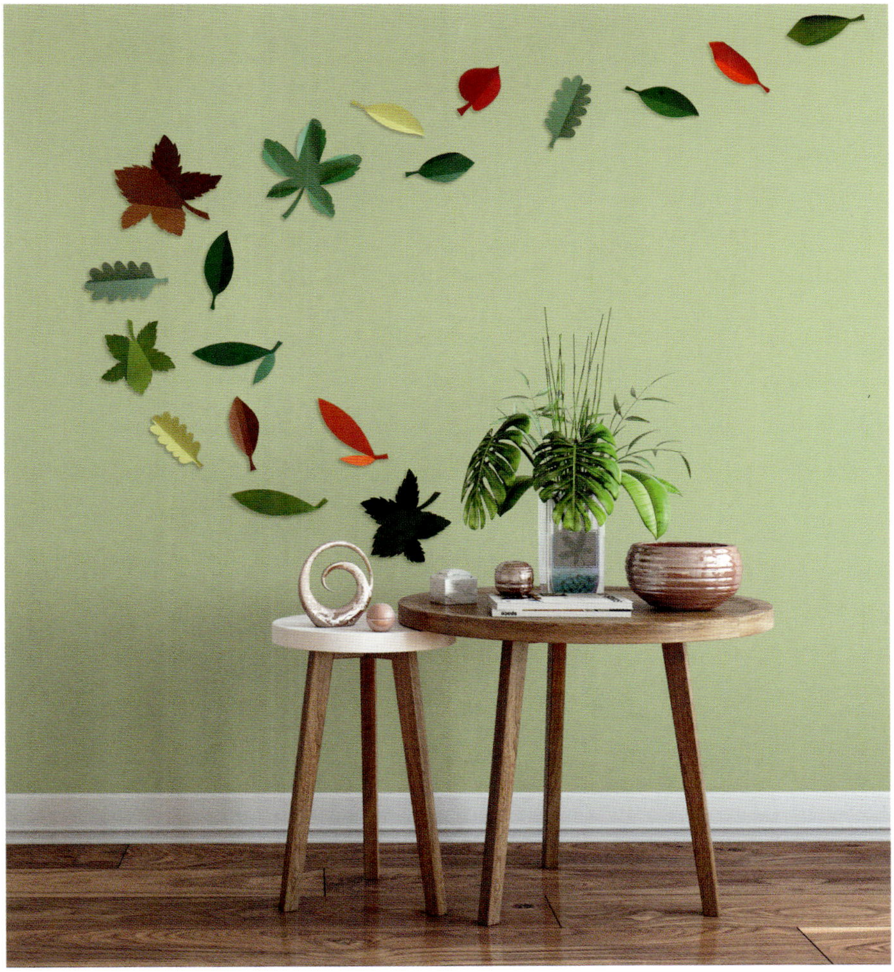

GRAND STAG TROPHY

In the past, taxidermy animal-head trophies lined the grand walls of big country houses on large estates. They were a way of showing off and symbolized power over the animal kingdom. These days, thank goodness, we have reversed the old status: now they celebrate the animal kingdom, and if you can use recycled cardboard boxes too, you can help save the planet.

Stags are magnificent creatures and have inspired artists since the Paleolithic-era cave paintings. They have been used in mythology, sculptures, and paintings ever since.

How about designing a whole family for your home? You can name them and put a little nameplate under each. First, follow the instructions for making the full-sized stag. To make a doe, size the templates a little smaller. Don't use the antlers, so ignore the antler slots. For the fawns, size the templates even smaller.

This would make a great art and craft project for family or friends. With younger children it may be wise to cut and assemble the stag, doe, and fawns yourself and then get each child to decorate their own trophy. Then they can name it either after themselves or create a new mythical family.

The templates can easily be sized up or down as required. Use firm cardboard, or for a substantial trophy make the pieces out of plywood (just adjust the slot widths) or create a tiny stag's head out of patterned thin card as a perfect handmade gift.

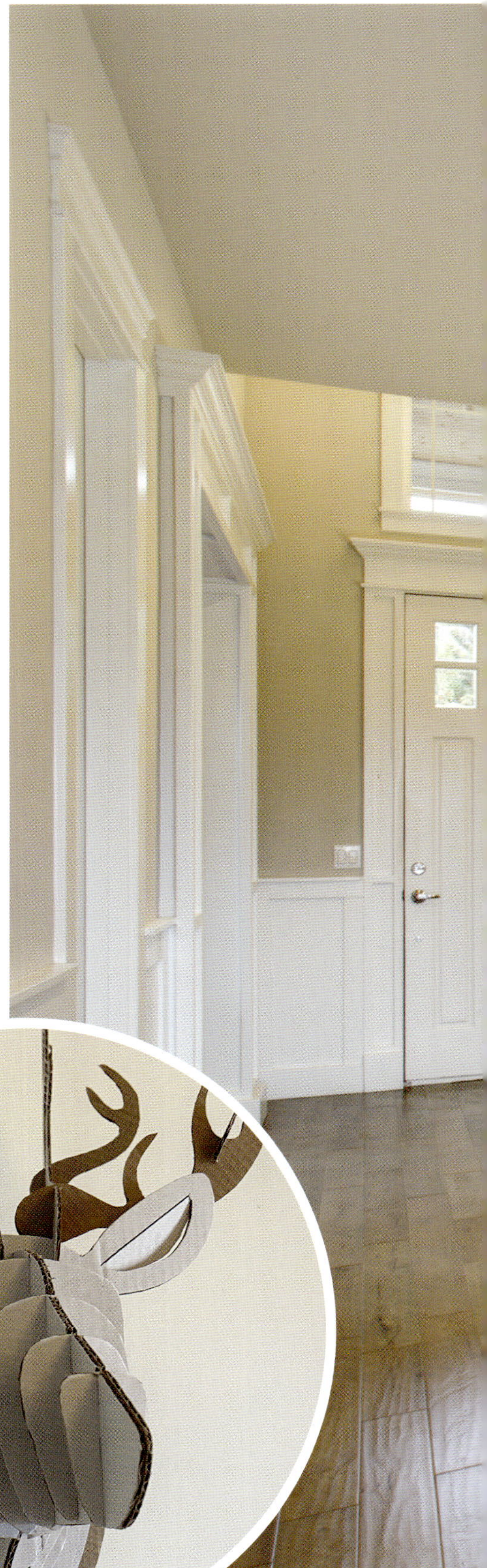

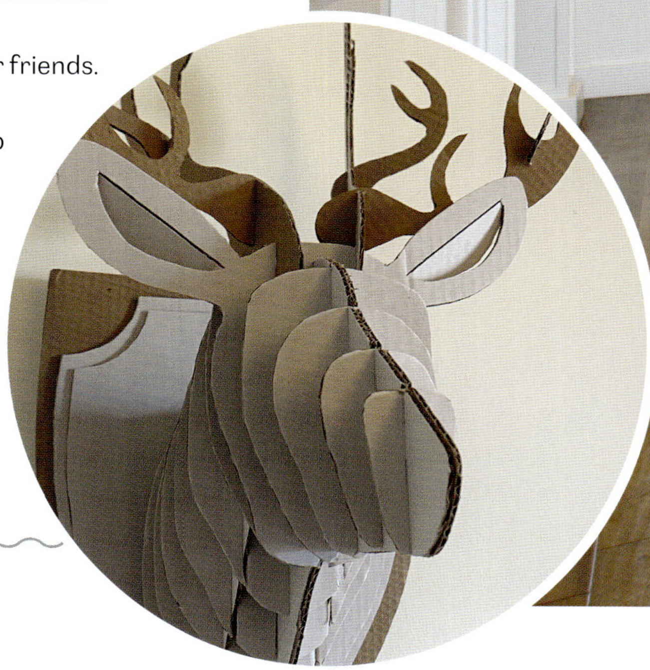

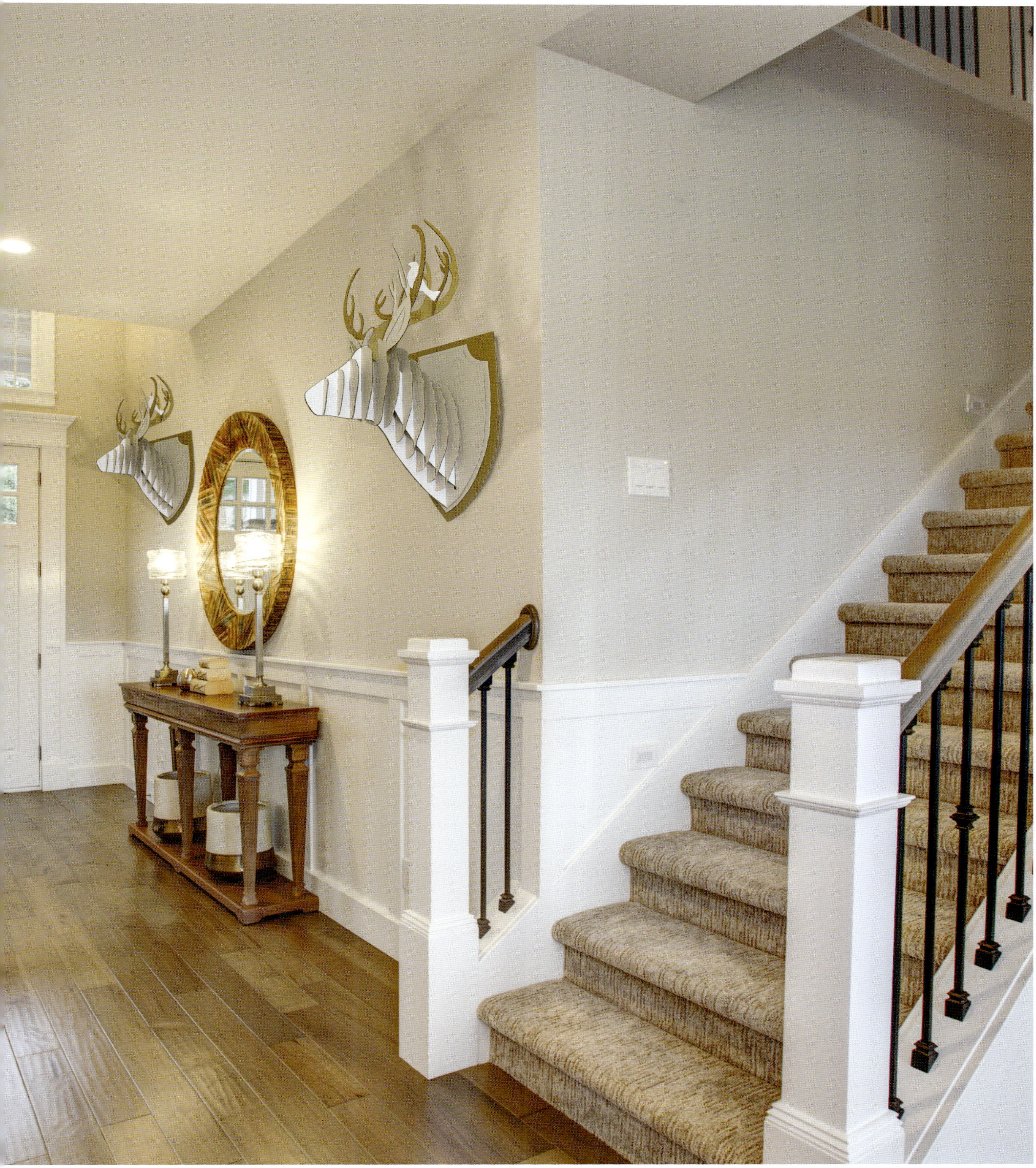

STEP-BY-STEP INSTRUCTIONS

YOU WILL NEED

- *Corrugated card—use recycled boxes if you can*

For cutting

- *Craft knife*
- *Cutting mat*
- *Metal ruler*

For sticking

- *Clear adhesive tape*
- *Strong paper glue*
- *Wall fixings*

STEP 1

CHOOSE THE BASE

For the stag we sourced corrugated card with one white side. This gives a great contrast to the sculpture, but you can use any card or foam board or even cut the shape out of plywood.

The larger you choose to make your stag, the stronger your base material needs to be.

STEP 2

PREPARE YOUR TEMPLATES

The stag we made measures 24 x 14.5 in. (61 x 37 cm). To get to this size, we enlarged the templates by 285 percent (see pages 10-11 on how to enlarge). Corrugated card has grooves inside it that run one way. Follow the brown arrows on the templates so that you make the stag structurally as strong as possible.

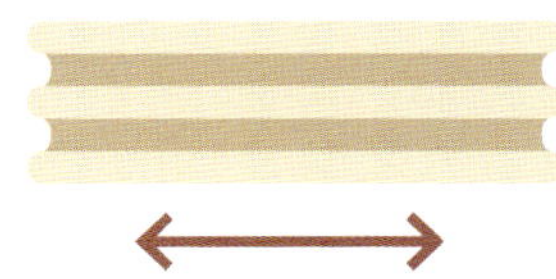

Direction of the corrugated grooves

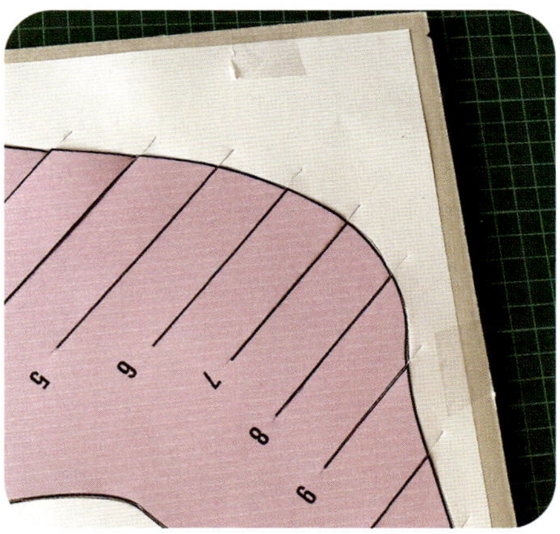

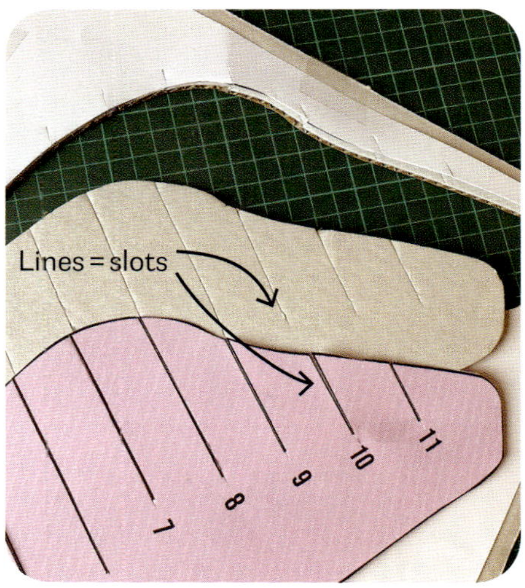

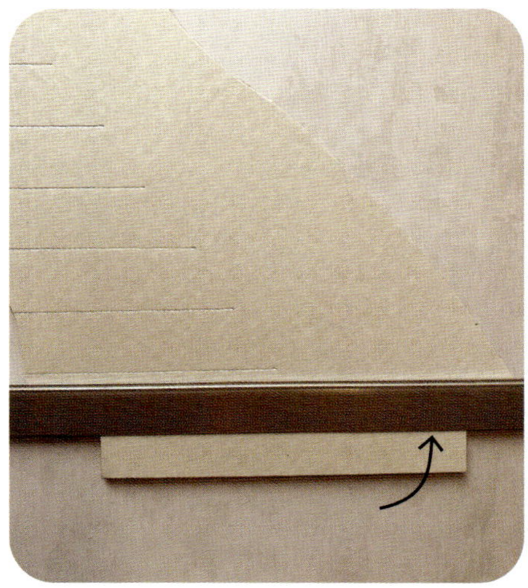

STEP 3

CUT THE PIECES

Get your templates and lightly tape them so they don't move while cutting. Carefully cut out all of the pieces by using a sharp craft knife and cutting mat. If your card has different colors on each side, use one side consistently faceup.

STEP 4

MARK THE SLOT POSITION

Before you remove the template, mark the slot positions, cutting lightly so that later you can clearly see where they are.

TIP

When cutting corrugated card, don't press too hard on your metal ruler or you may crush the card!

STEP 5

FOLD THE FIXING TABS

Take the four body support pieces, (the pink templates) and on the white side of the card, score along the tab.

Use the metal ruler to help bend the tab up to a 90-degree angle. These will attach to the shield base later on in the build.

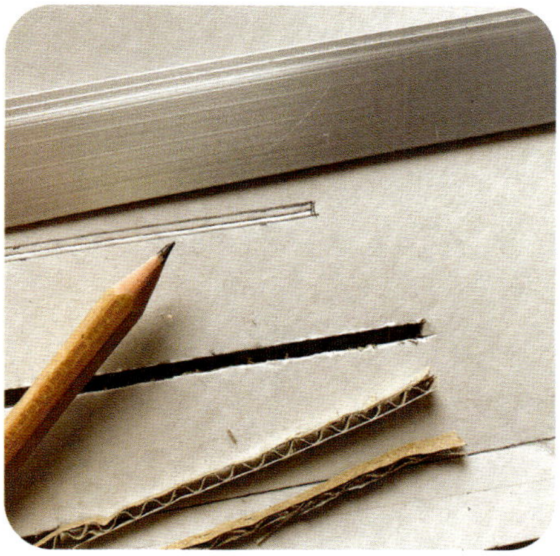

STEP 6

MAKE THE SLOTS

Take a couple of bits of spare board to do a quick slot test. Measure the thickness of your board and then divide the measurement in two and mark this on either side of the score you made for the slot. It is critical that the slots are not too large; otherwise the stag will not be structurally sound.

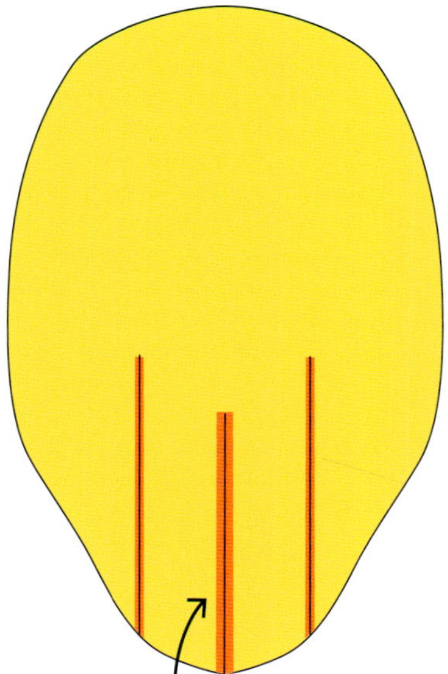

The central support is double-thickness card, so this slot needs to be wider than the two side slots.

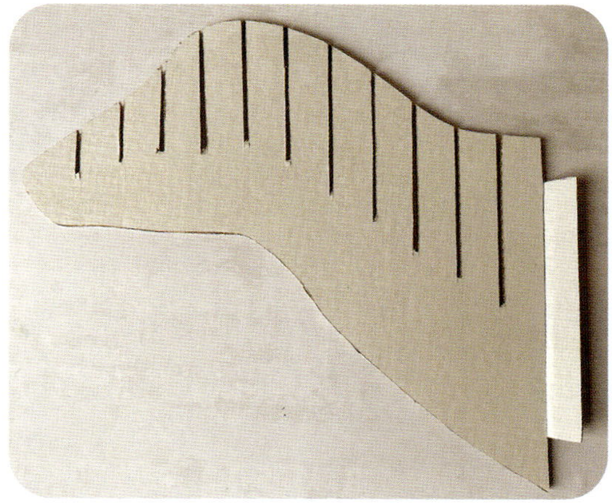

STEP 7

CENTER SUPPORT

Stick the two parts of the main support together (back to back) with glue. Then measure, mark, and cut the slots.

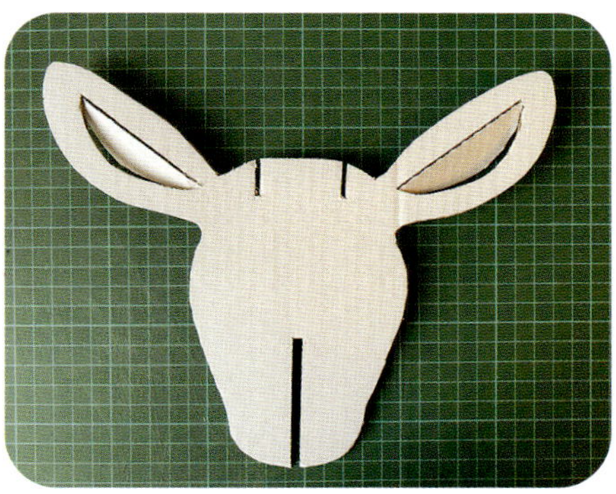

STEP 8

EARS

Cut the bottom curve inside each ear (as shown on the template), then score along the dotted straight line and gently bend back. Try to score lightly and not cut the fibers. If the card does not bend, score again until the card bends easily.

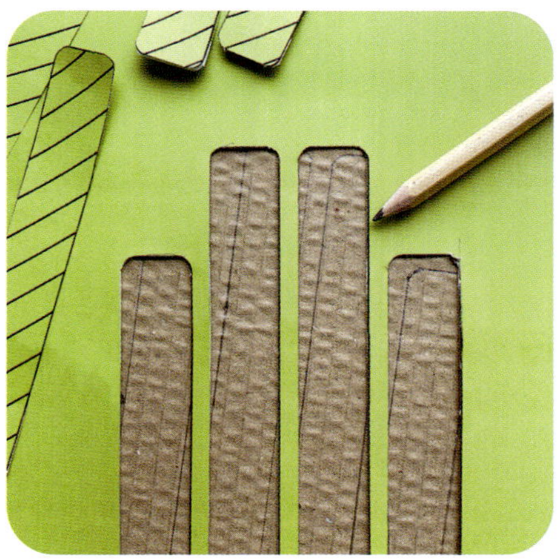

STEP 9

SHIELD GLUE POINTS

After sticking the two shield pieces together with glue, take the template and cut out the glue point sections from the template.

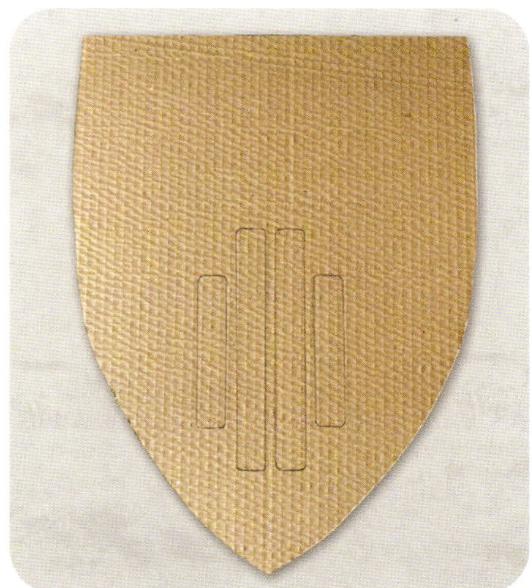

STEP 10

SHIELD GLUE POINTS

Lay the template over the shield and mark in pencil where the glue points are located.

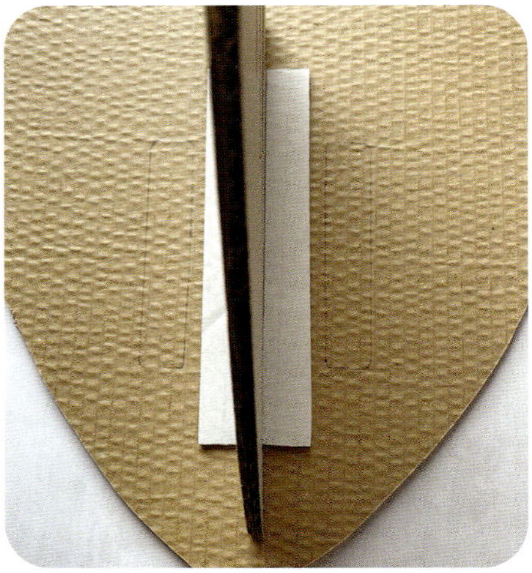

STEP 11

GLUE CENTRAL SUPPORT

Bend the tabs back on the central support piece (shield part A) and, using a strong paper glue, position and stick on the marked glue points.

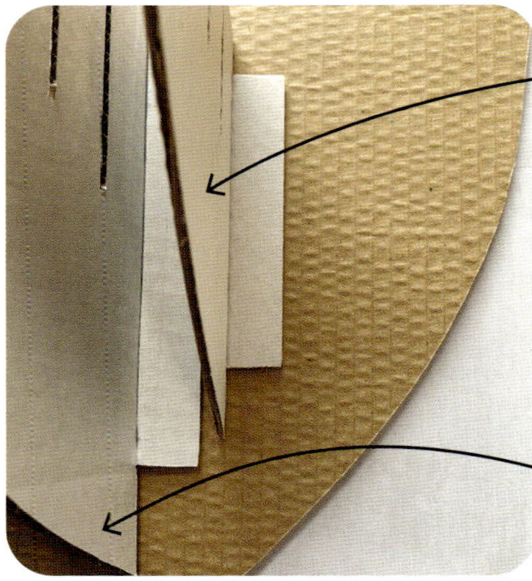

STEP 12

SIDE SUPPORTS

Take the two side supports and stick them over the glue points on either side of the central support, making sure that the white surface is on the outside. Leave to dry.

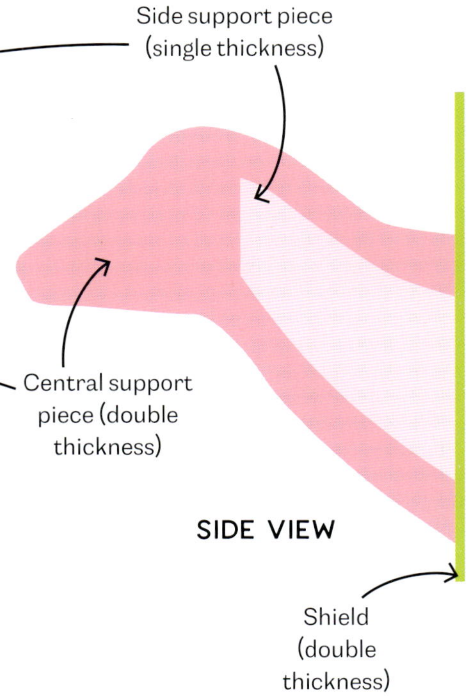

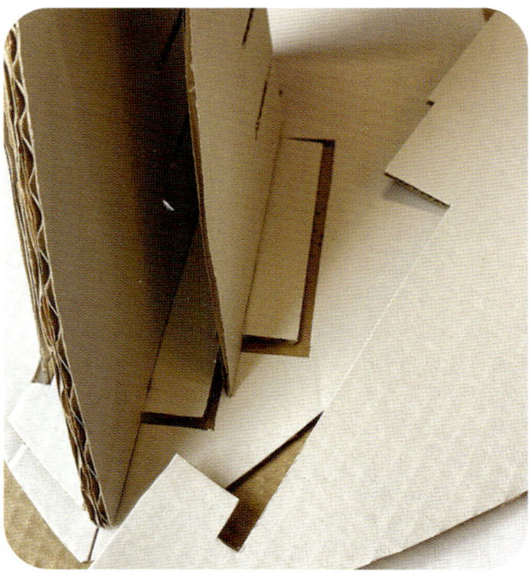

STEP 13

COVER THE SHIELD

Take the two pieces of shield part B and stick them over the base, making sure they are even. Then position and glue two shield part C pieces to cover the support tabs.

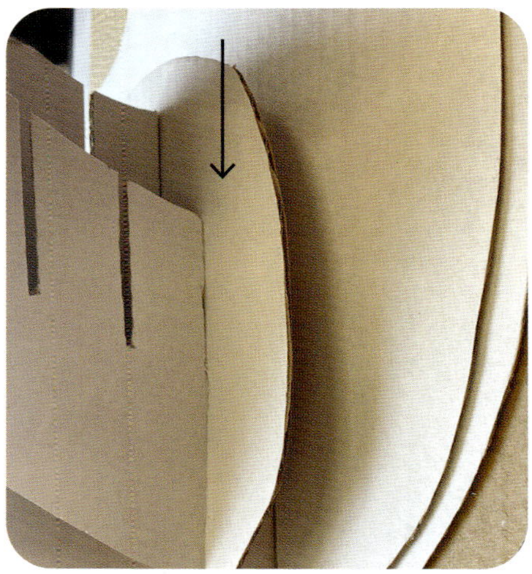

STEP 14

NECK & HEAD CONSTRUCTION

Starting with piece 1, gently slot it into the three supports matching the numbers. You'll notice that on the support templates there are numbers on each slot. Match the piece number with the slot number.

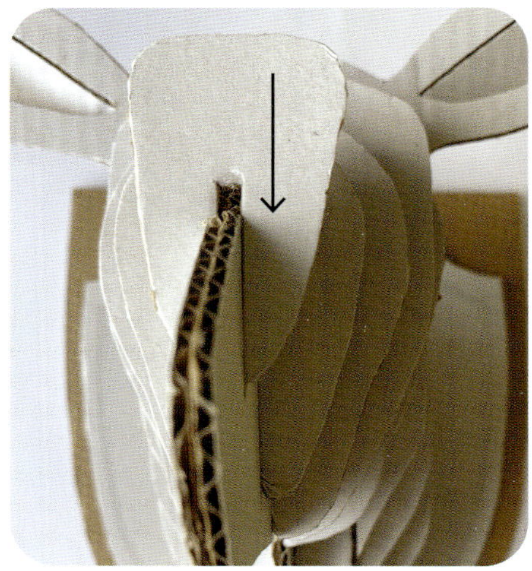

STEP 15

CONTINUE THE SLOTS

Continue slotting pieces. Gently push them onto the three structural parts. This might take a little bit of wiggling, and you may need to make tiny adjustments to the slots.

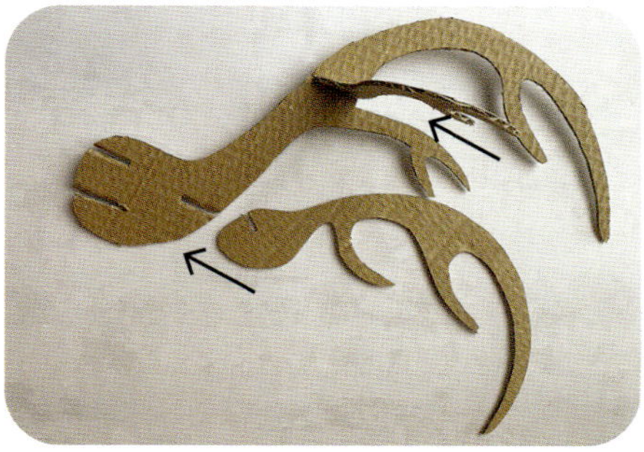

STEP 16

ANTLERS

Turn the three antler parts over to the brown side and build them before adding to the stag. Starting with the largest piece, match the letters next to each slot on the templates and slot them together. They should be at a 90-degree angle to each other. Repeat for the second antler.

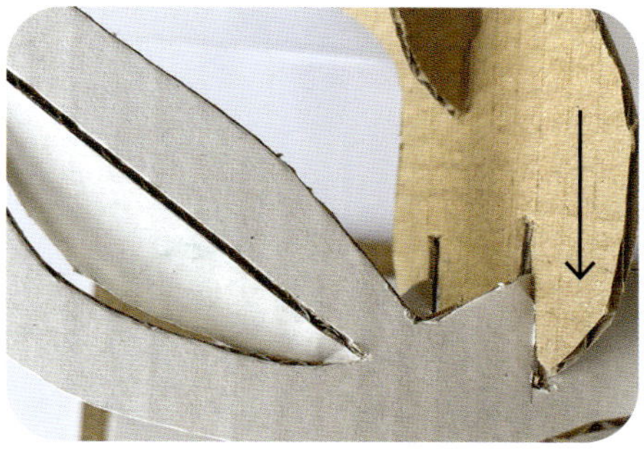

STEP 17

ATTACHING THE ANTLERS

Match A and B on the first antler, then match with A and B shown on the head pieces on the templates and slot the antler onto the head. Repeat for the other antler.

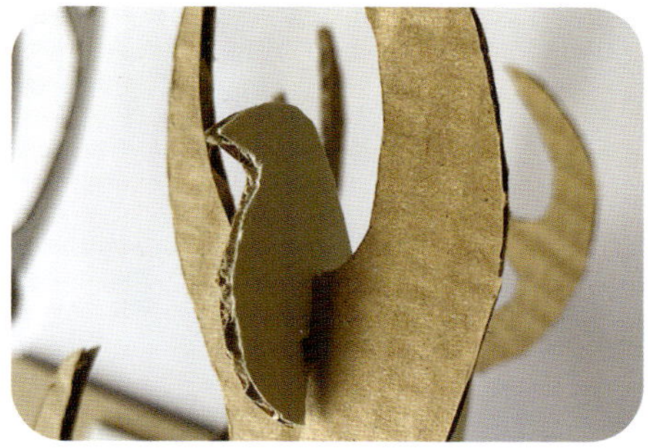

STEP 18

BIRD

Decide where you would like to put the bird, then remove the antler, cut a slot, add the bird, and replace the antler.

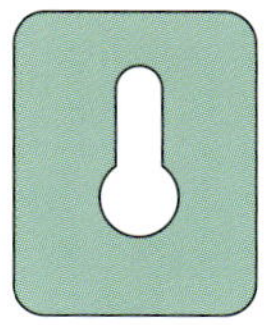

To attach it to the wall, cut two pieces of card with a nail hole, stick them together, then glue to the back of the shield.

VARIATIONS

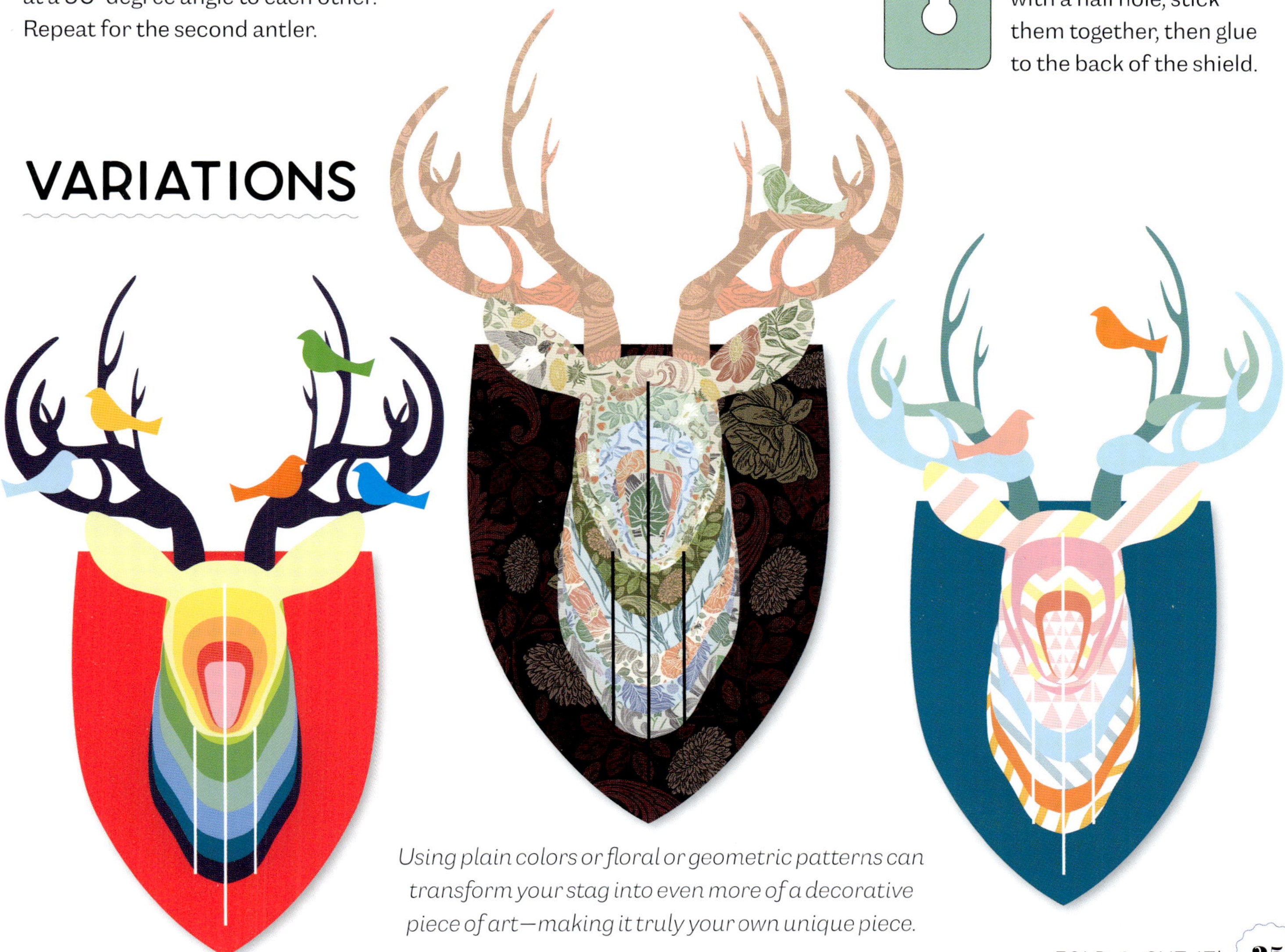

Using plain colors or floral or geometric patterns can transform your stag into even more of a decorative piece of art—making it truly your own unique piece.

TEMPLATES

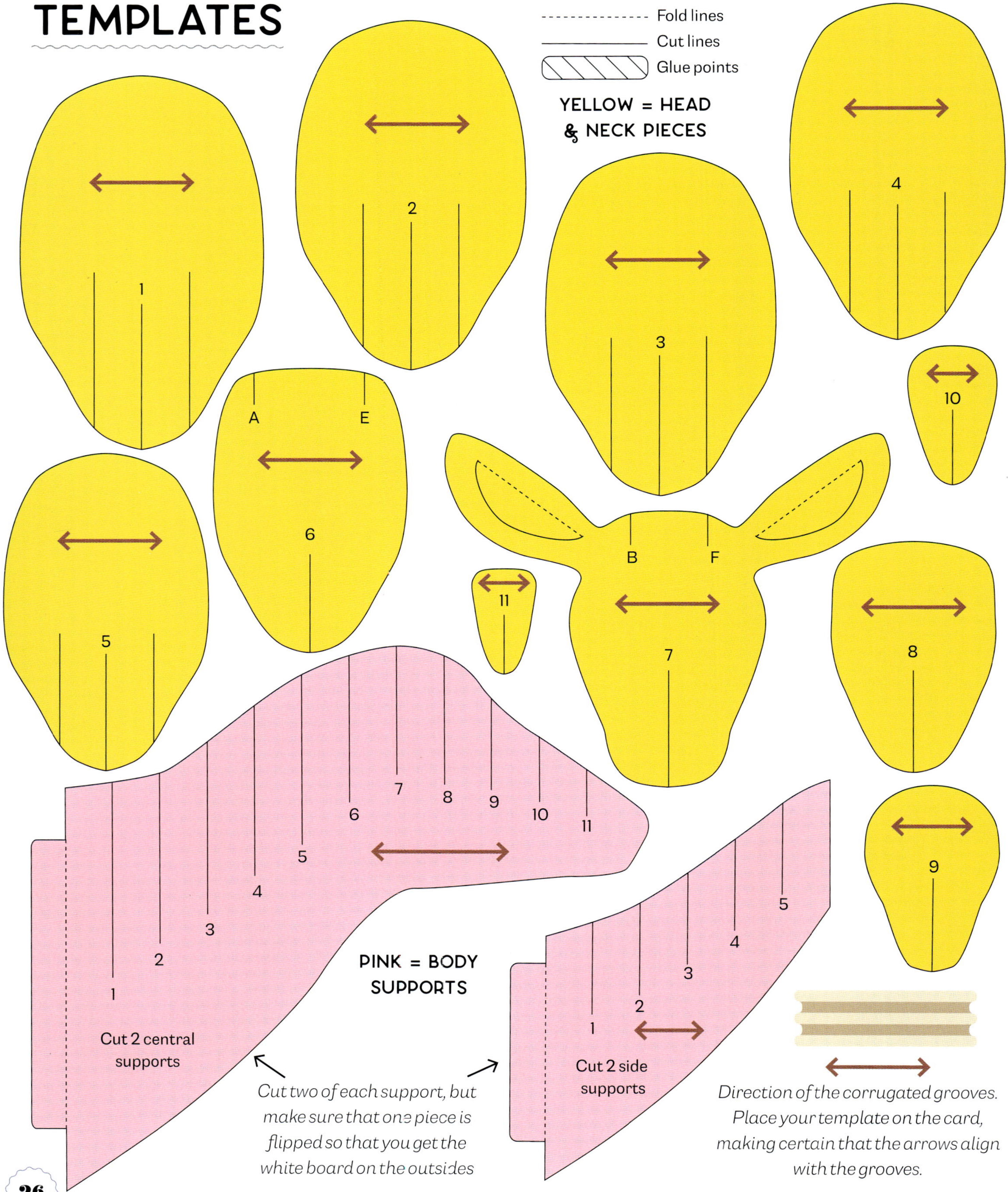

Cut two of each support, but make sure that one piece is flipped so that you get the white board on the outsides

Direction of the corrugated grooves. Place your template on the card, making certain that the arrows align with the grooves.

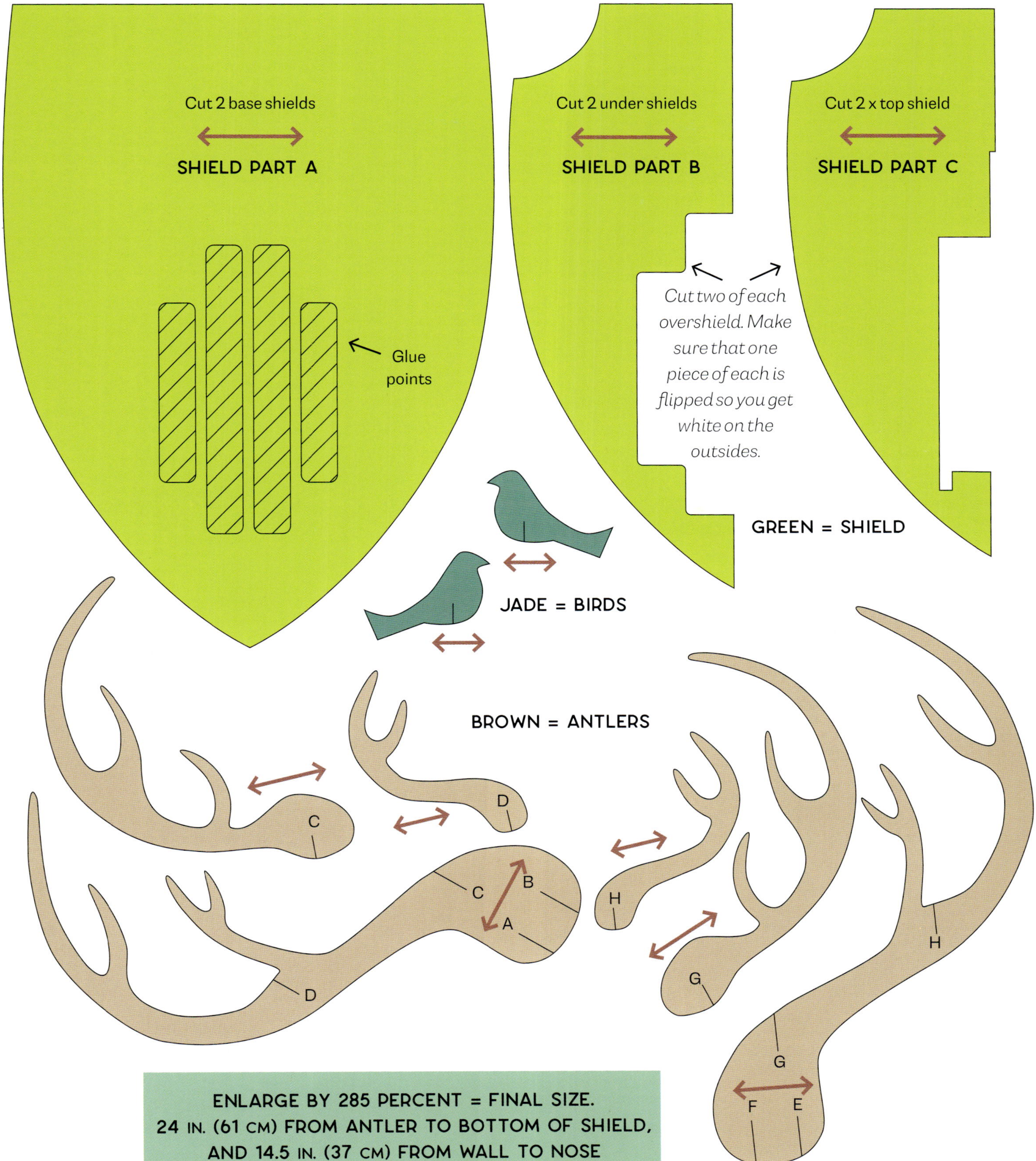

**ENLARGE BY 285 PERCENT = FINAL SIZE.
24 IN. (61 CM) FROM ANTLER TO BOTTOM OF SHIELD,
AND 14.5 IN. (37 CM) FROM WALL TO NOSE**

FLOWER PYRAMID TILES

These glorious tiles are so versatile! Each tile is made out of different types of simple origami pyramids. You can do so many exciting designs using this simple technique. It's so easy to change the color and design to suit your style.

When you start to think about what you would like to create, think about your overall color scheme and the other patterns or textures in your room. In our room we have a beautiful chaise lounge in a muted jade. We've given an extra splash of color with the vibrant yellow-ocher cushion. For our panels we thought that bringing natural colors and design into our room would work really well, so we researched photographic origami papers.

Once the papers arrived, we were inspired to create these abstract flowers and leaves. They pick up the colors in our room so beautifully and really brought the outside inside in a classy and sophisticated way. One of the most satisfying bonuses of making these panels is how relaxing we found building them. We didn't make them all in one go. We started with just three and then added to our collection gradually. Seeing the panels spread across the wall was quite magical and extremely satisfying.

In the other corner of the room, we went on to make three other panels; this time we used a pack of graduated-color origami paper. Have fun and enjoy the delicacy of this art.

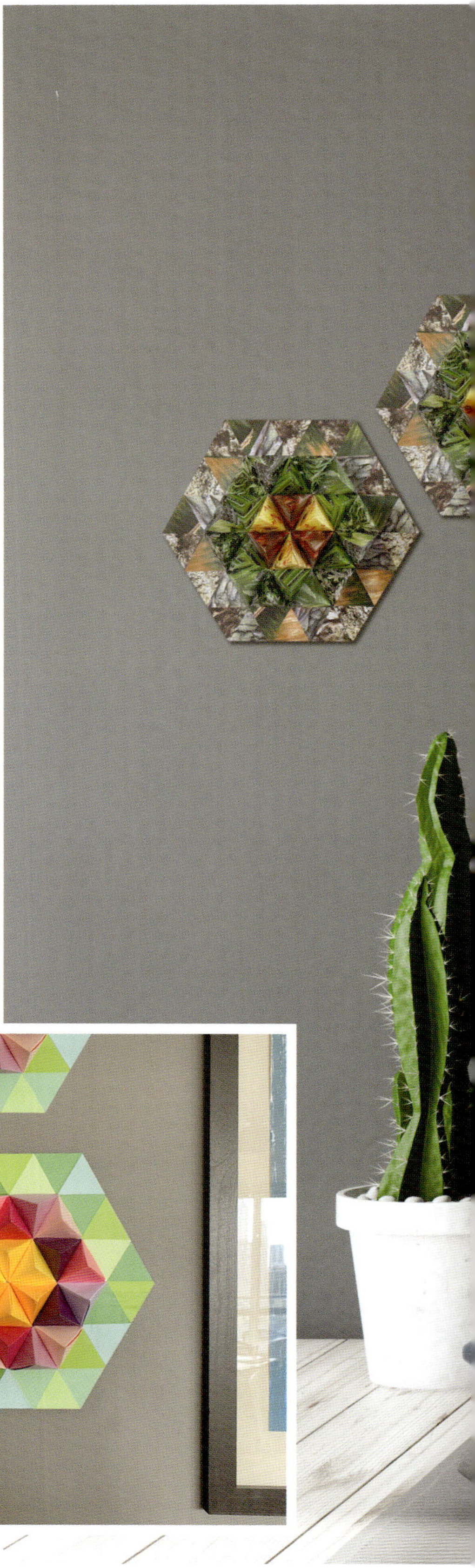

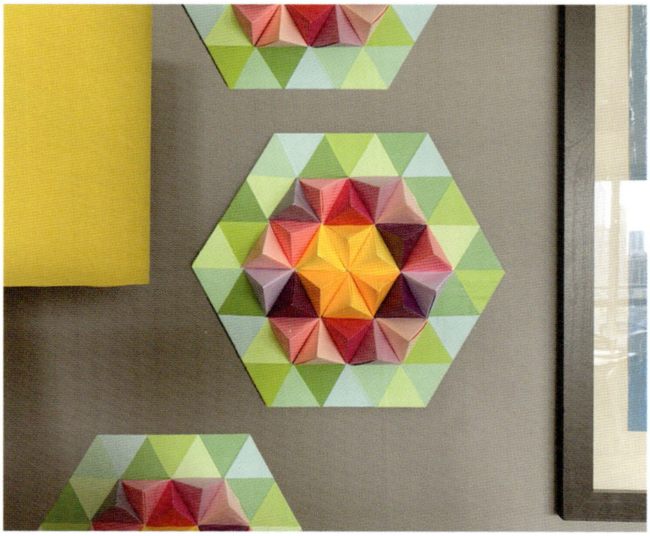

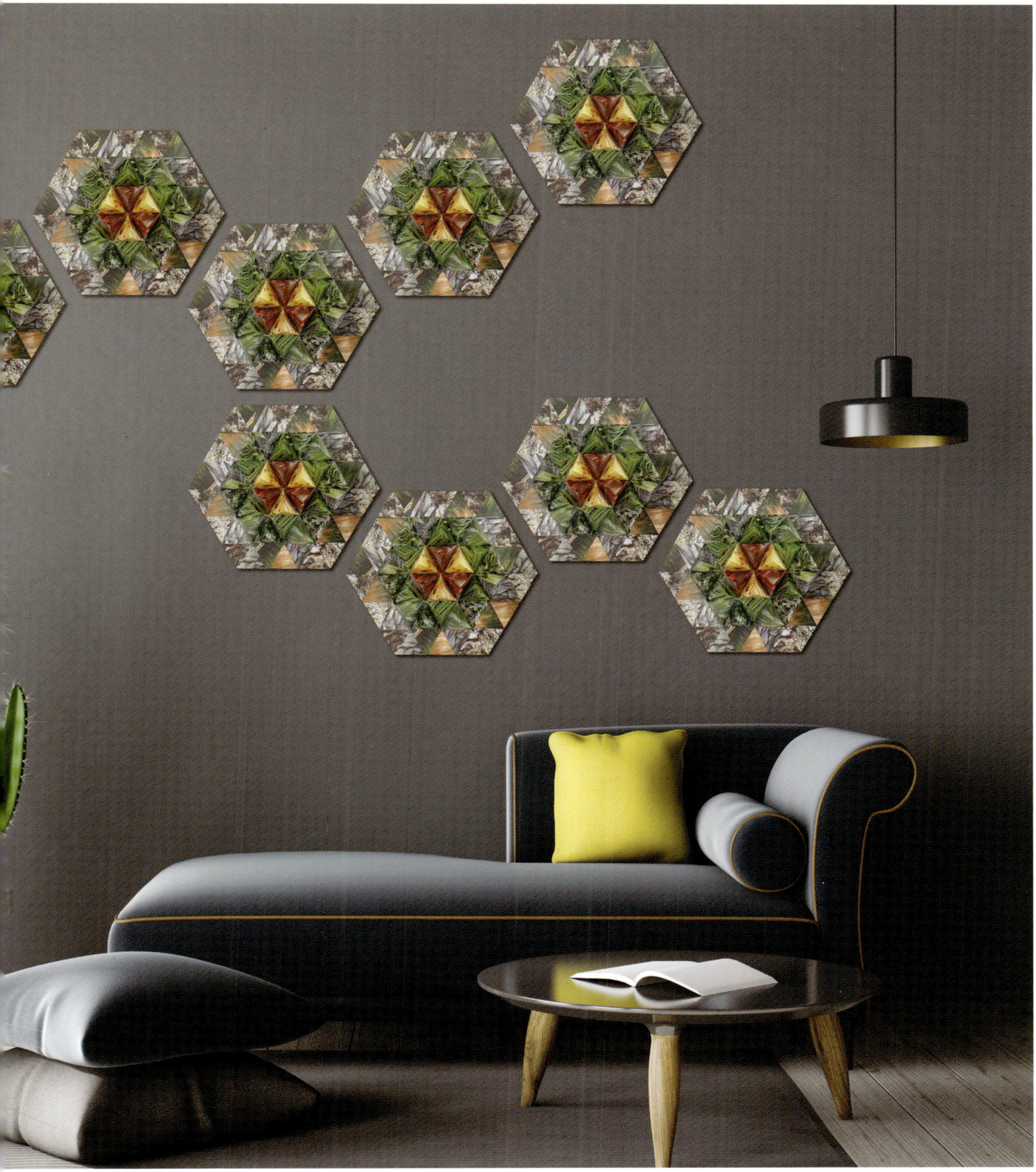

STEP-BY-STEP INSTRUCTIONS

YOU WILL NEED

- *Pack of origami paper 6 x 6 in. (15 x 15 cm)—we used photographic nature papers*

For cutting

- *Craft knife, cutting mat, and metal ruler*

For sticking

- *Clear adhesive tape and double-sided clear adhesive tape*
- *3 6 in. (15 cm) square thick card to make repeat template guides*
- *5 sheets of A2 (23.4 x 16.5 in. / 59.4 x 42 cm) 5 mm thick black foam board*

For hanging

- *Nail and hammer or Velcro®*

STEP 1
WHICH DESIGN?

First, decide which design to do: see the ideas on page 33.

Once you have decided which pattern to follow, think about which pyramid sizes to use. They all have the same base size, but there are three different heights, plus a flat triangle piece.

For our panels we have chosen to use three tall, three medium (for the center of our flower), eighteen small pyramids, and thirty flat triangles.

It will take eighteen to twenty origami sheets for each panel, depending on how many patterns or colors you want to use in your design.

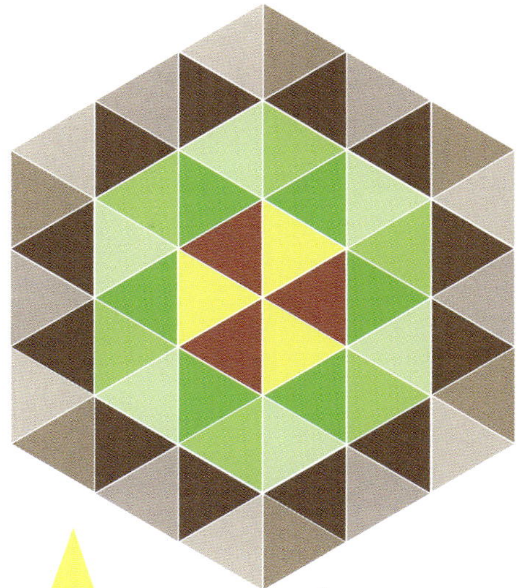

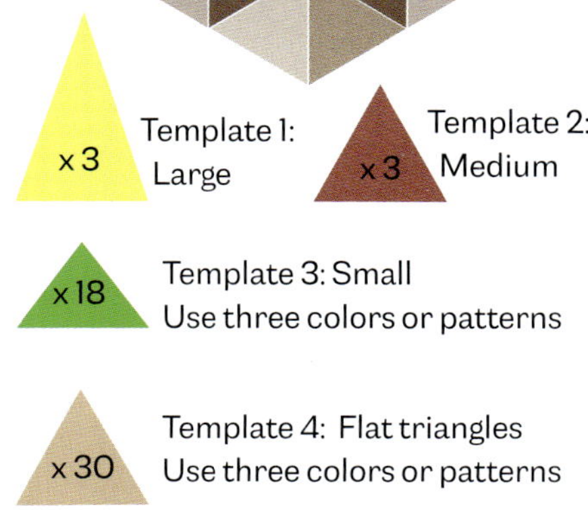

STEP 2
PREPARING YOUR TEMPLATES

We've used 6 x 6 in. (15 x 15 cm) photographic origami papers. To make larger or smaller pyramids follow the sizing info on pages 10–11.

NOTE The square borders around the templates are guides to use if you have 6 in. (15 cm) origami papers. Ignore this bounding box if you are using any other size of paper.

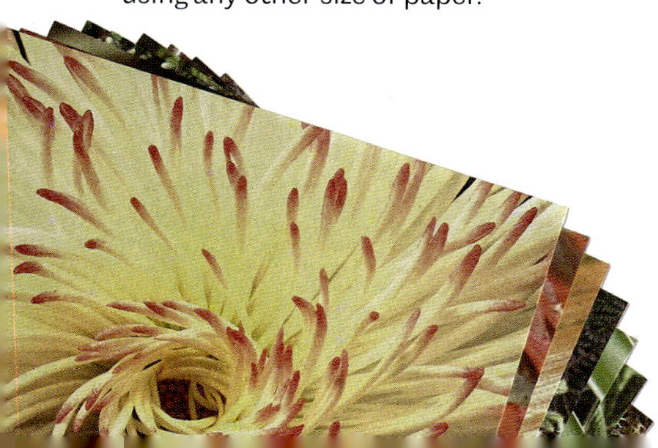

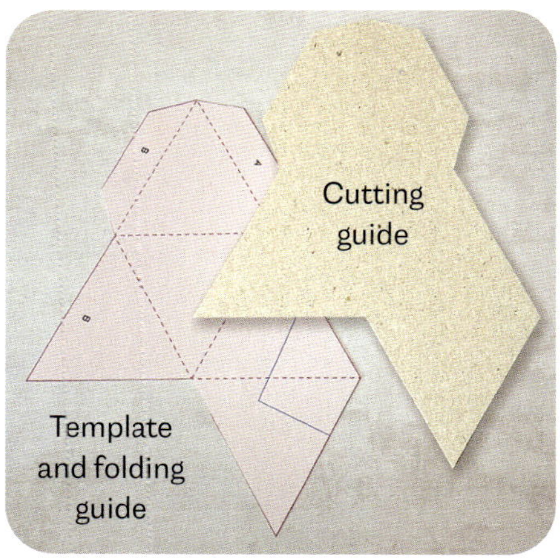

STEP 3
MAKE A CUTTING GUIDE

Using the template, place the paper over your piece of thick card and, with a craft knife, metal ruler, and cutting mat, cut around the edges to create a cutting guide.

Repeat for three templates. Keep the paper template because you'll use this as your folding guide.

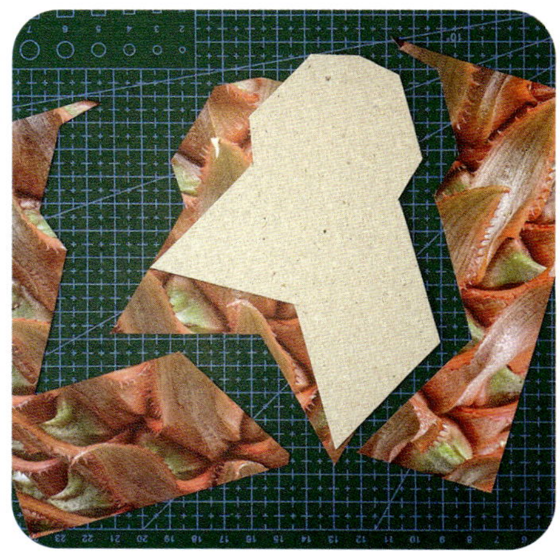

STEP 4
CUT THE PYRAMID PIECES

Take the cutting guide and lay it over your paper. Either draw round it and then cut using scissors or (a quicker method) staple a few sheets together and, using a craft knife and metal ruler, cut several sheets together. Cut the required number and shapes you need for your design.

STEP 5

FOLDING THE PYRAMIDS

All three differently sized pyramids use the same folding method. The smaller the pyramid size, the more fiddly they get. We are showing the medium-sized pyramid in the step-by-steps. Once you have done one, it's easy!

To illustrate the method for templates 1, 2, and 3, we used template 2 in the step-by-steps.

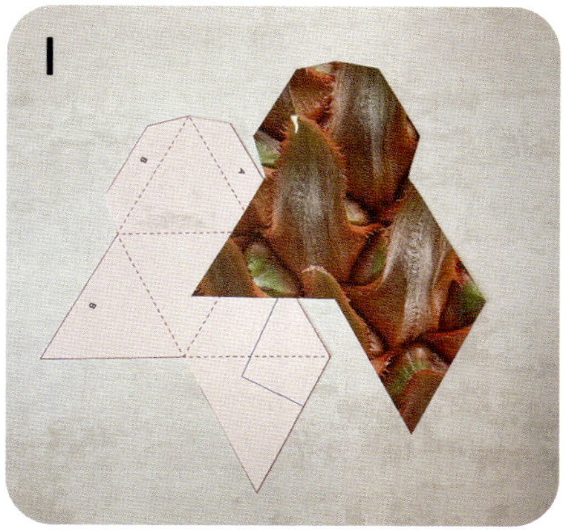

Keep your folding guide at hand for reference and follow the dotted fold lines carefully.

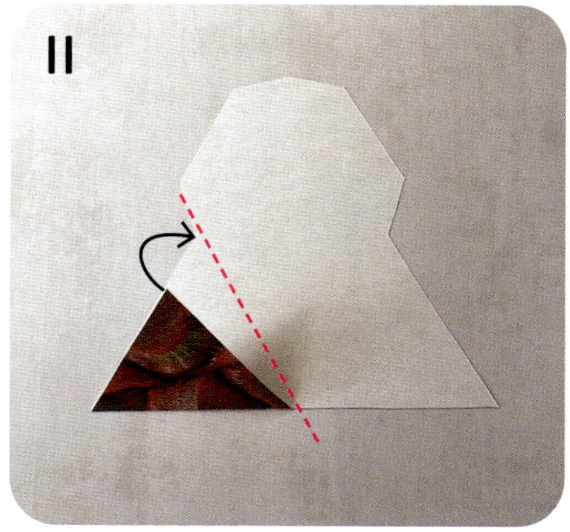

Turn your patterned paper over, fold over the first corner, and align the point with the angle.

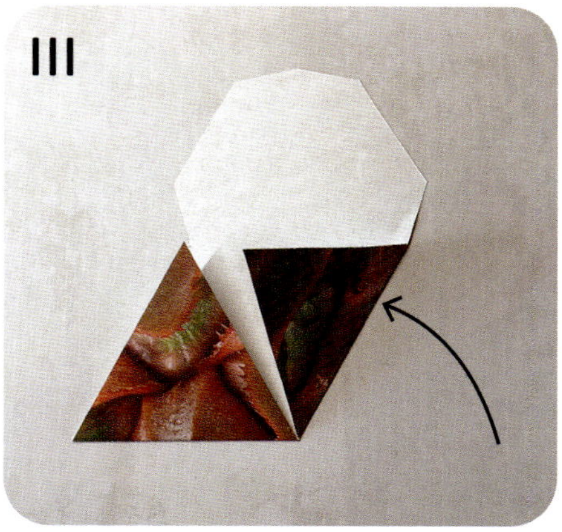

Next fold the other triangle into the center, making sure that the points align as above.

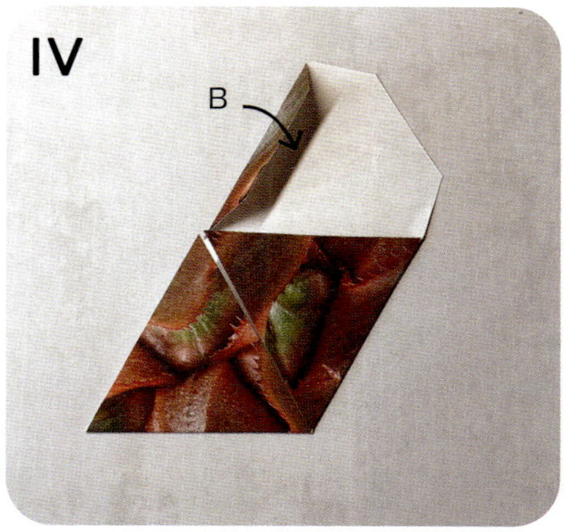

Fold in the top flap B.

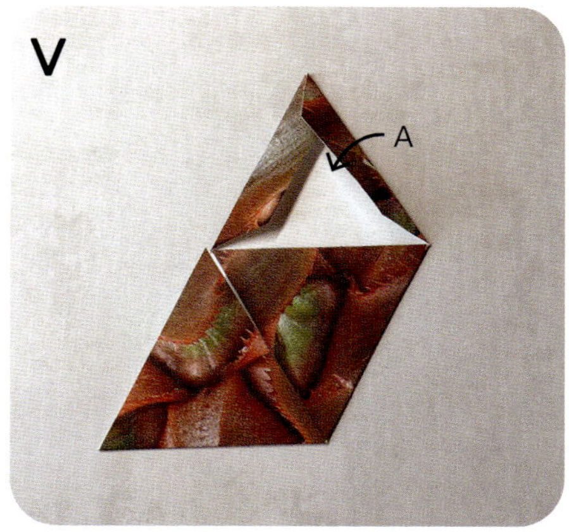

And then flap A inward.

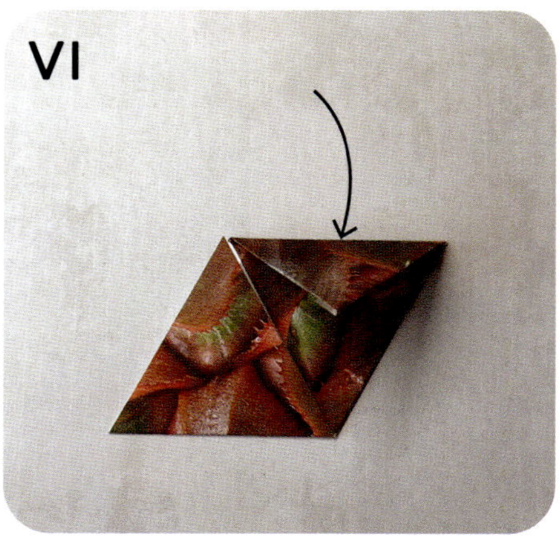

Fold the triangle with flaps over.

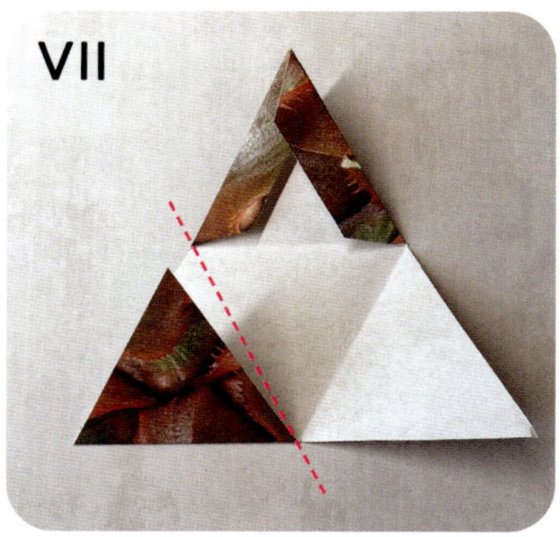

Open out as shown, ready for your final crease.

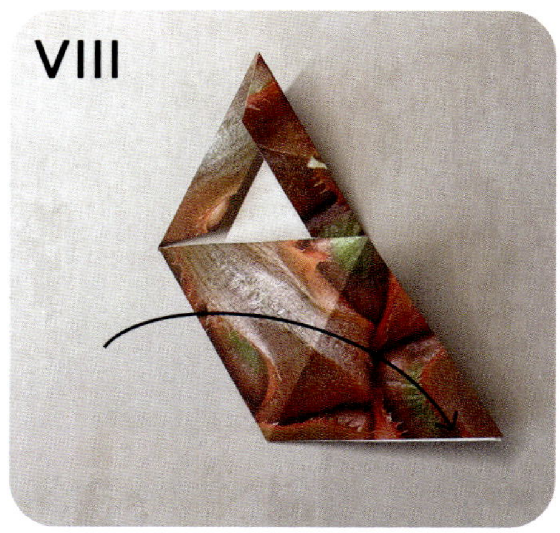

Fold over for your final fold. Unfold ready for construction.

STEP 6

PYRAMID CONSTRUCTION

All you need is clear adhesive tape and double-sided tape, or a dry glue stick to glue the final panel. When taping your pyramids, be gentle—your artwork is delicate. All three of the different-height pyramids are constructed in the same way.

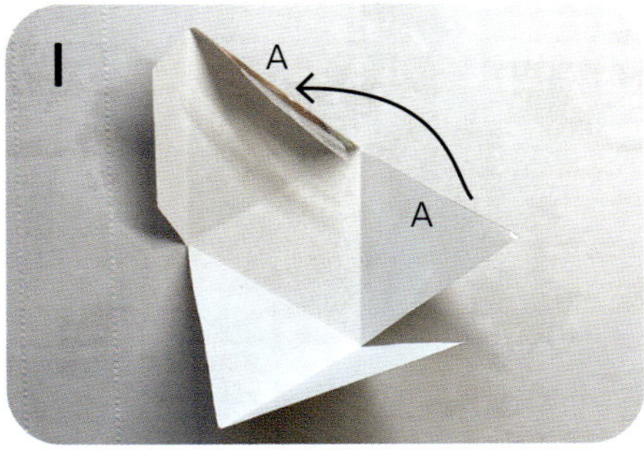

Place double-sided, clear adhesive tape on flap A and stick it to area A; see the folding guide.

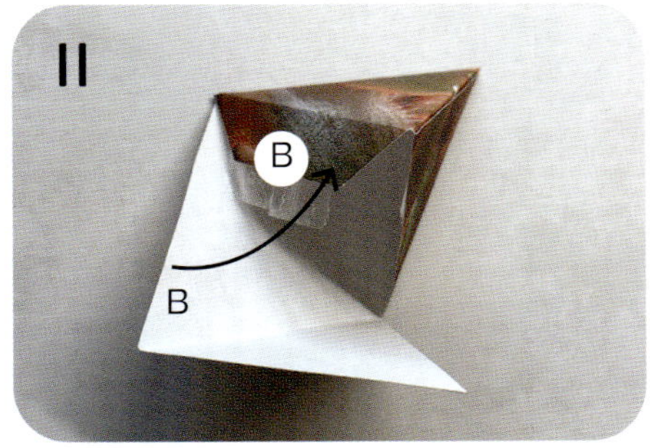

Flap B should be stuck to the corresponding flap B.

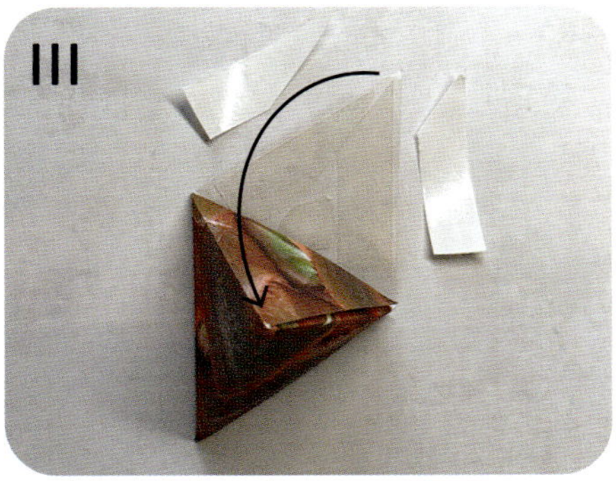

Put double-sided, clear adhesive tape onto the remaining free flap, then stick the flap over the pyramid, creating the final shape. Repeat the process and make the rest of the pyramids.

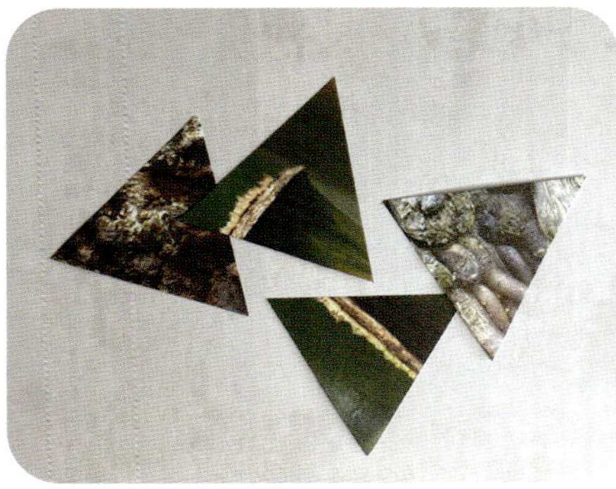

STEP 7

FLAT TRIANGLES

Using template 4, cut thirty flat triangles out of three different patterns of a similar color.

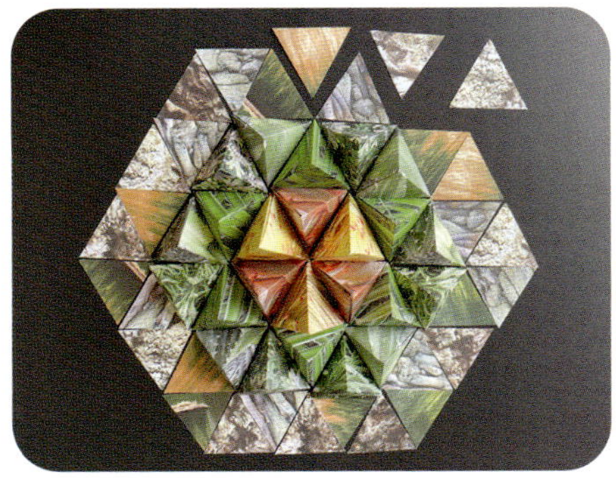

STEP 8

ASSEMBLY

Arrange the pieces into a hexagon on the foam board, making sure you distribute your colors evenly.

Rows of double-sided, clear adhesive tape

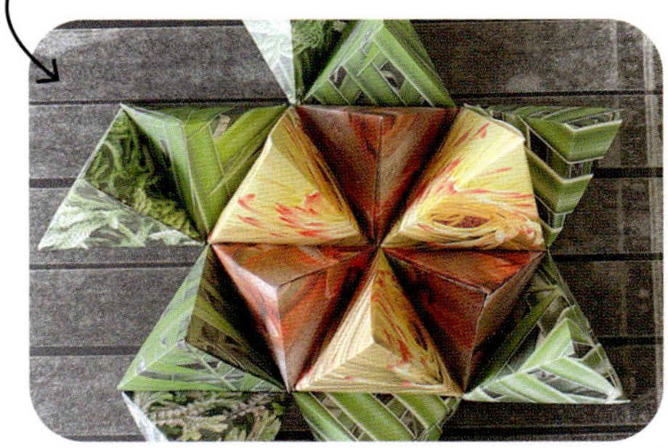

STEP 9

STICKING

Put double-sided, clear adhesive tape over the foam board, then stick the pyramids down, working from the center outward.

Place metal ruler along the edge

Trim the excess foam board

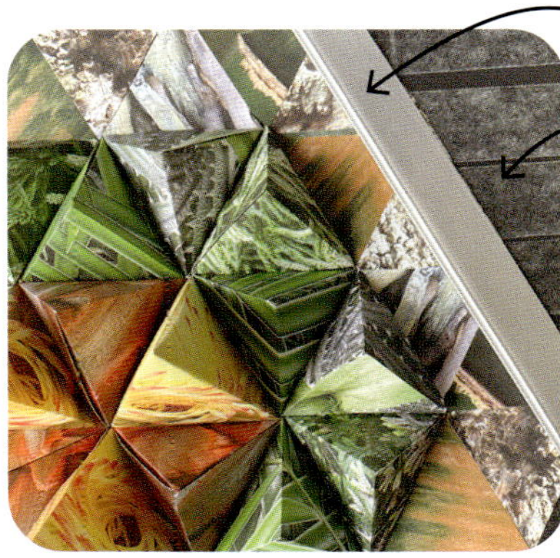

STEP 10

TRIMMING

Finally, evenly trim the edges of the foam board using a craft knife, metal ruler, and cutting mat.

Finished trimmed panel

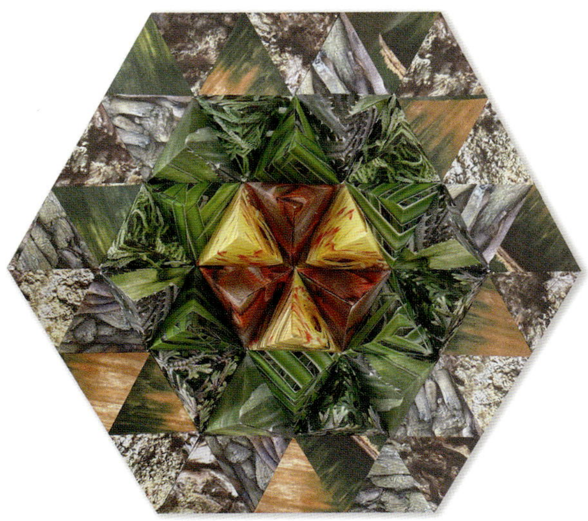

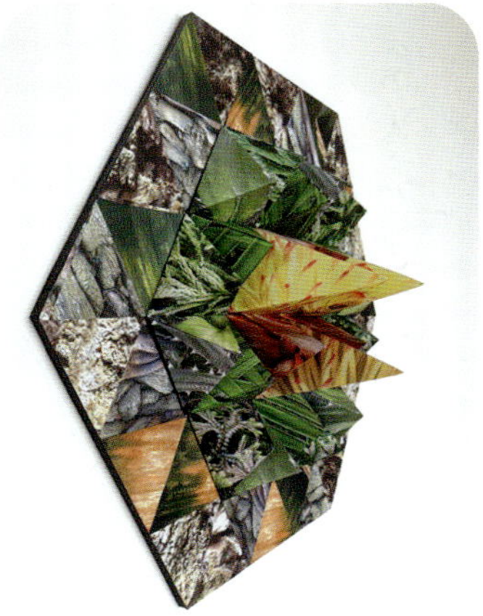

STEP 11

HANGING THE FLOWER PANELS

Position your artwork with low-tack putty to get the spacing and design just right.

Your panels are very light so won't need much to hold them on your wall. Use a small piece of Velcro® tape or carefully make a small hole in the back of your foam board that a nail can fit in, but make sure the hole isn't too deep and damages your artwork.

TIP

Not all of your flowers need to be 3-D. Make some as flat artwork too. This will give your wall different textures and profiles and also speed up the folding process

VARIATIONS

You can arrange the pyramids in hundreds of designs and color schemes. Try using traditional origami designs or graduated-color papers so the shades and tones vary.

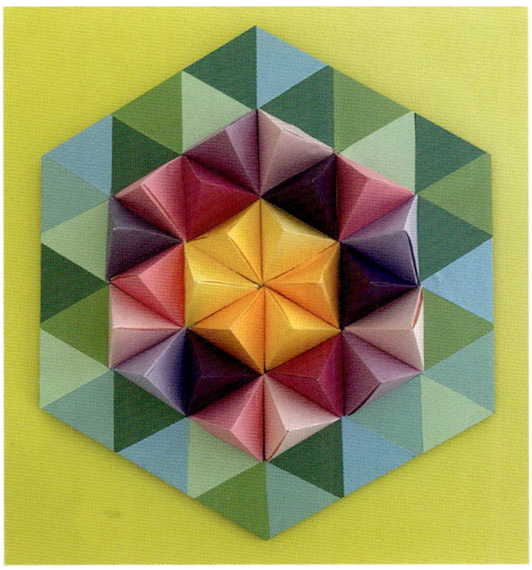

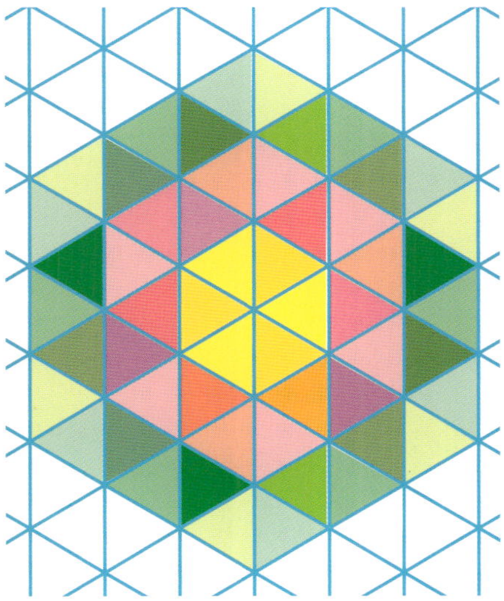

Left: *Try using just one pyramid height rather than three. For example, on the left we used the middle-height triangle for all of the pyramids and a pack of multicolored origami papers.*

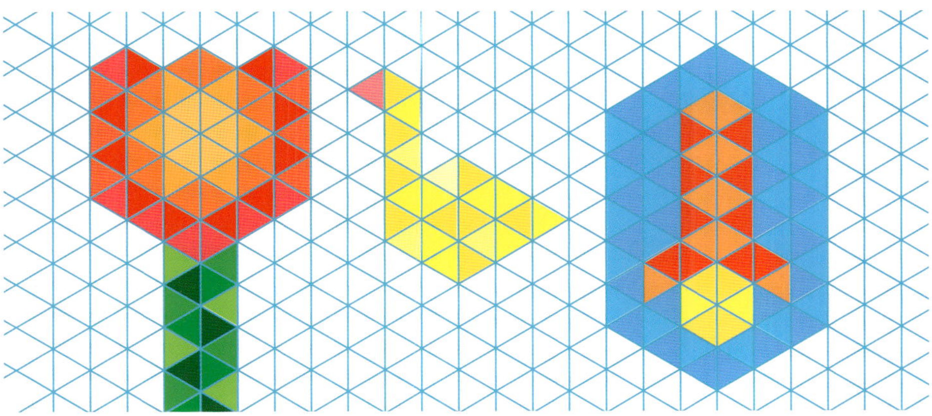

Left: *Triangles are so adaptable, how about trying some simple-shape designs for a child's bedroom?*

Try drawing a simple isometric grid (left) and create your own designs.

TEMPLATE 1
LARGE (BLUE)

One per 6 in. (15.3cm) sheet.
Shown at 100 percent

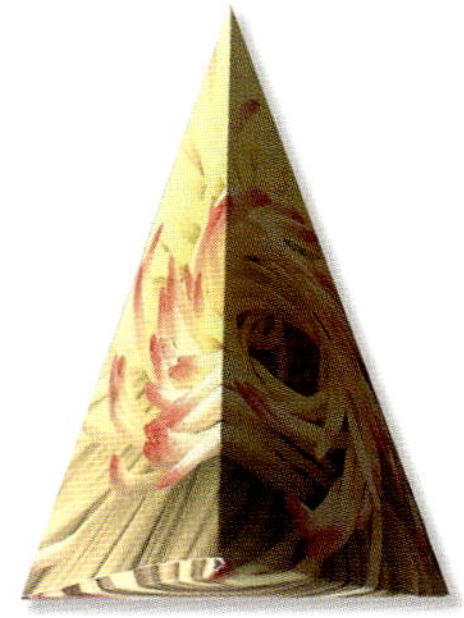

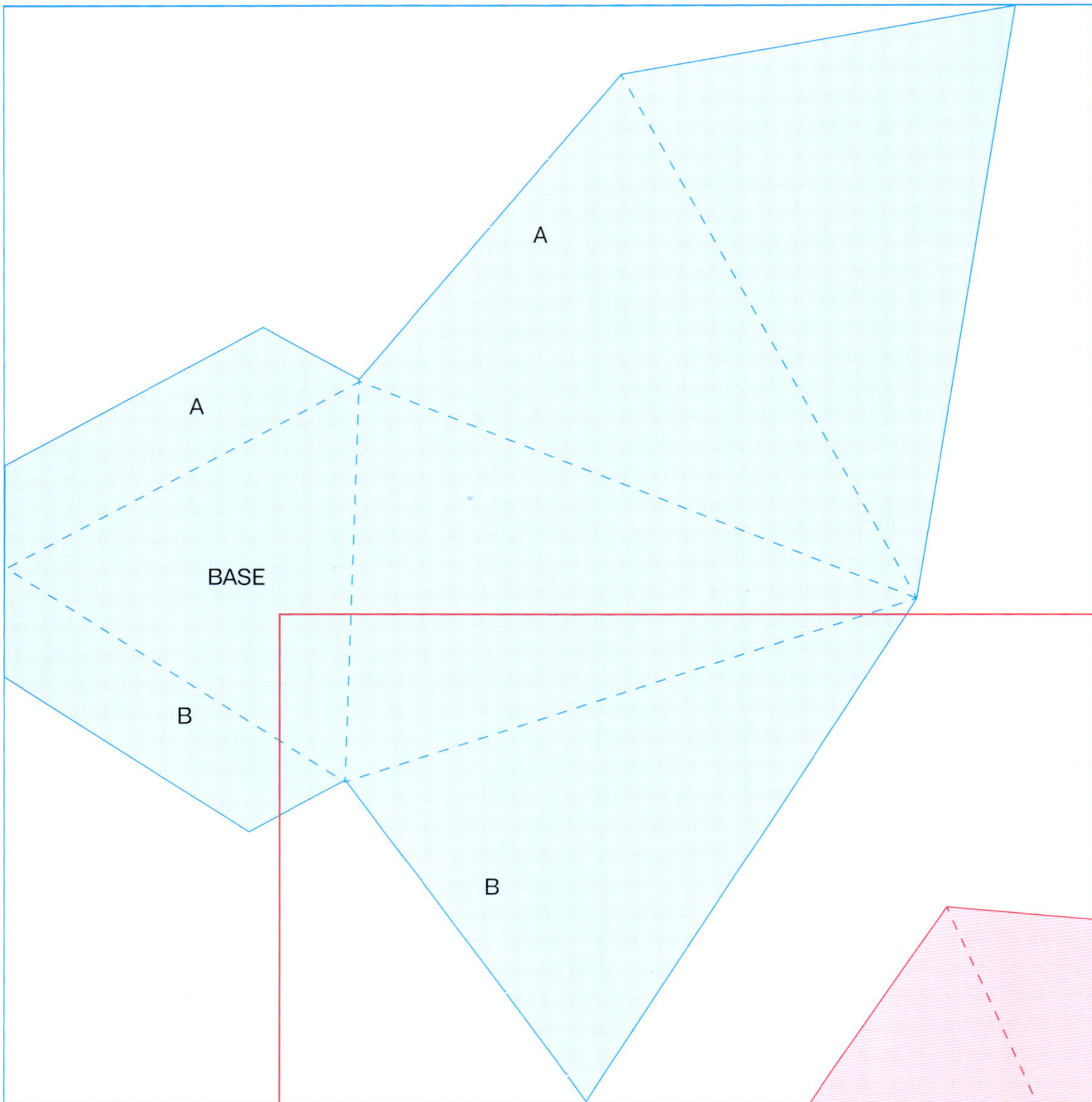

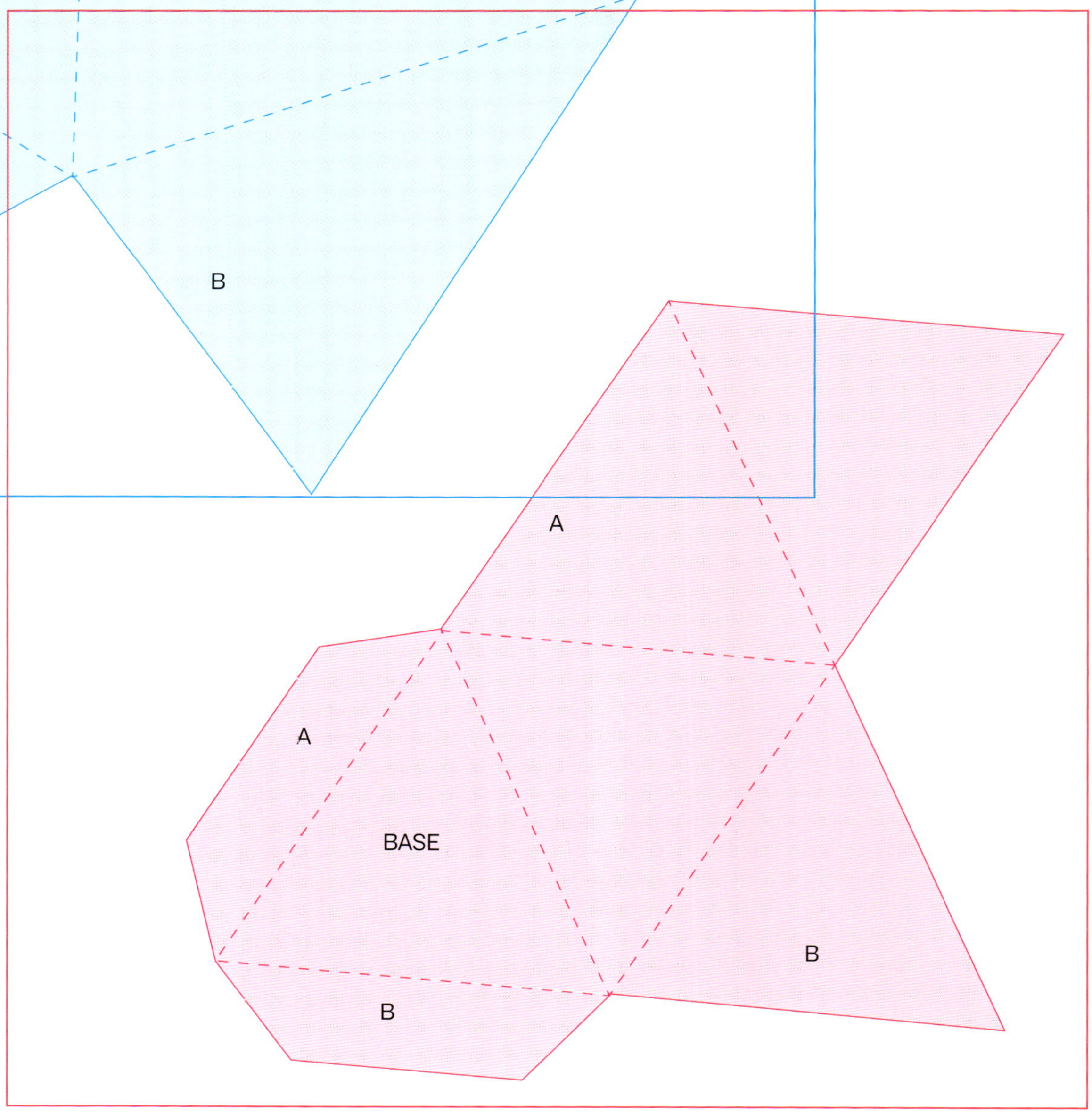

TEMPLATE 2
MEDIUM (PINK)

One per 6 in. (15.3 cm) sheet.
Shown at 100 percent.

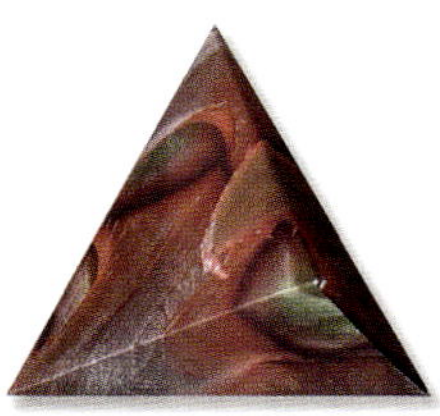

TEMPLATES

NOTE The square borders around the templates are guides to use if you have 6 in. (15.3 cm) origami papers. Ignore this bounding box if you are using any other size of paper.

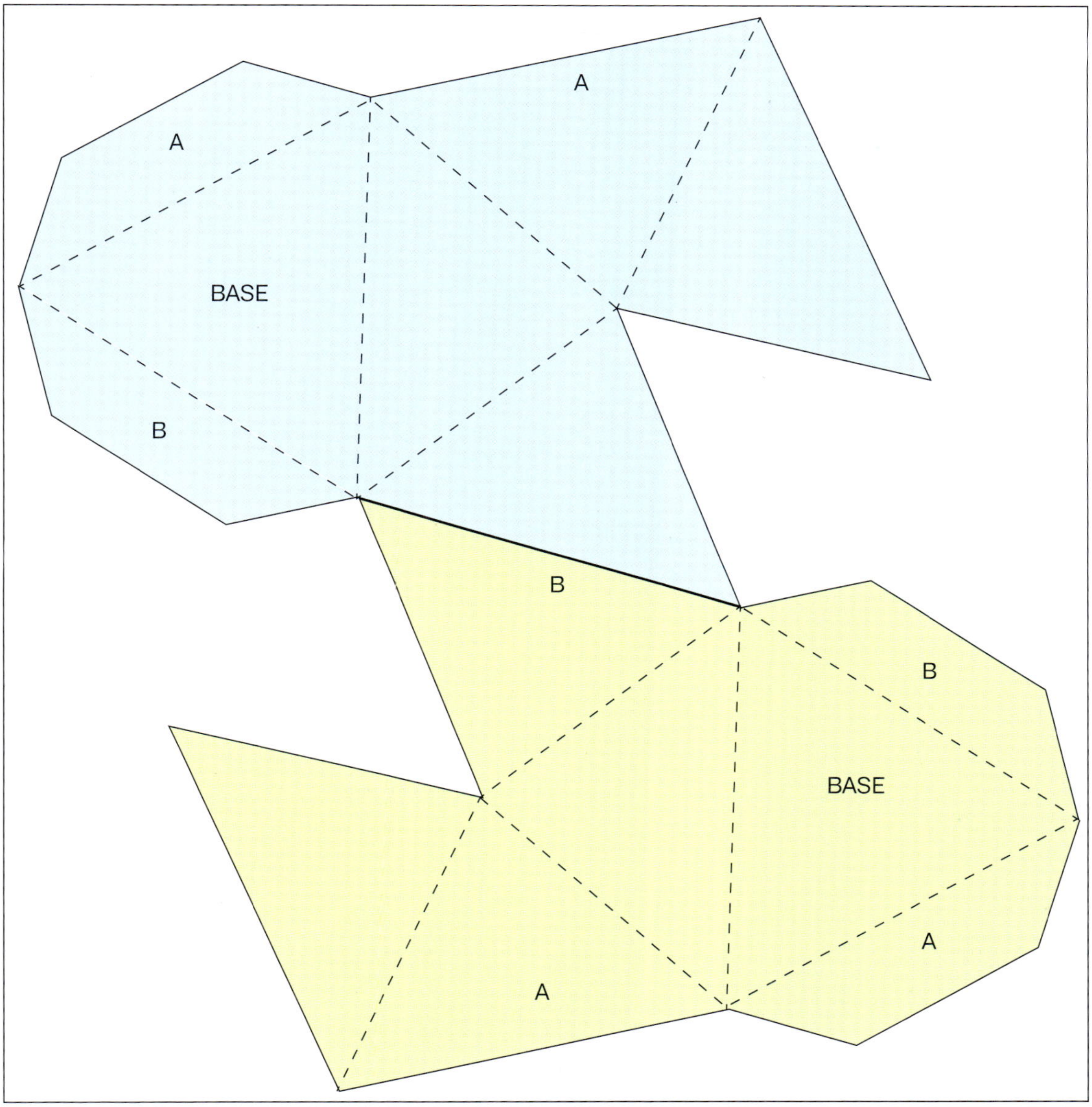

TEMPLATE 3
SMALL

Two per 6 in. (15.3 cm) sheet.
Shown at 100 percent

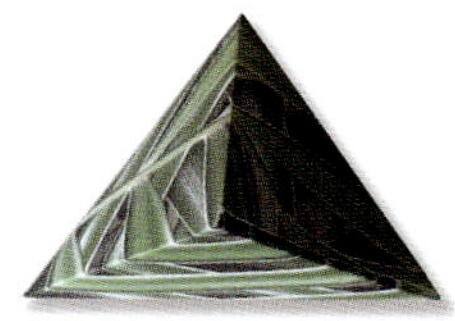

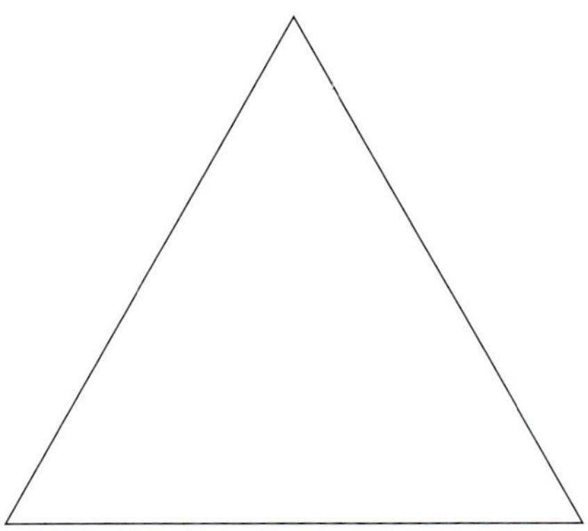

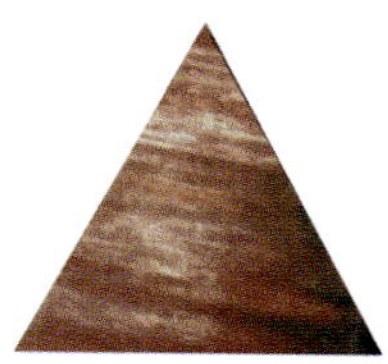

TEMPLATE 4

Flat triangles.
Shown at 100 percent.
You should be able to get twelve flat triangles out of a 6 in. (15.3 cm) sheet

TEMPLATES ARE 100 PERCENT = FINAL TILE SIZE OF 13 IN. (33 CM) AT THE WIDEST POINT

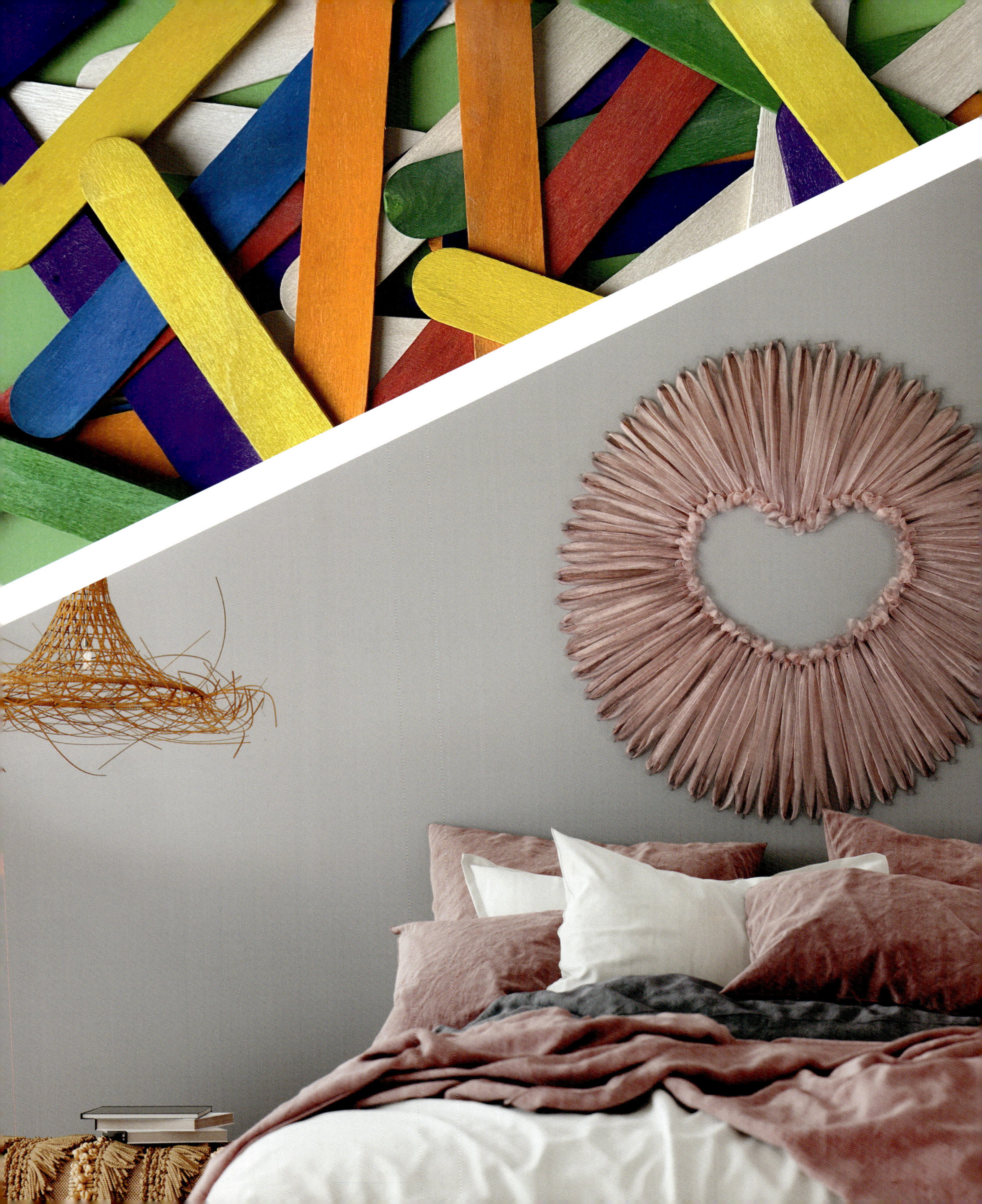

3-D FOUND OBJECTS

Making use of the things that we find!
There are so many objects that we have, things we collect or find, and these can be put together to make the most-glorious art for our walls. We have picked three projects that use items that you can either find or buy in quantity, easily and cheaply, from popsicle sticks and corks to torn-up fabrics.

2

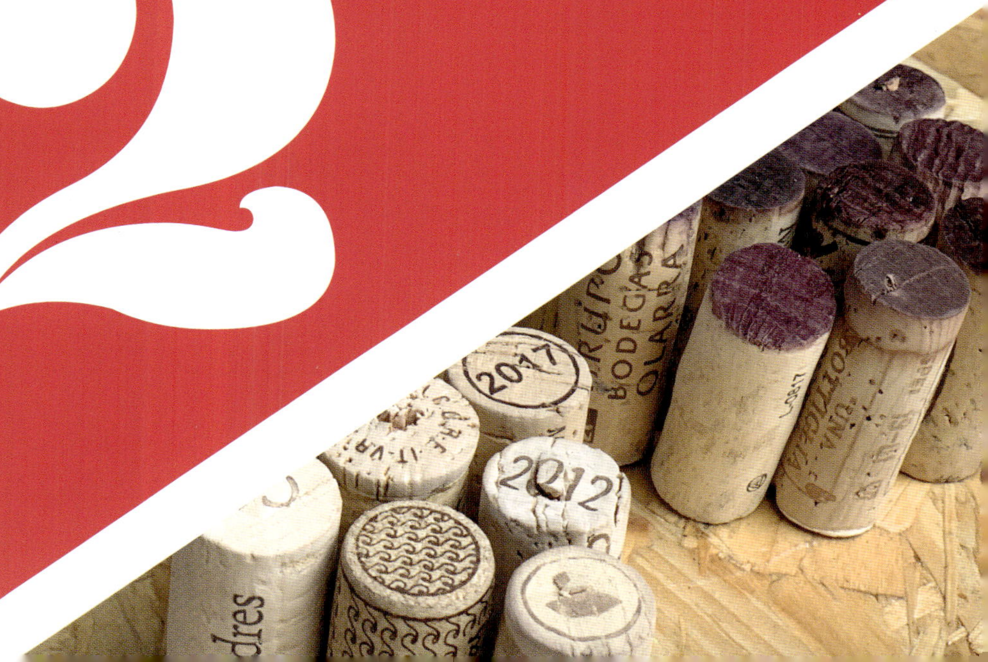

NEW-MOON OMBRÉ CORK PLAQUE

Is it Wine O'Clock, yet?

With this crescent moon plaque hanging on your wall, the sun is always over the yardarm . . . and so, the right time for a tipple whenever you please!

Cork is an amazingly versatile material that has been used in clothing, footware, and building materials for a very long time. In Egypt, natural-cork stoppers have been found in tombs dating back thousands of years. Most cork growing and manufacturing takes place in southern Europe and is harvested from the bark of the cork oak tree, *Quercus suber*.

This project takes advantage of the delightful color of wine itself when it stains the tips of the corks in the bottle. The stains range from deep burgundy blacks through rich rosy flushes to the palest of tints. Sort them into colored stacks of these tones, and see the lovely ombré effects that appear.

We're also very fond of the interesting graphics and illustrations that are found on corks, and really like the way the printing on them responds to the texture of the corks themselves.

This project can use a LOT of corks! For the sake of your health, we suggest asking your local restaurant or bar to save theirs for you, rather than drinking all the bottles yourself. Alternatively, bundles of assorted used corks can be sourced from online retailers and craft suppliers.

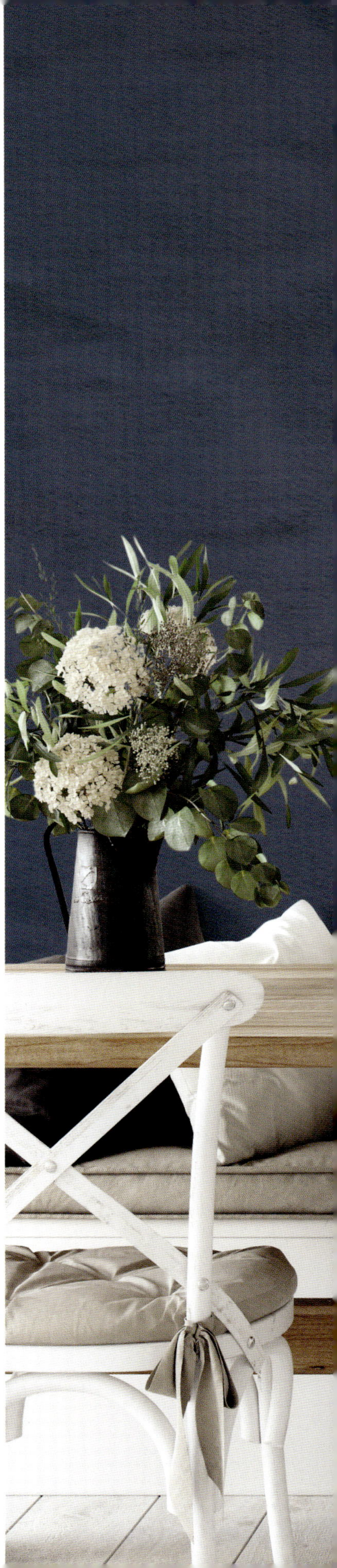

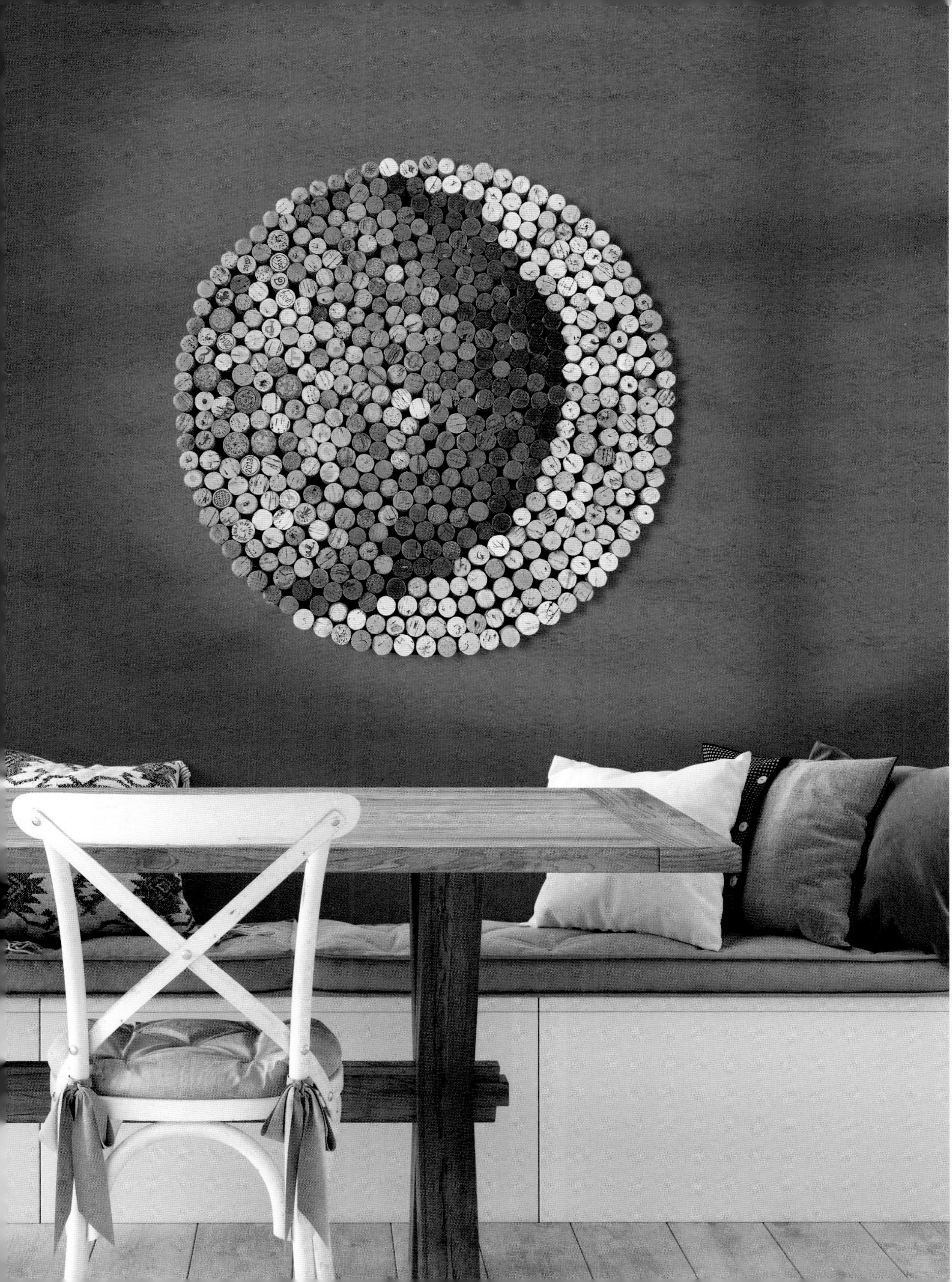

STEP-BY-STEP INSTRUCTIONS

YOU WILL NEED

To make

- *General-purpose adhesive*
- *Lots of wine corks (real cork, not plastic ones!)*
- *Pencil*
- *Ply or chipboard circle*

OPTIONAL

- *Brushes and acrylic, watercolor, or metallic paint*

To display

- *Two screw-in hooks and string for display*

STEP 1

PLAN THE SIZE OF YOUR PIECE

The first thing to do is get a rough idea of the area the corks you have will take up. We stood all of ours up on a worktop and squashed them into a rough circle. This doesn't have to be a perfect circle; we're just getting a ballpark figure for the size of base that's needed. This suggested a base circle of around 22 in. (56 cm) diameter.

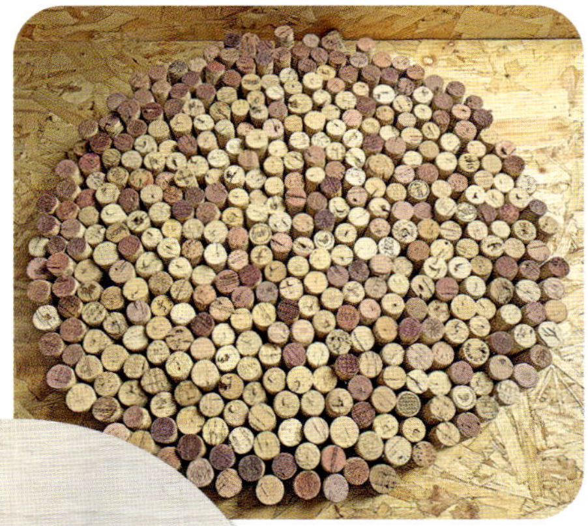

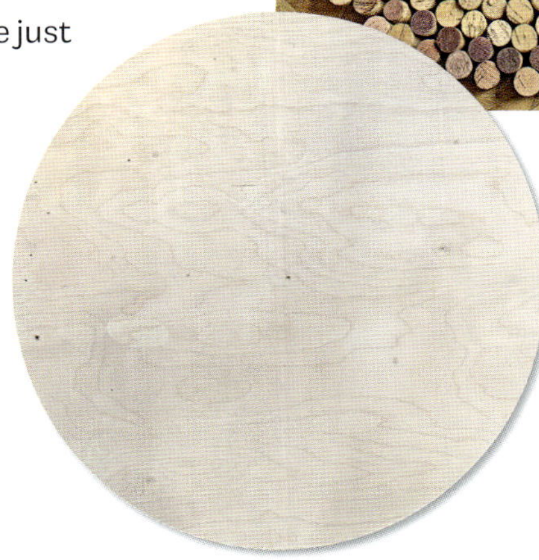

Purchased ply base 22 in. (56 cm) in diameter

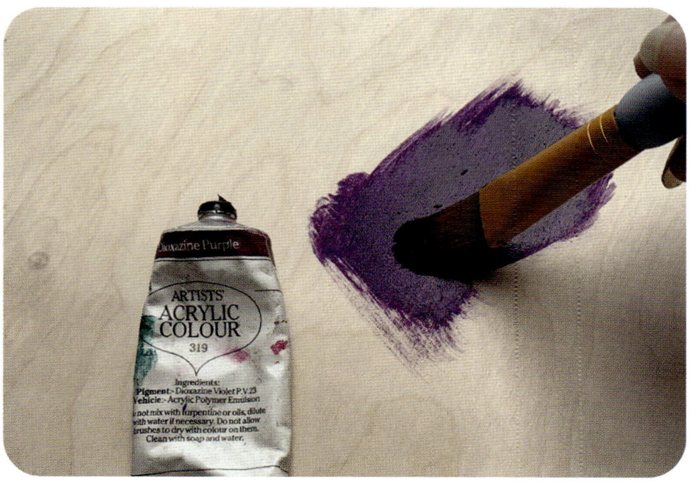

STEP 2

PREPARE THE CIRCLE BASE

You can make your own circle base from any firm material such as chipboard or ply that you have handy. They can also be easily sourced from online retailers as plywood circles and are usually available in a large range of sizes.

It's an option to paint the base circle in a nice deep color of acrylic paint. It doesn't have to be perfect. It just adds a little bit of interest should you be able to see down any gaps between the corks. Set aside to dry.

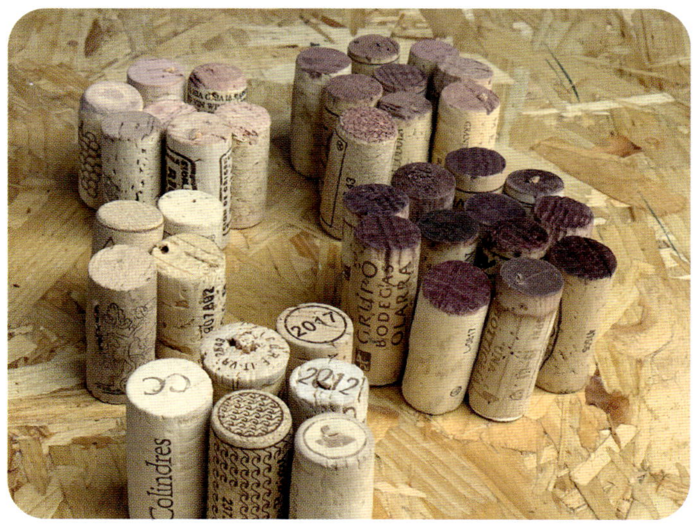

STEP 3

SORT THE CORKS

A good time to sort the corks is while the background is still drying. You'll need to sort them into five groups shown counterclockwise here: dark stained, medium stained, lightly stained, no stains or graphics, and unstained but with graphics.

STEP 4

STICK THE OUTER EDGE OF THE MOON

For the moon part, we're going to use corks that have no staining or graphics on the ends. Since these will be placed on the outside edge, it's most effective to use corks that have graphics on the long edge, since this will add real interest to the finished piece. Turn the cork so that these graphics face the outside edge, and glue each cork so that it hangs a tiny bit over the edge of the backing circle (*picture B*).

Glue these corks for just over half of the circumference. Let this row of corks set completely. Then draw the inside shape of the moon in pencil.

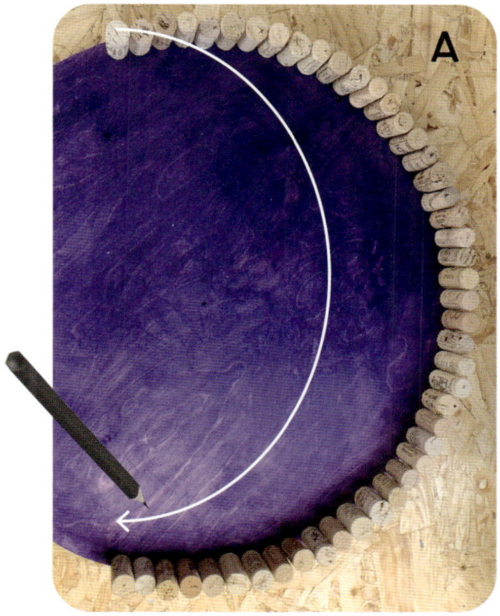

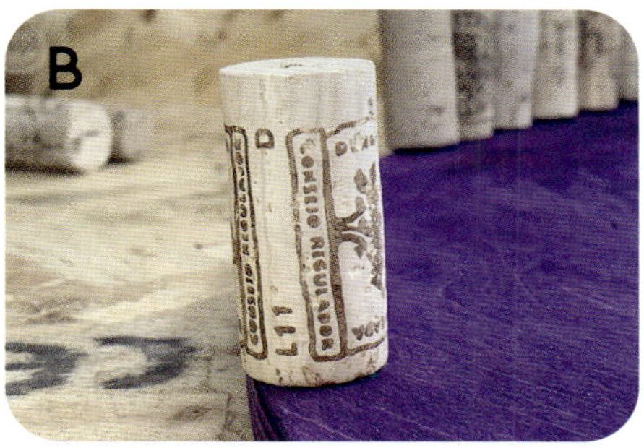

TIP

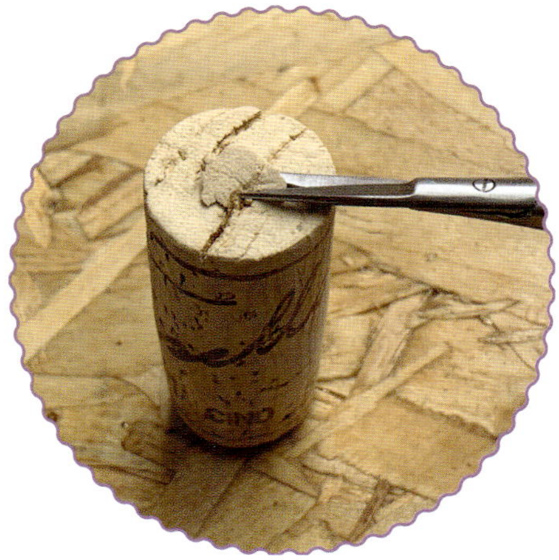

Sometimes you might need to snip or pull the pierced end of the corks off to help them stand up.

STEP 5

FILL IN THE SHAPE OF THE MOON

Fill in the moon shape with corks that have plain ends showing upright. Put down squiggles of glue in small areas and fill in a bit at a time. The glue won't set completely for a good few minutes, so there'll be time to push and adjust the layout slightly to get a good fit. Don't even attempt to get the tops level: uneven is good and adds texture.

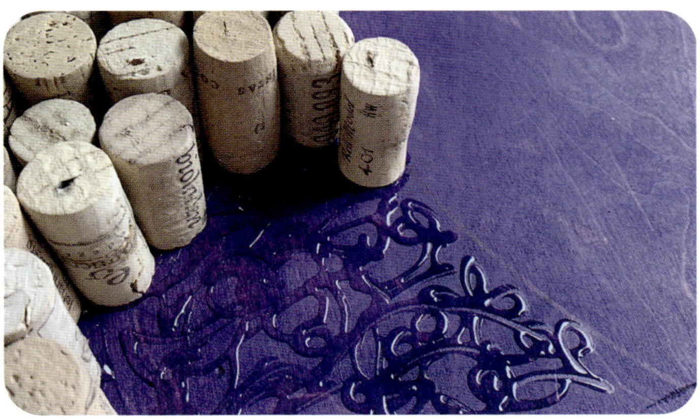

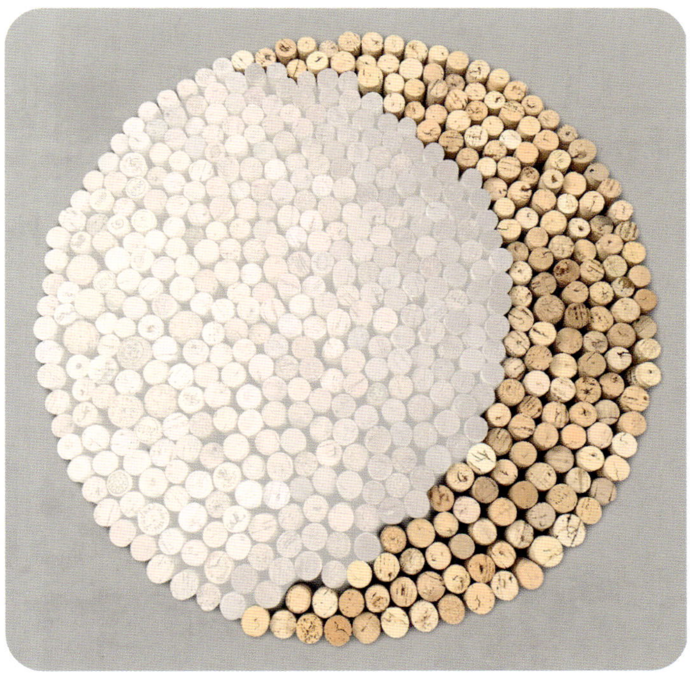

STEP 6

FILL IN THE REMAINING EDGE

Using the lightly stained corks in the middle, and the medium-stained ones at the top and bottom, complete the outside edge of the circle. Plan them, glue them, then leave to set.

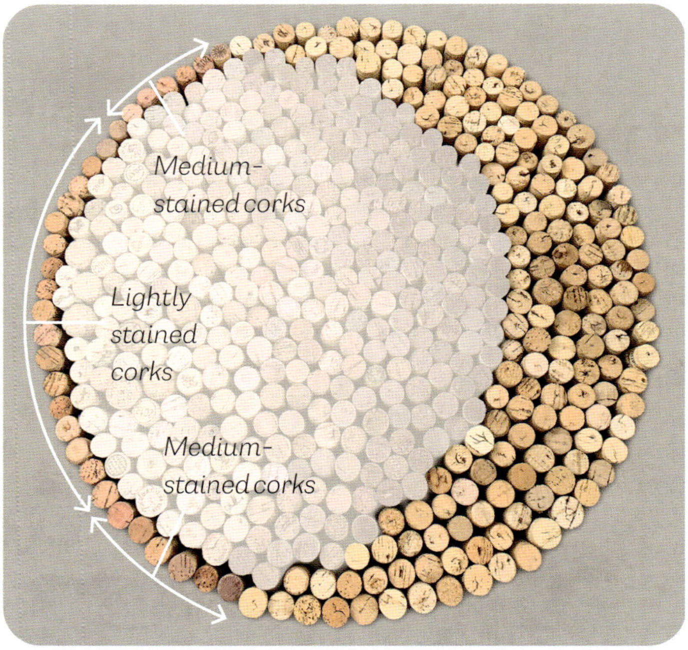

STEP 7

PLAN THE OMBRÉ EFFECT

With a firm ring of set corks to work against, the ombré effect can now be made. Fill the remaining area with corks that fade from the darkest tones on the right, to the palest on the left.

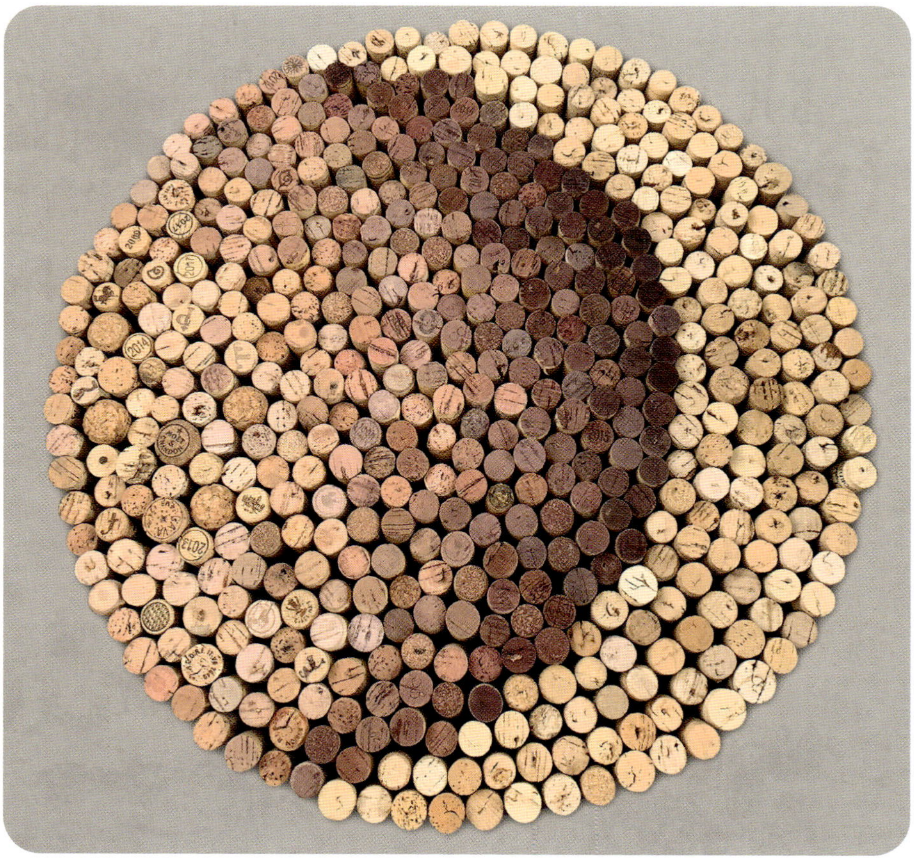

Once you are happy with your design, glue any loose corks to the base individually.

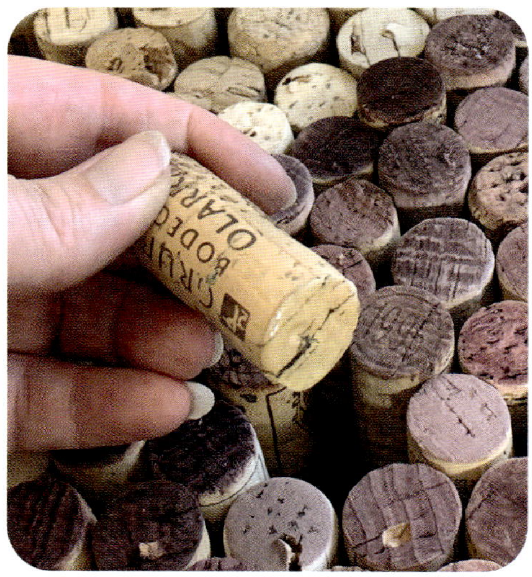

STEP 8

ATTACH THE FIXINGS

The piece is now finished. Screw the eye fasteners into the rear and tie the string between them to display.

TIP

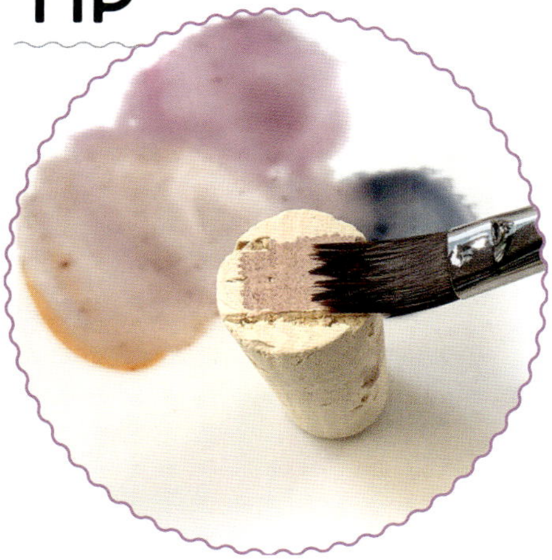

You may find you don't have enough of the right type of corks for each area. For extra unstained corks, flipping a stained cork will give you an unstained edge to display.

For extra stained corks, you can create your own. Mix up a watercolor wash made from indigo, burnt sienna, and purple lake to replicate wine color. Make as many extra pieces as you need.

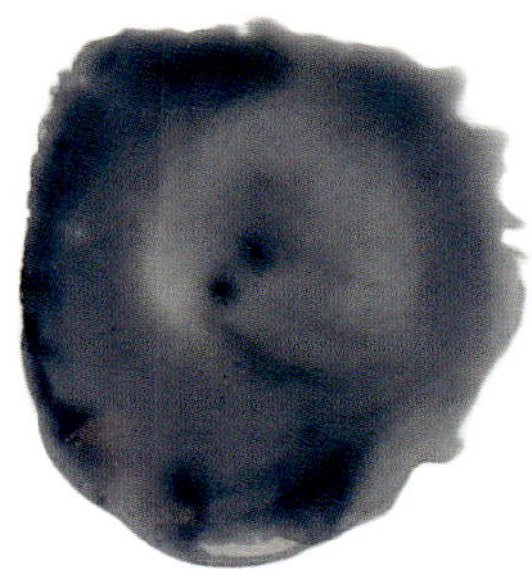

Indigo

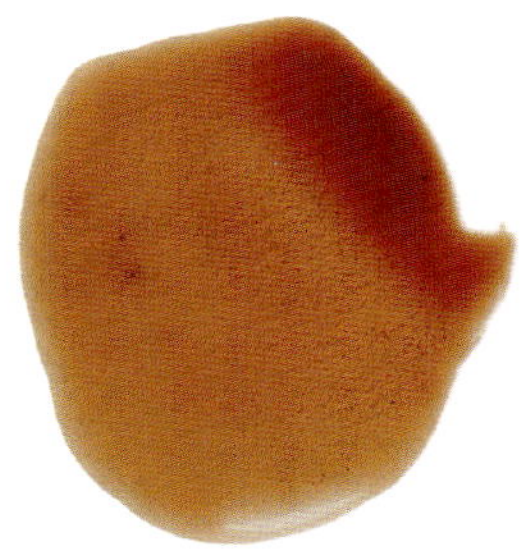

Burnt sienna

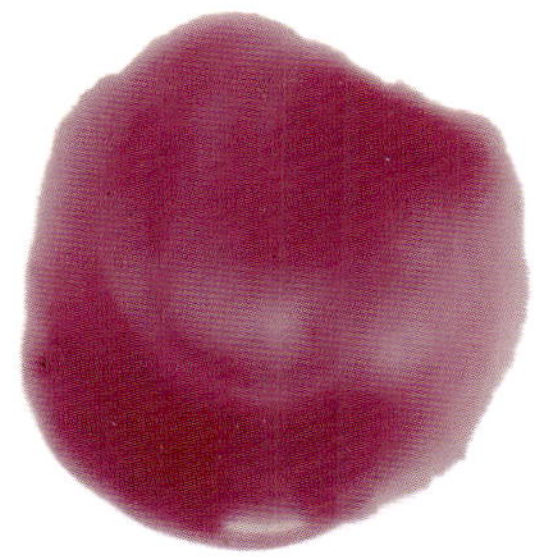

Purple lake

VARIATIONS

Watercolor washes can be added to the ombré parts to provide a subtle variation in color. Using watercolor rather than acrylic paint will allow both the color of the wine stain and the graphics to show through.

Add a translucent glaze of metallic acrylic to the section that makes up the moon. This will give a subtle shimmer to those corks.

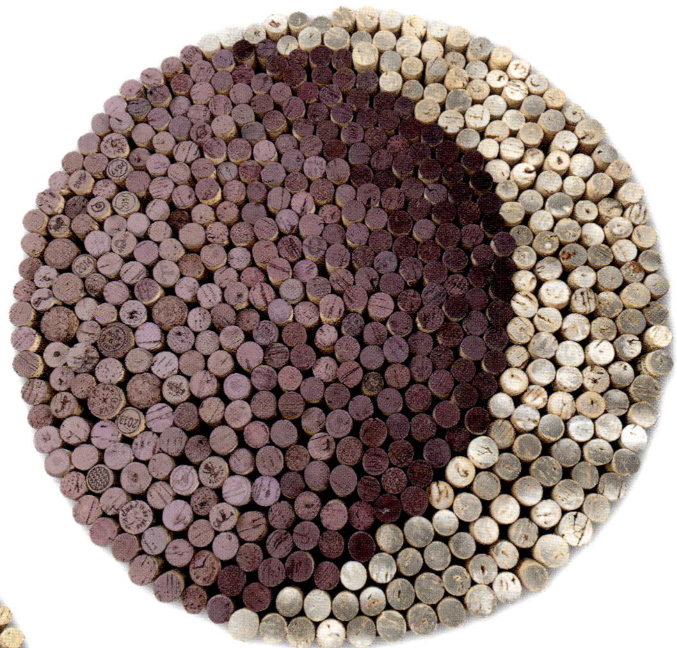

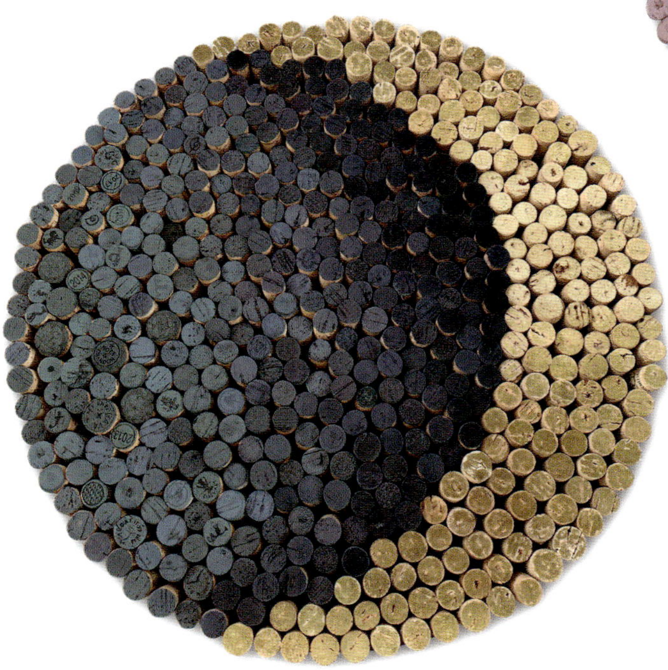

STRING ART HEART

Homemade string wall art was a really popular pastime and decoration form in the 1970s. It was just pins or nails driven into a backing board, with the string wound in patterns between them. The designs were often abstract and geometric and created with metallic thread over a black background—simple but effective. More recently, in contrast to those geometric designs, simple shapes are wound in an informal way.

For this project we are going to use wall-friendly adhesive cable clips, rather than battering in some nails—less risk of sore thumbs too!

This design takes a heart shape, but as a cutout negative. The design then bursts rays out to fill an outer circle.

The instructions show 100 percent cotton butcher's twine (a.k.a. cooking twine). This results in a very crisp, graphic piece and makes it easier for you to see what's going on with the weaving. However, the main image (*right*) uses two shades of organza ribbon, which gives the design presence. The extra bulk of the material makes for a more solid shape, but any heaviness is avoided by the sheerness of the organza.

This idea also makes a fabulous upcycling project by using fabric torn from favorite worn-out clothing. If your budget can run to it, you could even use LED lights to really emphasize the design. The great thing is, once the clips are in position, you can change what you choose to thread them with, and how. The possibilities make for a lot of fun and variety.

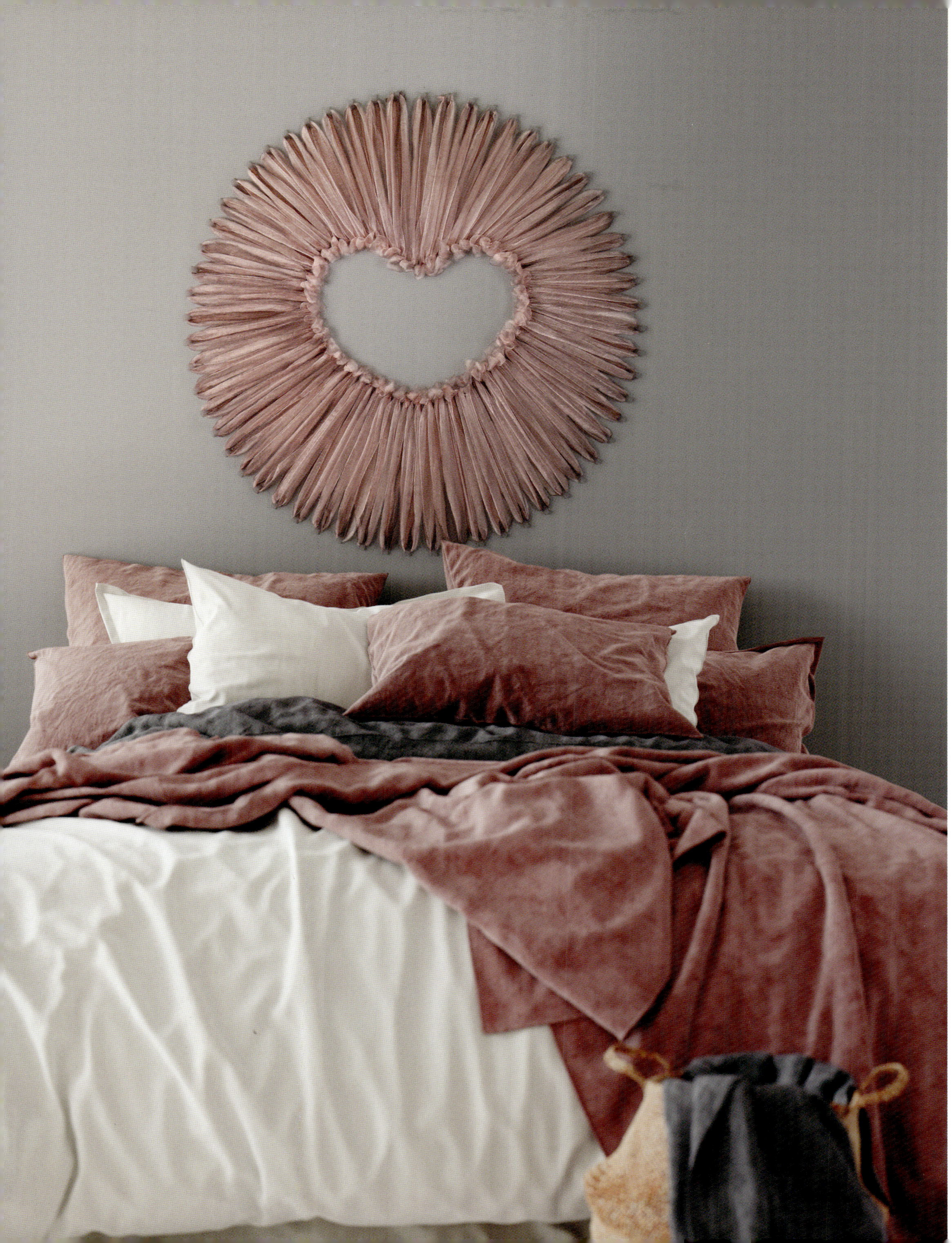

STEP-BY-STEP INSTRUCTIONS

YOU WILL NEED

To prepare the design

- *120 small adhesive cable clips*
- *Long ruler with a circle punched out at one end*
- *Rubbing alcohol for degreasing the wall*
- *Stationery: pencil, thumbtack, scissors, masking tape*

To weave the heart

- *Around 164 ft. (50 m) of material to weave the design*

OPTIONAL

- *Paint for blending clips*

STEP 1

PREPARE THE WALL

Following the method shown in the introduction, mark out the horizontal and vertical centers of where you want your design to sit on the wall. Using rubbing alcohol, clean the wall in the area where the heart will be, and leave to dry.

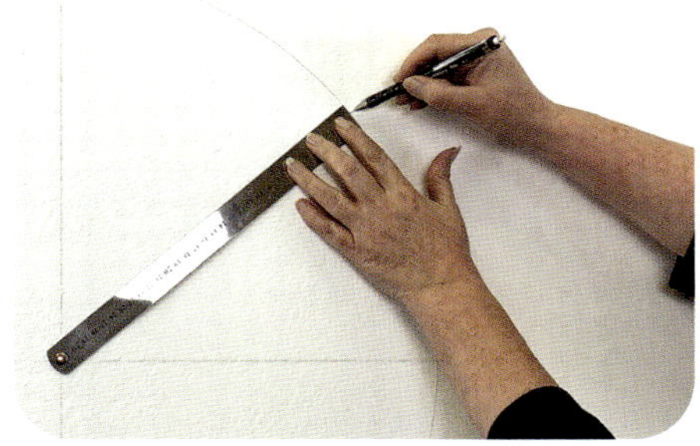

STEP 2

MARKING THE OUTER CIRCLE

Push the thumbtack through the hole in the ruler at the center point marked on the wall. Keeping your pencil resting on the edge of the ruler, rotate it to draw a circle.

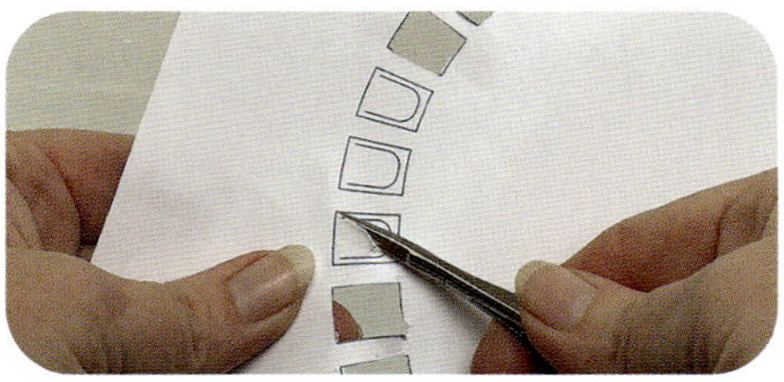

STEP 3

PREPARE THE TEMPLATE

Print the template. Cut out inside the rectangles, and around the pale gray lines Box B. Join up the vertical centerline with the two Center Dash C lines right to the edge of the page.

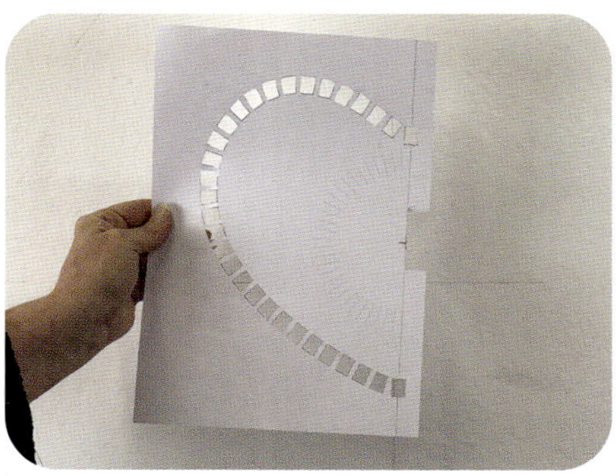

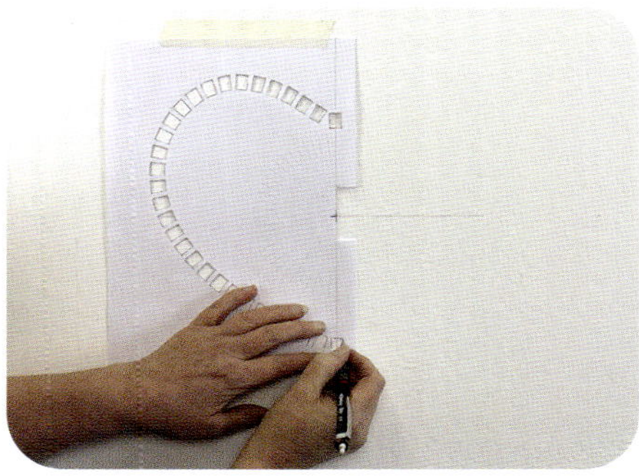

STEP 4

MARK OUT THE HEART

Align the center marks on the template with the one on the wall. Draw inside each rectangle onto the wall. Flip the template over, align the red rectangles on the template with the ones drawn on the wall, and complete the heart.

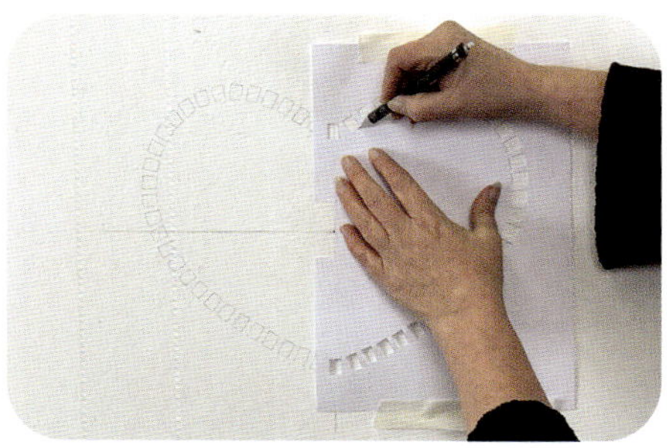

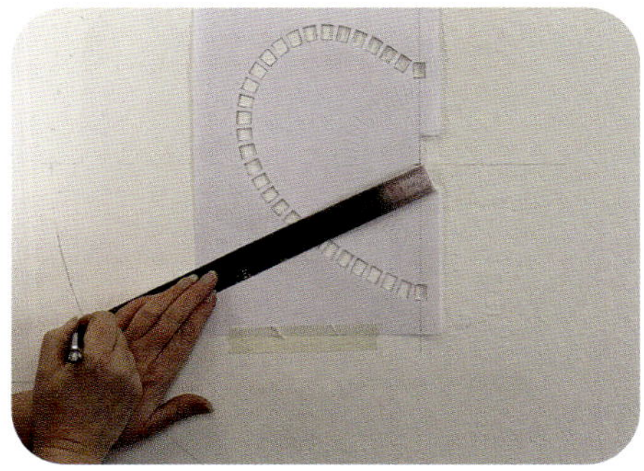

STEP 5

PLOT OUTER CIRCLE POSITIONS

Place the template back as it was in the first part of step 4. Using Protractor Marks D, mark the positions where these would hit the outer circle. For the second side you will need to rotate the template as shown in the picture below.

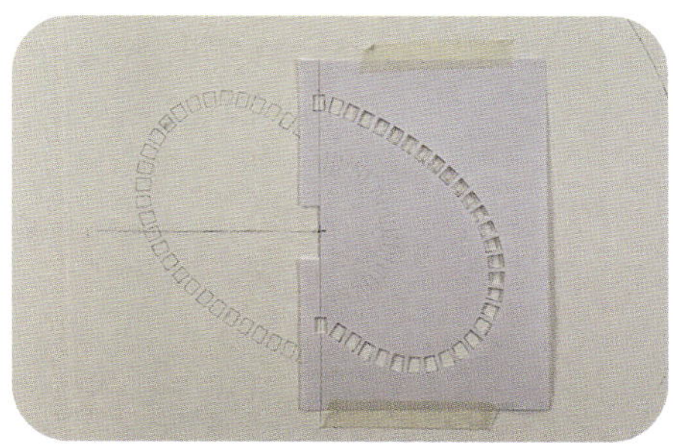

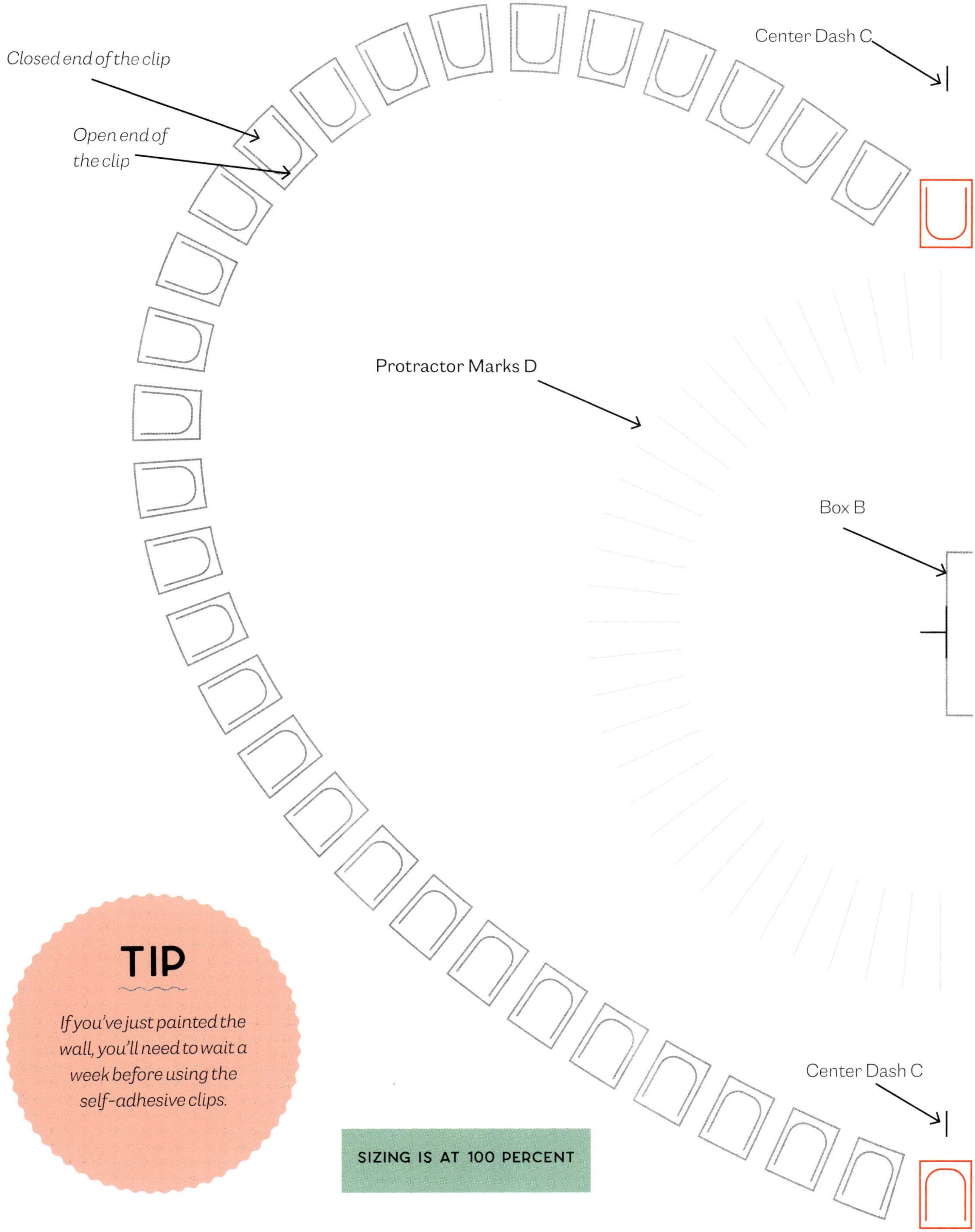

TIP

If you've just painted the wall, you'll need to wait a week before using the self-adhesive clips.

SIZING IS AT 100 PERCENT

STEP 6

ATTACH THE CLIPS INTO PLACE

Stick a clip on each rectangle you drew for the heart, plus one centered on each mark on the outer circle. It's very important that the clips are stuck so that the thread can pull against a closed end. Make sure the closed ends face the outer edge of the heart and the inner edge of the circle. Leave them to bond for a day.

Optional: If you're going to paint the clips to a color that's closer to your wall, now is the time to do it.

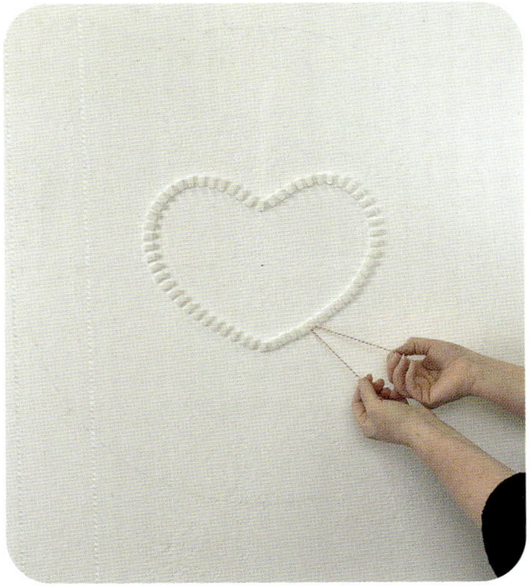

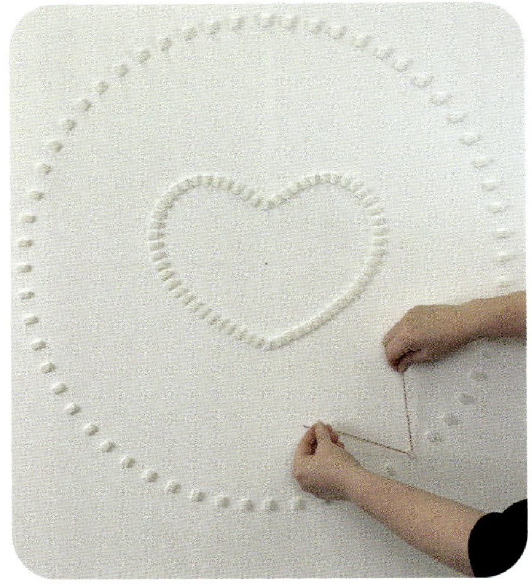

STEP 7

THREADING THE DESIGN—CLOCKWISE ROW

I've used butcher's twine (a.k.a. cooking twine) for clarity in the photographs, but the finished design has been done using organza ribbon. Here's the threading order.

Start with the clip to the left of center at the top. Weave the thread down under the center clip of the heart, then up around the center clip of the circle. Continue until you reach the clip you started with, then tie off the string.

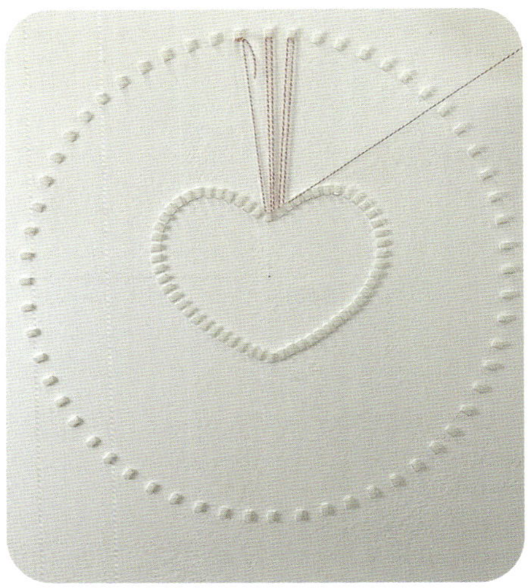

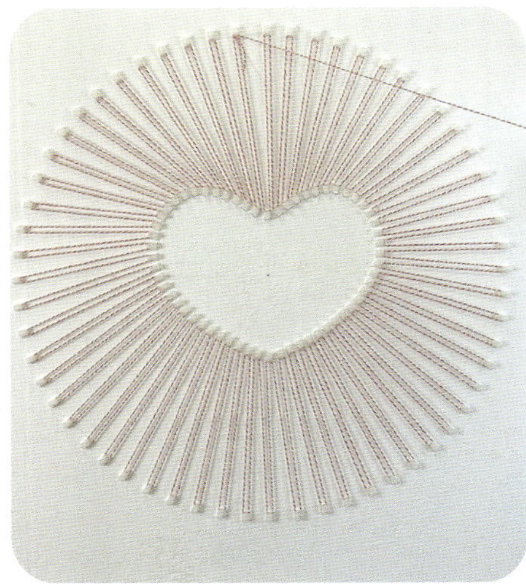

STEP 8

THREADING THE DESIGN—COUNTERCLOCKWISE ROW

Weave in the opposite direction. Start with the clip to the right of center at the top. Weave the thread down under the center clip of the heart, then up around the center clip of the circle. Continue until you reach the clip you started with, then tie off the string.

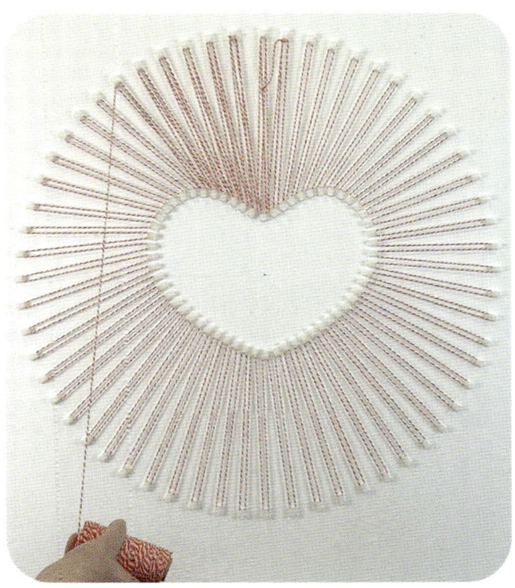

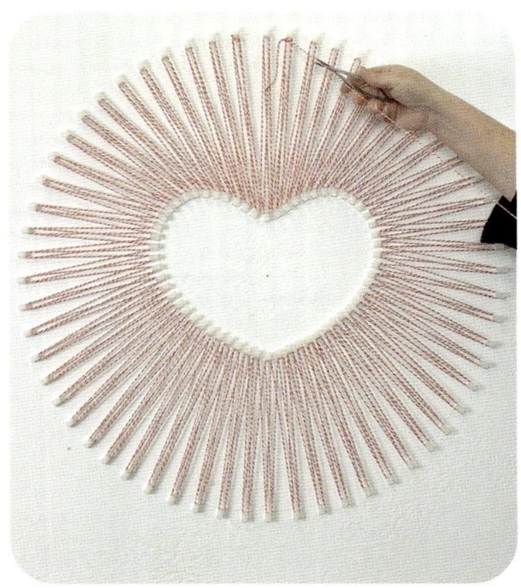

ORGANZA OPTIONS

Using organza ribbon—with its bouncy movie star sheen—changes the look of the design from a modern stark graphic to one with luscious Hollywood glamour. Two shades of ribbon were used, with the darker one for the first row. An additional decorative touch was added by teasing a length of ribbon around the heart clips. The ribbon is wound around each clip while adjusting the tension to give a little flounce or loop in between the clips.

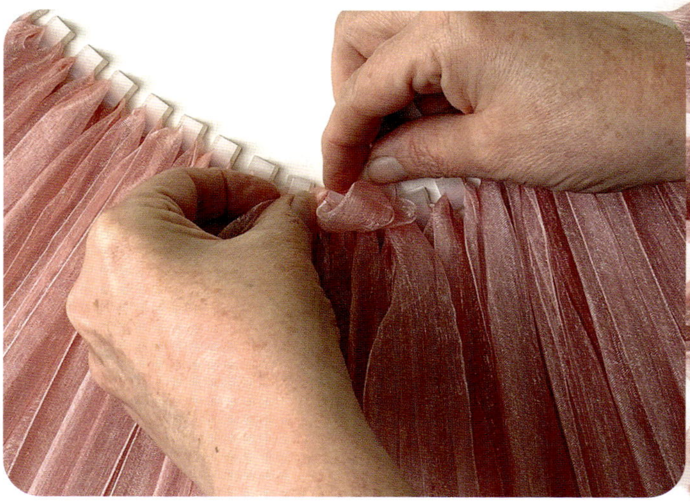

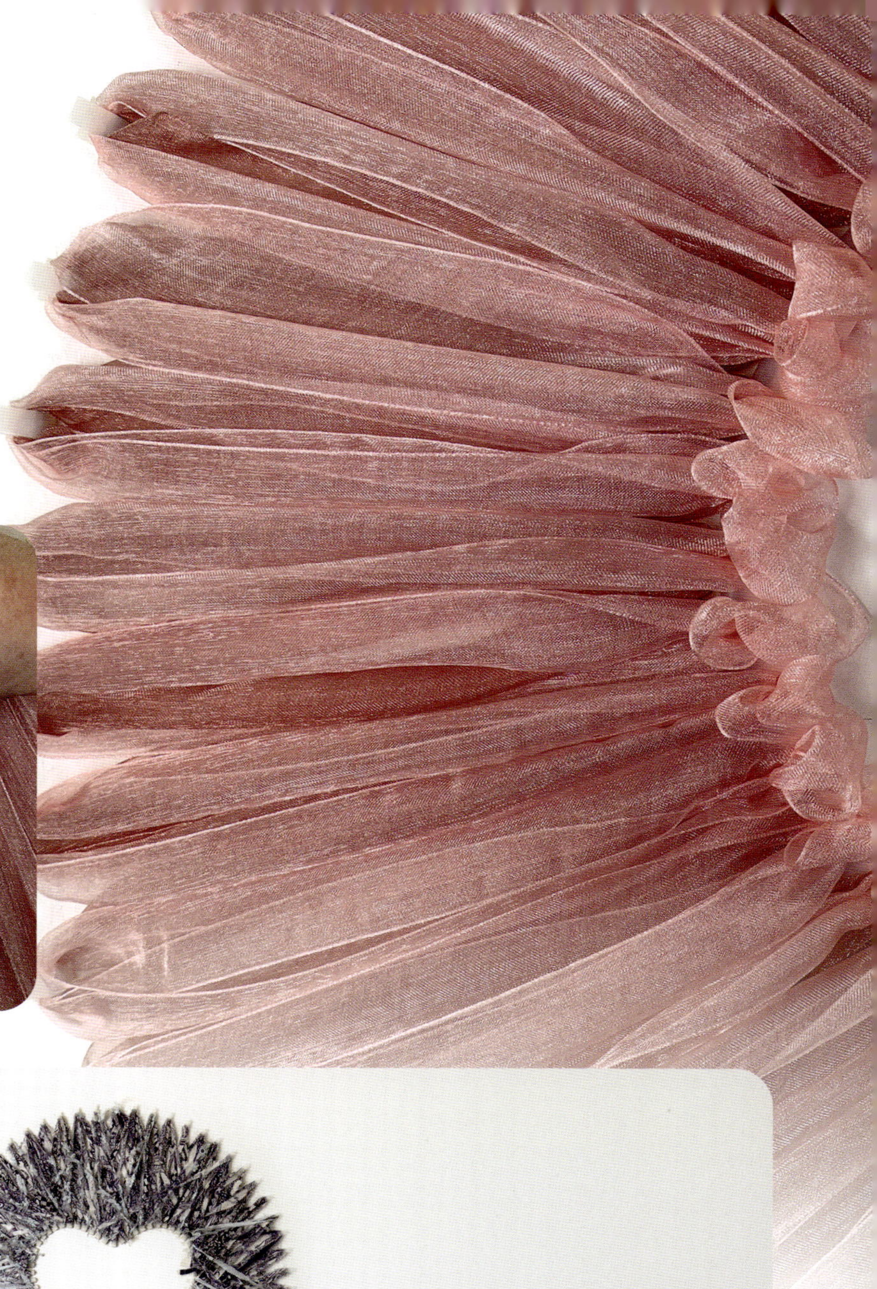

ALTERNATIVE WORKINGS

This is the same design worked with a free-form weaving technique using strips of cloth. First, lengths of thin strips of fabric are tied together. The frayed edges and tied ends suit the casual approach of the technique.

Weaving is done between the clips in a random manner, filling in any thin areas as you go. This is a lovely way to use old clothes that a child may have grown out of, or as a memorial piece for a special textile.

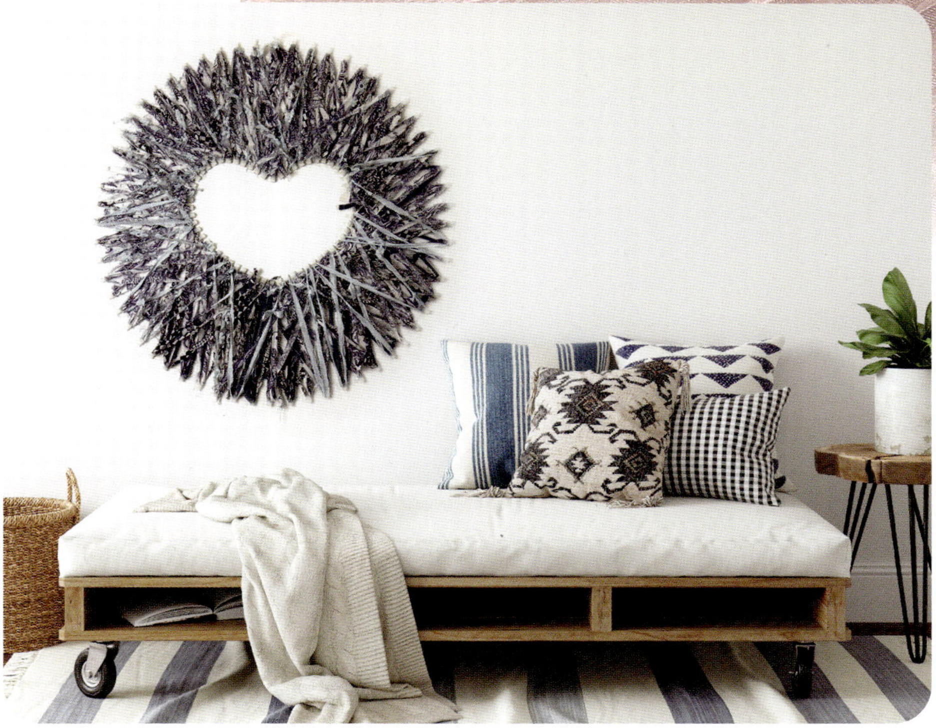

THE GREAT MARBLE RUN

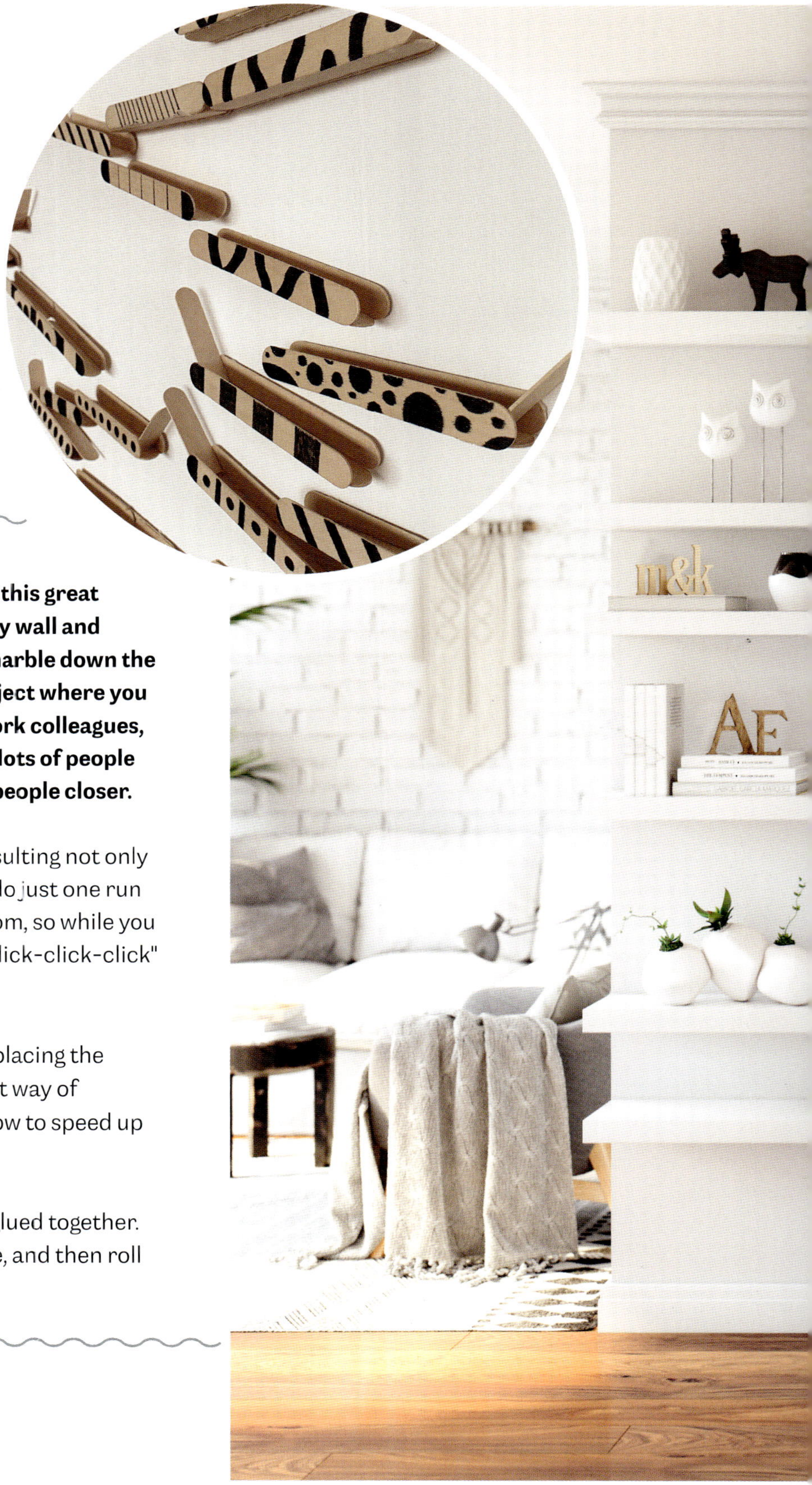

Your walls can be playful as well as artistic with this great marble fun run! This fab project will liven up any wall and make you smile every time you pass and roll a marble down the run. If you are searching for a collaborative project where you can work as a team with your family, friends, work colleagues, or class, then try this! It's a great way of getting lots of people involved, having a laugh together, and bringing people closer.

For our run we created three starting points, resulting not only in a run, but also in a race! You might choose to do just one run that goes from the top of your stairs to the bottom, so while you are going down the stairs you can listen to the "click-click-click" as the marble jumps between the pieces.

Working out how the run works, adjusting, and placing the pieces so that the marbles don't pop off is a great way of teaching children about gravity and velocity—how to speed up the marble with angles and how to slow it down.

The marble run is made from giant craft sticks glued together. You make your pieces, design your run, decorate, and then roll those marbles!

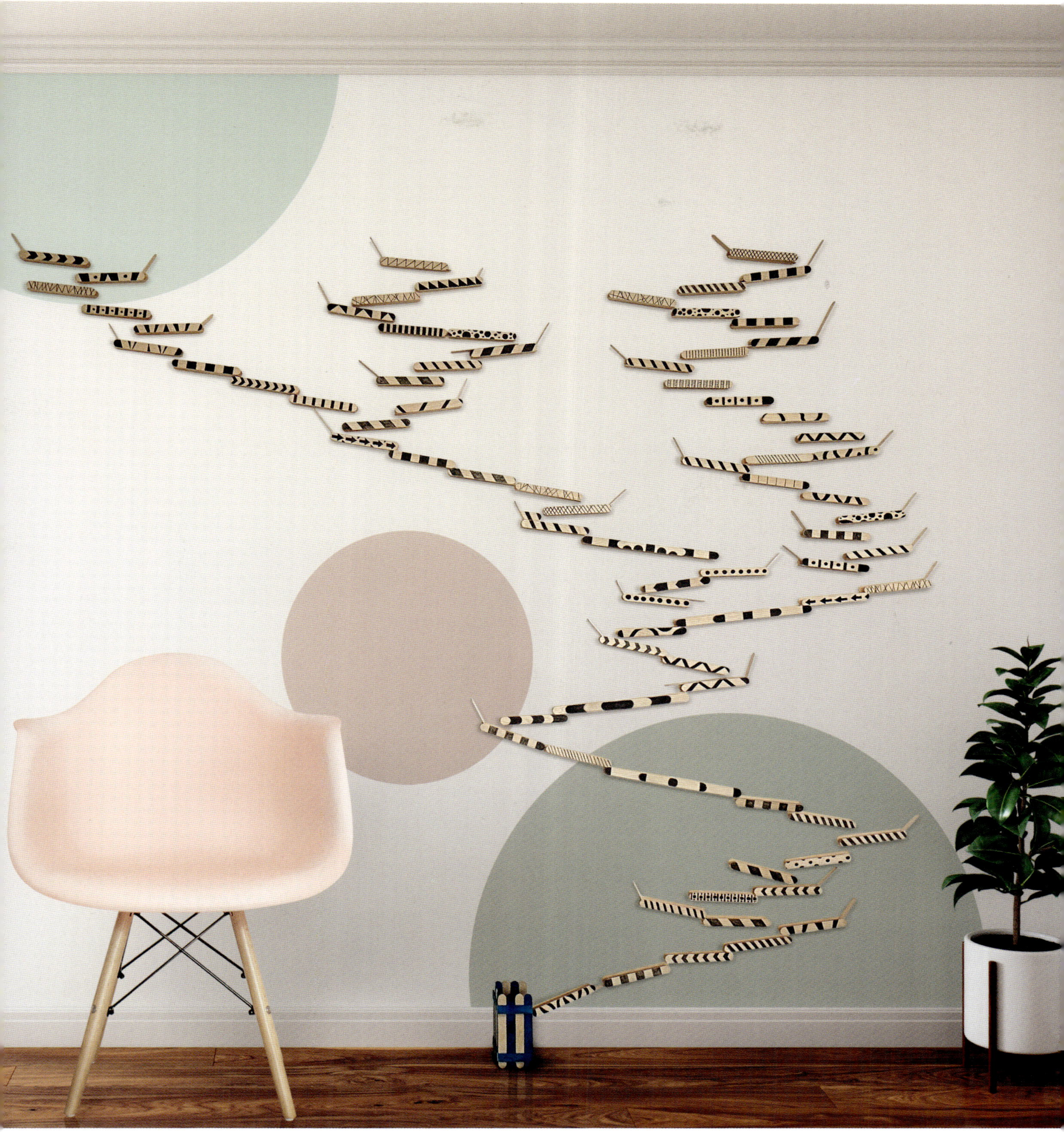

STEP-BY-STEP INSTRUCTIONS

YOU WILL NEED

- *100-150 craft sticks 6 x 0.75 in. (15.3 x 2 cm), plain or colored, or more if you want a big run!*
- *A few small marbles (smaller than the width of your popsicle sticks)*
- *Marker pens for decoration*

For marking and sticking

- *Glue gun and glue sticks*
- *Heavy-duty knife and cutting mat*
- *Pencil and metal ruler*
- *Reusable adhesive putty and grip tape*

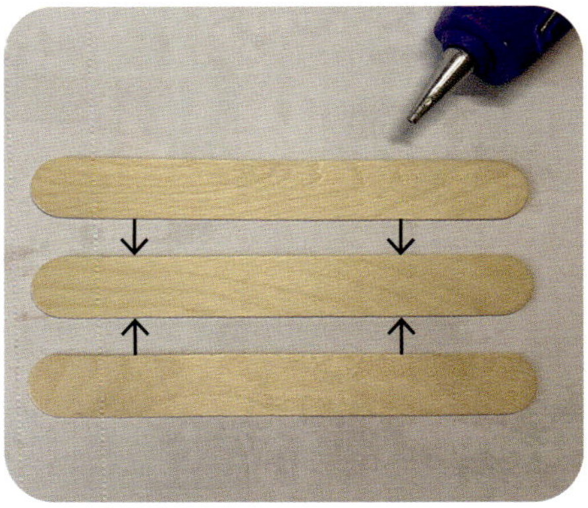

STEP 1

BASIC RUN

Take three craft sticks and heat up your glue gun.

Be very careful when using a glue gun, since the glue and metal tip get extremely hot. Keep well out of the reach of children.

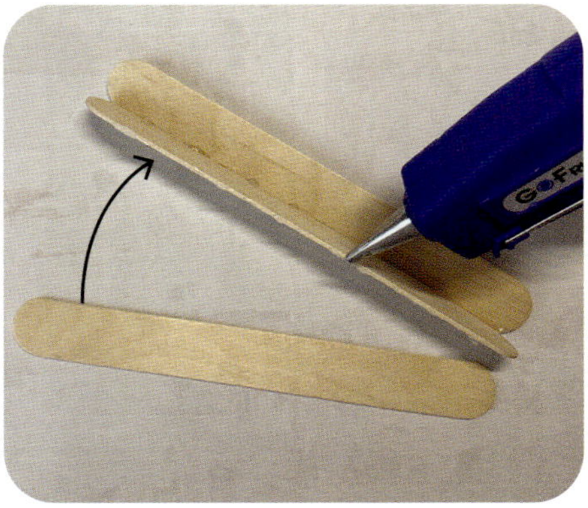

STEP 2

BASIC RUN SIDES

Glue along one edge at a time (the glue sets very quickly, so act fast) and fix each of the side pieces at 90 degrees to form a "U" shape once you have glued the two sides on.

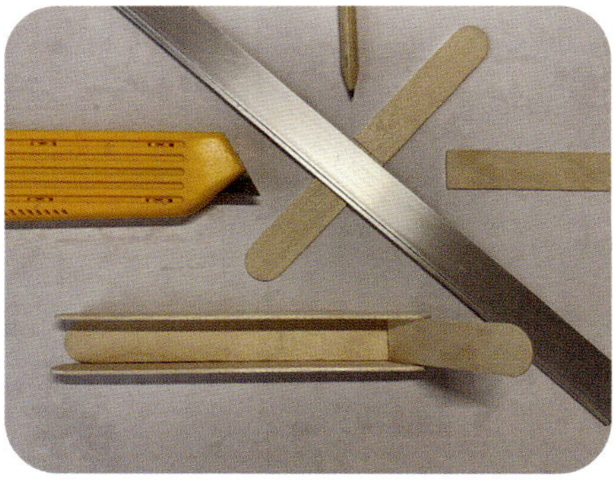

STEP 3

STOPPER

This stops the marbles falling off the run when the direction changes. Mark with a pencil where to cut, about halfway, then cut using a heavy-duty knife on a cutting mat. Lightly sand the cut edge if needed, then stick the stopper at an angle into the end of the run.

Leave space for the marble to drop if using when changing direction

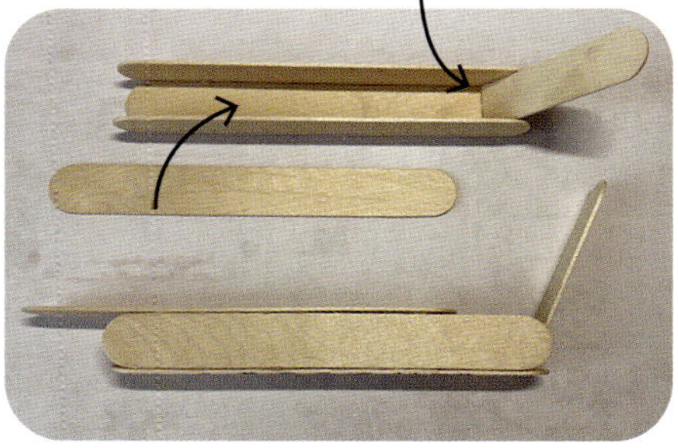

VARIATION 1

TUNNEL

The tunnel hides the marble as it travels! You can make the tunnels as long as you like by joining tunnel pieces together (see step 6).

Take a run with or without a stopper, and glue a stick to the top of the run, creating a box.

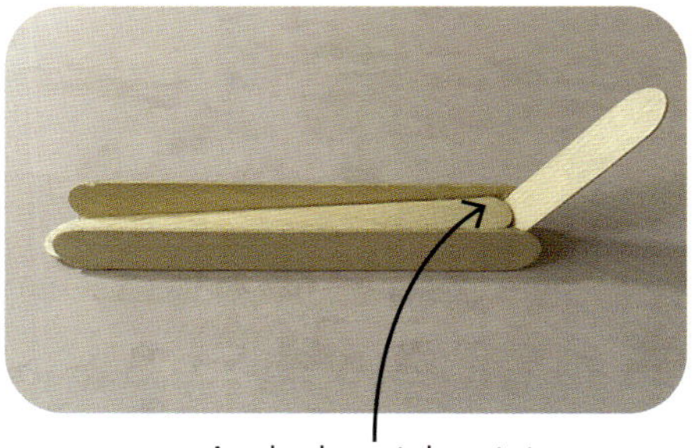

Angle the stick so it is higher near the stopper

VARIATION 2

INNER SLOPE

This changes the speed of the marble and creates an overhang by gluing a stick at an angle inside a run. When gluing, angle the stick so that it is higher near the beginning of the run and lower at the end.

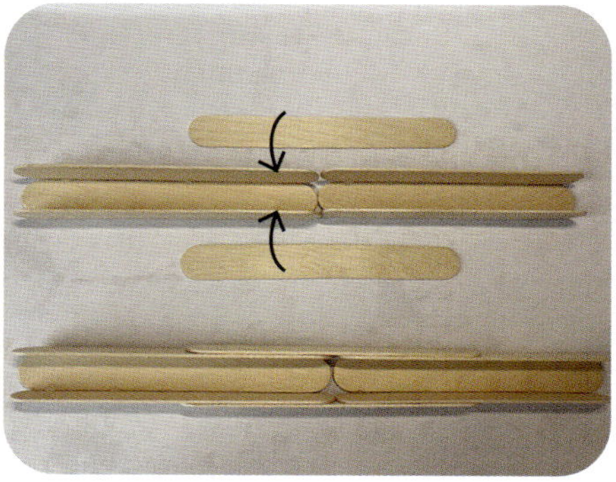

VARIATION 3

LONG, STRAIGHT RUN

To make one continuous straight run, glue a stick each side of a single run. You can make your runs as long as needed.

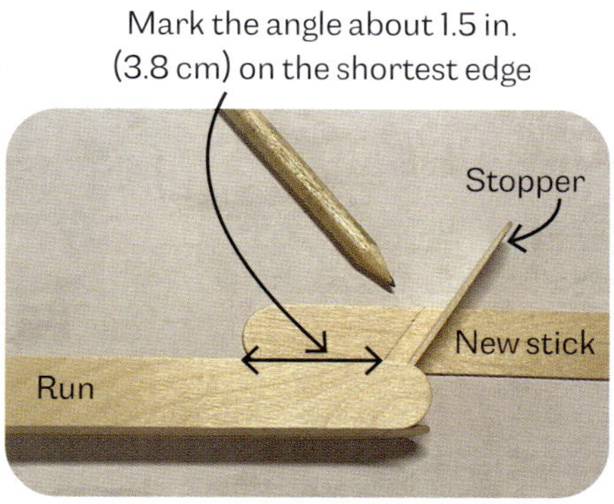

STEP 4

THE STAIRS: MARK ANGLE

Take a run with a stopper and a new stick and mark with a pencil the same angle as the stopper, about 1.5 in. (3.8 cm) at the shortest from the end.

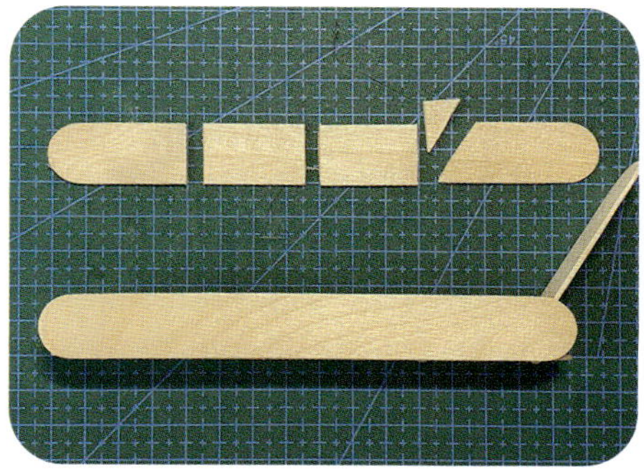

STEP 5

THE STAIRS: CUT STEPS

Mark the rest of the steps about 1.25 in. (3 cm) apart. Use a heavy-duty knife, metal ruler, and cutting mat to divide the stick into five parts. Discard the small triangle. Sand the ends if they are a little rough.

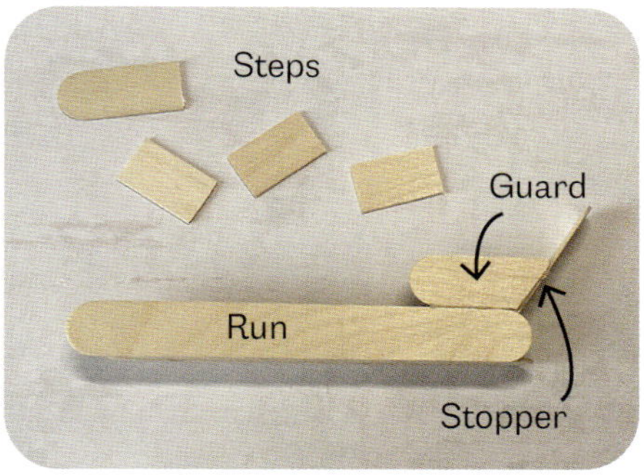

STEP 6

THE STAIRS: ATTACH GUARD

Taking the angled piece, attach it to one side of the run, on the outside. Glue to the top of the run and the side of the stopper.

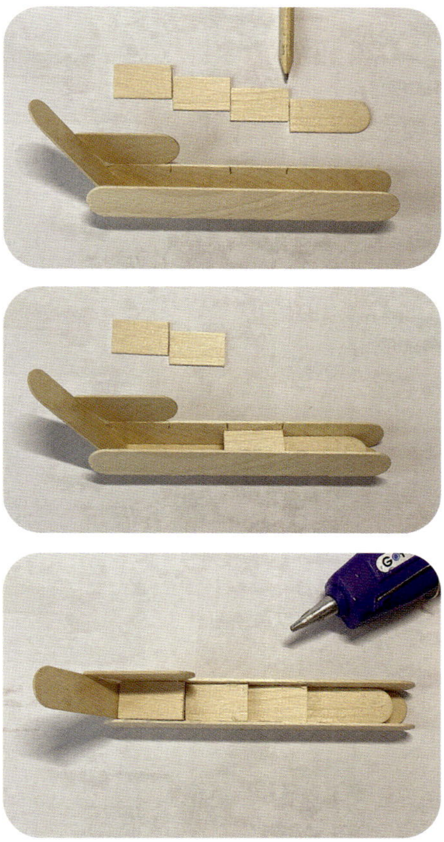

STEP 7

THE STAIRS: GLUE THE STEPS

First, start at the stopper mark where your steps align on the inner edge of the run.

Beginning with the lowest step, glue it to the inside of the run, then continue with the other three steps, raising each a little until you get to the top step that can align with the top of the run. The guard will stop the marble from escaping.

TIP

Make around thirty or so basic runs, and twenty with stoppers, plus a few of the special runs such as doubles, tunnel, or stairs. Start building your run and add more as you need them

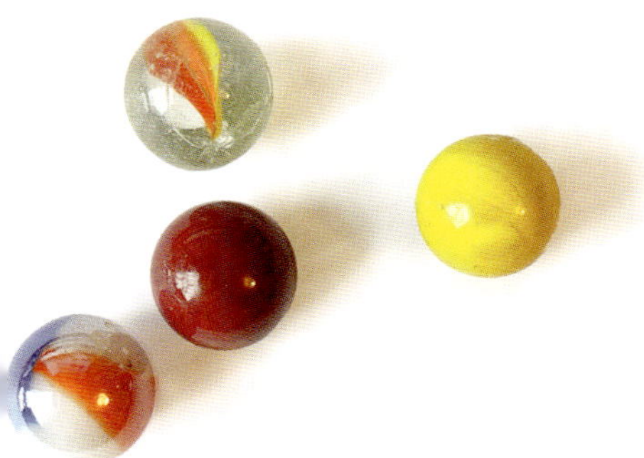

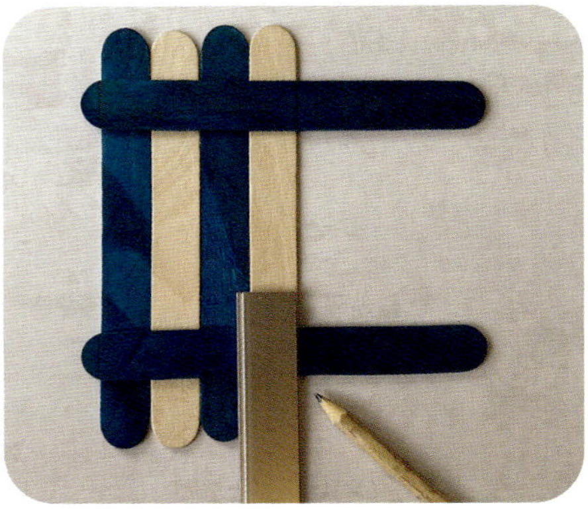

STEP 8

BOX: MEASURING THE BEAMS

For contrast we chose to use natural and dyed sticks for our box. Place four sticks alongside each other and put another stick on top, marking the edges so you know where to cut. Repeat for the bottom beam. You will need two side panels and four beams.

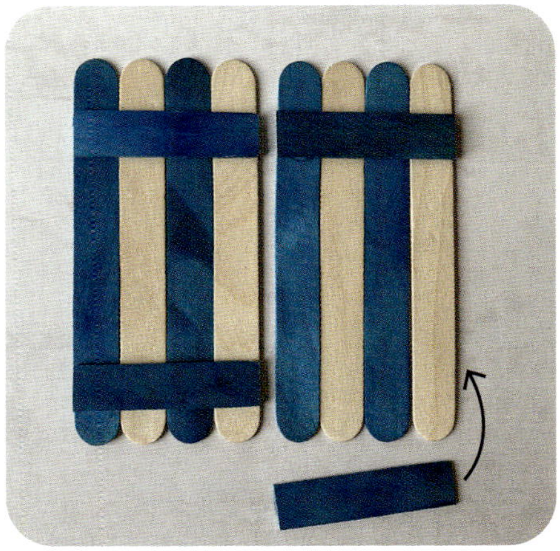

STEP 9

BOX: MAKE THE TWO SIDES

Cut the beams to size and glue top and bottom onto the box side beneath. Make sure that the beams are the same height position on each of the two side panels.

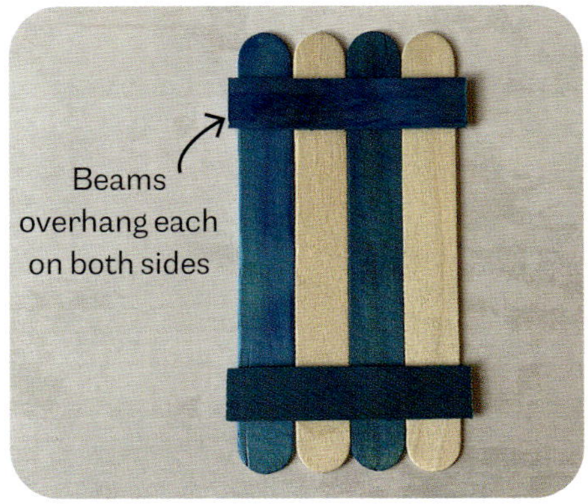

STEP 10

BOX: BACK PANEL

For the back panel the beams need to be slightly longer than the four sticks. On each side they need to overhang by the thickness of your sticks multiplied by two. When glued to the sides, this will make the corners neat.

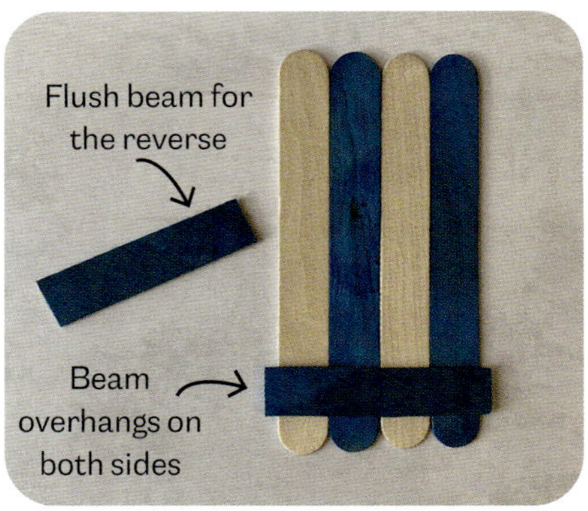

STEP 11

BOX: FRONT PANEL

The front panel also needs the beam on the front to overhang by the thickness of your sticks multiplied by two. Glue the overhang beam to the bottom of the front panel, making sure it aligns with the other beams on the other panels

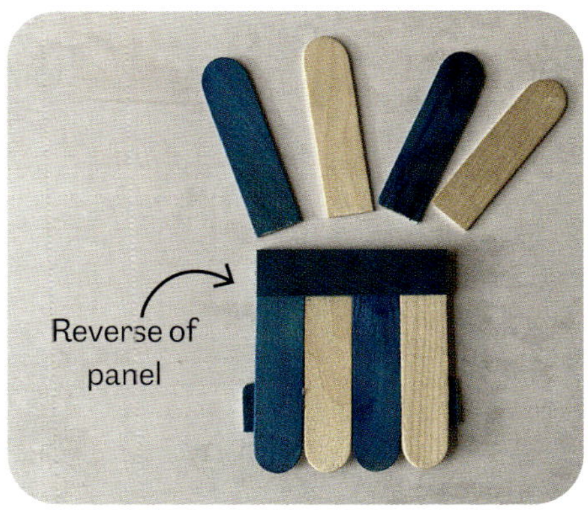

STEP 12

BOX: FRONT PANEL INNER BEAM

Turn the panel over and glue the shorter (flush) beam about halfway down.

Once dry, trim off the tops of the sticks flush with the beam.

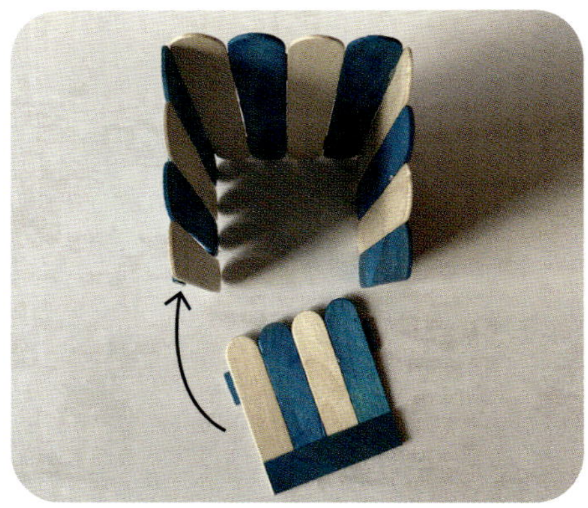

STEP 13

BOX: ASSEMBLE

Glue the two side panels to the back panel at 90 degrees to form a "U" shape. Add the front panel. The tops and bottoms of the panels should align so that it stands up properly. If you want to add a base, just cut more sticks to length and glue to the bottom.

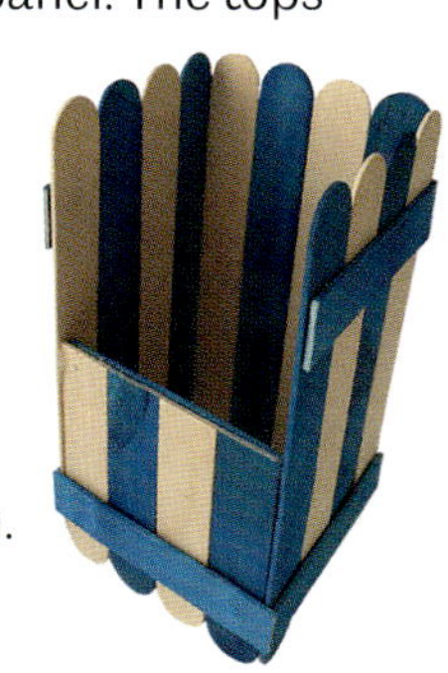

BUILD YOUR RUN

This is the most fun part of the project—you can design any layout you like! We chose to have three starting points that all run into each other. Who will win?

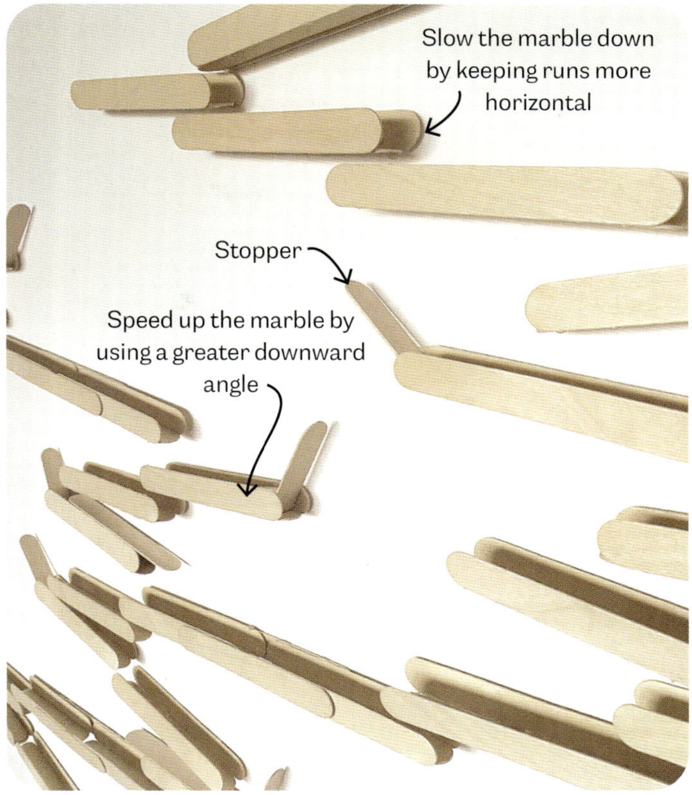

STEP 14

DESIGN YOUR RUN

Start at the top and work your way down, sticking the pieces gently to your wall by using reusable adhesive putty. Test every few runs with a marble and adjust the angles if the marble goes too fast or falls off the run. To slow the marble down, reduce the angle of the run and have a few pieces where the runs are almost horizontal. To speed up the run, increase its downward angle. Use a stopper to stop the marble from falling off the run.

Wait to decorate your run until after you have planned it out; otherwise you won't know which side of each run to decorate.

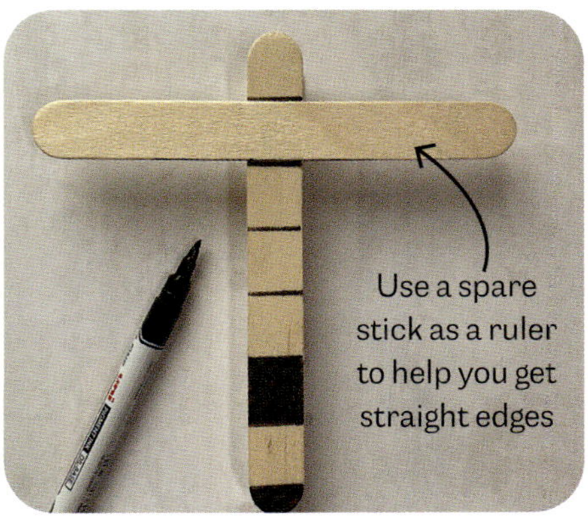

STEP 15

DECORATION

Once you have designed your run and it works, take each piece off the wall and decorate it. We have used marker pens and kept the design monotone, just using black and a variety of designs. We also have two runs that meet in the middle. You could have a different color for each run and then a third where the two runs meet.

Turn the page for ideas.

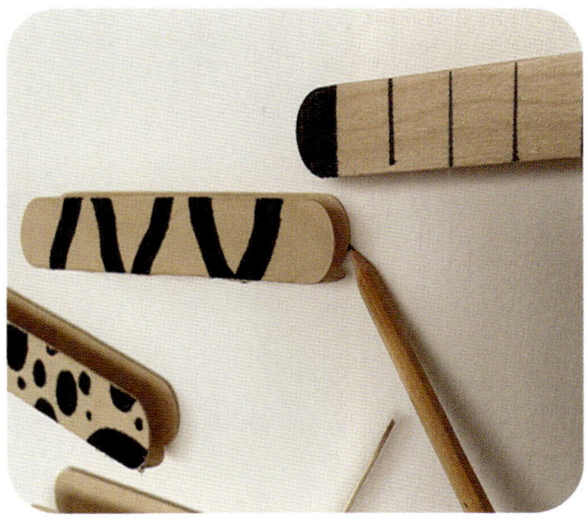

STEP 16

FIXING

After you have decorated a run, put it back on the wall and test it again with a marble. Mark the final position lightly with a pencil underneath. Use grip tape to permanently stick it to the wall. If you want to keep creating, you can just use reusable adhesive putty, but at some point a run might fall off the wall!

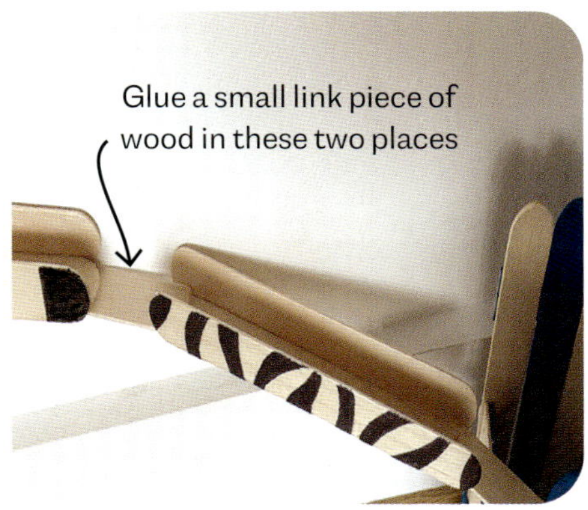

STEP 17

FLOOR BOX TO CATCH MARBLES

If your box is on a table then you don't need to do this, but ours in on the floor, and the skirting board pushes the box out of range.

Cut two short pieces of popsicle stick and glue between the last run stuck on the wall and the "hanging run" to maneuver the marble into the box.

PATTERN DIRECTORY

We chose to keep our piece monochrome—just black and white. It gives uniformity when using so many different designs, but you can use any color or colors you like.

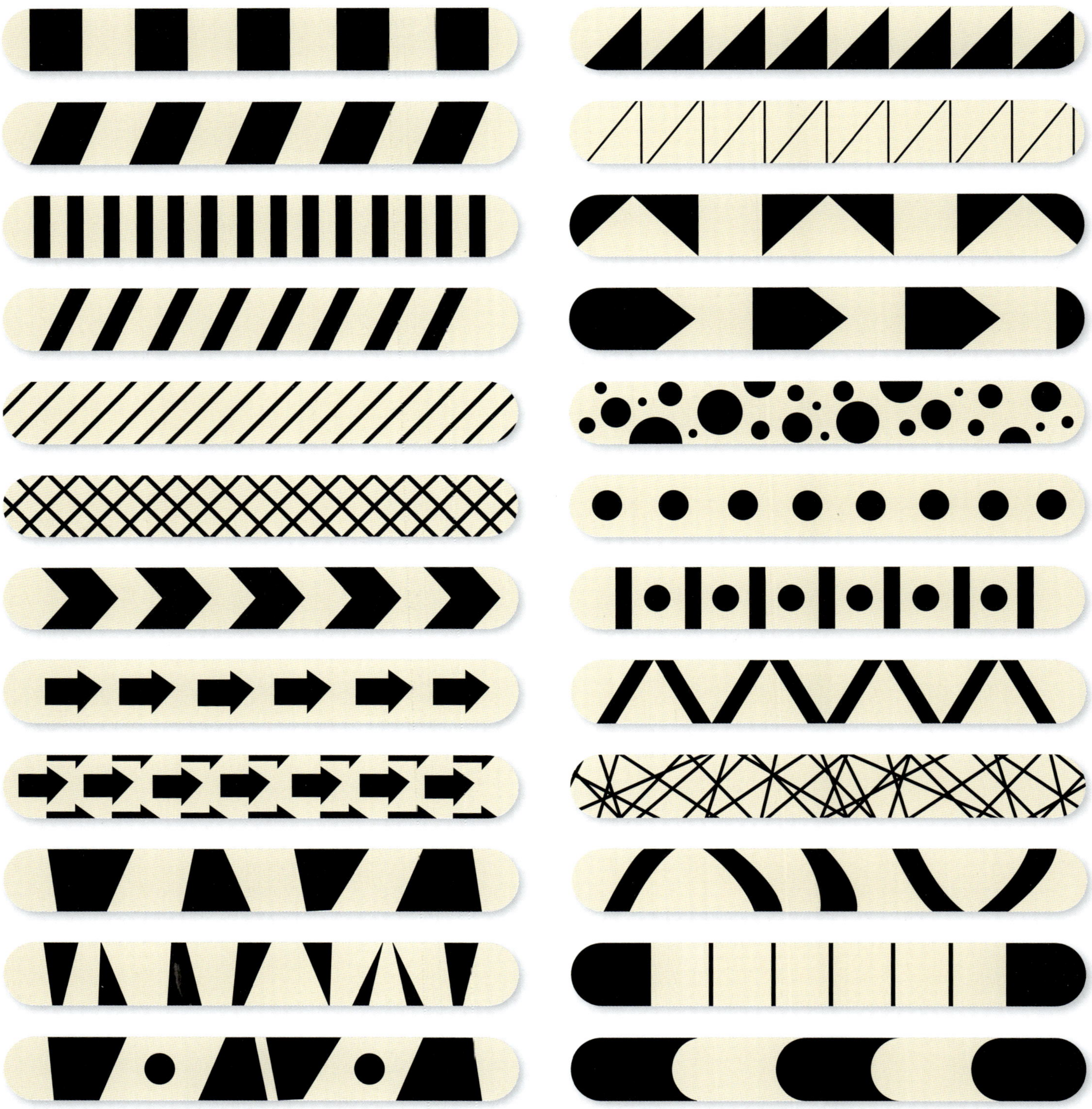

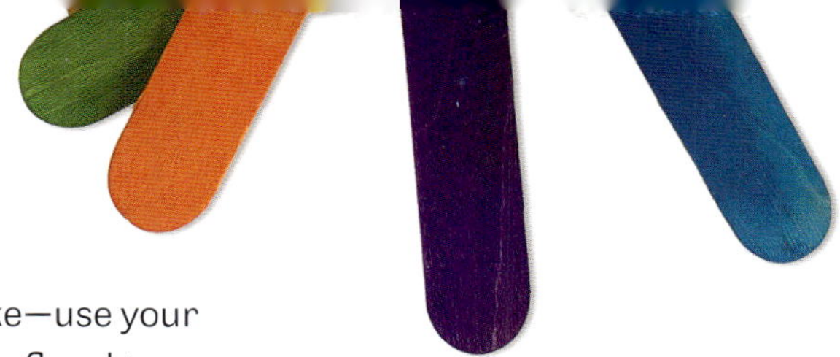

VARIATIONS

You can decorate your run anyway you like—use your imagination! Any color or any design, from floral to childlike, rainbow to plain, or for simplicity, just use colored popsicle sticks that are already stained.

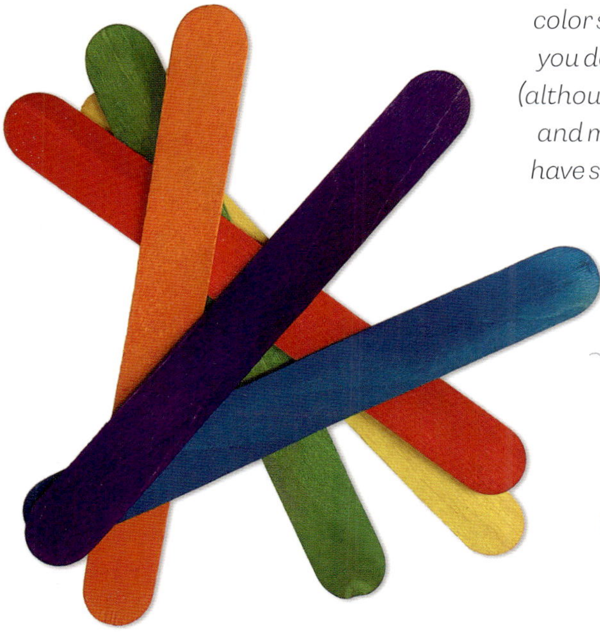

Left and right: Ready stained color sticks are very effective and you don't have to decorate them (although you still can). You can mix and match colors on each run or have solid color runs. What about a rainbow run?

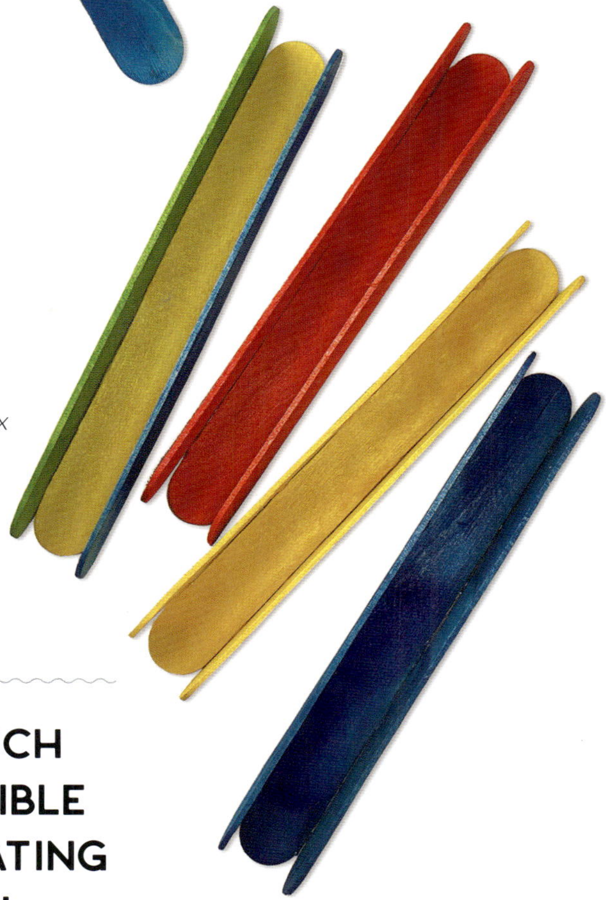

HAVE AS MUCH FUN AS POSSIBLE WHEN DECORATING YOUR RUN

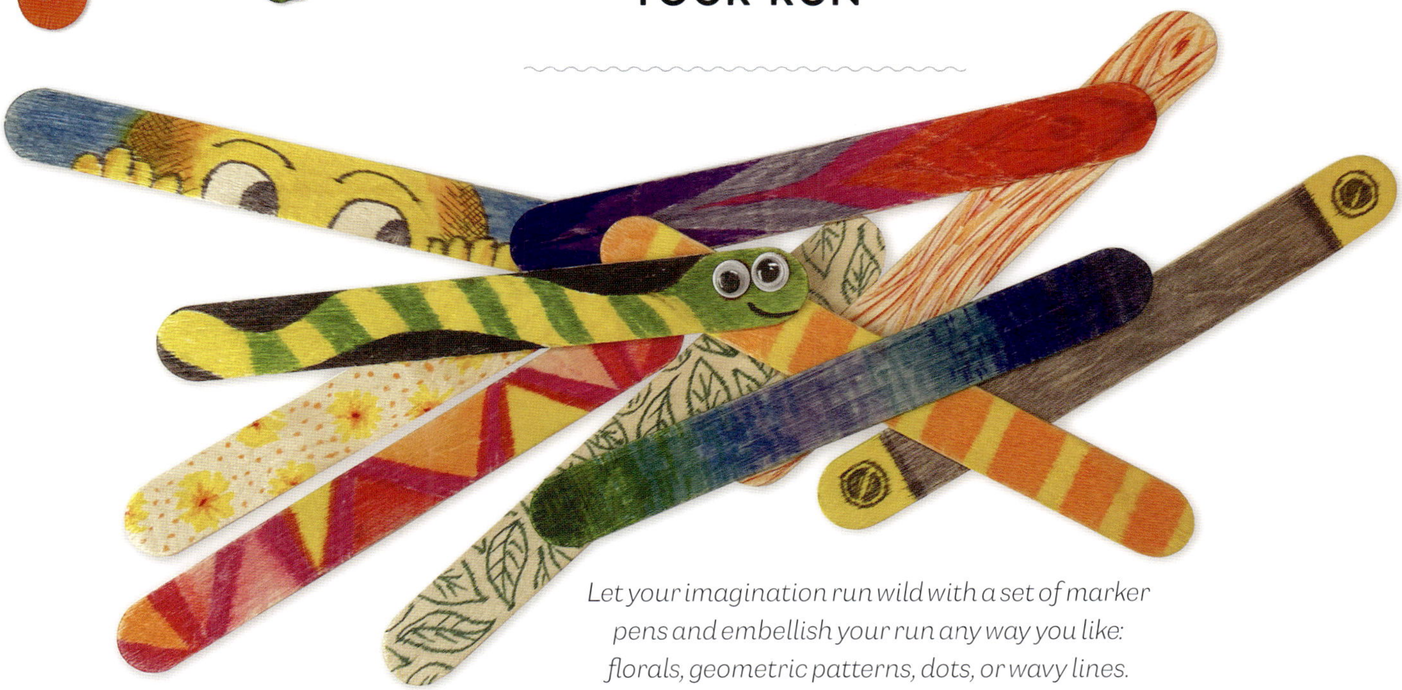

Let your imagination run wild with a set of marker pens and embellish your run any way you like: florals, geometric patterns, dots, or wavy lines. Or make it fit into your existing decor for artistic sophistication. Alternatively, how about using googly eyes, or theme it as a pop art installation?

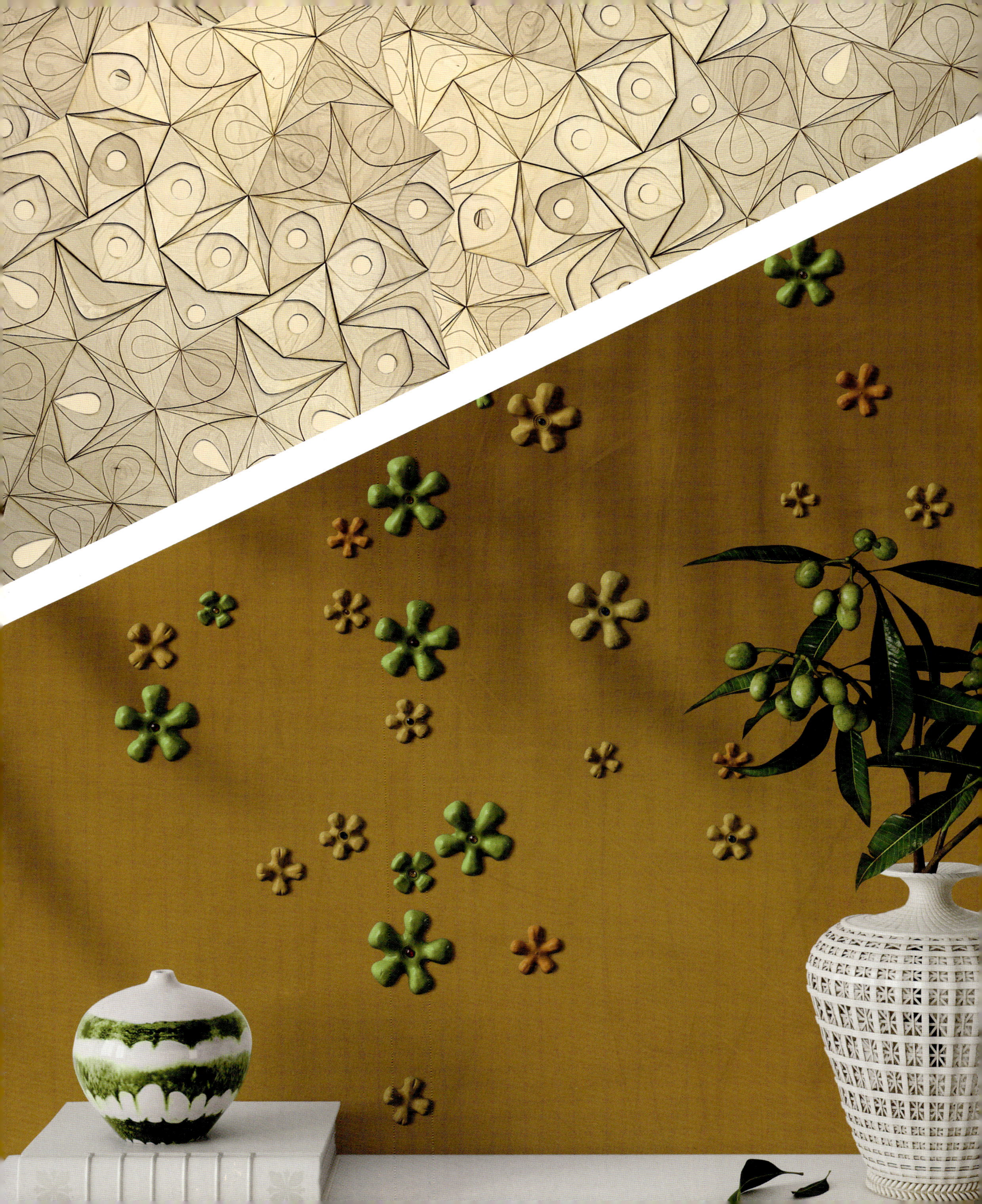

CAST & CONSTRUCT

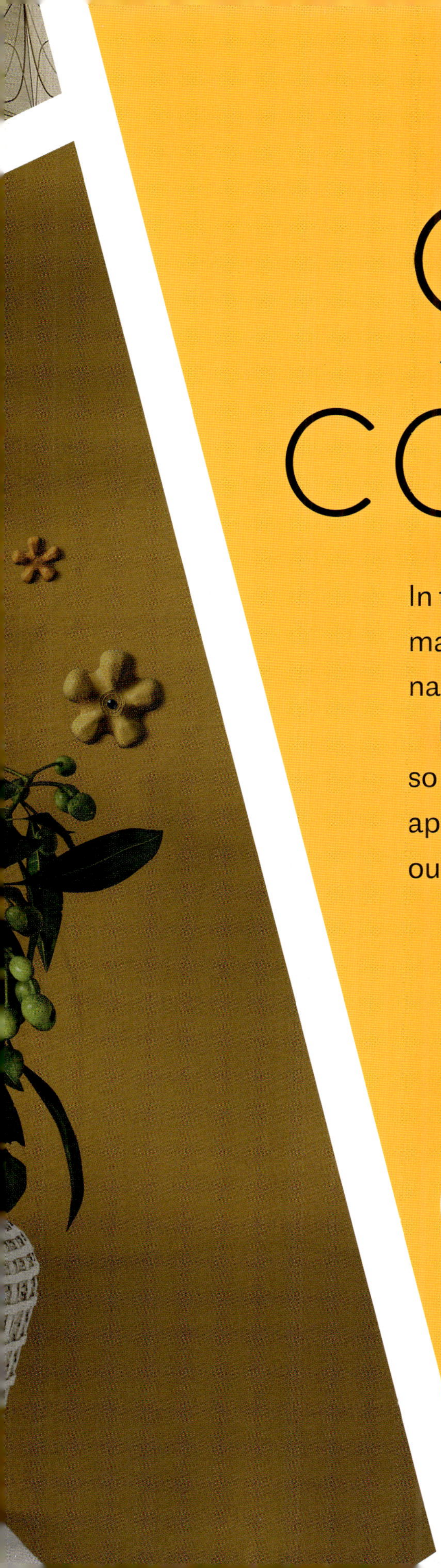

In this section, we'll be making new objects from materials more commonly found in the building trade: namely, plaster and wood.

It's always exciting to experiment with new materials, so we hope this section will introduce you to some fresh approaches or enable more-experienced crafters to try out some unusual ideas and approaches.

3

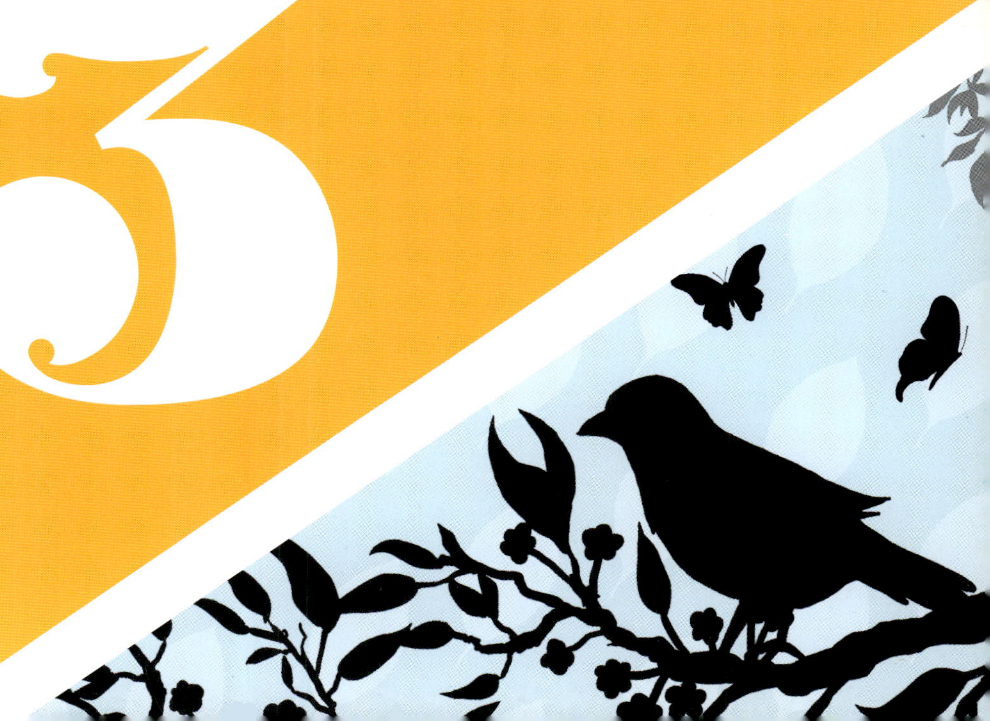

PLY PENROSE TILES

Penrose tiles are named after the English mathematician and physicist Roger Penrose, who investigated them in the 1970s. Unlike ordinary tiles, which have repeating patterns when placed together, Penrose tiles—also known as aperiodic tiles—grow out from a starting point.

These tiles can cover a large area in similar patterns, but it's also possible to get stuck and not be able to place more tiles in a given direction. Your project will need careful planning!

We love midcentury architecture and interiors. Alongside the futuristic shapes and exciting new materials, there was often extensive use of ply in furniture, and particularly for large wall panels. When we use these ideas as inspiration, the tiles in this project take the geometric shapes and use ply as the material and so will fit right in to any 1960s- and '70s-inspired interior. The 3 mm ply sheets are easily sourced online if you can't find a local supplier.

We're not lucky enough to have our own laser cutter, so instead we went along to our local community Makerspace. Makerspaces are popping up everywhere and are perfect for accessing expensive pieces of equipment that you'll use only now and again.

Alternatively colored card versions, with printed lines rather than engraved, would look equally stunning.

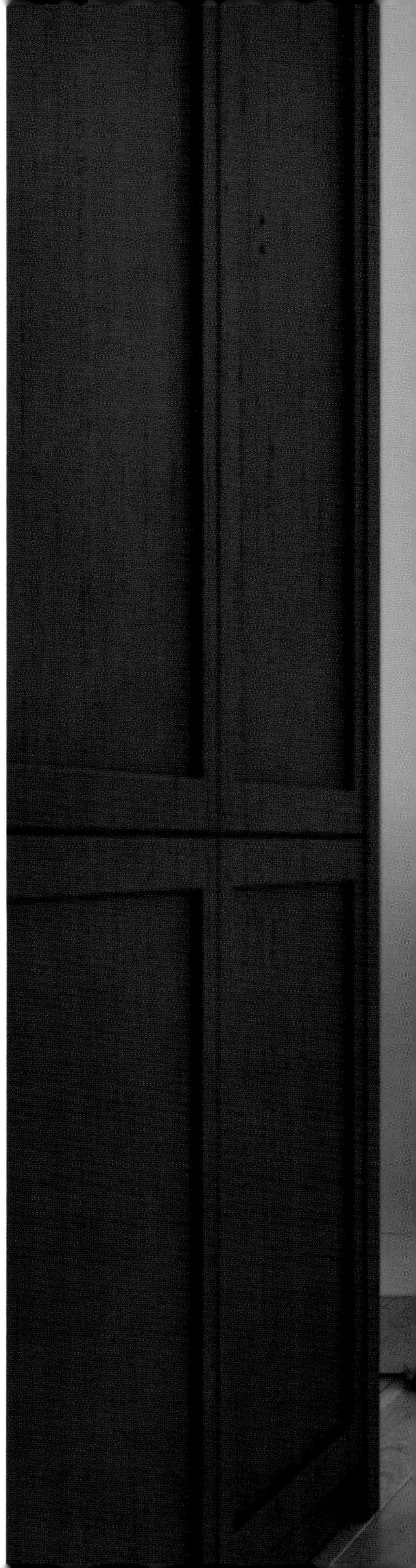

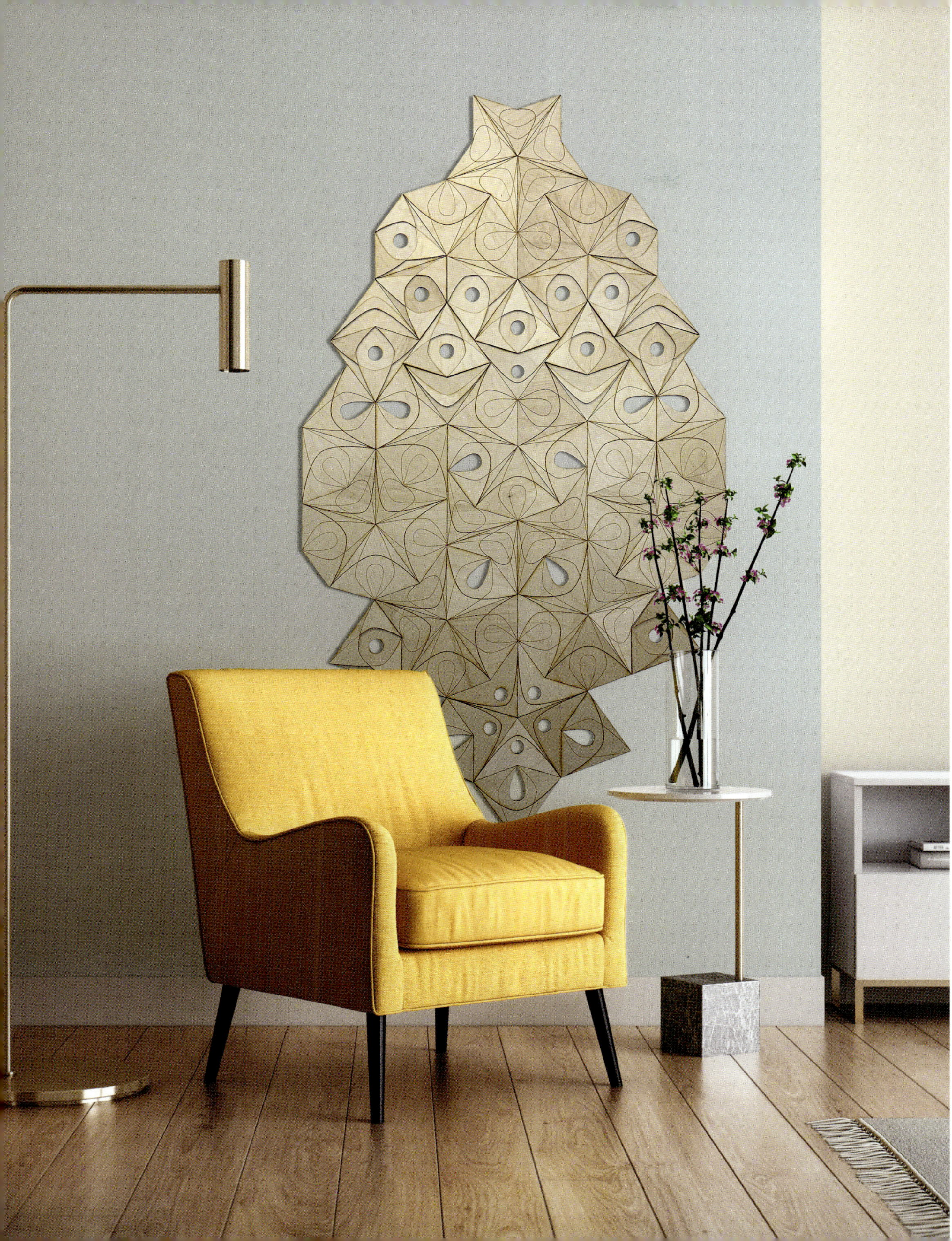

STEP-BY-STEP INSTRUCTIONS

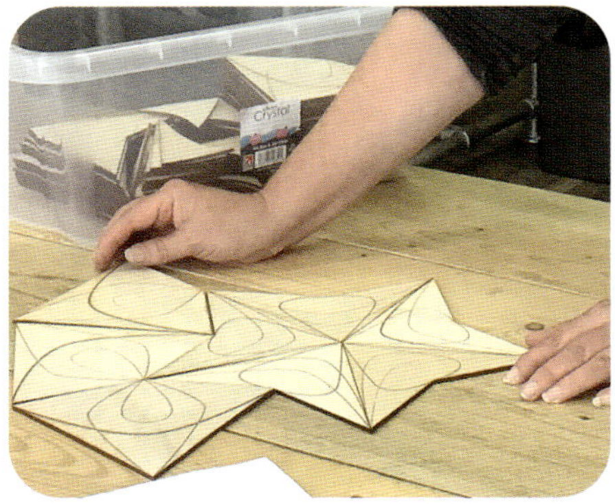

YOU WILL NEED

To prepare the wall
- *Spirit level and pencil*

To attach the tiles
- *At least 280 tabs of small double-sided sticky pads*

To make the tiles
- *47 A4 (11.7 x 8.3 in. / 29.7 x 21 cm) sheets of 3 mm ply; access to a laser cutter*
- *Wood glue*

STEP 1
MAKE THE TILES

Laser-cut and engrave the ply, using the templates on pages 66–69. The settings we used are in the green box below. The quantities needed for each tile can be found on the layout on page 64. Templates 5 and 6 will need gluing, so leave these to rest overnight before starting to stick the design to the wall.

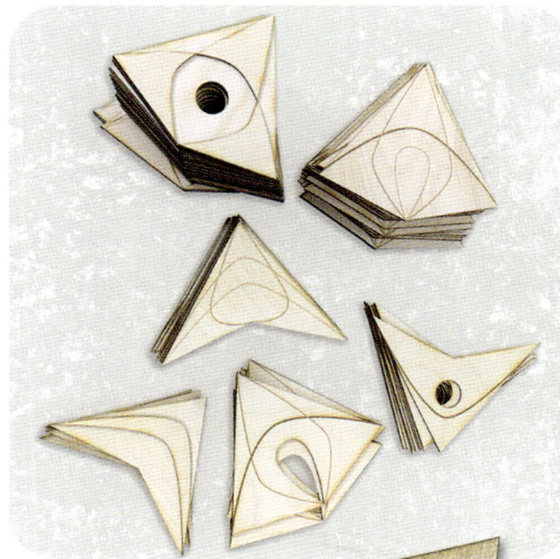

STEP 2
ORGANIZE YOUR TILES

Once you have made all the tiles you need, sort them into piles according to type, ready to hang on the wall.

TIP

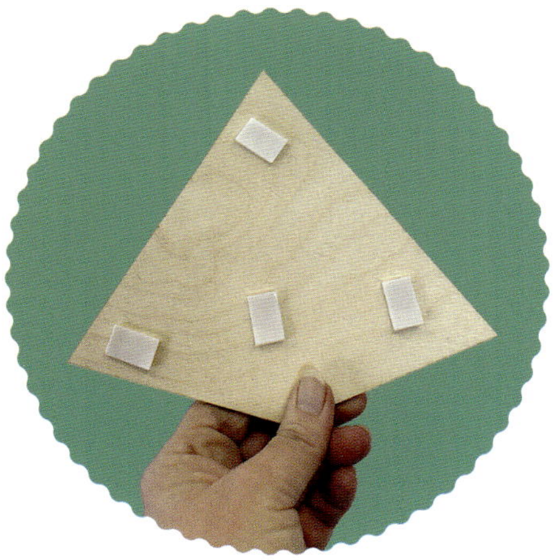

Use three to four sticky pads per tile, spaced evenly across the back

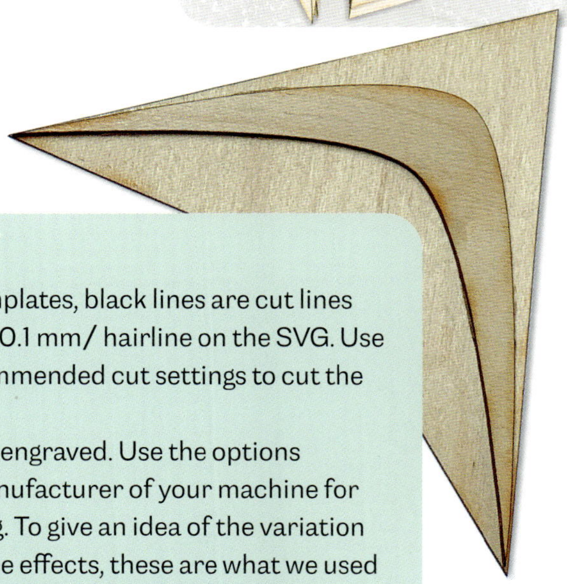

LASER CUTTERS

On the downloadable templates, black lines are cut lines (vector) and will be set at 0.1 mm / hairline on the SVG. Use the manufacturer's recommended cut settings to cut the materials you are using.

Colored lines are to be engraved. Use the options recommended by the manufacturer of your machine for the material you are using. To give an idea of the variation between settings to get the effects, these are what we used on the 30-watt machine at our local Makerspace:

	Speed	Power	Frequency
Red	30%	100%	500
Green	80%	100%	500
Blue	50%	100%	500

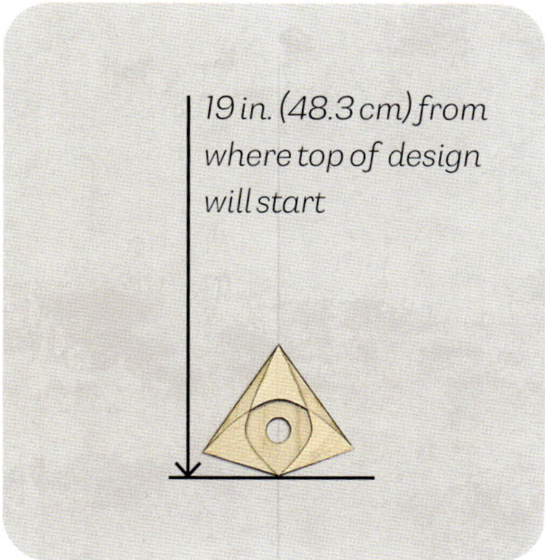

STEP 3

ASSEMBLE THE DESIGN

Pencil a vertical line at the center of where your design will be, using the spirit level to ensure it's true. Place the first tile (marked on page 64) on the wall. Check that the top of the design will fit comfortably in the remaining space, and align the center through the pencil mark.

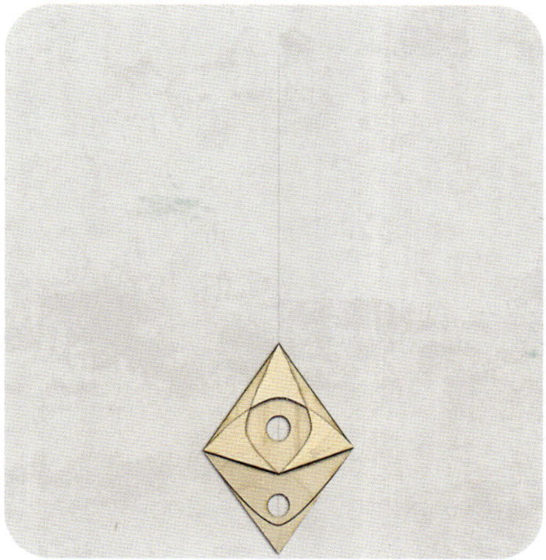

STEP 4

CONTINUE ASSEMBLING

Place the tile underneath, checking its alignment with the pencil mark. Make the two fit snugly together and align the ends.

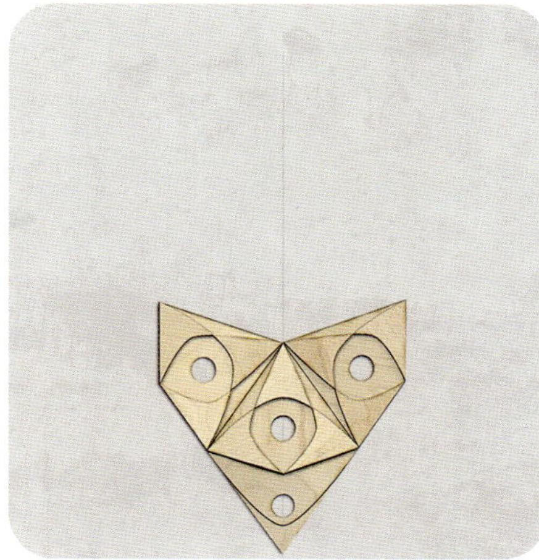

STEP 5

Add the two tiles flanking the top of the first tile.

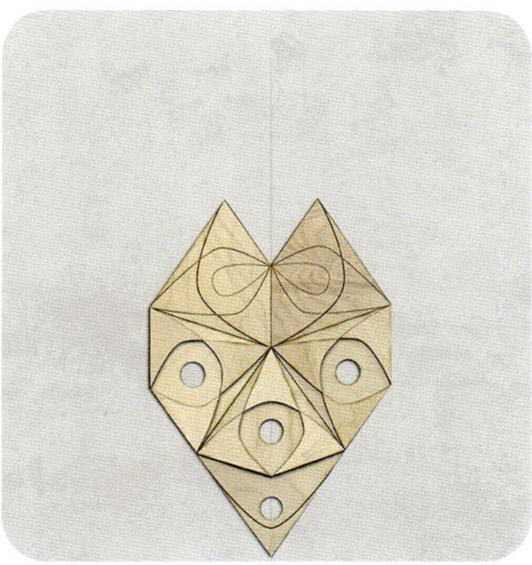

STEP 6

Fill in more tiles above the ones you have already placed. Keep all the fits snug and the alignments correct.

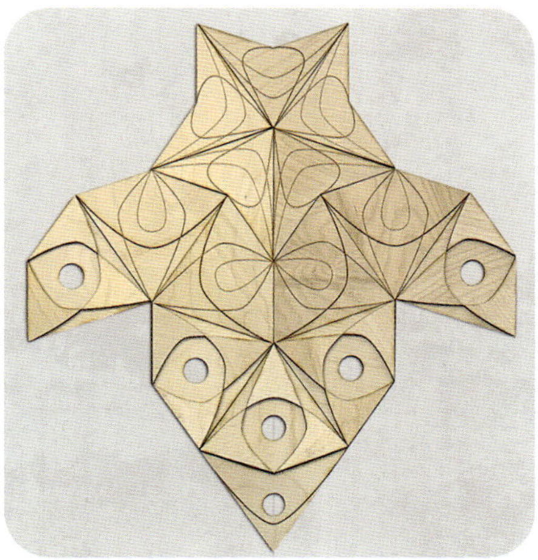

STEP 7

Placing the next four tiles should give you a solid shape that allows the fitting of the remaining tiles.

STEP 8

Continue placing the tiles in the correct shapes and patterns to complete the design.

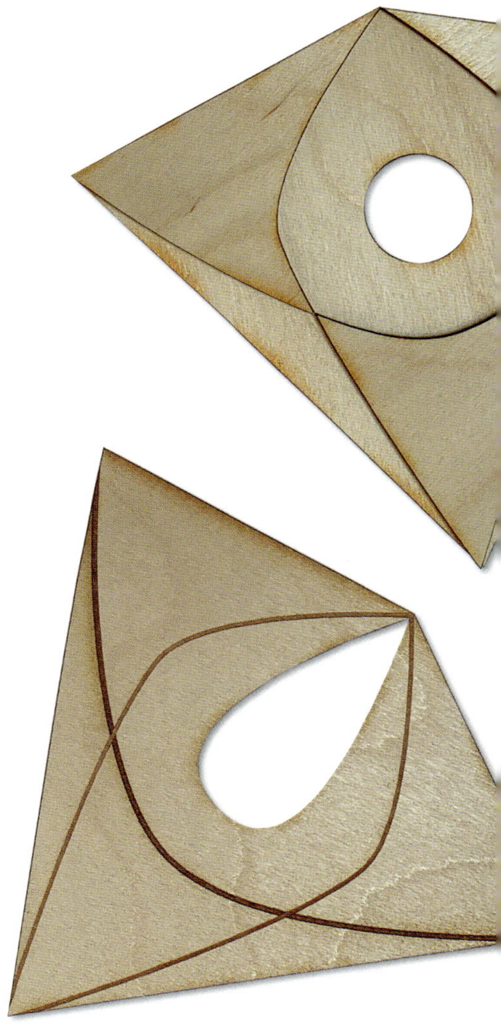

LAYOUT OF THE TILES

This is the layout of our design for the tiles. along with an indication of how many of each type of tiles is needed.

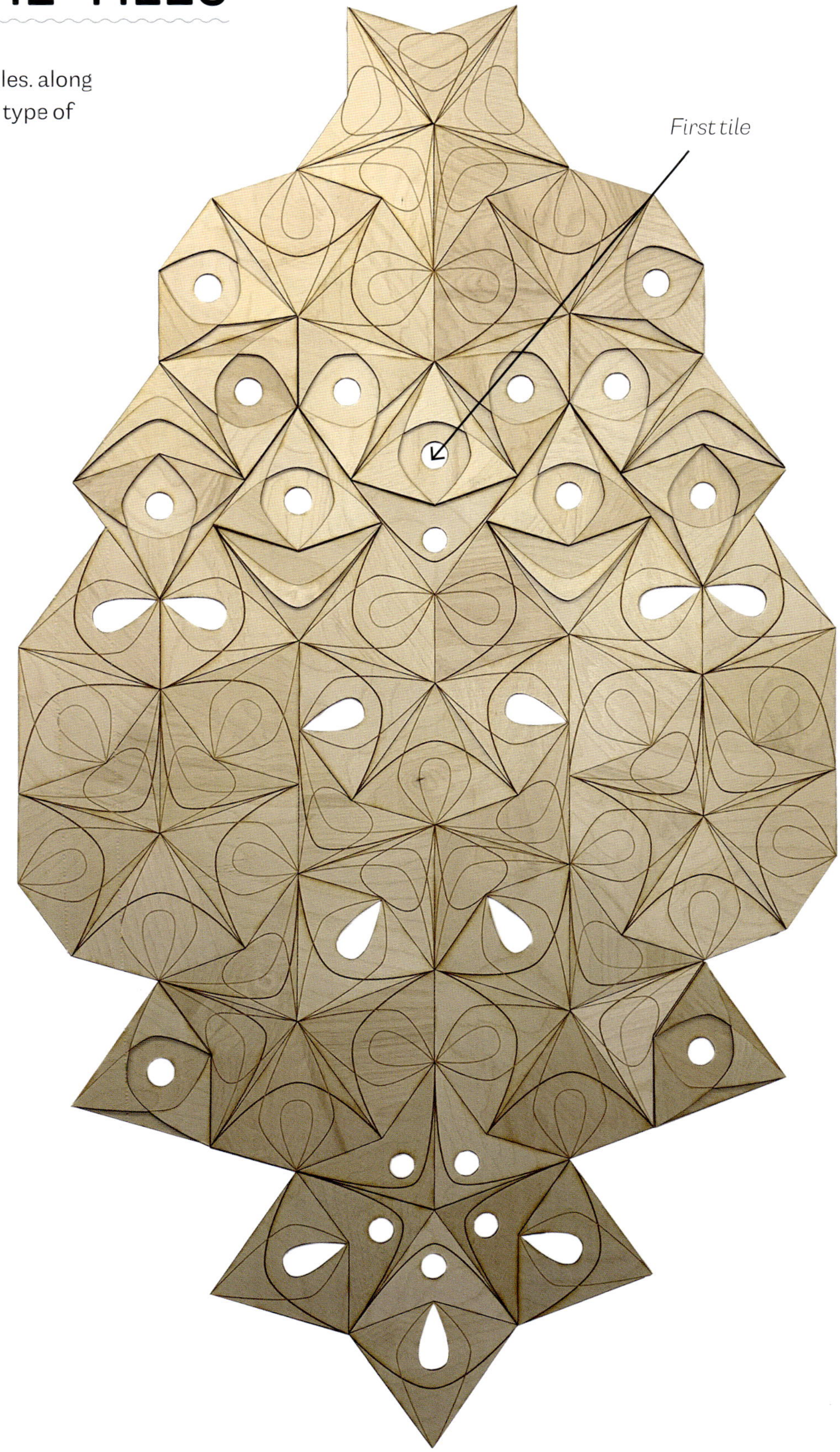

TEMPLATES 1 AND 2

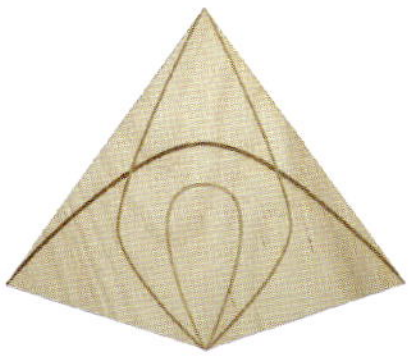

Engraved kite: 21 tiles

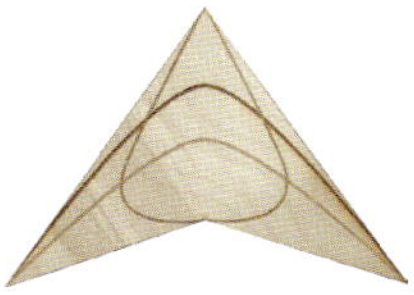

Engraved dart: 17 tiles

TEMPLATES 3 AND 4

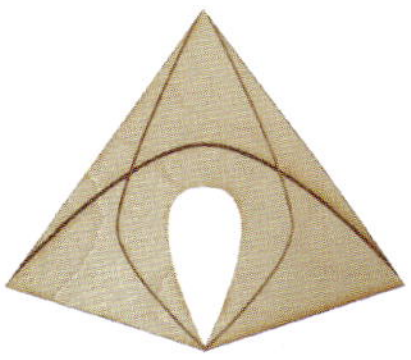

Engraved and pierced kite: 11 tiles

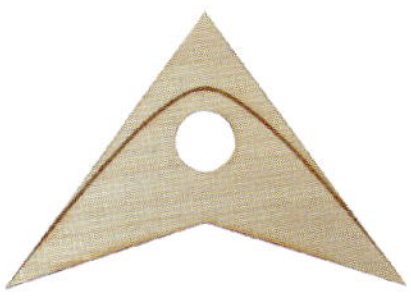

Engraved and pierced dart: 6 tiles

TEMPLATES 5 AND 6

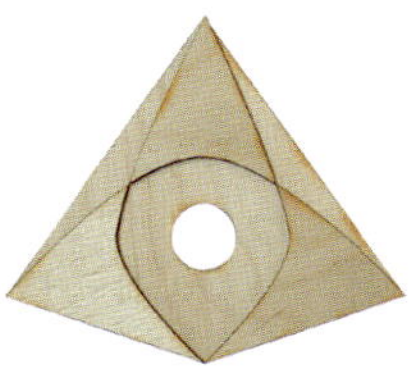

Stacked and pierced kite: 11 tiles

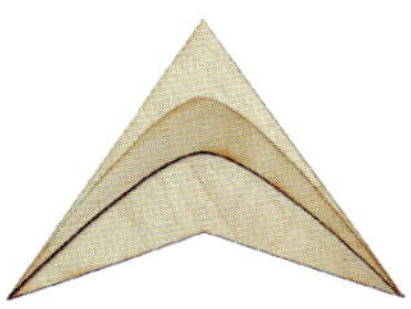

Stacked dart: 4 tiles

SAMPLE PATTERN STARTERS

By changing the set of tiles at the core, a completely different pattern will emerge. Here are some starter shapes to experiment with. Can you identify the starter shape in our design?

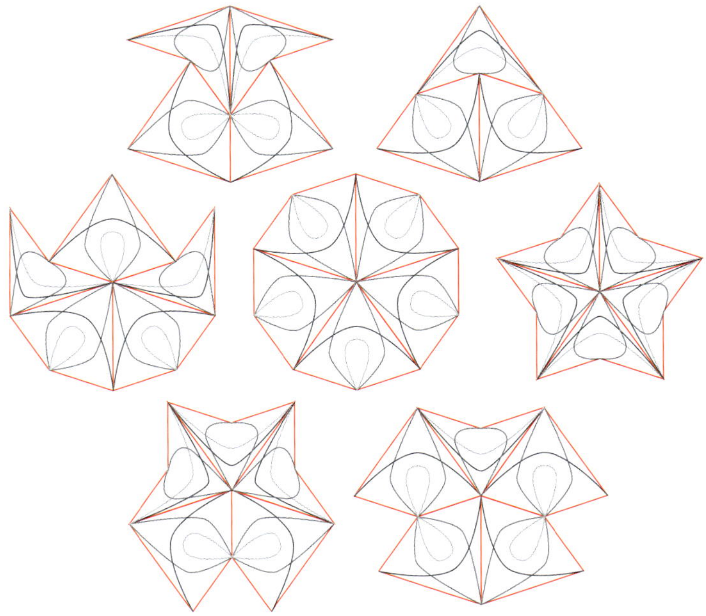

ALTERNATIVES

For a fantastically folksy take on some serious mathematics, try cutting tile shapes out of felt. There's a file of this simplified design available to download.

The design below and right is an example of a regular pattern made with Penrose tiles. For this, equal numbers of kites and darts were cut out of various colors. The parts were then swapped about before being needle-felted in position onto a backing piece of strong felt.

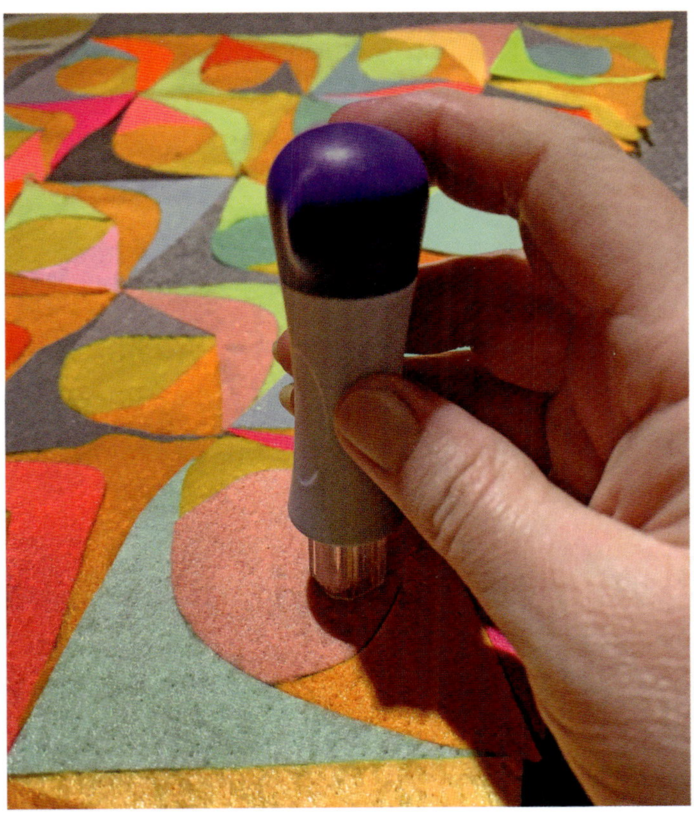

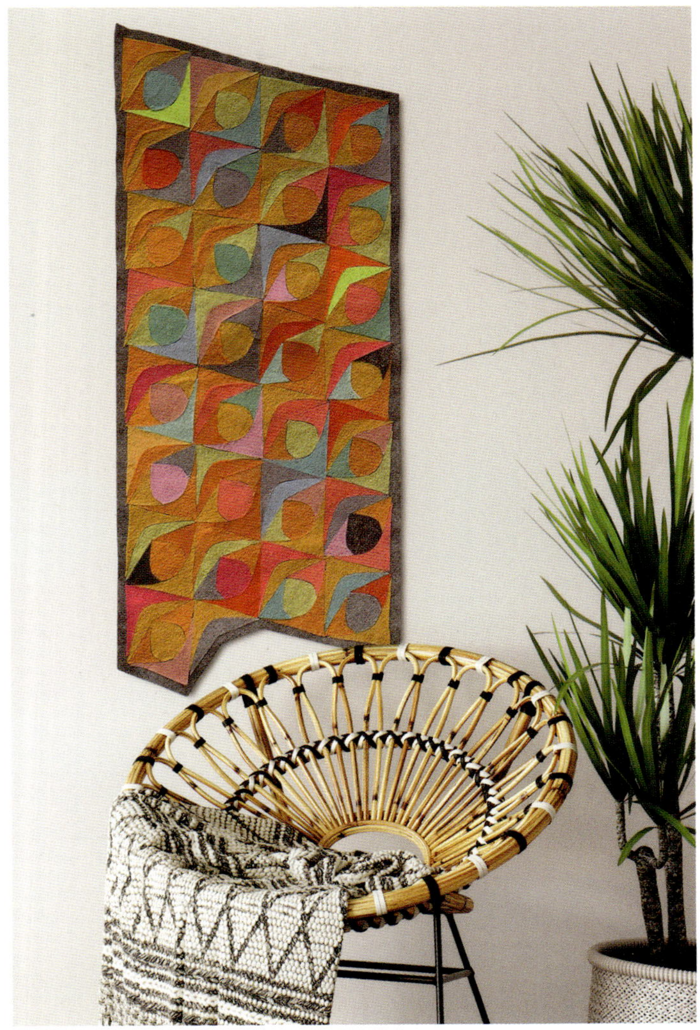

TEMPLATES 1 AND 2

Engraved Kite and Dart

Scan and convert to SVG or download a file. Colored lines are raster and are to be engraved. Use the options recommended by the manufacturer of your machine for the material you are using. These are engrave and cut only, with no assembly required.

On page 62 we've given the settings to engrave the colored lines on the 30-watt machine we used. You may have to adjust for the machine you use, but the green lines involve the lightest engraving and the red the deepest.

To make the same design as us, make twenty-one kites and seventeen darts.

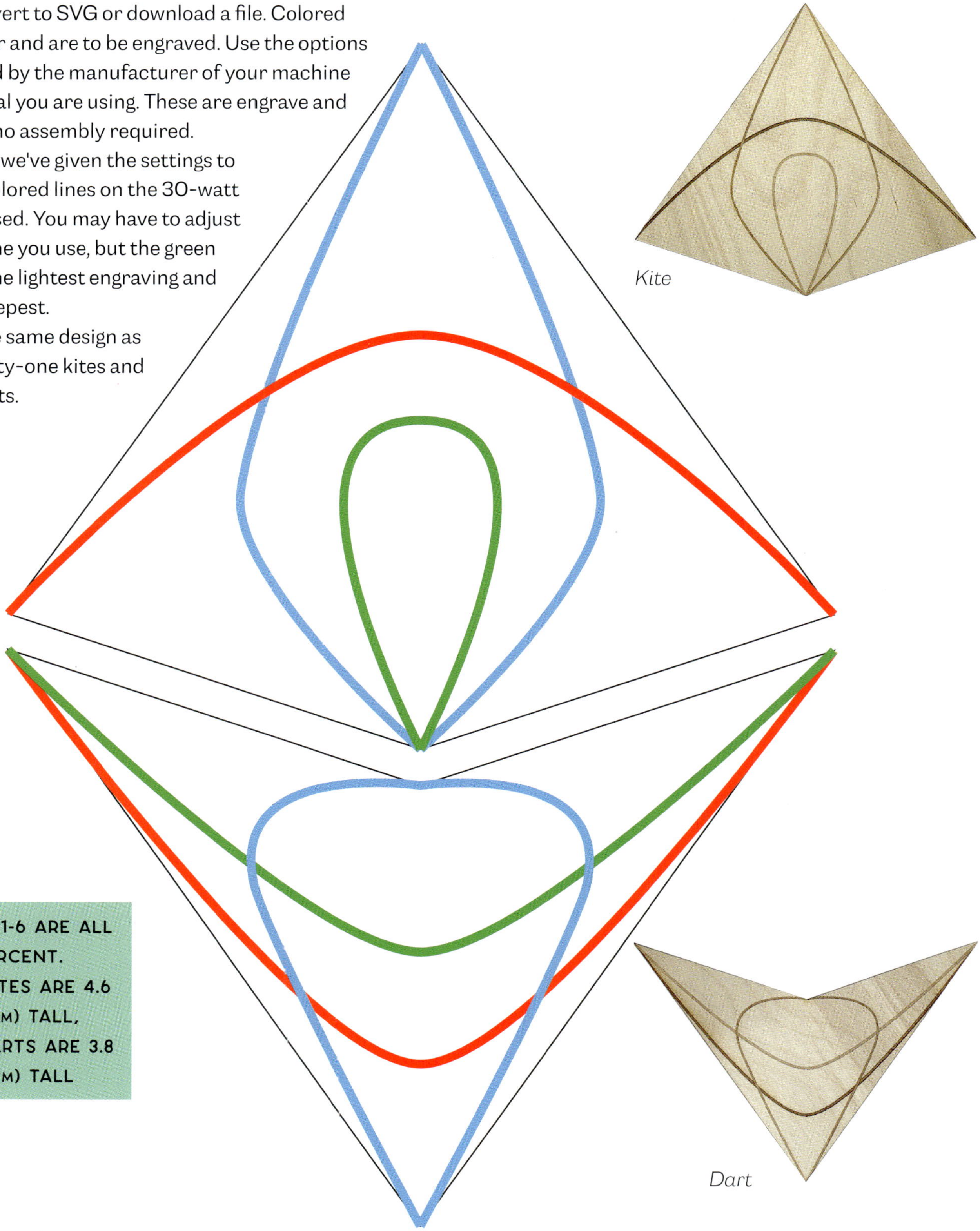

Kite

Dart

TEMPLATES 1-6 ARE ALL 100 PERCENT. FINISHED KITES ARE 4.6 IN. (11.6 CM) TALL, FINISHED DARTS ARE 3.8 IN. (9.6 CM) TALL

TEMPLATES 3 AND 4

Engraved and Pierced Kite and Dart

Scan and convert to SVG or download a file. Colored lines are raster and are to be engraved. Use the options recommended by the manufacturer of your machine for the material you are using. These are engrave and cut only, with no assembly required.

On page 62 we've given the settings to engrave the colored lines on the 30-watt machine we used. You may have to adjust for the machine you use, but the blue lines involve the lightest engraving and the red the deepest.

To make the same design as us, make eleven kites and six darts.

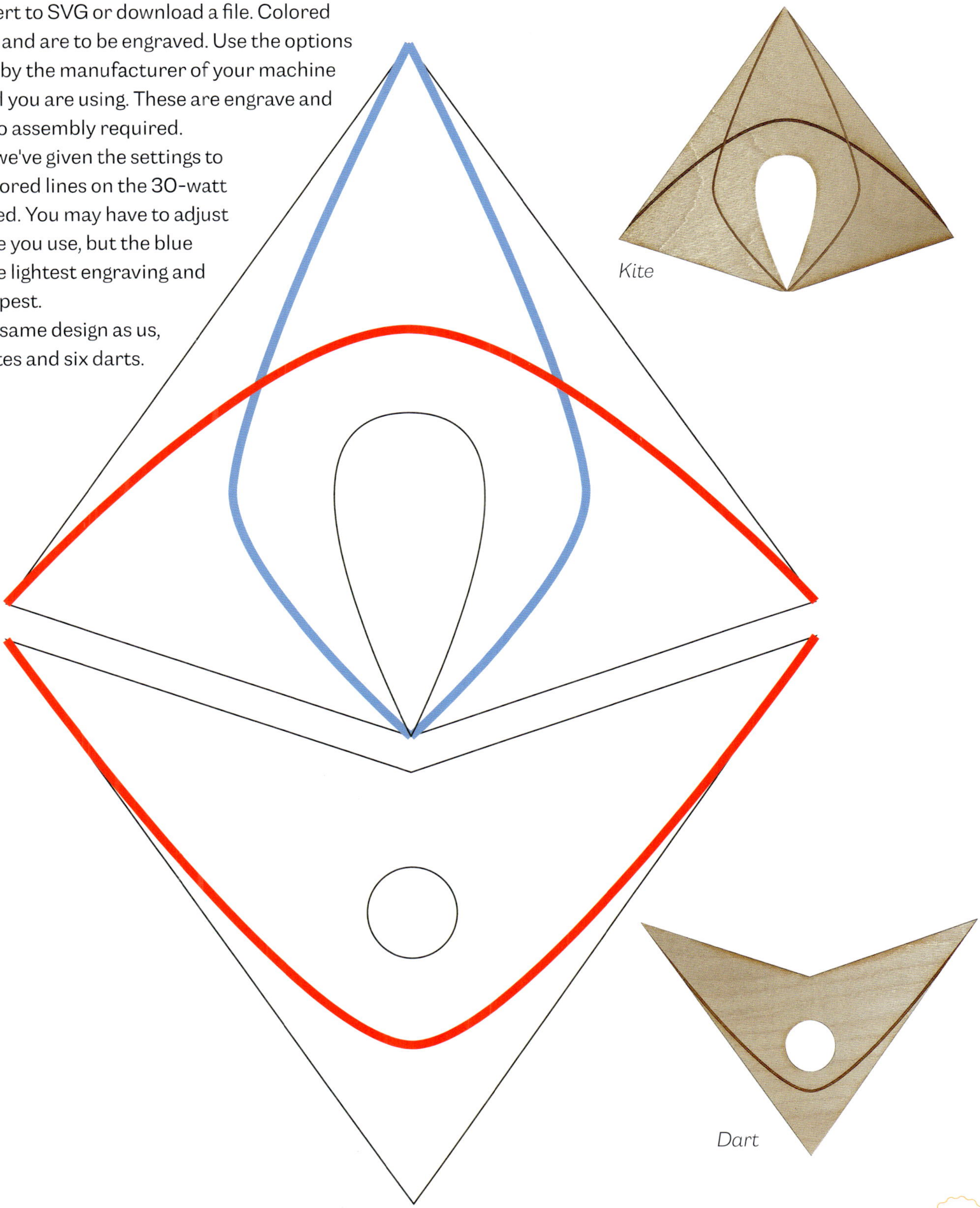

Kite

Dart

TEMPLATE 5

Stacked and Pierced Kite

Scan and convert to SVG or download a file.

These are cut only and need to be glued.

To make the same design as us, make eleven kites.

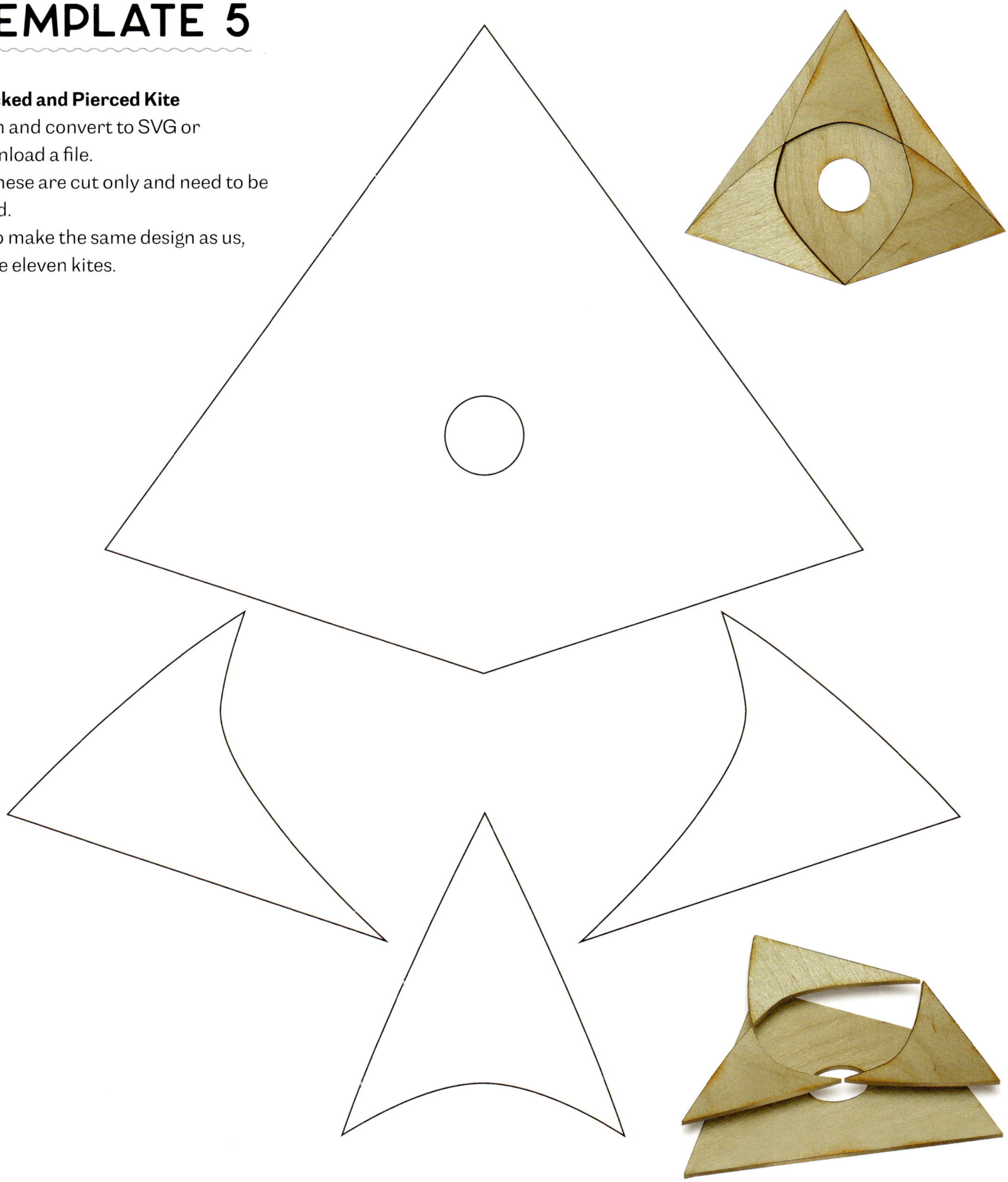

Glue the three triangles to the base dart. Align their edges with the edges on the base.

TEMPLATE 6

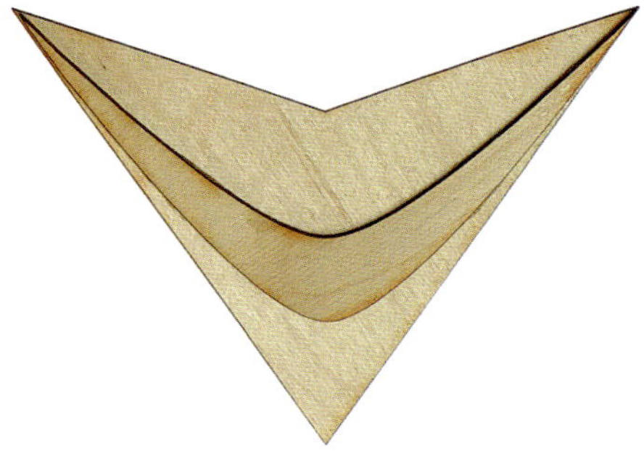

Stacked Dart

Scan and convert to SVG or download a file. These are cut only and need to be glued.

To make the same design as us, make four darts.

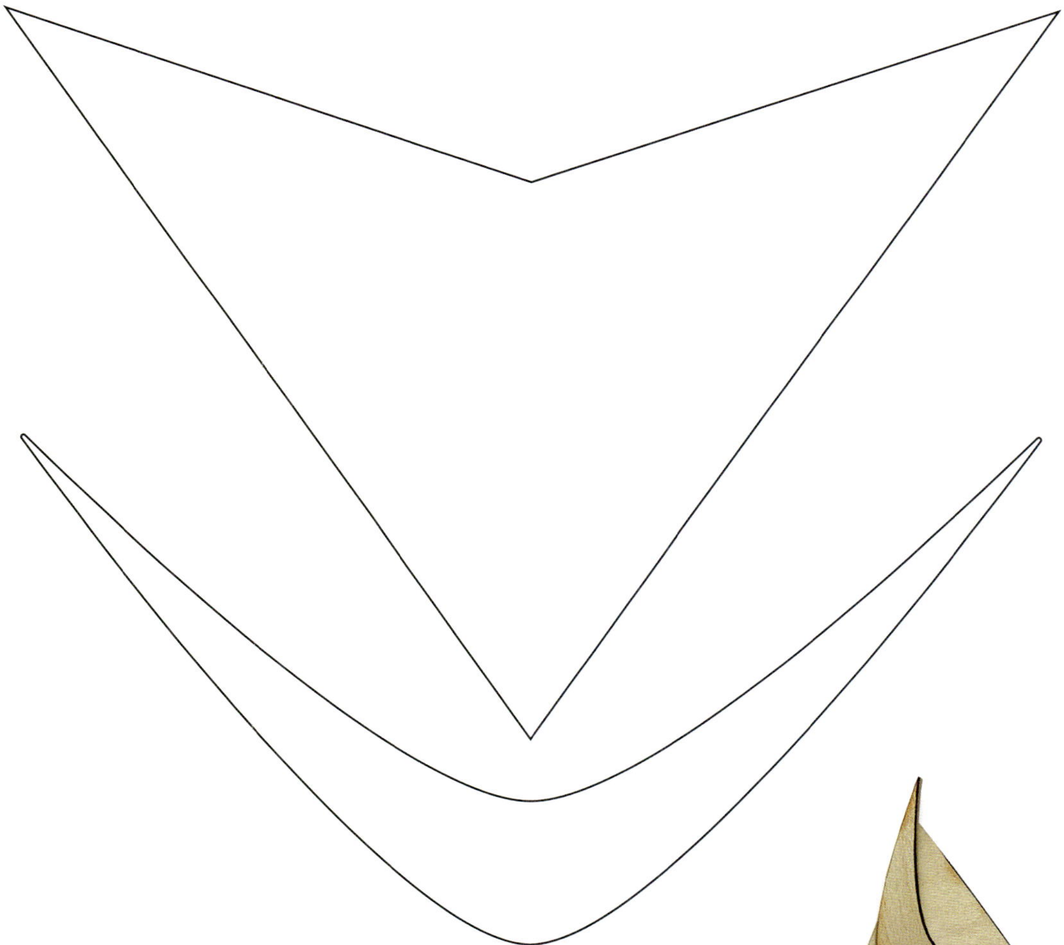

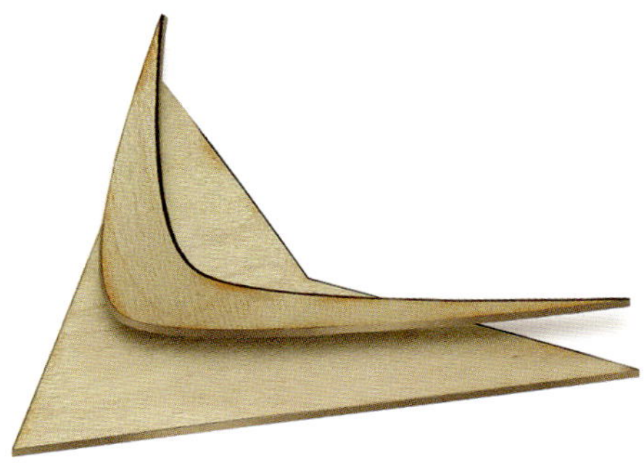

Glue the boomerang shape to the base dart. Align its points with the points on the base on either side of the indent.

BOTTLE BOTTOM FLOWERS

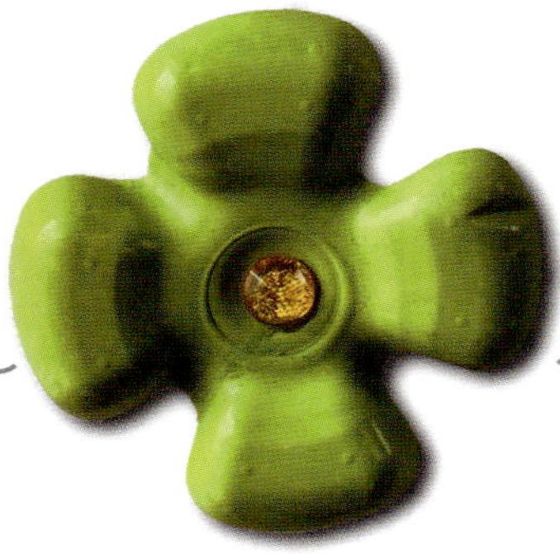

Sometimes beautifully decorative shapes can be found in the most-surprising places. At the bottom of many soda pop bottles are structural forms that add strength to the bottle. With fresh eyes, and taken in isolation, these shapes look like stylized flowers.

Super cute and fresh, these flower shapes remind us of the Swinging '60s and the exciting designs of Mary Quant. The shapes between brands can be subtly different, and there are some gorgeous four-petaled designs in the smaller-volume bottles.

The plastic of the bottles is so smooth that the results are shiny and very touchable. We've chosen to cast these in plaster of paris since it sets quickly and the resulting casts are very light. For use outdoors, you could try using white cement or concrete.

It's great to develop the habit of looking at packaging for potential casting projects —boxes of chocolates and cookies often have interesting dividers. At the very least, this gives waste products one turn at being useful before they go to be recycled.

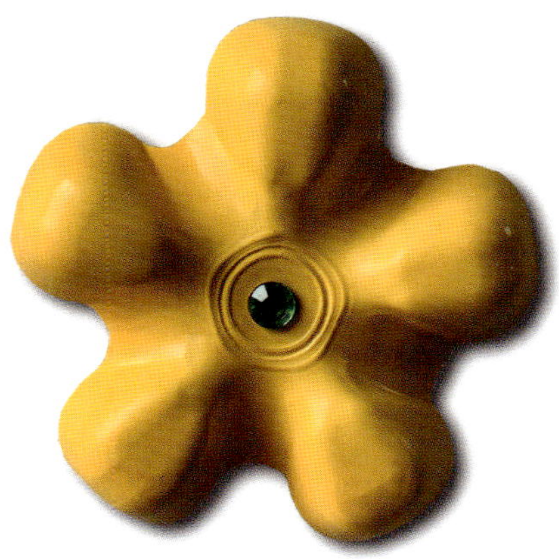

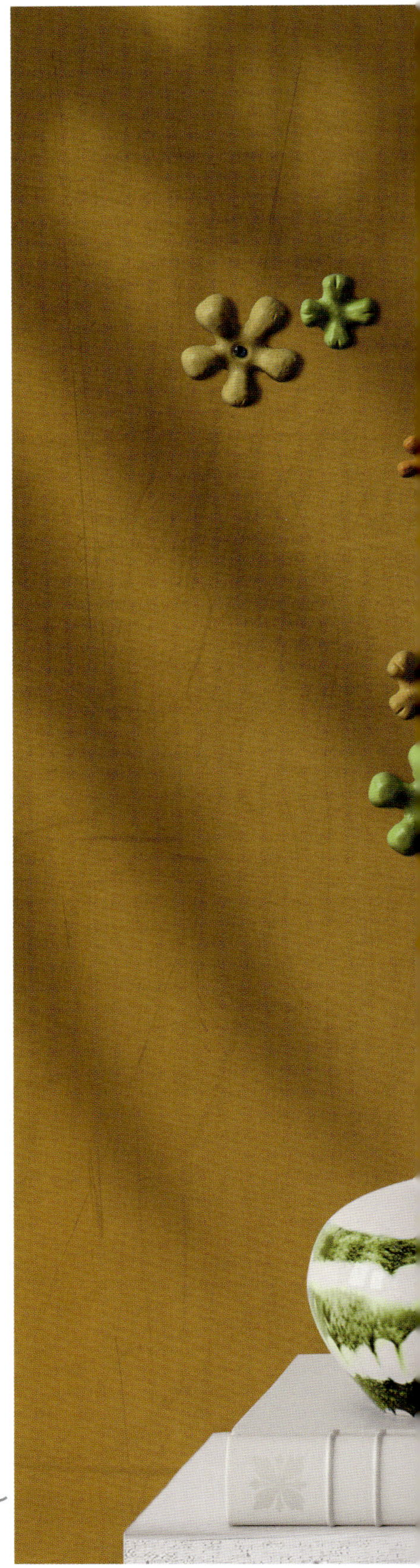

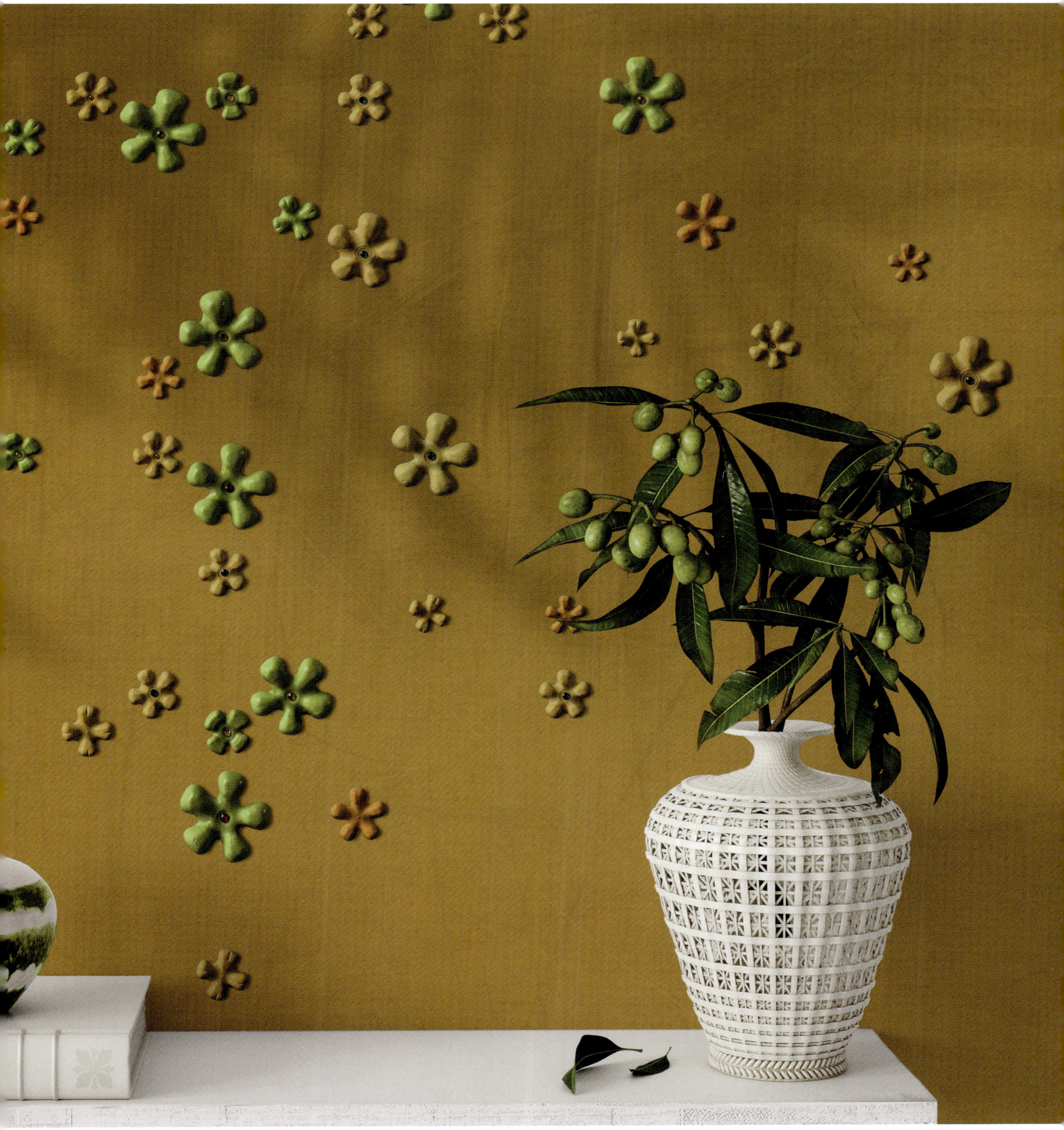

STEP-BY-STEP INSTRUCTIONS

YOU WILL NEED

For the flower molds
- *A selection of soda pop bottles*

For the casting
- *White plaster of paris*
- *Pigments for color*
- *Bamboo skewers for mixing*
- *Empty 1-pint plastic pots*
- *Water for mixing*

To unmold
- *Marker pen and small scissors*

To attach to the wall
- *Double-sided foam tape*

Optional
- *Round decorative gems and all-purpose glue*

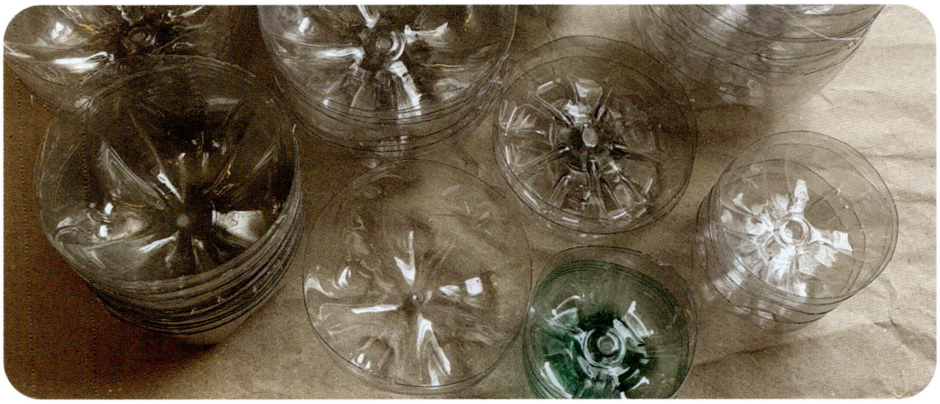

STEP 1

TRIM THE BASES OF YOUR BOTTLES

Gather together your soda pop bottles. A collection of various sizes with a good mix of four- and five-lobed bases look great together, since there'll be lots of variety. Trim each one to about 2 in. (5 cm) in depth.

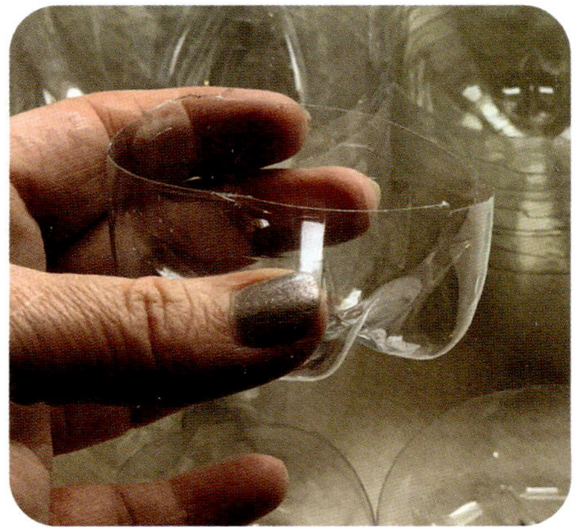

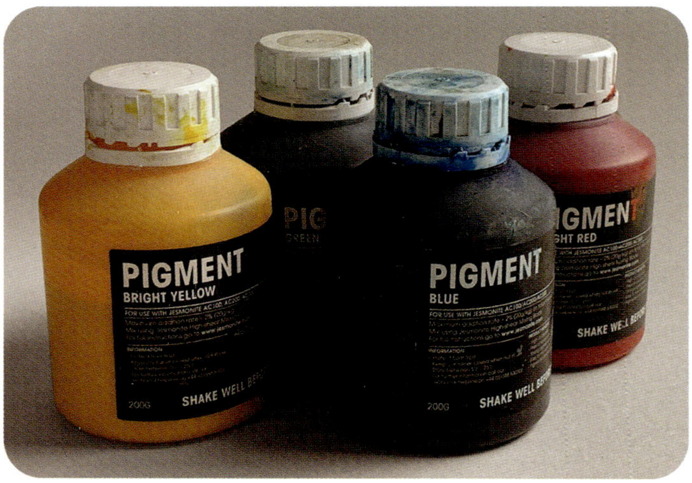

STEP 2

MIXING UP THE COLORS

We've used concentrated pigment colors developed for casting since they were what we already had in our stock cupboard. It's possible to use many things to color your casts—inks of various colors, food coloring, pigment powders, or acrylic paint.

Whatever you choose to use, it's a good idea to do any color mixing first in a separate container. This is because plaster sets very quickly, and by mixing the color first, you're breaking the process into stages and the mix won't go solid before you are ready.

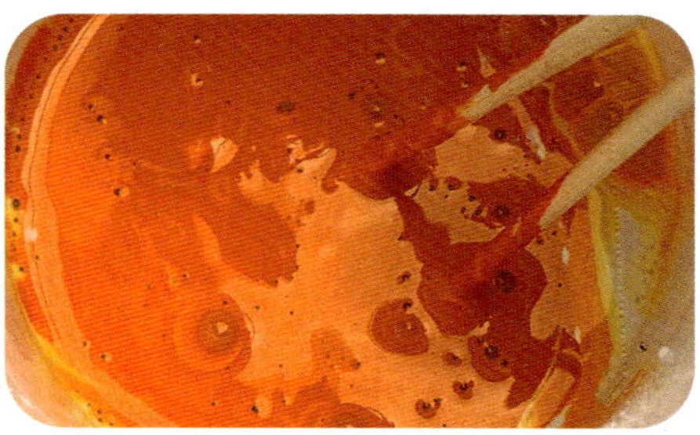

Here's a pot of orange mixed from the base colors of red and yellow liquid pigment. Very little red was needed in the yellow, so it was good to get that right first. It's now ready to be added in the next step.

STEP 3

THE CASTING MIX

Start by working in small batches. A cup of plaster mix will make enough medium for around four or five flowers, depending on the mold size.

First add water, then the pigment to a cup of plaster until it's the consistency of cake frosting. While you do this, stir it like crazy with two bamboo skewers, making sure you get at the dry stuff right at the bottom.

If you overdo the water, don't panic; just add in some more plaster mix and stir well.

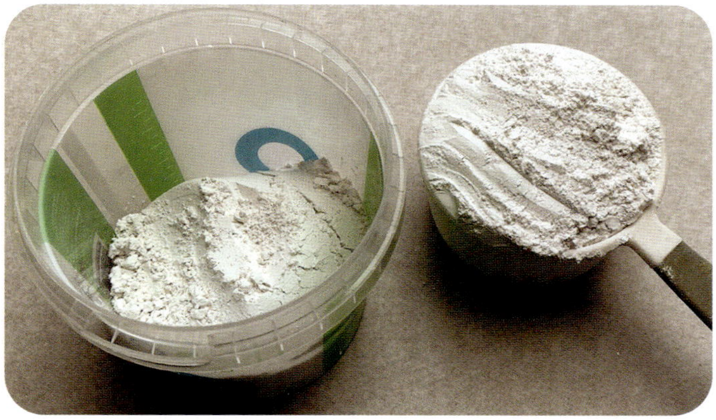

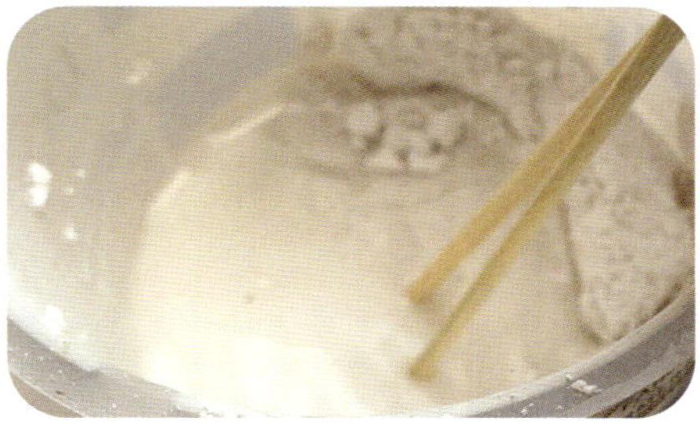

STEP 4

FILL THE BOTTLE BOTTOMS

In order to get the lovely petal shape, it's important not to cast the flowers too deeply. Quickly scoop about 0.5 in. (1.25 cm) of casting mix into four or five bottle bottoms.

When first put in, the mixture will have peaks and be really uneven. Pick up each mold in turn, and tap it repeatedly on your work surface. This will both even out the mix to a flat, smooth surface and burp out any trapped air bubbles.

You can see in the photo on the right the difference between the molds before and after tapping.

Continue with different colors until you have made all your flowers.

NOTE: Expect around 10 percent of the casts to break during demolding, so make enough to allow for this.

Leave everything to set for at least twenty-four hours.

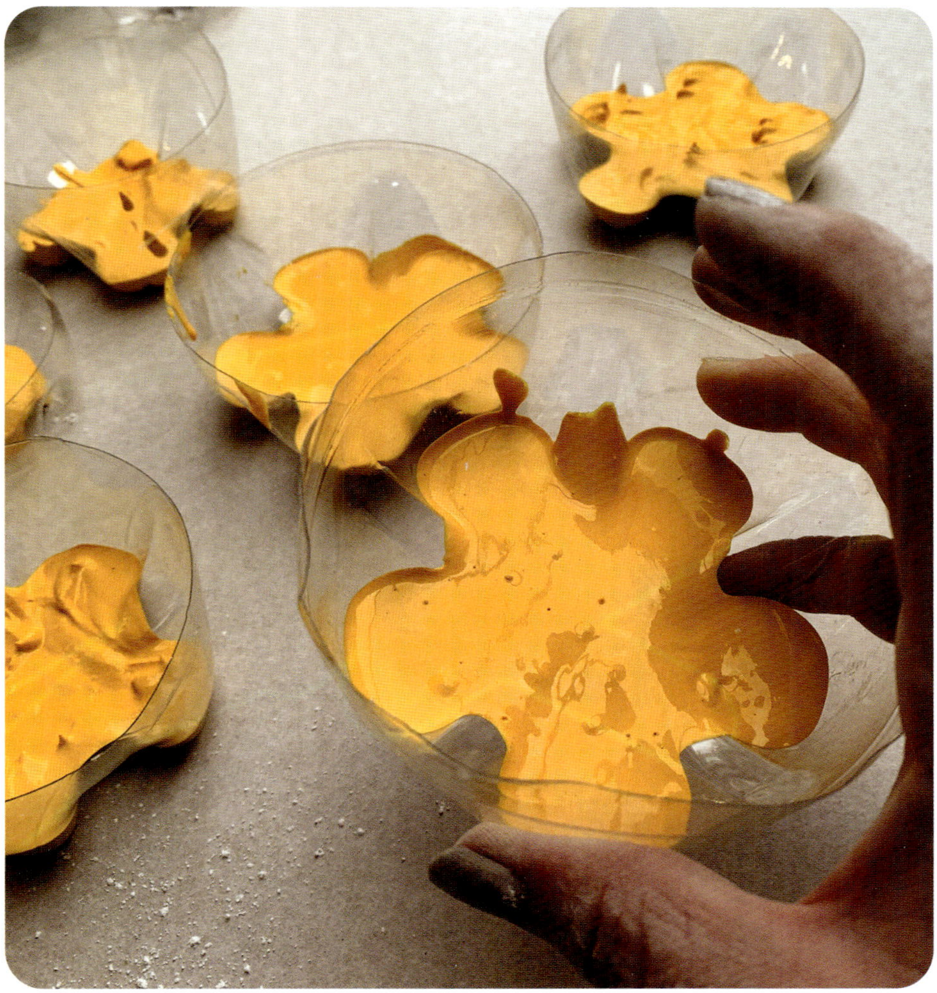

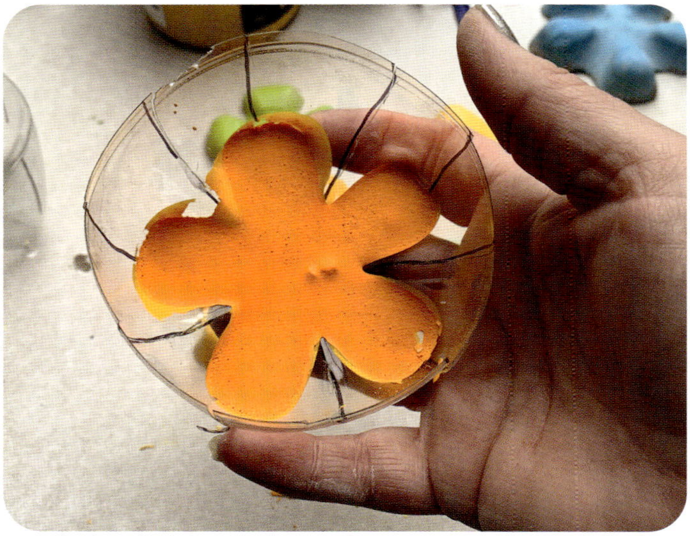

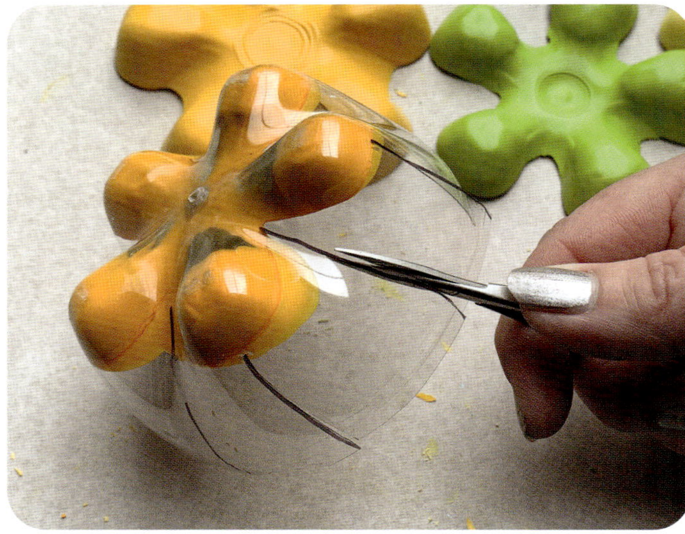

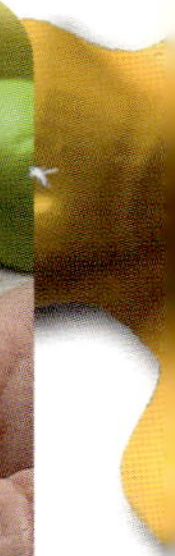

STEP 5

PREPARING TO UNMOLD

Once the castings have had at least twenty-four hours to set thoroughly, the time will have come for the exciting unmolding!

Look at your casting. For the first one, draw lines on the bottle at the fattest points and the pinch points of the flower. Once you've gotten the idea, there'll be no need to draw lines each time—just make the cuts.

STEP 6

RELEASING THE TENSION

Start by cutting down all the lines at the fattest points, then cut down the lines at the pinch points. The purpose of this is to release the tension by the smallest amount—it's just enough to free the flower from its mold.

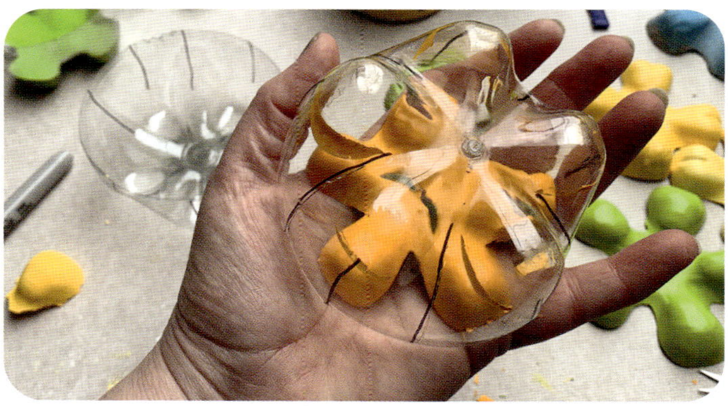

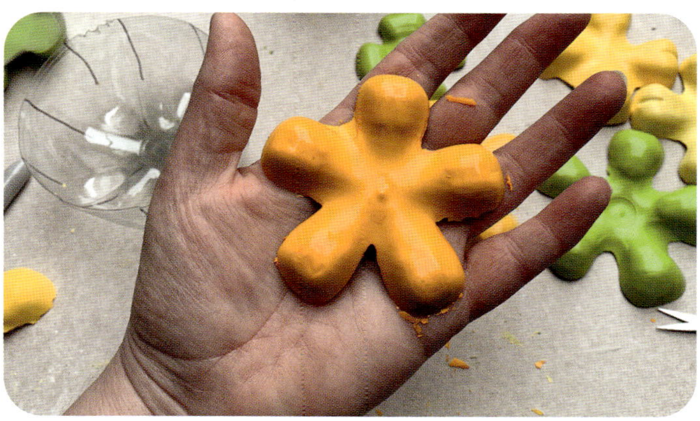

STEP 7

UNMOLDING AND TIDYING

Flipping the bottle onto your hand should be enough to release the flower!

There'll be some fine crispy bits at the edges of the petals, and possibly some between them, a bit like webbing. This can be removed with a light touch with your fingers.

Give the flowers a day of rest to dry out, with the cast surface exposed to the air.

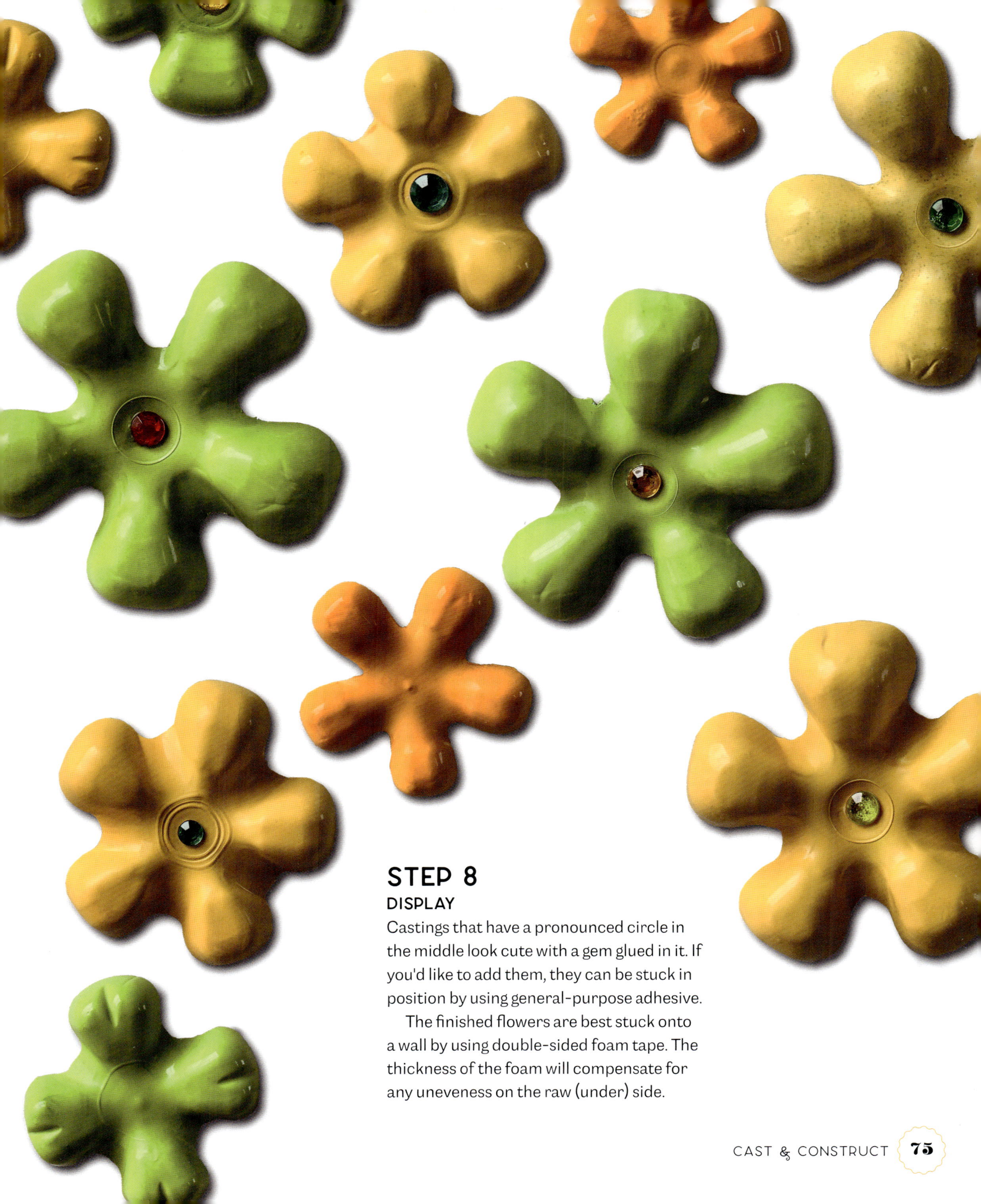

STEP 8

DISPLAY

Castings that have a pronounced circle in the middle look cute with a gem glued in it. If you'd like to add them, they can be stuck in position by using general-purpose adhesive.

The finished flowers are best stuck onto a wall by using double-sided foam tape. The thickness of the foam will compensate for any uneveness on the raw (under) side.

THROUGH THE WINDOW

A home can never have enough windows or views to inspire us. Looking outward into the distance away from the rigors of everyday life can be good for our mental health. Having elements on our walls that make us pause to think, rest, or invigorate our minds helps keep us all healthy and creative.

Your real-life view from your window of that brick wall is unlikely to inspire you, so take control of your environment and change your view. It's far cheaper than moving home after all!

Before you start, take a few days to think about what you need to see from your room—maybe a relaxing countryside scene? Perhaps you crave nature, or does the sight of the sea make you feel calm? Would you like to feel energized or relaxed? Or do you want to be reminded every day of your last vacation and that stunning view from the balcony?

Once you have thought through which feeling you would like, start thinking about the design you would enjoy seeing. We chose a blue sky, birds, butterflies, and trees in silhouette as our art piece. After we hung our window on the wall, we then customized all the other frames around it with elements we used in our main window. This design trick unifies the room, expands the concept, and extends the theme.

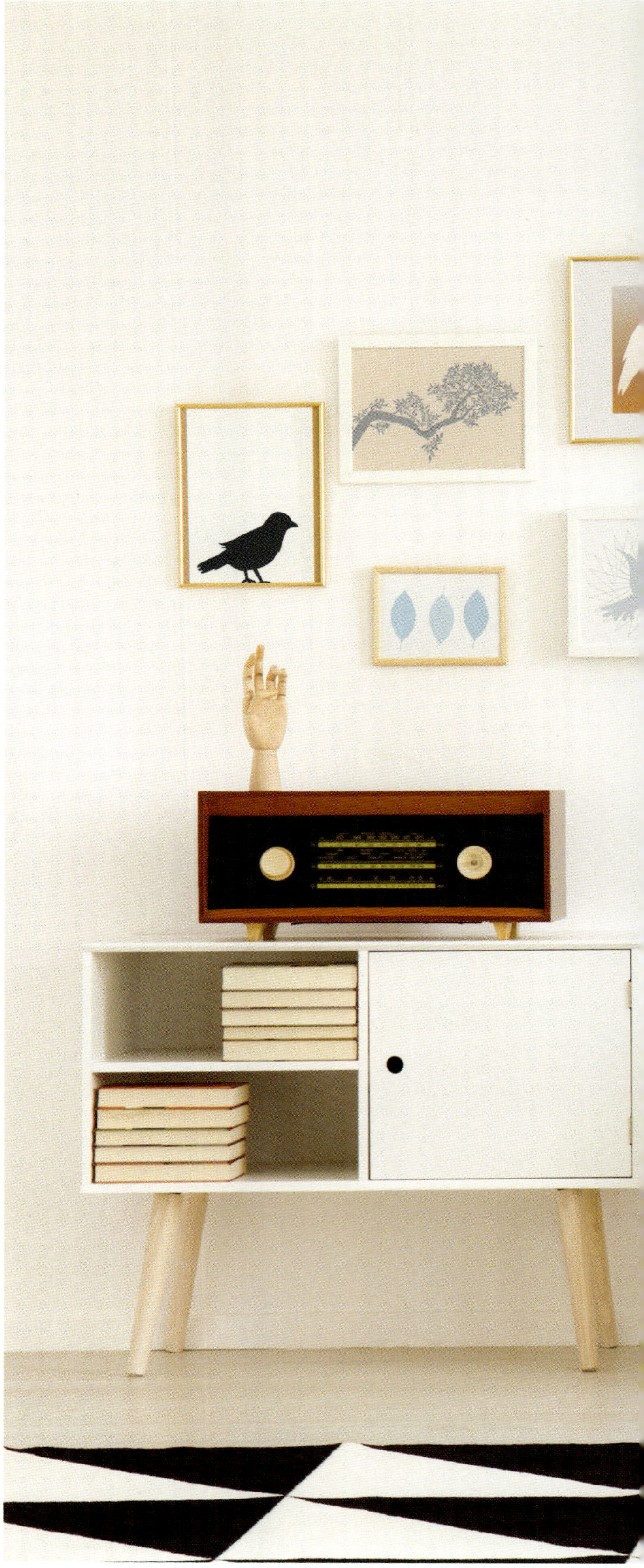

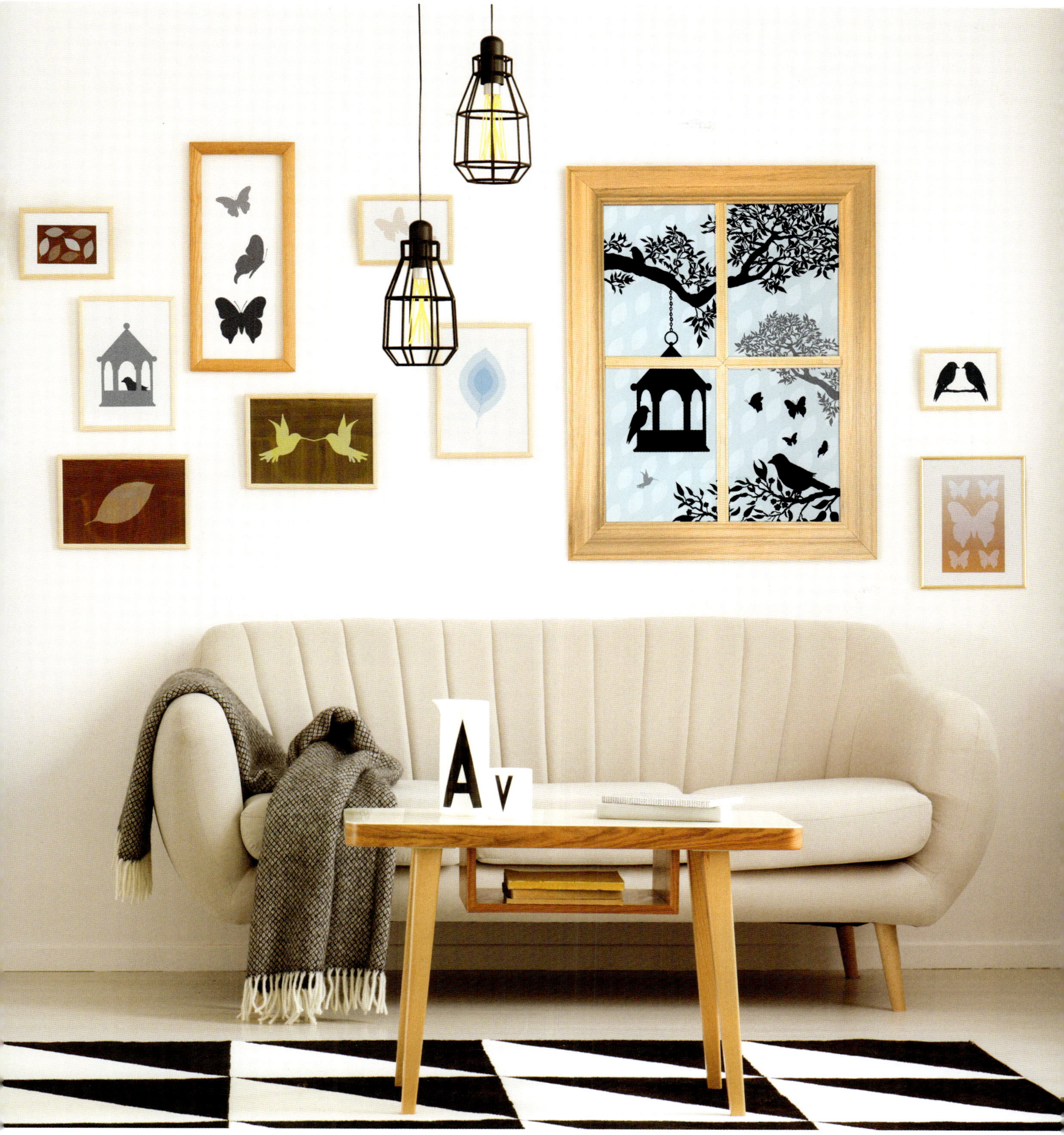

STEP-BY-STEP INSTRUCTIONS

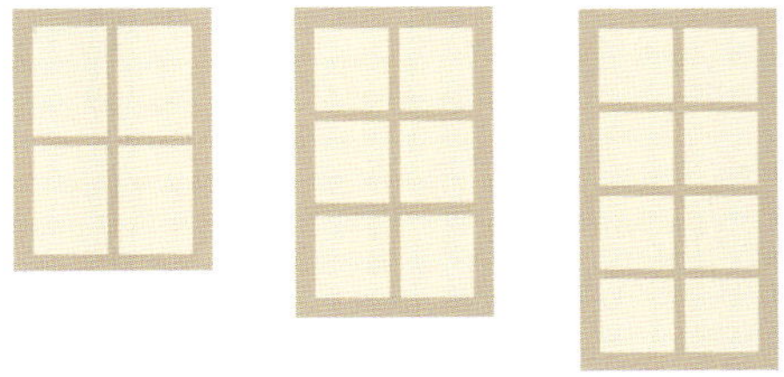

YOU WILL NEED

For the frame

- *A3 (11.75 x 16.5 in. /29.7 x 42 cm) sheet of thin card (any color)*
- *8–10 clips*
- *Craft sticks *see note below*
- *2 D rings*
- *Frame fixings: 4 L-shape brackets and 16 screws*
- *Hardboard for the frame backing*
- *Heavy-duty knife*
- *Miter box and hacksaw*
- *Molded picture frame wood 8.5 ft. (2.6m) long*
- *Pencil*
- *Point-driving tool and push points*
- *Safety googles and gloves*
- *Set square*
- *Tape measure and ruler*
- *Wood glue and paper glue*

For the image

- *Artwork or photograph for your window*

For the wall

- *Hanging fixings suitable for your wall type (if uncertain, consult a specialist)*
- *String*

OPTIONAL

- *Clear plastic "glass" for your frame, cut to size*

* Cross-beam craft sticks; once you have chosen the picture wood, see steps 7 and 8 and measure the inner lip to know what length and thickness craft stick to buy.

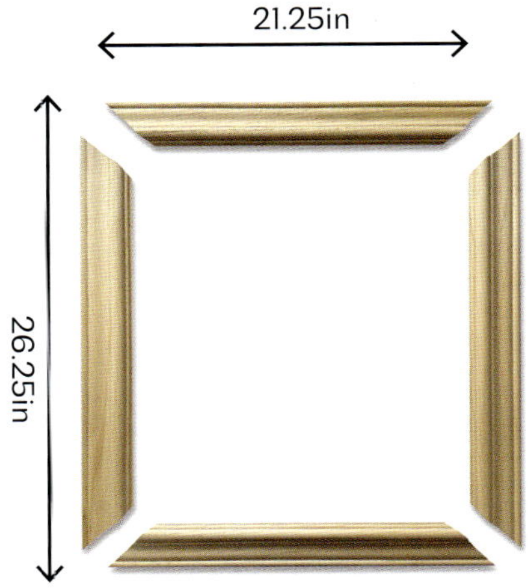

STEP 1

WHAT SIZE?

Our final frame will be 21.25 in. (54 cm) wide by 26.25 in. (66.7 cm) high. You can make the window any size you like. We have chosen four inner panes, but you could do six or eight or make a landscape window.

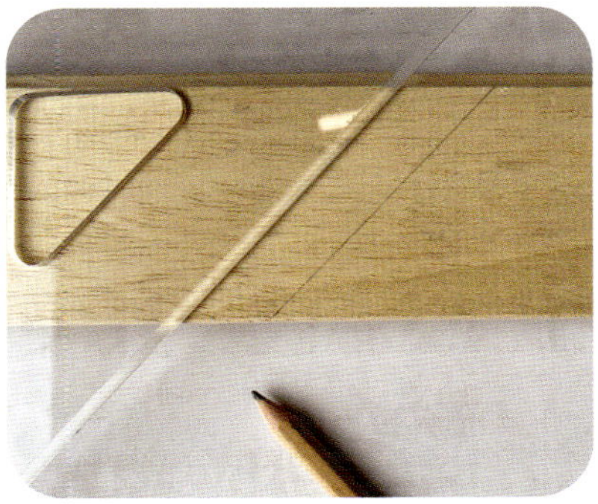

STEP 2

MARK THE CUT

It is important to mark the pieces correctly. Using a set square, mark on the back of the frame with a pencil the 45-degree angle. The outer molding on every piece should match, so before you cut, check that the molding will match along the outer edge when cut.

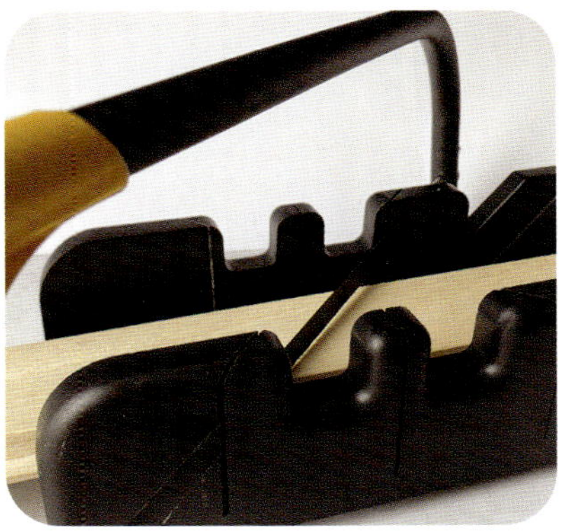

STEP 3

CUTTING THE FRAME

Wear safety goggles and protective gloves and cut using a wood saw. Ideally, use a miter box to cut your 45-degree angle—it will be more accurate—but you can just follow your mark carefully after clamping the molding.

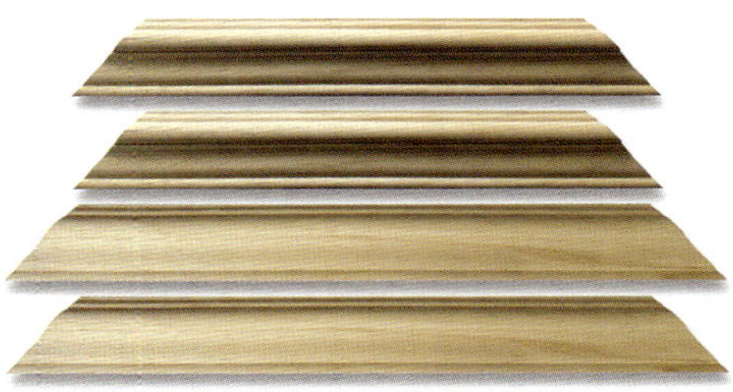

Top

Bottom

Right

Left

Make sure you mark and cut the angles correctly; you should finish with four pieces like this.

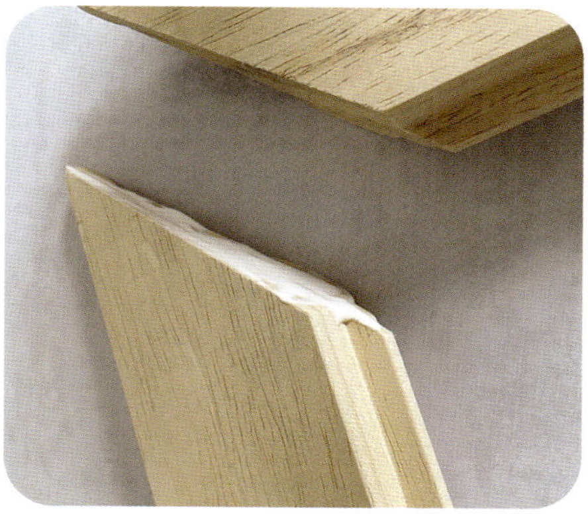

STEP 4

GLUE THE JOINTS

Glue the corners with wood glue, making sure that the corners align exactly. Once in position, wipe away any excess, clamp, and wait for it to fully dry.

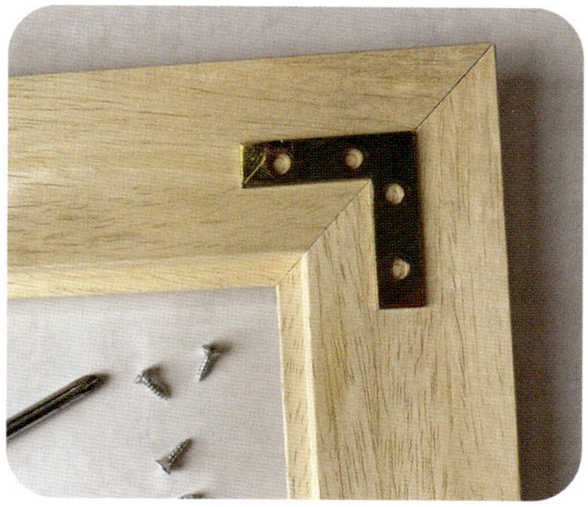

STEP 5

SECURING THE JOINTS

When the glue has set, add the L plates and screw them in to secure each corner of the frame.

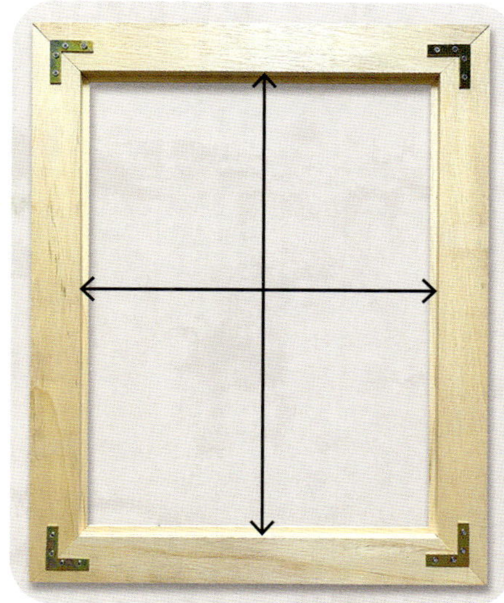

STEP 6

BACKING BOARD

Place the frame facedown on a flat surface. Measure inside the lip where the backing board will sit, and cut the baseboard to fit. Keep the backing board for later.

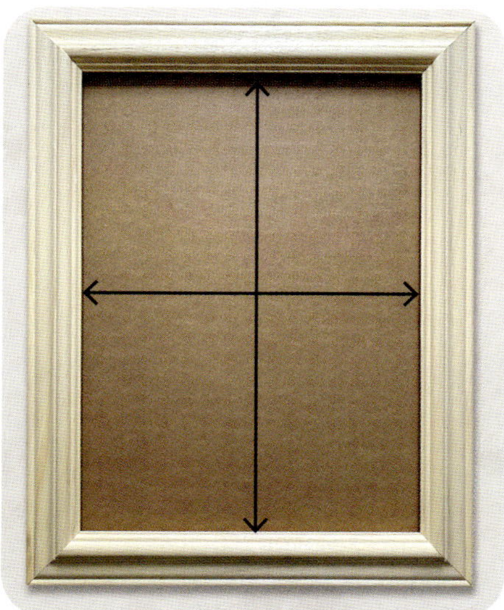

STEP 7

MAKING THE CROSS

Measure the internal dimensions of the front of the frame. Divide both measurement in half—this is the measurement for the length of your inner crosspieces.

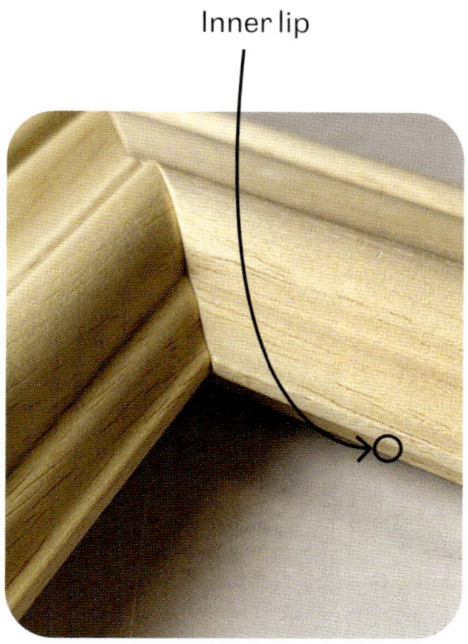

STEP 8

CROSS BEAM THICKNESS

Measure the depth of the small inner lip on the inside of the frame edge. Your cross thickness should not be higher than this; otherwise it will protrude from the frame.

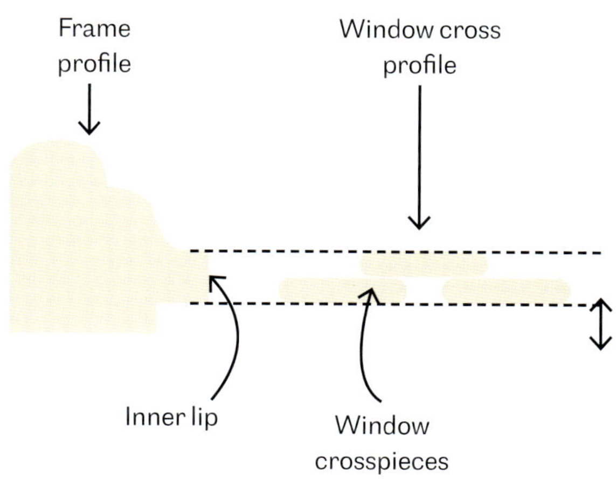

The height of the inner lip of the frame should be the same height as your window crosspieces when stacked.

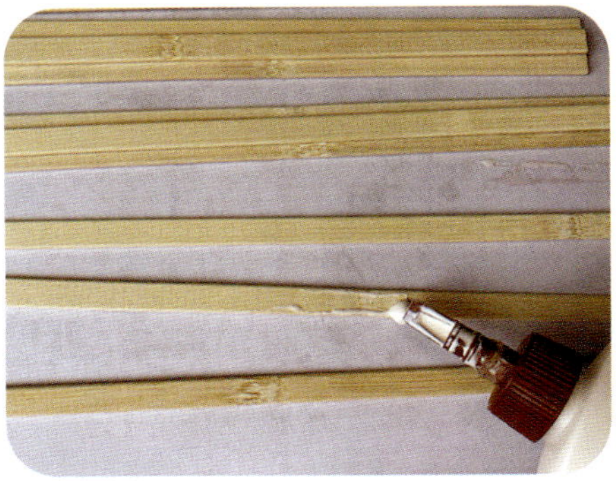

STEP 9

GLUE CROSSPIECES

Glue three pieces of the craft sticks together (*see below*) leaving a gap in the center. Make four; wait for the glue to dry.

Cross section of how to glue the three craft sticks together.

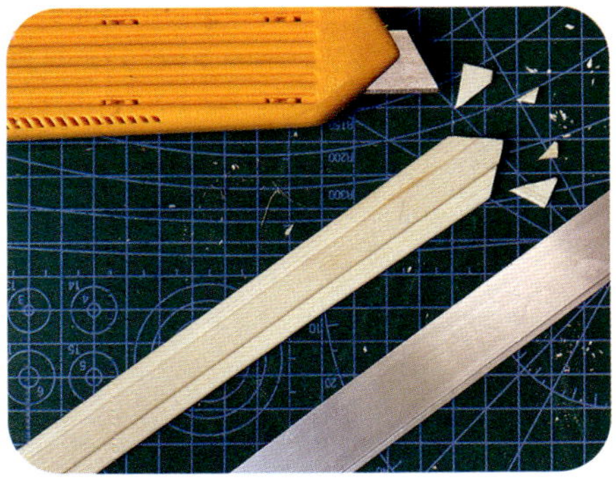

STEP 10

CUT THE CENTER MITER

Mark the center point of each stick, and then the 45-degree angle on each edge. Use a heavy-duty knife or small hacksaw to cut the end into an arrow shape. Repeat the process for the other three pieces.

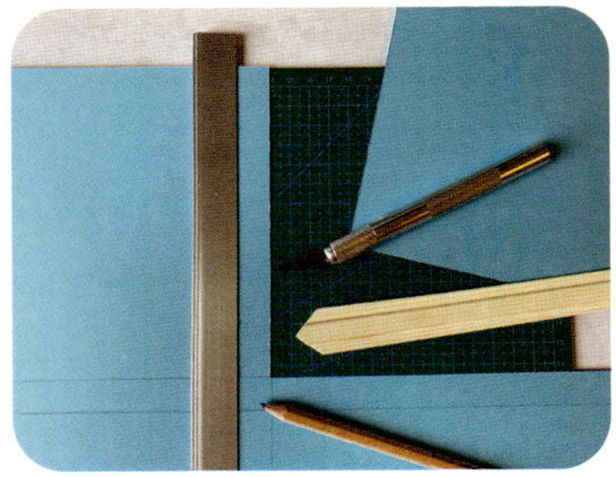

STEP 11

MAKE A PAPER CROSS

Measure the width of the crosspieces and cut a cross from a very light card that is thinner than the crosspieces (so that the card doesn't show when you glue them together).

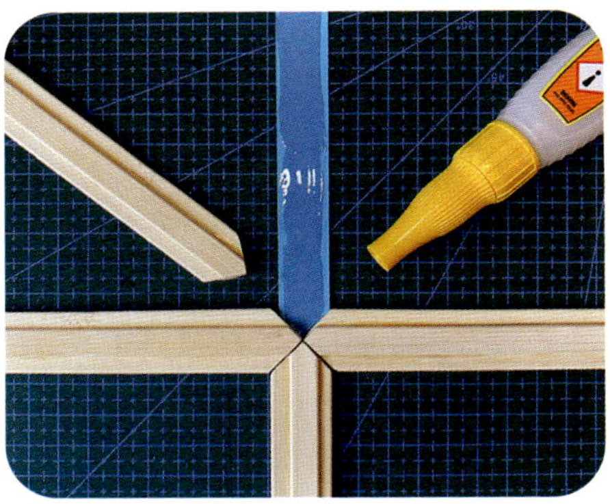

STEP 12

GLUE TO THE CARD

Now glue the four pieces onto the thin card. If you use a cutting mat, you can use the lines to make sure that you align the pieces so they are all at 90 degrees to each other. Leave to dry thoroughly.

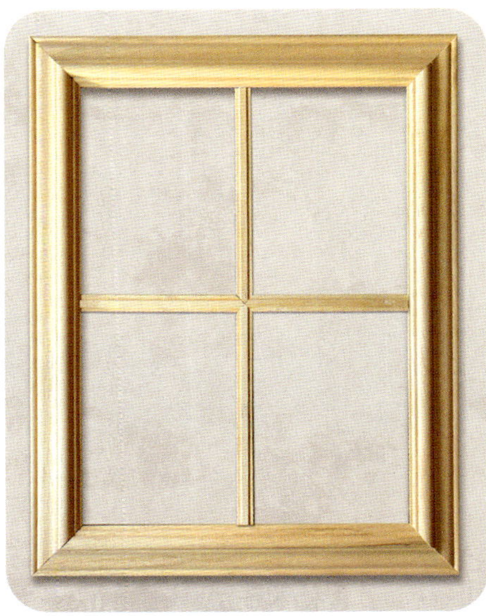

STEP 13

STAIN, PAINT, OR LEAVE?

Now you've made your window frame, you'll need to decide if you want to stain, paint, or leave the wood bare. If you are going to paint or stain it, you have to do it before you put the artwork in and fix the cross on.

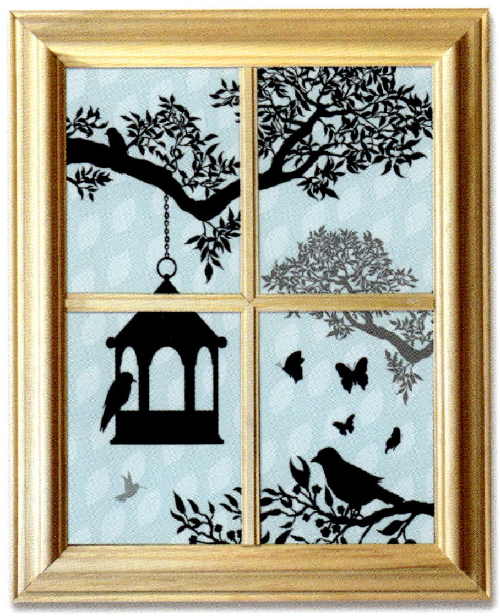

STEP 14

CHOOSE YOUR VIEW

On pages 82 and 83 there are two templates. You can enlarge the blue design and print it out, or use the white one; enlarge and cut out the delicate design on a piece of colored paper, then glue on a background of your choice.

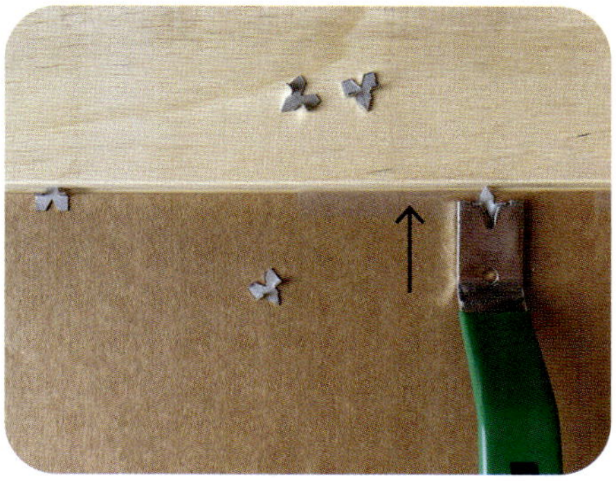

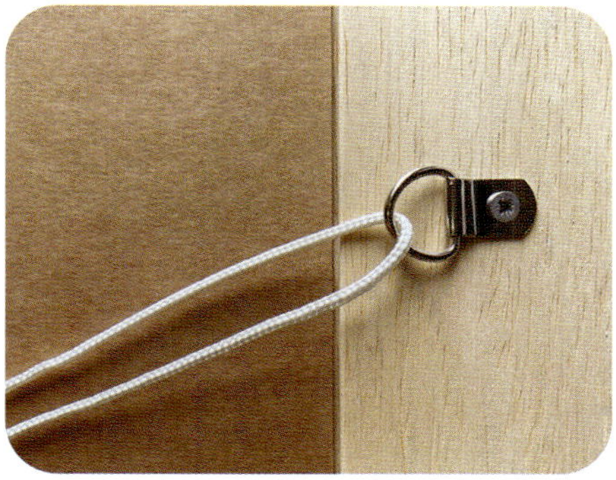

STEP 15

FRAME IT!

Once you have completed the artwork, put it onto the backing board, gently sticking the edges to hold it in position.

Insert the backing board with your artwork into the frame and fix the backing board to the frame, using a point-driving tool and clips. Position around four clips on the long side and two on the top and bottom.

STEP 16

ADD FRAME FIXINGS

Turn the frame over and screw a D ring to both sides of the frame about a quarter of the way down the frame from the top. Attach string to the D rings to hang the frame.

TIP

If you want to keep changing your view, then buy some clear acrylic "glass," insert it into the frame, and glue the cross to the acrylic. You can change the art every season if you like!

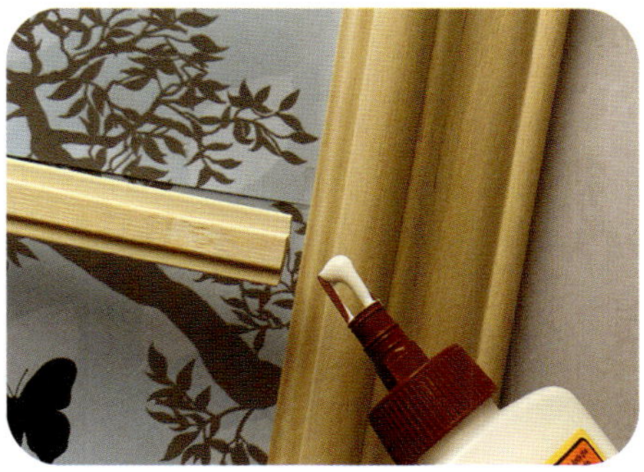

STEP 17

FINALLY... ADD THE CROSS

With wood glue, stick the ends to the edges of the frame. Make sure you don't get glue on your artwork. Hang it up and admire your new view!

IDEAS FOR YOUR VIEW

Let your imagination go wild with the view! You could enlarge and print your favorite holiday photograph or use an old map or a colorful textile. What about creating your own silhouette artwork from a photograph?

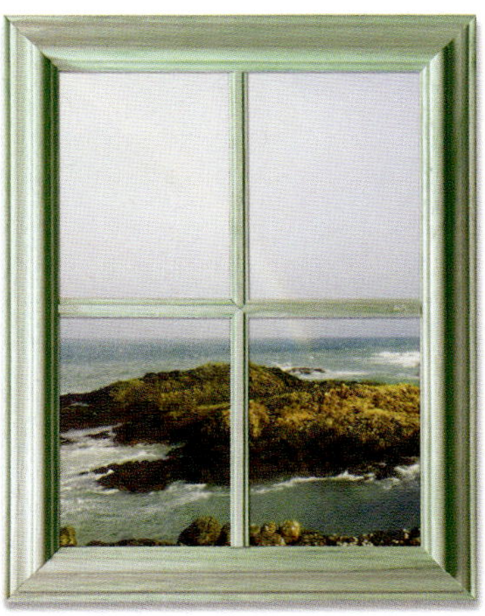

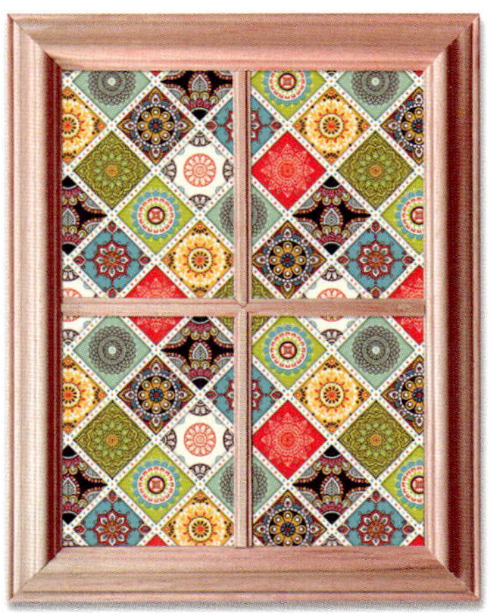

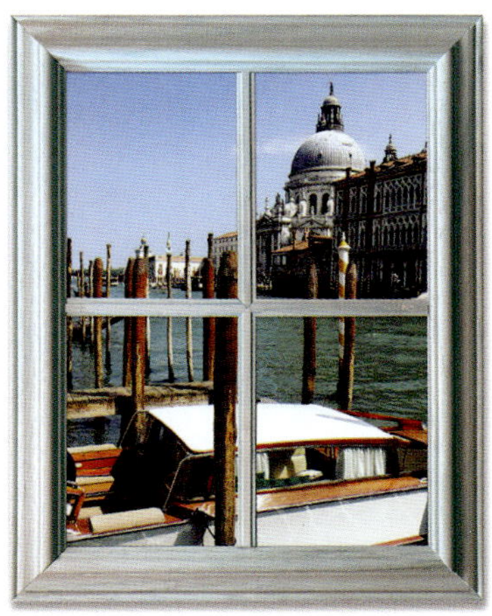

ARTWORK

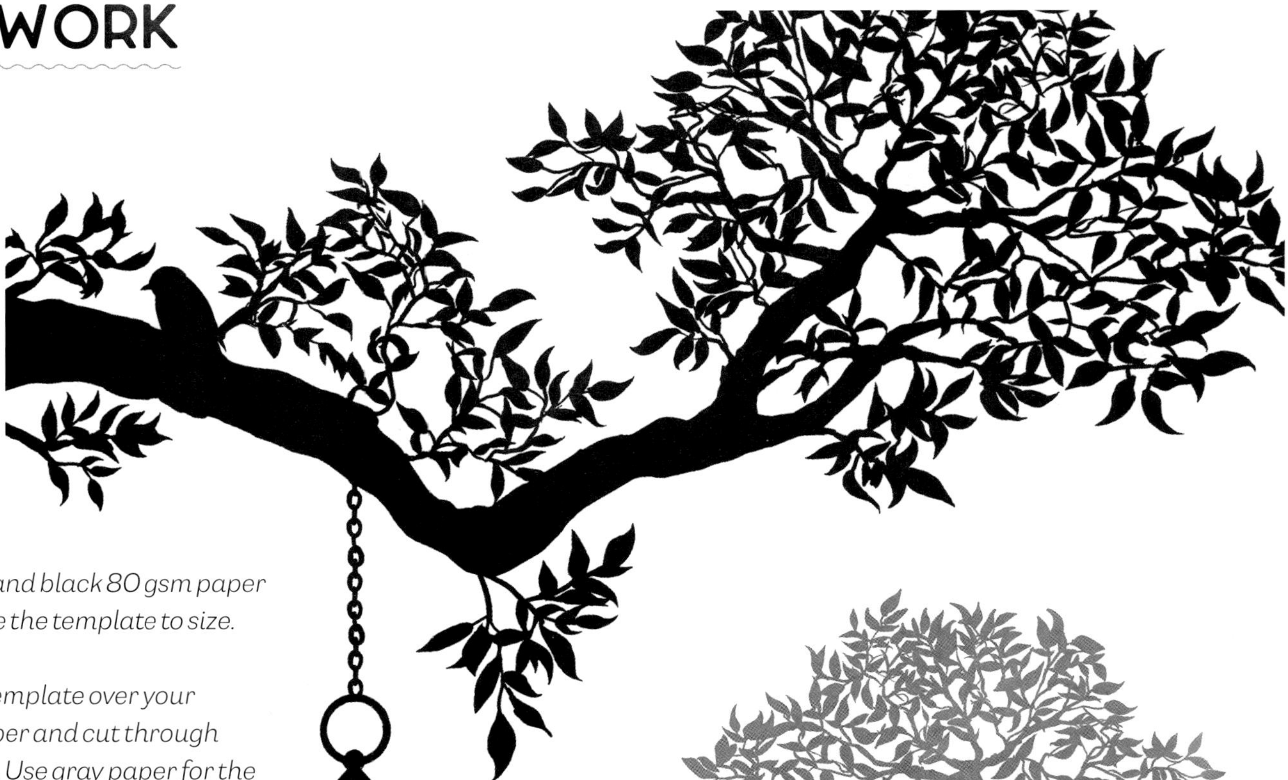

Use a gray and black 80 gsm paper and enlarge the template to size.

Place the template over your colored paper and cut through both layers. Use gray paper for the background objects and black for the foreground.

Once cut, stick it onto a background of your choice.

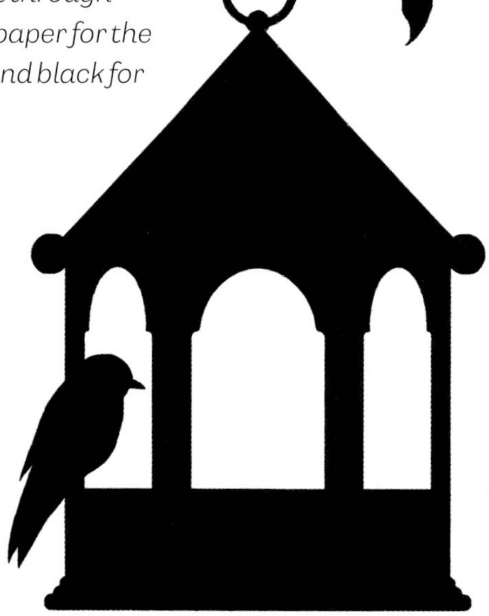

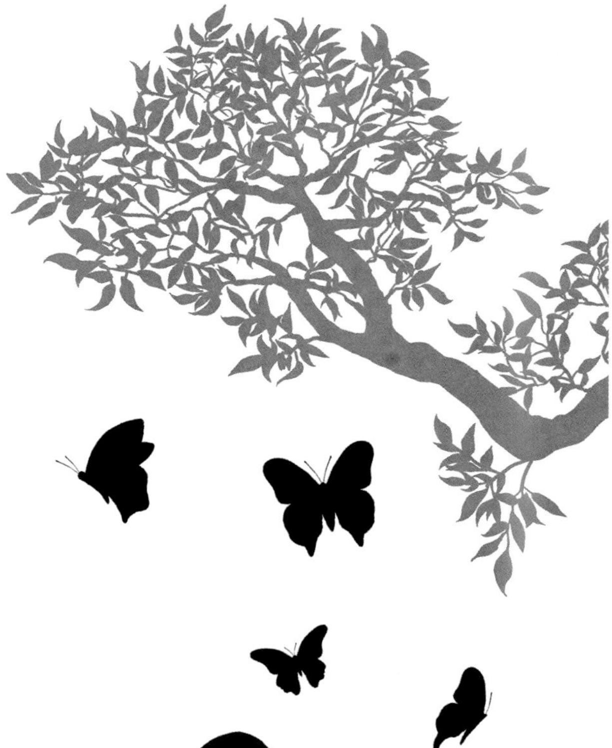

For the background, use a very slightly lighter tone of blue paper and stick the leaves onto it in a repeat pattern, as on page 83.

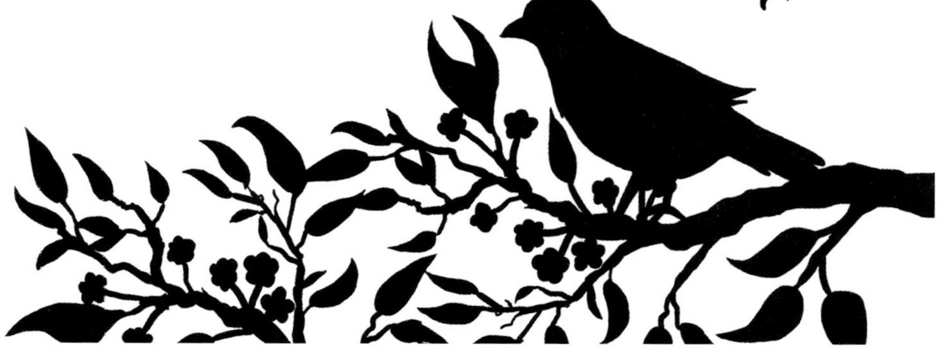

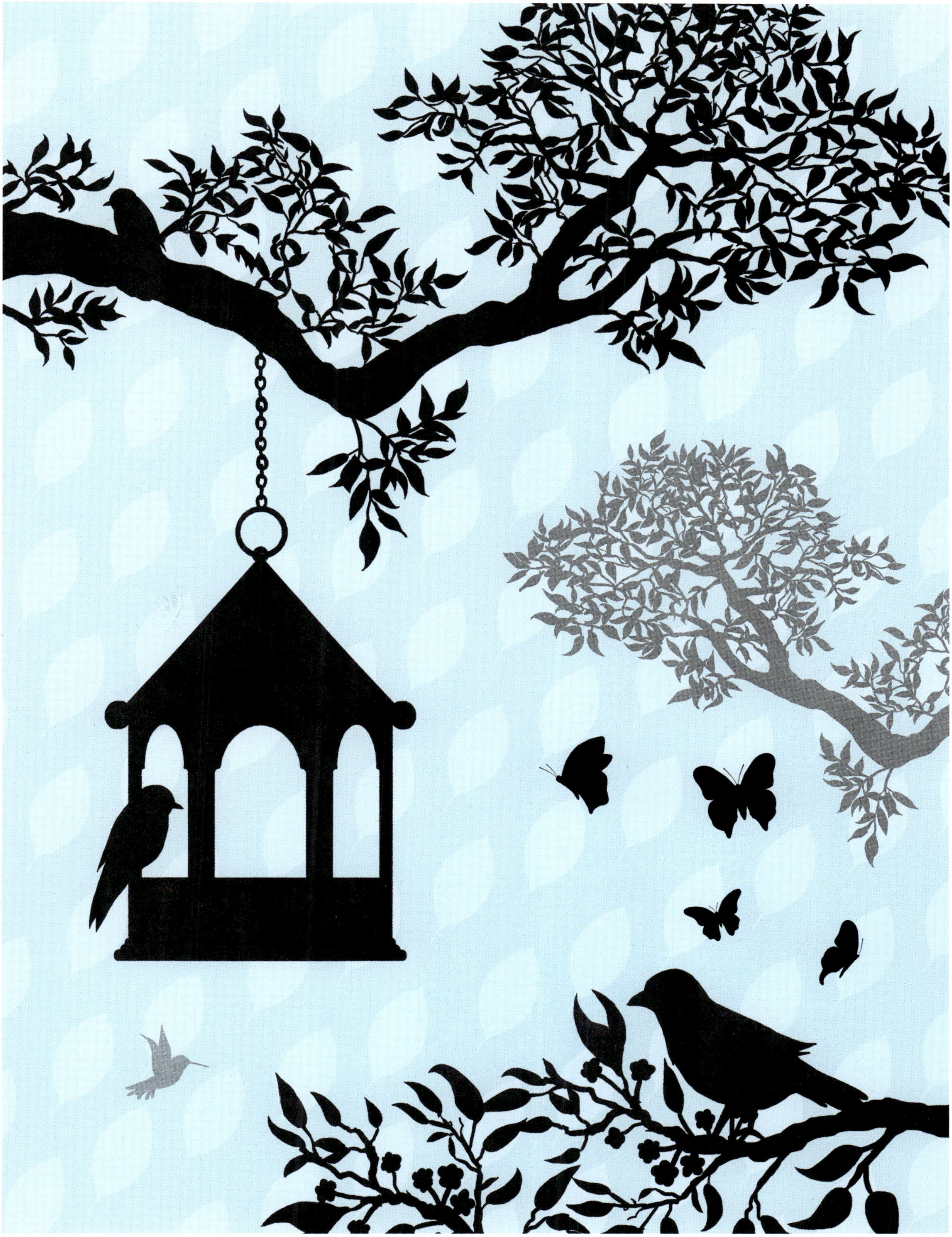

SIZING: ENLARGE BY 250 PERCENT = FRAME SIZE

You can just enlarge this design to the size of your window frame.

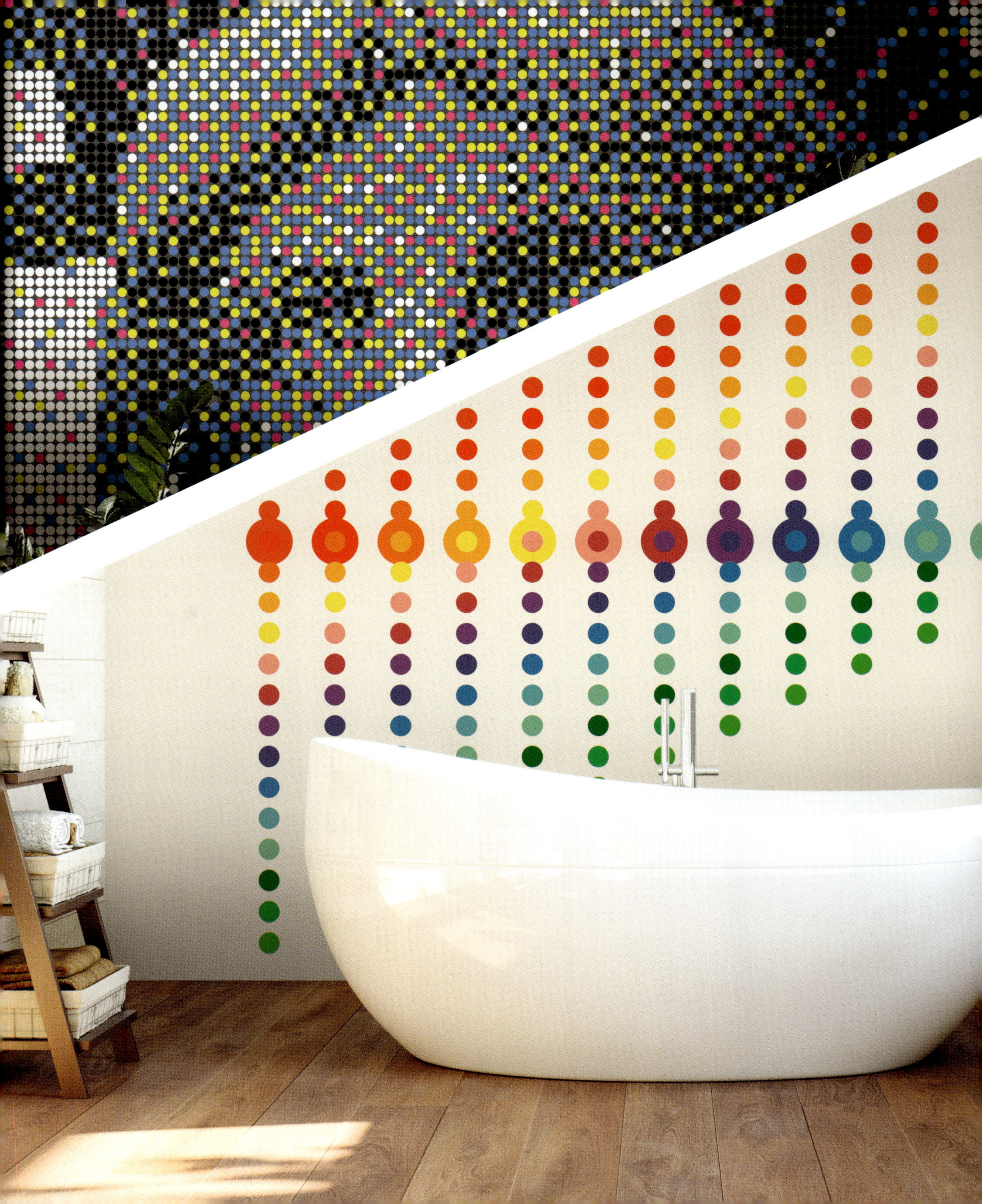

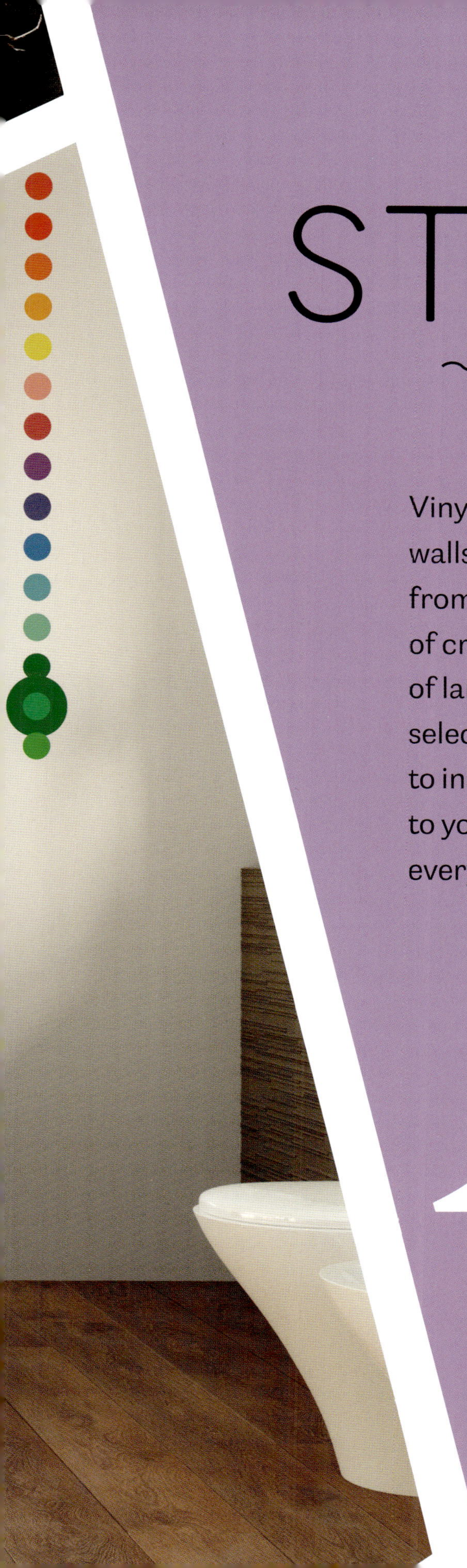

STICK IT!

Vinyl and stickers are easy ways to transform your walls. It can be as simple as buying large stickers from a stationery store. Think about the vast amount of creativity you can have with mixed color packs of large, round stickers! We have chosen to do a selection of ideas to get your imagination working, to inspire you to create artworks that are unique to you and create a visually impactful room to wow everyone who walks in.

4

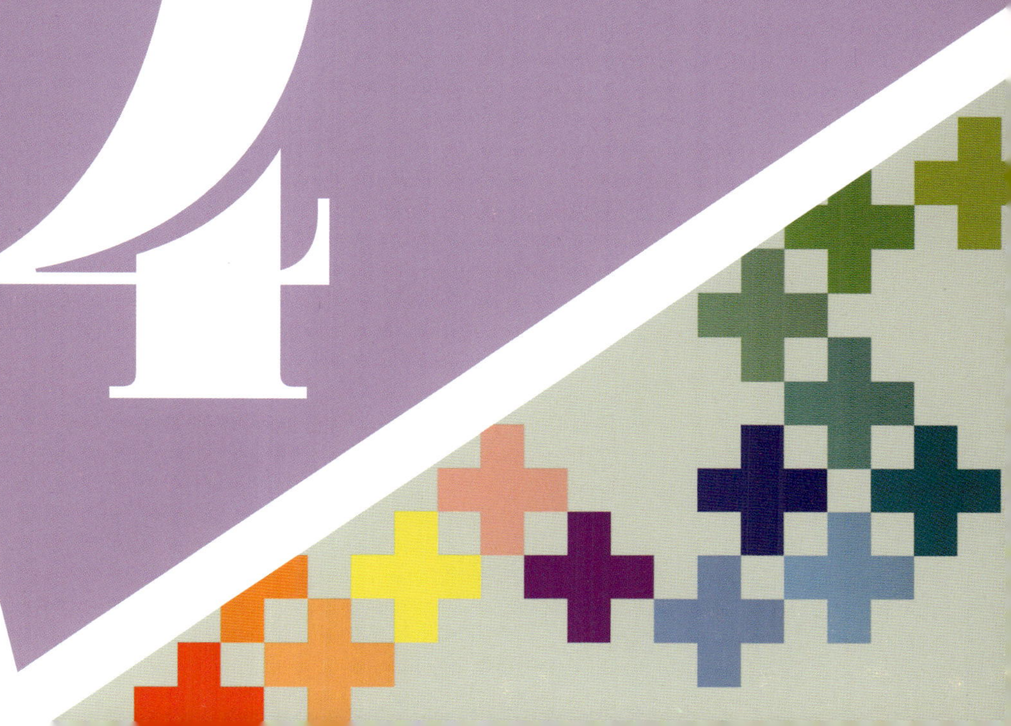

BIG PIXEL MURAL

Have you ever looked really closely at your television set or computer monitor and been fascinated by the way the colors break up? There are just three colors of dots, yet our eyes and brains mix and merge them into a full spectrum when viewed from a distance.

This project takes advantage of the way our eyes work to resolve images in this super-scaled image of the Statue of Liberty. Lady Liberty is made from just five colors. The result is super cool and pop arty.

Our instructions guide you on how to re-create this image by using ordinary store-bought stickers. This design uses just five colors, which blend and mix when seen from farther away. The five colors are easy and economical to source: they are red, blue, yellow, white, and black. Stickers that are around 2 in. (5 cm) in diameter are perfect for a mural like this.

If you have a cutting machine, you can go one stage further and make your own out of self-adhesive vinyl or sticker paper—and you can make them any shape you like. The mural can also be made with card, map pins, or even plastic bottle tops or metal beer or soda caps.

The step-by-step instructions show you how to take an area from the template to re-create, using ready-made stickers. If you refer to the scale and cropping information in the Tools & Equipment section on page 8, and the How to Print When Enlarging Massively on page 11, you could start by selecting the area you want to re-create and make your own stickers to fit.

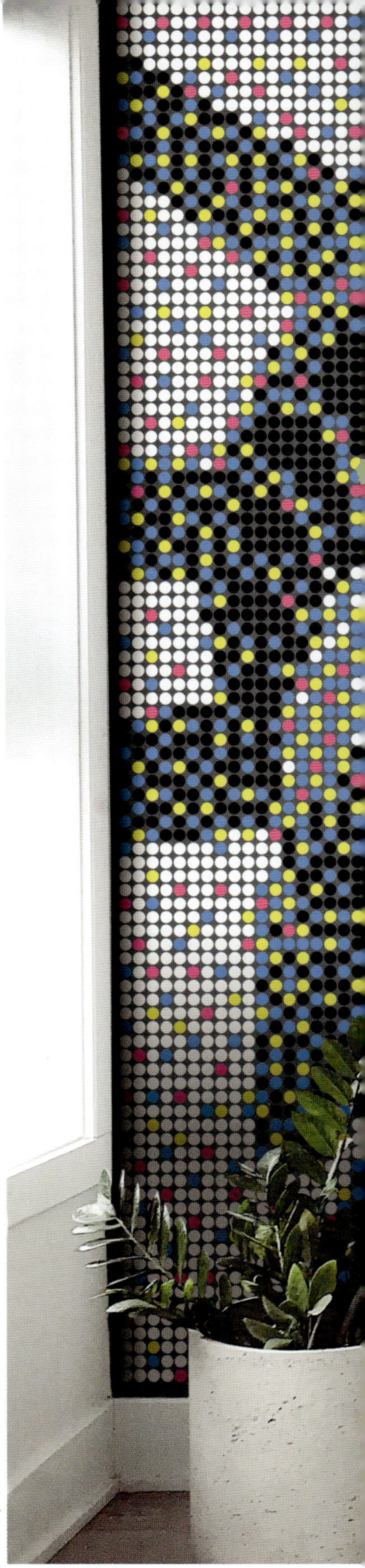

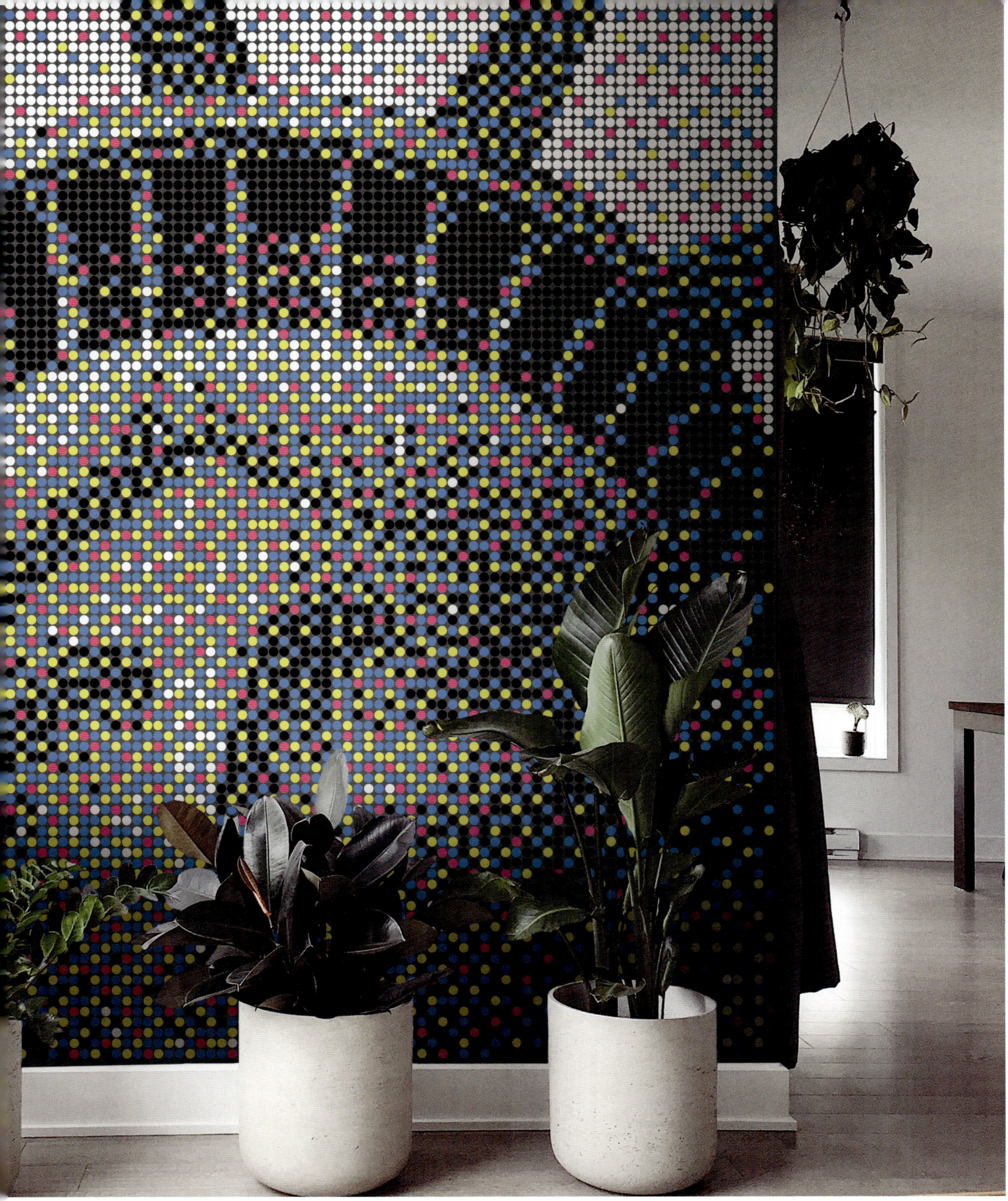

STEP-BY-STEP INSTRUCTIONS

YOU WILL NEED

To prepare the wall

- *Pencil*
- *Spirit level*
- *Tape measure*

For the positional template

- *A4 (8.25 x 11.75 in. / 21 x 29.7 cm) sheet of card*
- *Craft knife*
- *Cutting mat*

To make the mural

- *Lots of stickers in black, white, red, yellow, and blue*

STEP 1

USING THE STICKERS AS PIXELS

In this example, imagine that we'll use stickers with 7/8 in. (0.875 cm) diameter. They're going to placed so that there is 1/8 in. (0.125 cm) between each row and column of stickers. This gives us a neat 1 in. (2.5 cm) per column or row.

TIP

The proportions of 7/8 sticker and 1/8 gap work well whatever size of sticker you choose to use.

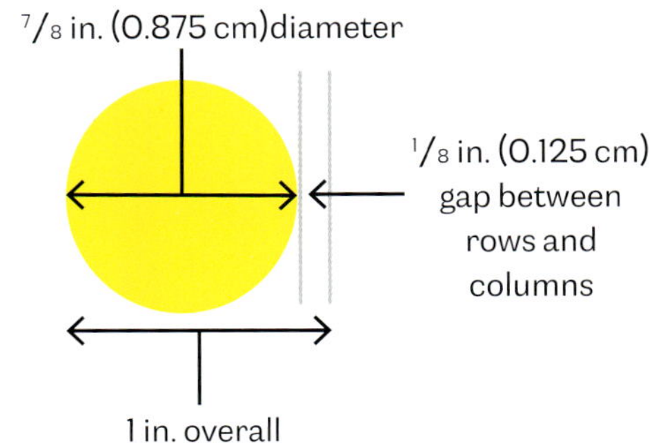

TIP

To calculate how many of any-sized stickers needed to fill your wall: divide the size of the wall in inches (or centimeters) by the size of your sticker, including the gap.

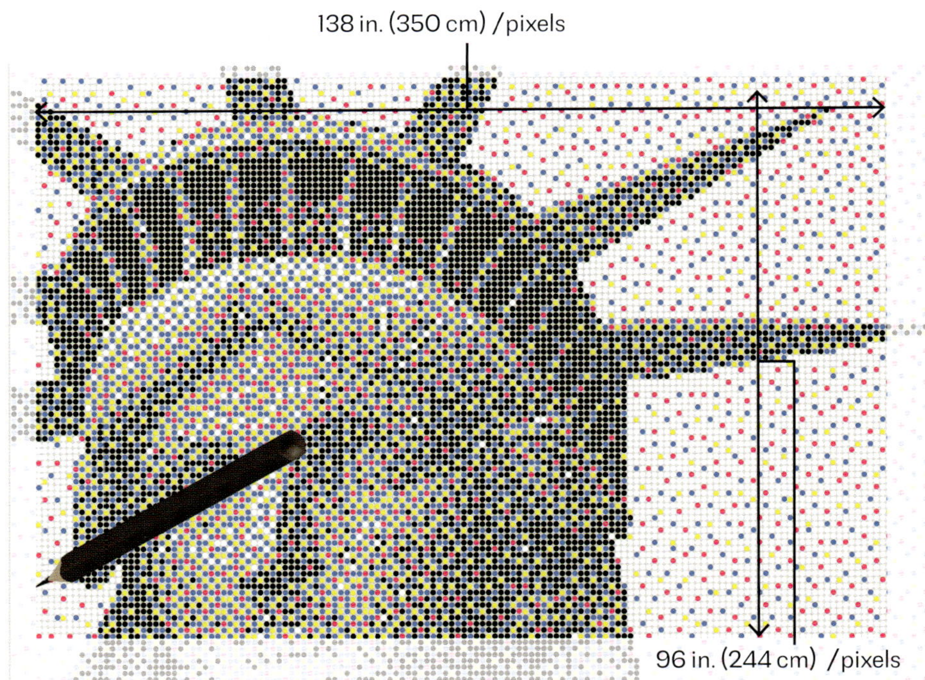

STEP 2

CHOOSING A PART OF THE TEMPLATE IMAGE TO RE-CREATE

Let's imagine our wall is 8 ft. (2.4 m) high and 11.5 ft. (350 cm) wide. That makes it 96 in. (2.4 m) high and 138 in. (350 cm) wide. So to fit the wall, I need to select an area of the template that is 96 pixels high by 138 pixels wide.

Measure out your pixels by width and height on the template and cut a window out of a sheet of paper to that size.

Move the window over the template until you are happy with the crop that you see, and draw lines on the template in pencil.

Mark the center of the design.

STEP 3

PREPARING THE WALL

Find the middle of the wall with the tape measure. Using the spirit level and pencil, mark the horizontal and vertical with 12 in. (30.5 cm) lines in a cross.

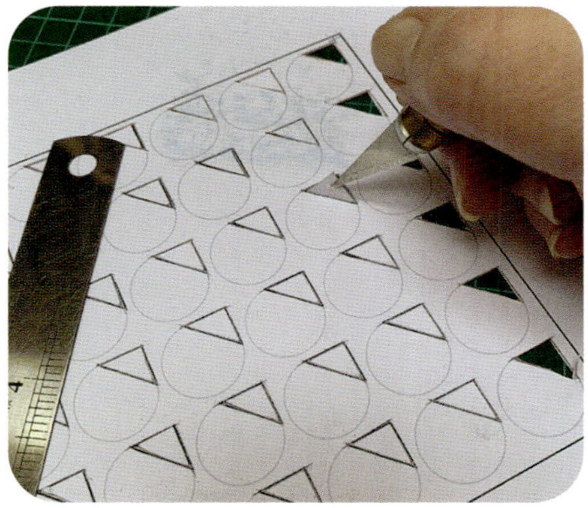

STEP 4

CUTTING THE TEMPLATE

Download or scan and print the template at the correct scale—see tip on page 90. Cut out all the triangles and around the outer black box.

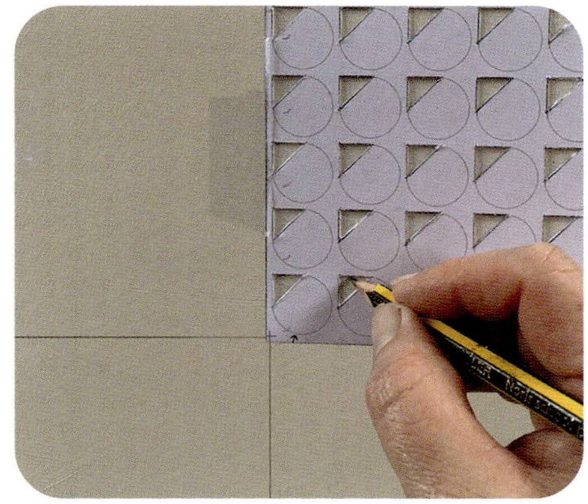

STEP 5

Start top right of the center cross. Align the blue lines on the left and bottom of the template with the centerlines on the wall. In each triangle, draw with faint pencil lines at the top and left of each triangle. Follow below the center cross, using the blue lines at the top and left of the template. Look at the template overleaf if you are confused.

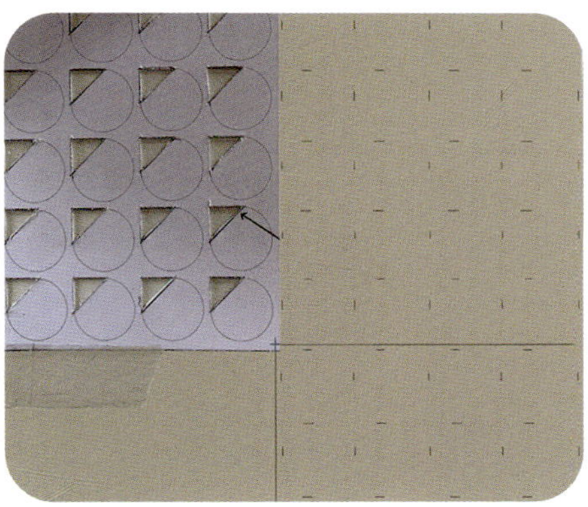

STEP 6

Top left of the center cross. Align the blue lines on the right, and the bottom of the template with the centerlines on the wall. In each triangle draw with the faint pencil lines at the top and left of each triangle. Follow below the center cross, using the blue lines at the top, and right, of the template.

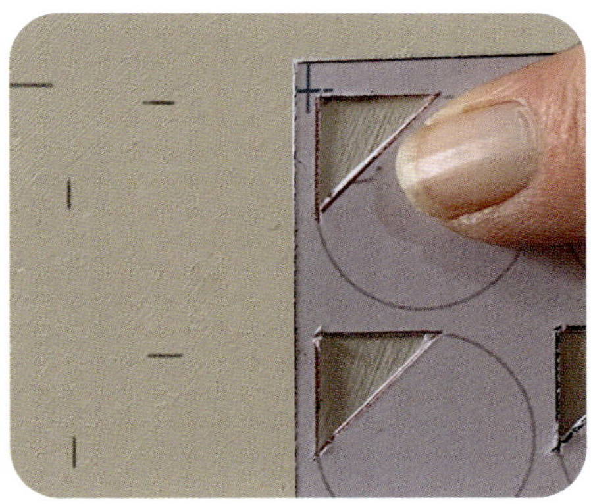

STEP 7

Continue to fill the wall in all directions with marks made from inside the triangles. You can use the triangles on the outside to overlap your existing pencil marks each time to get the new marks in the correct position.

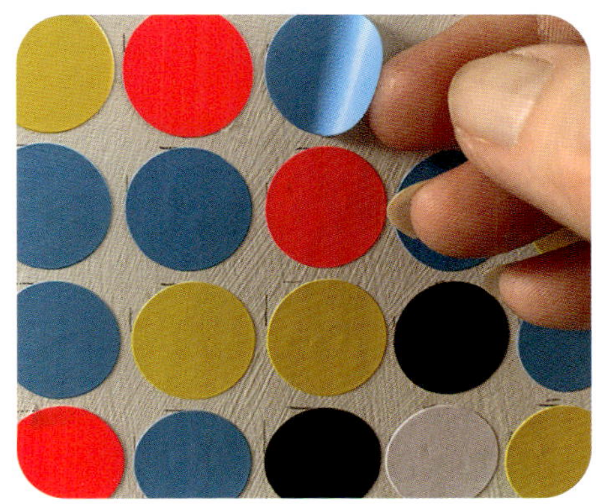

STEP 8

Using the template as a color guide, align each sticker to the pencil marks and fill the wall from the center out.

TIP

It may help to write the number of each row and column where the stickers will go, in order to keep track.

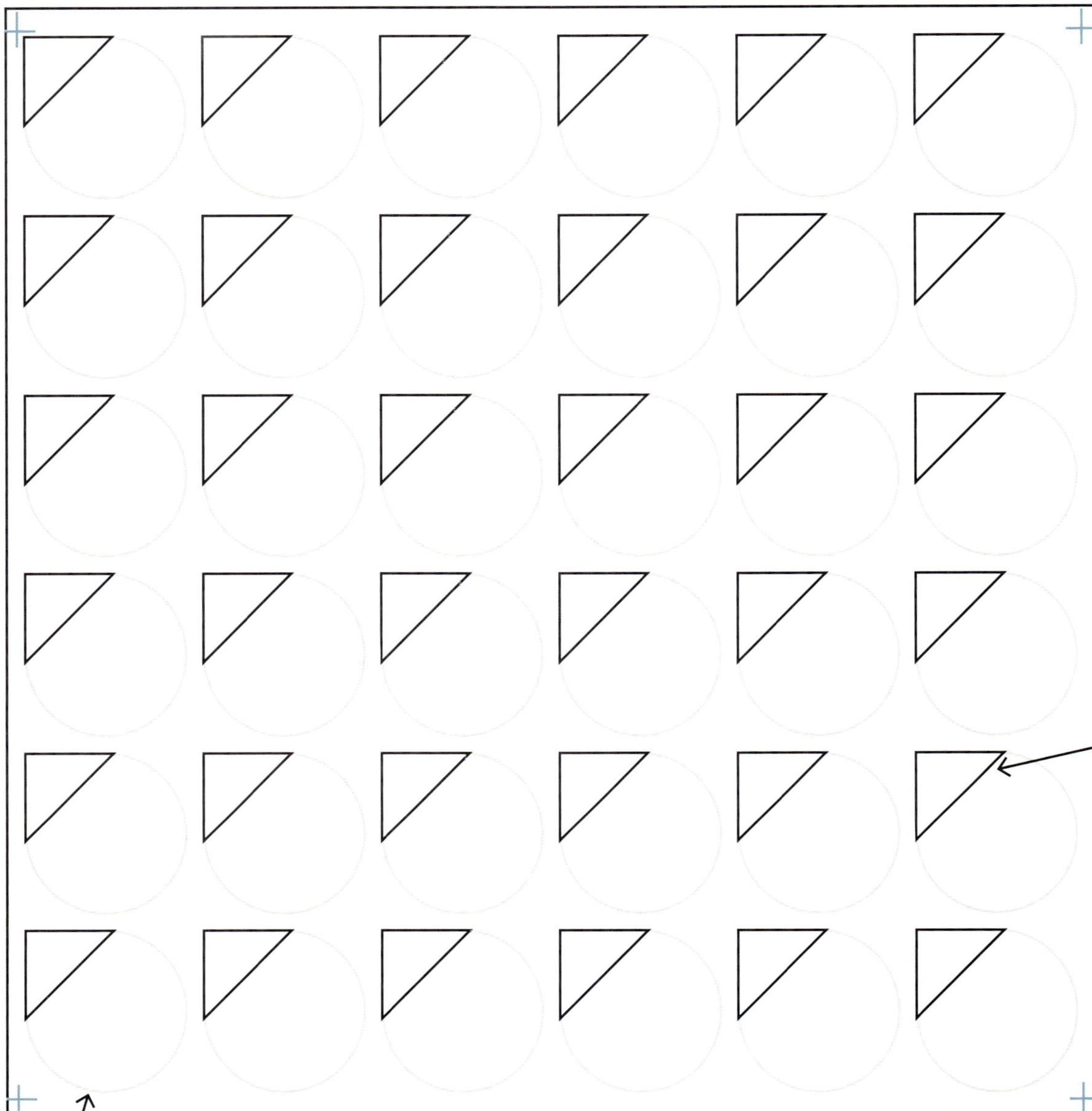

Blue lines align with penciled center marks on the wall

Cut around the black box to make the template

Cut out all the triangles; pencil marks will be drawn through them, top and left, and the stickers aligned to them.

The gray circle shapes are just an indication of how the stickers align

TIP

For the correct scale to print the template at for your stickers: divide the diameter of your stickers in mm by 22, then multiply it by 100. This will be the percentage to print the template at.

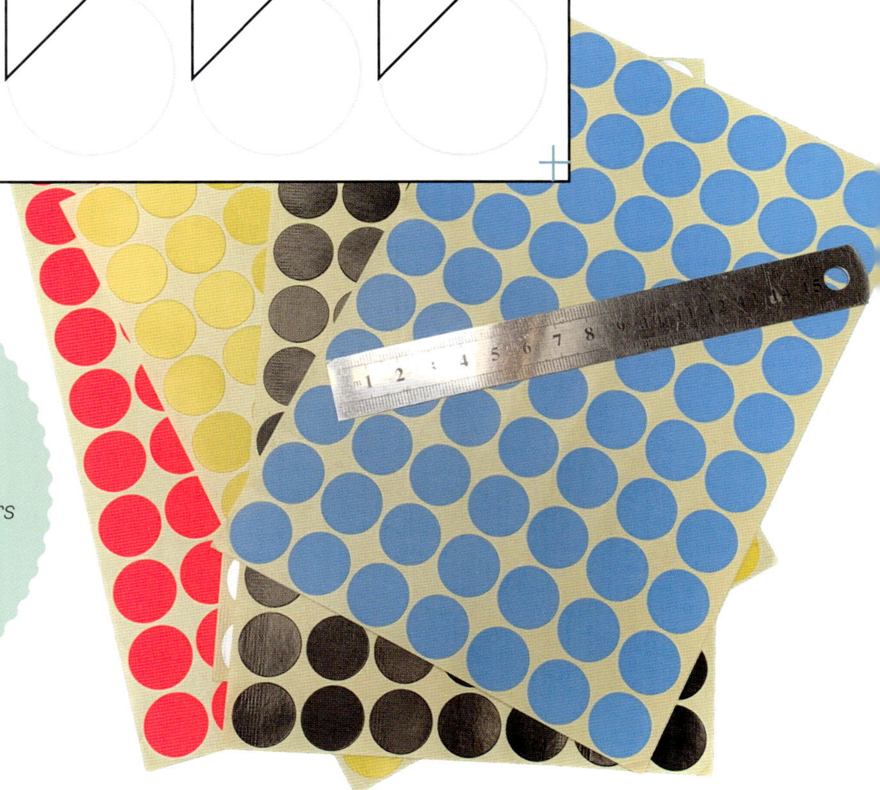

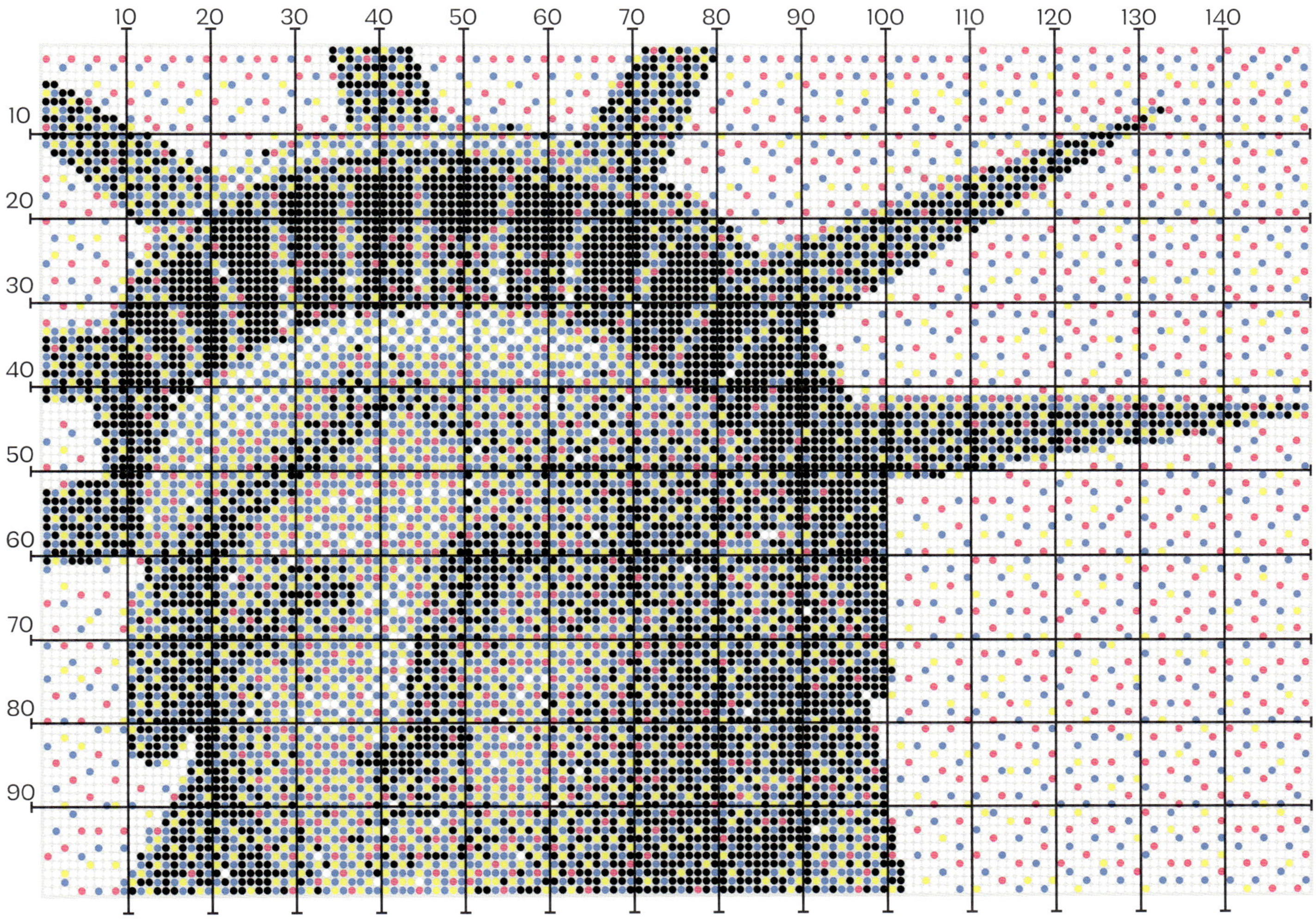
10 20 30 40 50 60 70 80 90 100 110 120 130 140
10 20 30 40 50 60 70 80 90

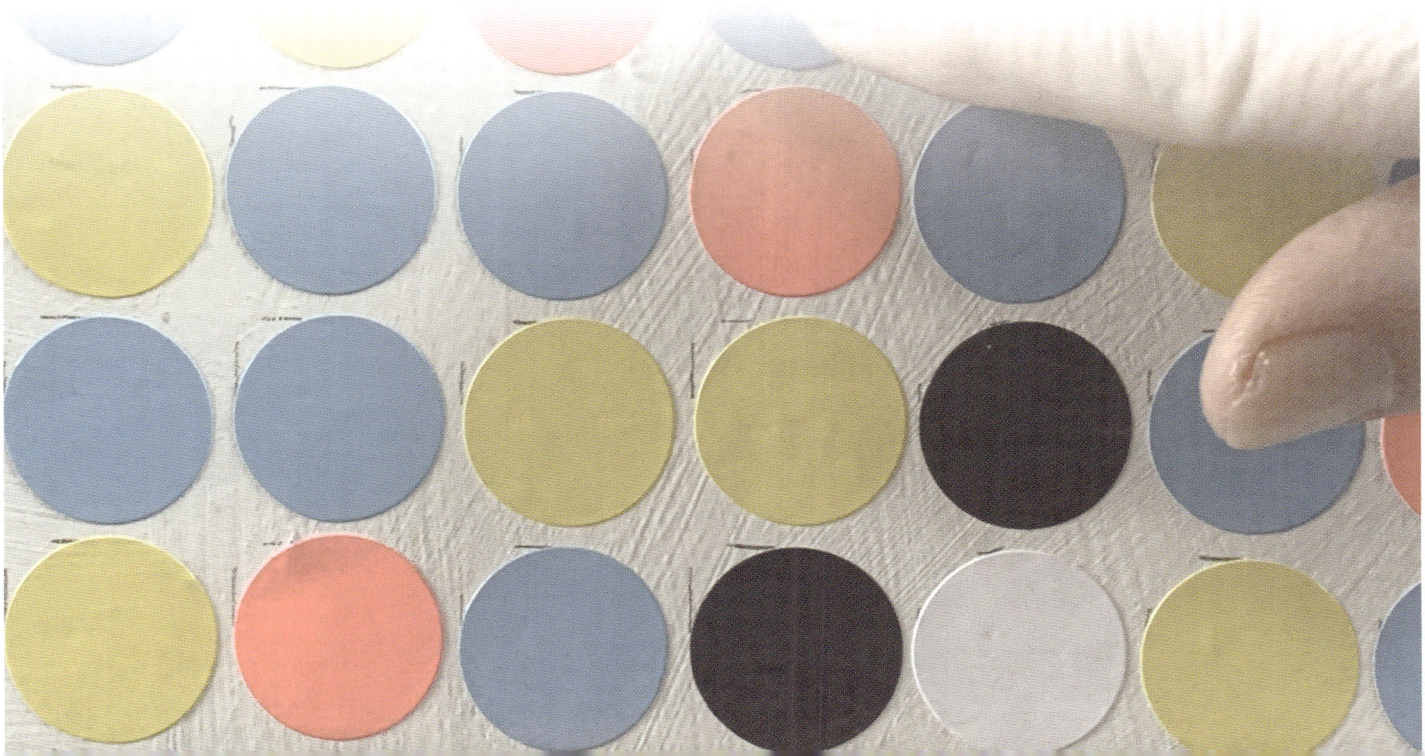

DOTTY SPOTTY WALL

Vinyl is the perfect material for the bathroom, dramatically changing a wall and the overall look of the room. It provides a terrific focal point, drawing the eye to the best features, such as this beautifully shaped bathtub. As well as attracting the eye, wall art can be used to distract away from things you don't want people to notice.

There are so many kinds of vinyl to choose from in various colors, shades, and finishes. There's matte or glossy, indoor or outdoor, and removable or permanent, plus vinyl you can put on windows. Many suppliers stock a wide range of colors and shades, plus special finishes like glitter, opals, metallics, and sometimes even printed patterns. You can get chalkboard vinyls and even some that are heat sensitive and change color as they warm up! There are so many gorgeous ones that it's hard to select, but check that the vinyl you buy is suitable for your room conditions before you hand over your money.

Like all of the wall art ideas in this book, spend some time thinking about your design before you purchase the materials. Alternatively, buy a variety pack of colors and be inspired when you get your first look at them.

If you have a cutting machine, then this project is even easier. Get the machine to do the hard work for you, and it will certainly speed the project up. If you are cutting by hand, then circles do take some time, but if you find circles hard, then use squares since they are easier to cut accurately.

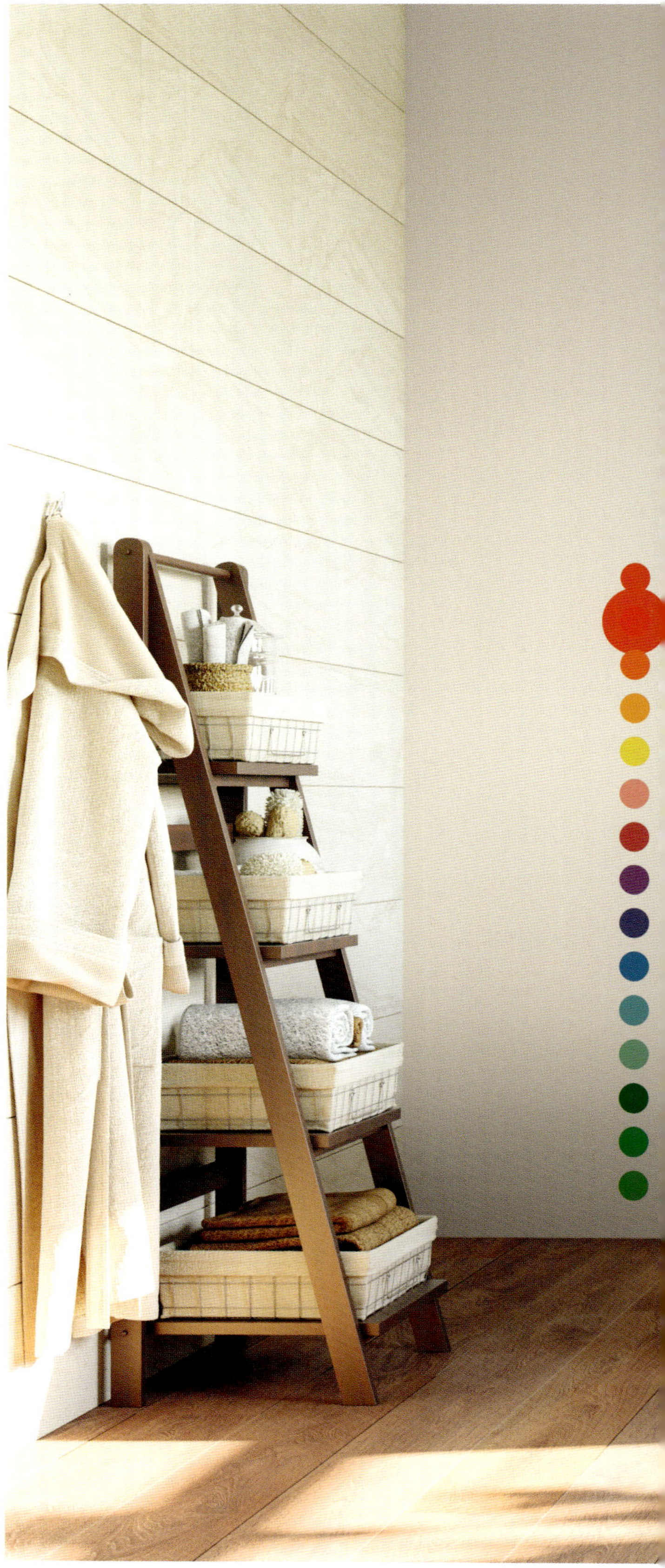

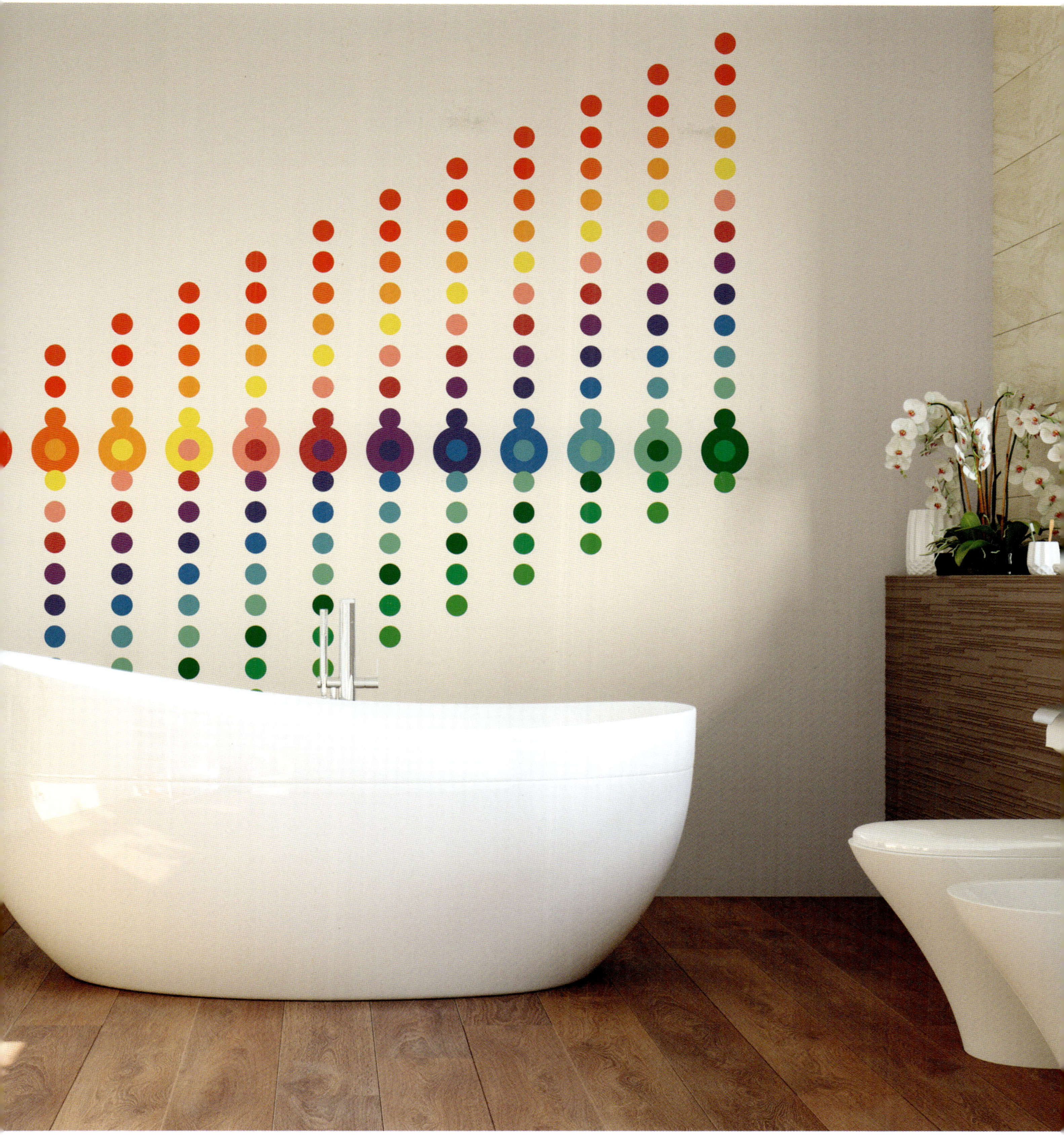

STEP-BY-STEP INSTRUCTIONS

YOU WILL NEED

- *Pack of assorted-color permanent vinyl sheets 12 x 12 in. (30.5 x 30.5 cm) We used fifteen colors in the main design, one sheet of each color*
- *Cutting mat and craft knife*
- *Masking tape and low-tack tape*
- *Pencil and eraser*
- *Smoothing tool or thick, sturdy card that won't bend*
- *Tape measure and spirit level*

OPTIONAL

- *Vinyl-cutting machine and manufacturer's software*

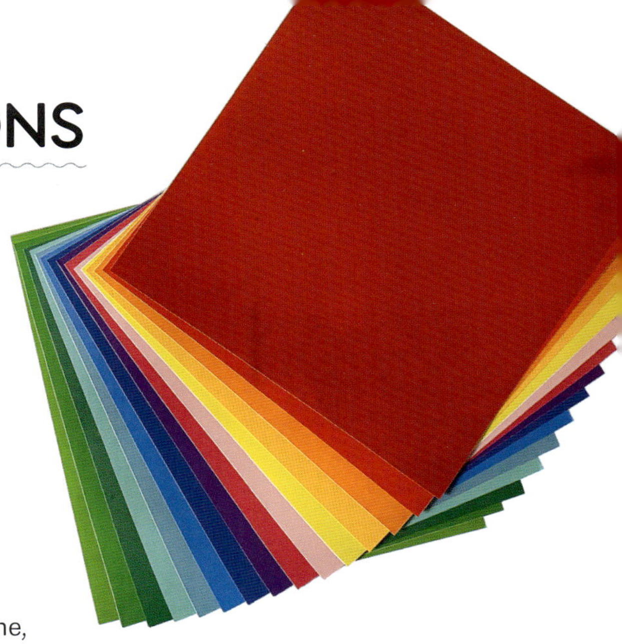

STEP 1

CHOOSE YOUR METHOD

If you have a die-cutting machine, then you can either scan in the circle templates on page 97 and convert to an SVG file or create your own file (see page 11 for how to download). If you do want to use a cutting machine, go to the jade box on the right-hand side for instructions.

STEP 2

CHOOSE YOUR COLORS

Choose and order your fifteen colors, so as to get a rainbow effect and color wheel in your wall piece.

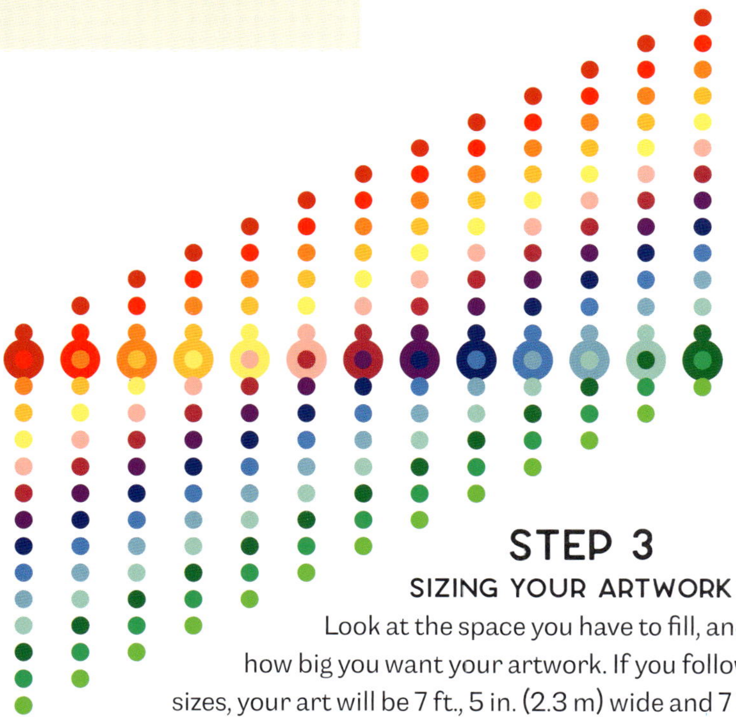

STEP 3

SIZING YOUR ARTWORK

Look at the space you have to fill, and decide how big you want your artwork. If you follow our sizes, your art will be 7 ft., 5 in. (2.3 m) wide and 7 ft., 2.5 in. (2.2 m) high. However, you can size your artwork to fit any space. Print out a paper template for each sheet you cut (fifteen). You can cut one and reuse, but it won't be as accurate or look as good.

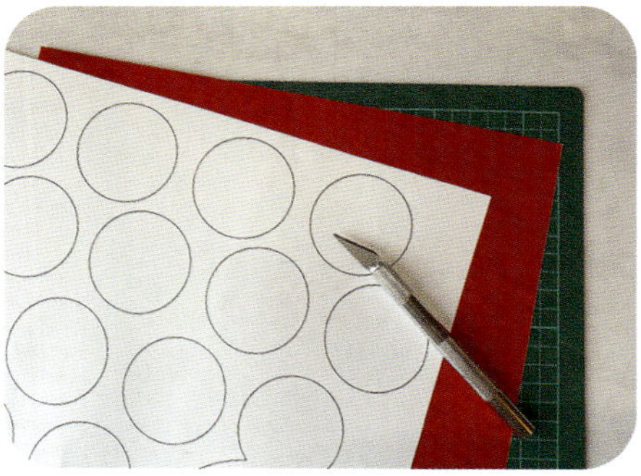

STEP 4

TEMPLATE

Gently put a small piece of low-tack tape on all four sides of your template to attach it to your vinyl sheet; this will stop it slipping when you cut. Now you are ready to cut.

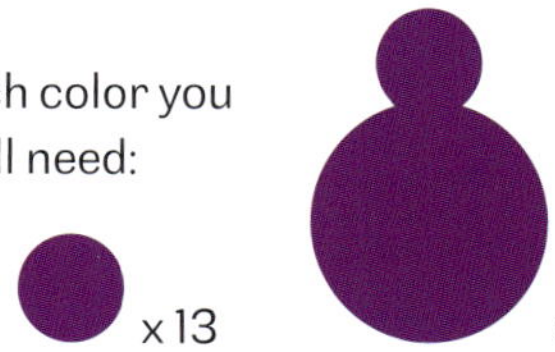

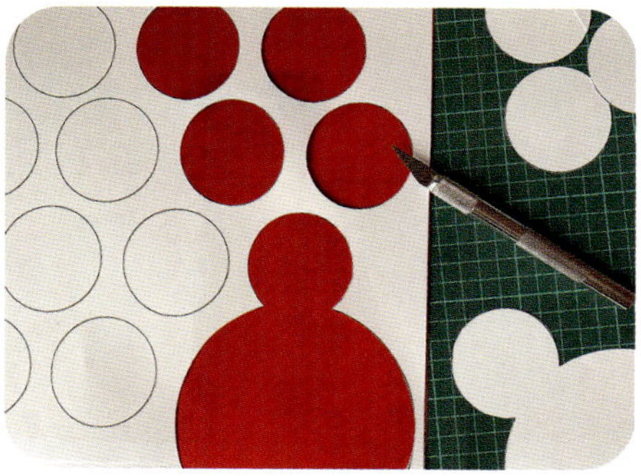

STEP 5

CUTTING THE VINYL CIRCLES

It can be quite hard to cut circles, but go slowly and carefully; it will be worth it! Test one circle to see if you are using enough pressure to cut through the template and vinyl but not the backing paper. Don't worry if you do go through all the layers, since you can still peel off the vinyl easily.

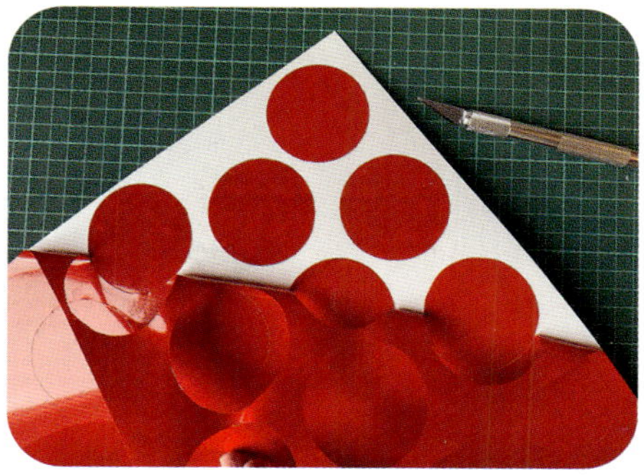

STEP 6

WEEDING

Weeding is a lovely term used by crafters, and means to peel off the waste vinyl around the circles. Do this carefully so you are left with just the circles and double circle on the backing paper. Repeat steps 4–6 for the entire range of colors.

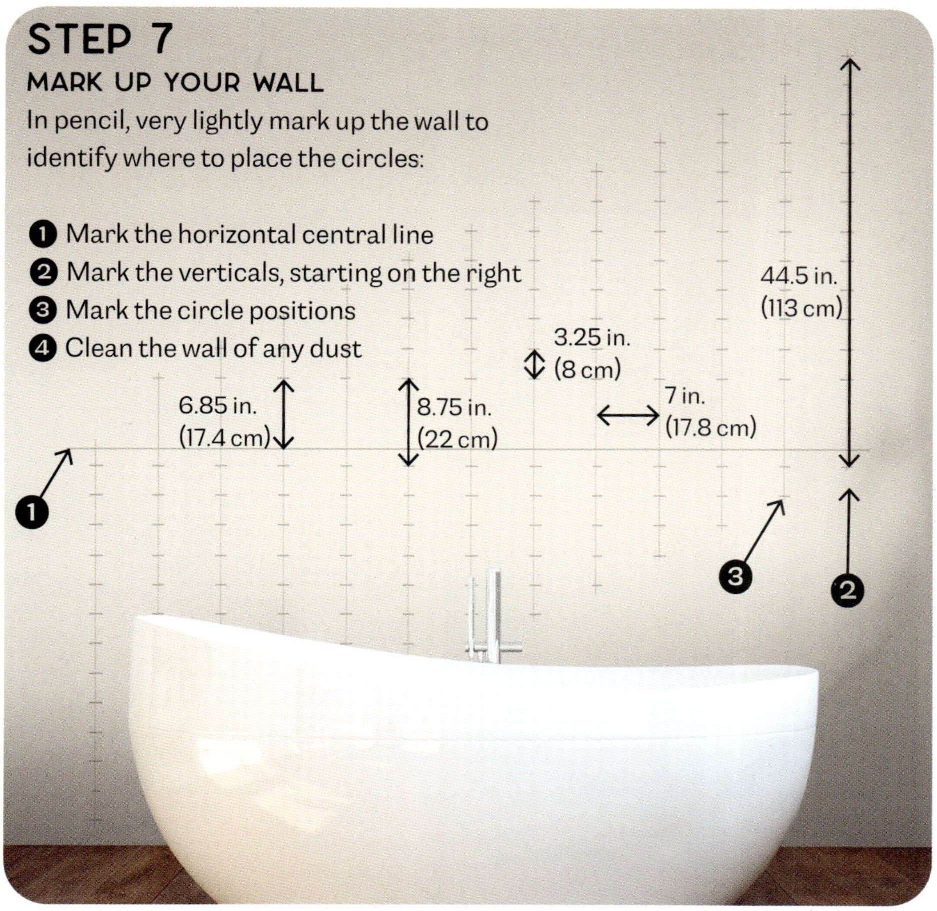

STEP 7

MARK UP YOUR WALL

In pencil, very lightly mark up the wall to identify where to place the circles:

1. Mark the horizontal central line
2. Mark the verticals, starting on the right
3. Mark the circle positions
4. Clean the wall of any dust

USING A CUTTING MACHINE

Each manufacturer uses slightly different software and has a range of machines, so follow their instructions. Importantly, before buying the vinyl sheets, make sure they are compatible with your machine.

1. First, work out the maximum size of vinyl sheet your machine can use.

2. Scan in the template on page 97 (or download an SVG; see page 11 for guidance) and size to 12 in. (30.5 cm) (200 percent), or draw the circles in a drawing program on the computer. Save your template as either an SVG or see the manufacturer's requirements for your machine.

3. Import your template into the software that the cutting machine uses. Follow the manufacturer's sizing and correct the artwork if needed.

4. Make sure you switch the machine manually to the vinyl setting or use the software so that the correct blades are used.

5. Stick the vinyl sheet on the manufacturer's cutting mat, feed into the machine, and cut.

6. Go to step 7 and follow the steps from there.

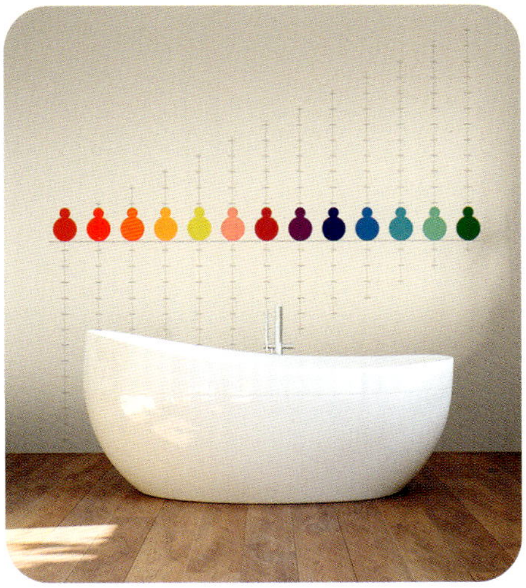

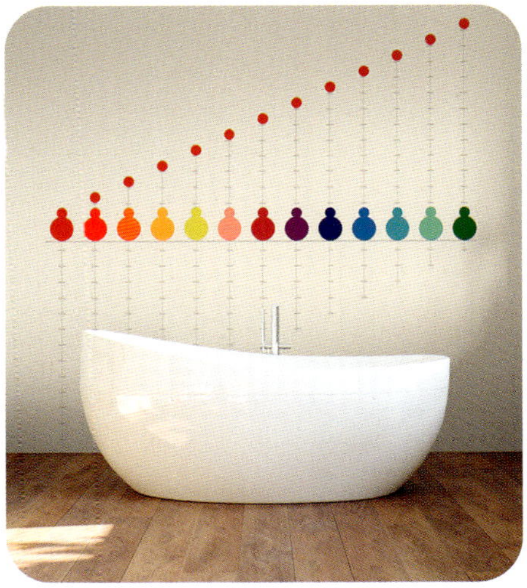

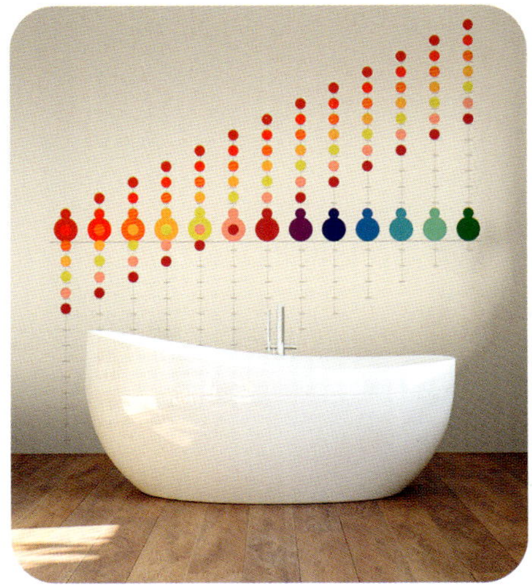

STEP 8

START WITH DOUBLE CIRCLES

Begin by placing the double circles on the centerline. Tack them lightly on the wall; once positioned correctly, use a piece of thick card with a flat edge or a smoothing tool to get any bubbles out.

STEP 9

WORK WITH EACH COLOR

Starting with the second column from the left, place a small circle (in the color of the double circle on the first column) on the topmost mark of each column. Continue for the other columns, working to the right.

STEP 10

FILL IN THE GAPS

Keep going and stick all of the colors on the diagonal.

Once finished, carefully rub out the pencil marks with your eraser and check that all the circles are smoothed down firmly on the wall. Check again that there are no trapped air bubbles remaining.

VARIATIONS

Using a simple geometric shape like a cross makes the cutting far easier to do. You can create your own shapes and designs in any formation you like! Do you like our crosses?

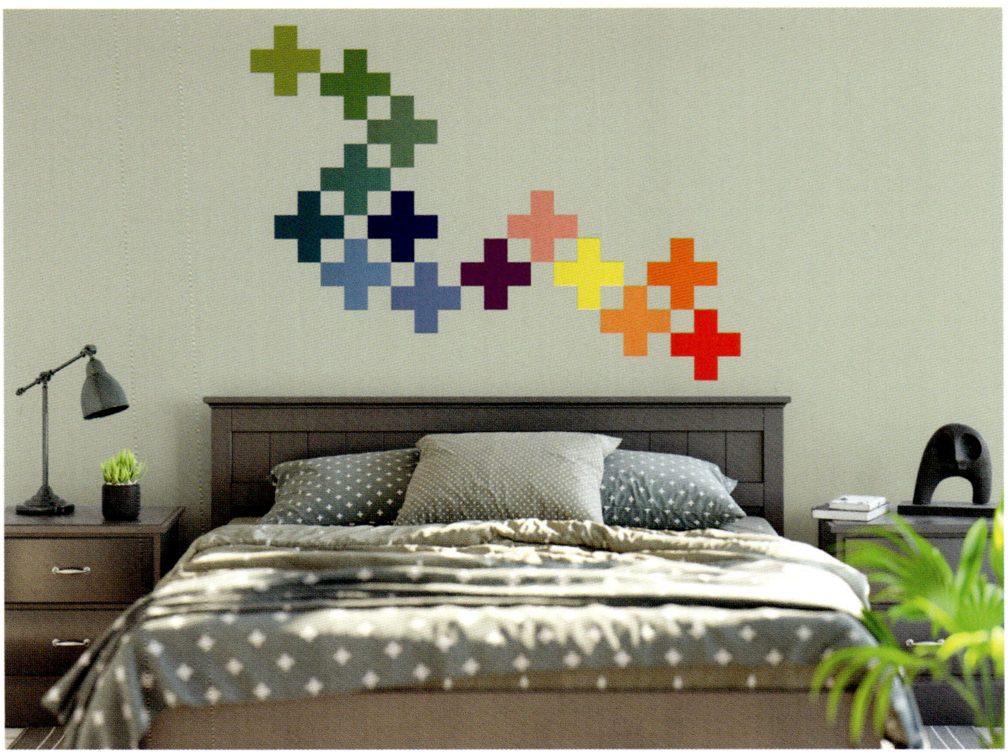

13 small circles 2 1/4 in (57 mm) in diameter per color

1 double-circle shape per color

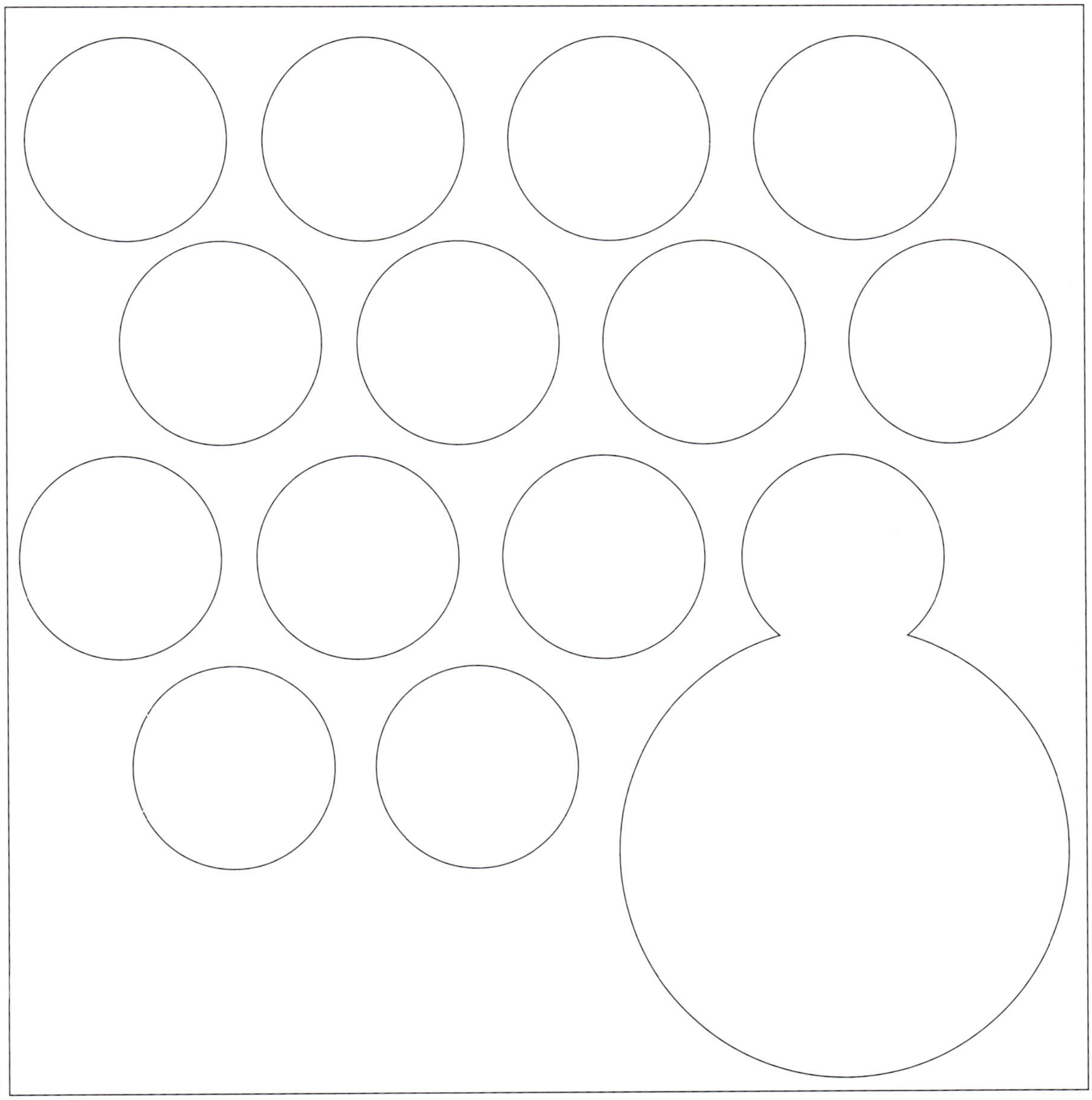

SIZING: ENLARGE BY 200 PERCENT = FINAL SIZE

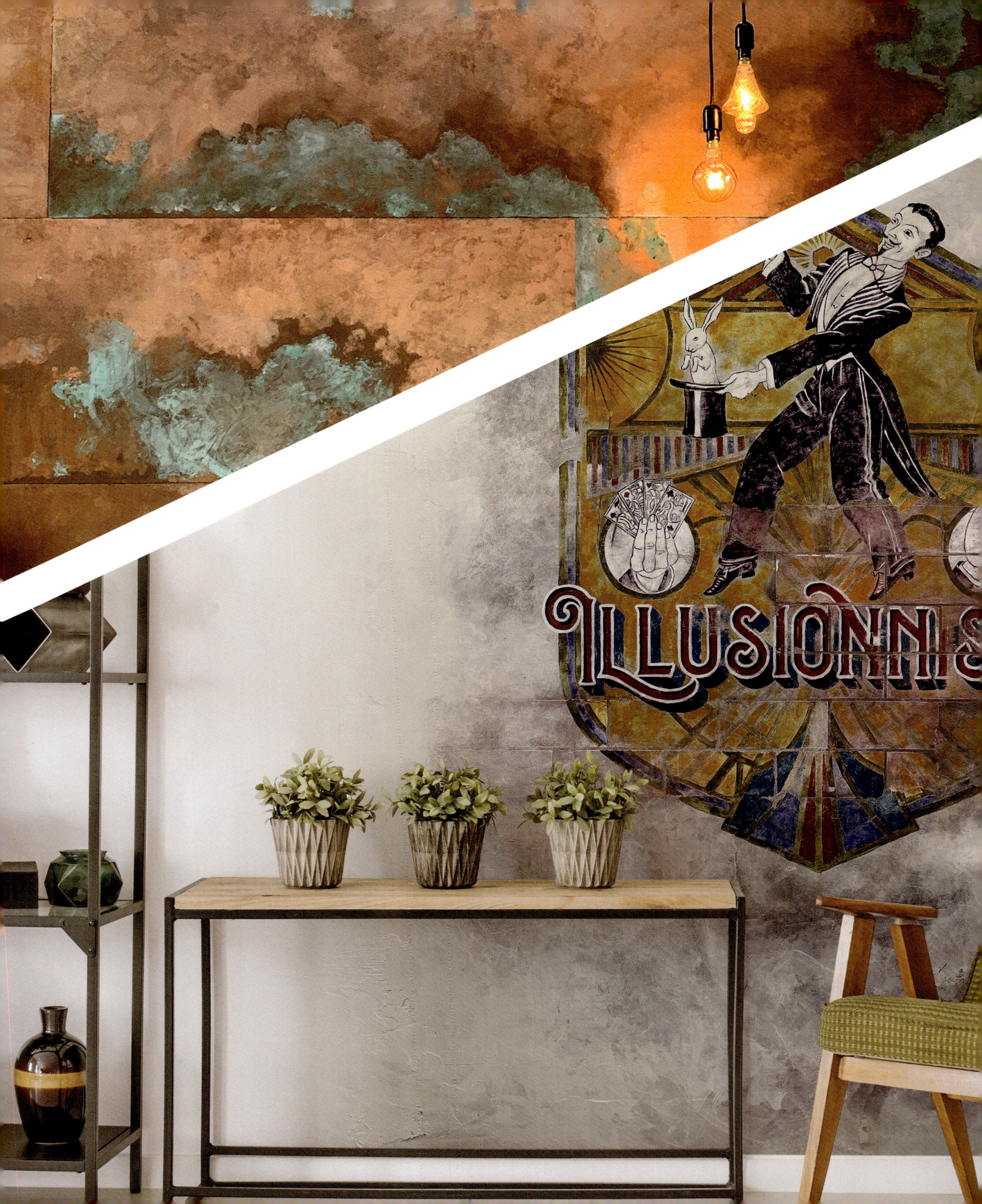
ILLUSIONNIS

PAINT ON WALLS

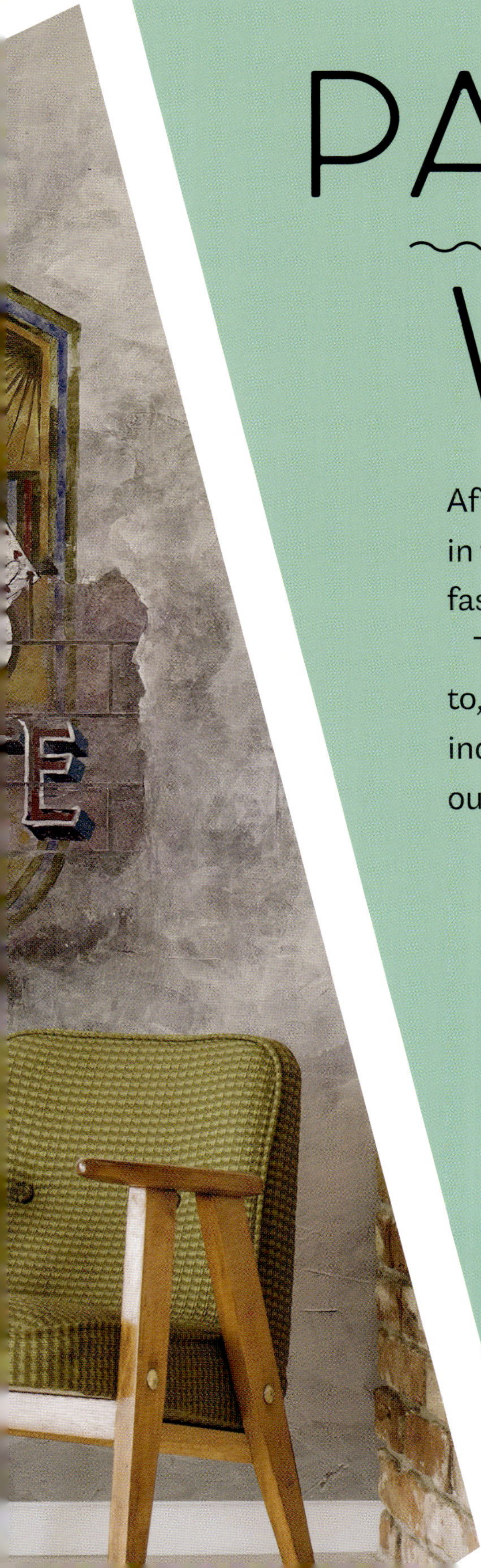

After exploring making and forming, and then fishing about in the recycling bin, we're going to finish up with good old-fashioned paint on walls!

The earliest humans blew ocher dust against their hands to, literally, put their own mark on their walls. You may indeed end up with equally messy hands, but we'll be trying out three different looks here.

5

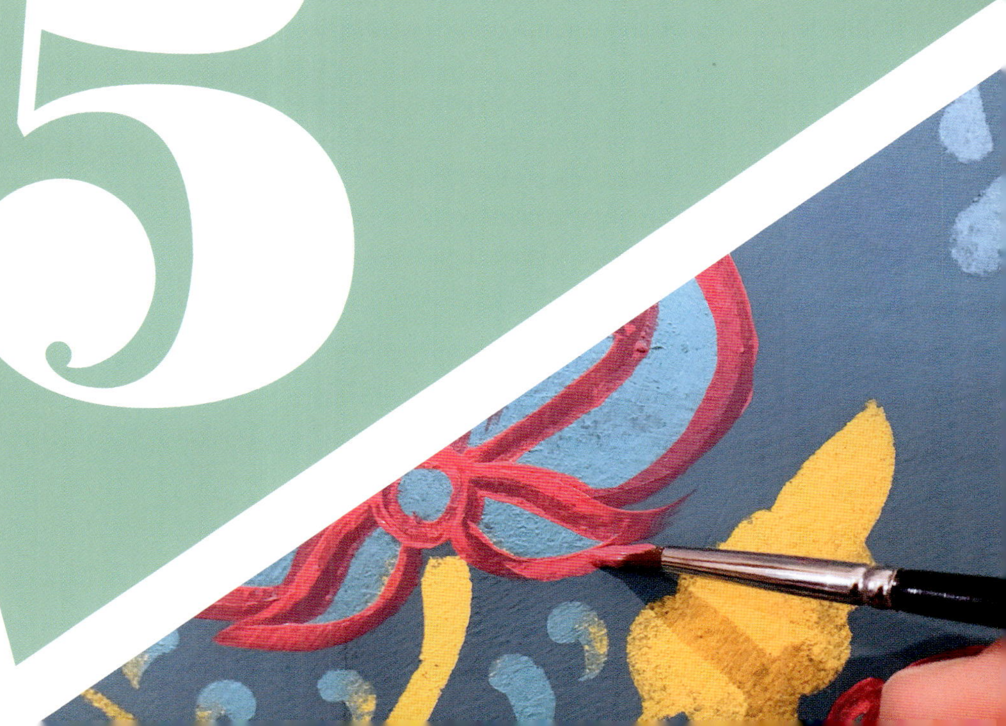

FAUX COPPER WALL

Copper is such a beautiful metal with its pinkish gleam. It can appear in various guises over time, from pink and scrubbed, dulling to a bronze color, then oxidizing through turquoise to pale blue-gray.

In this project you can really let go and enjoy the exciting textures and layering of the pigment mixes. It's all about the marks and enjoying being playful. The layers are quick to set down, and the joy is in letting one effect set, then working back into it.

This project uses acrylic wax, with decorative mica pigment powders mixed into it. The powders are usually sold in pouches of 100 g, but a little goes a long way.

Copper verdigris techniques can be done with paint, but using acrylic wax means that there's the opportunity to model the surface with tools and work back into it. The use of the metallic mica pigments also builds to a deep, authentically metallic shine quite unlike that achieved with paint alone.

In the example project the wax has been applied straight onto chipboard. This is an ideal base, since the surface already had broken color in a midtone. If you're going to be working on a painted wall, then start by painting the wall with a coat of mid- and deep-brown matte paint roughly rolled into each other to make a kind of camouflage pattern.

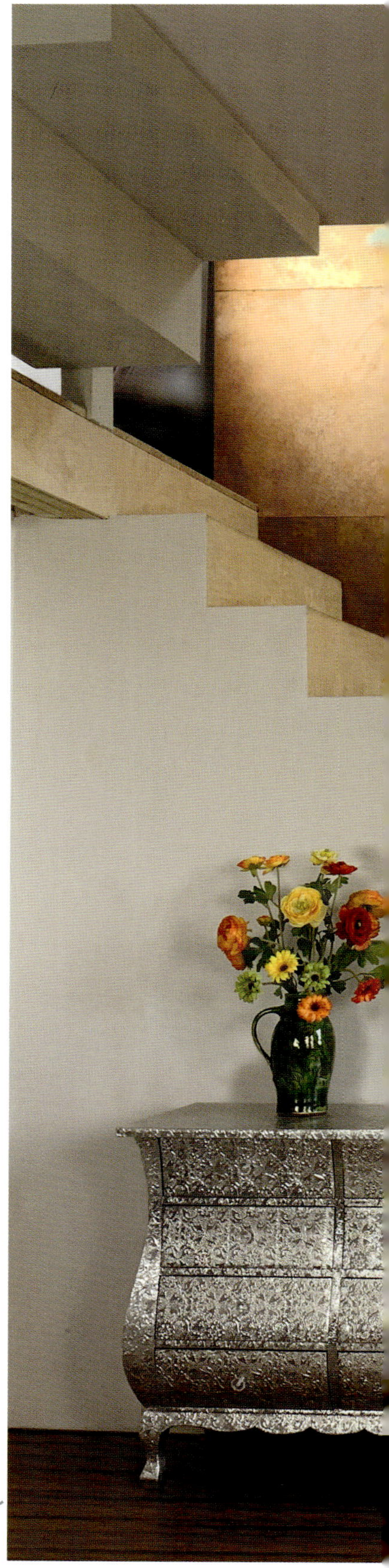

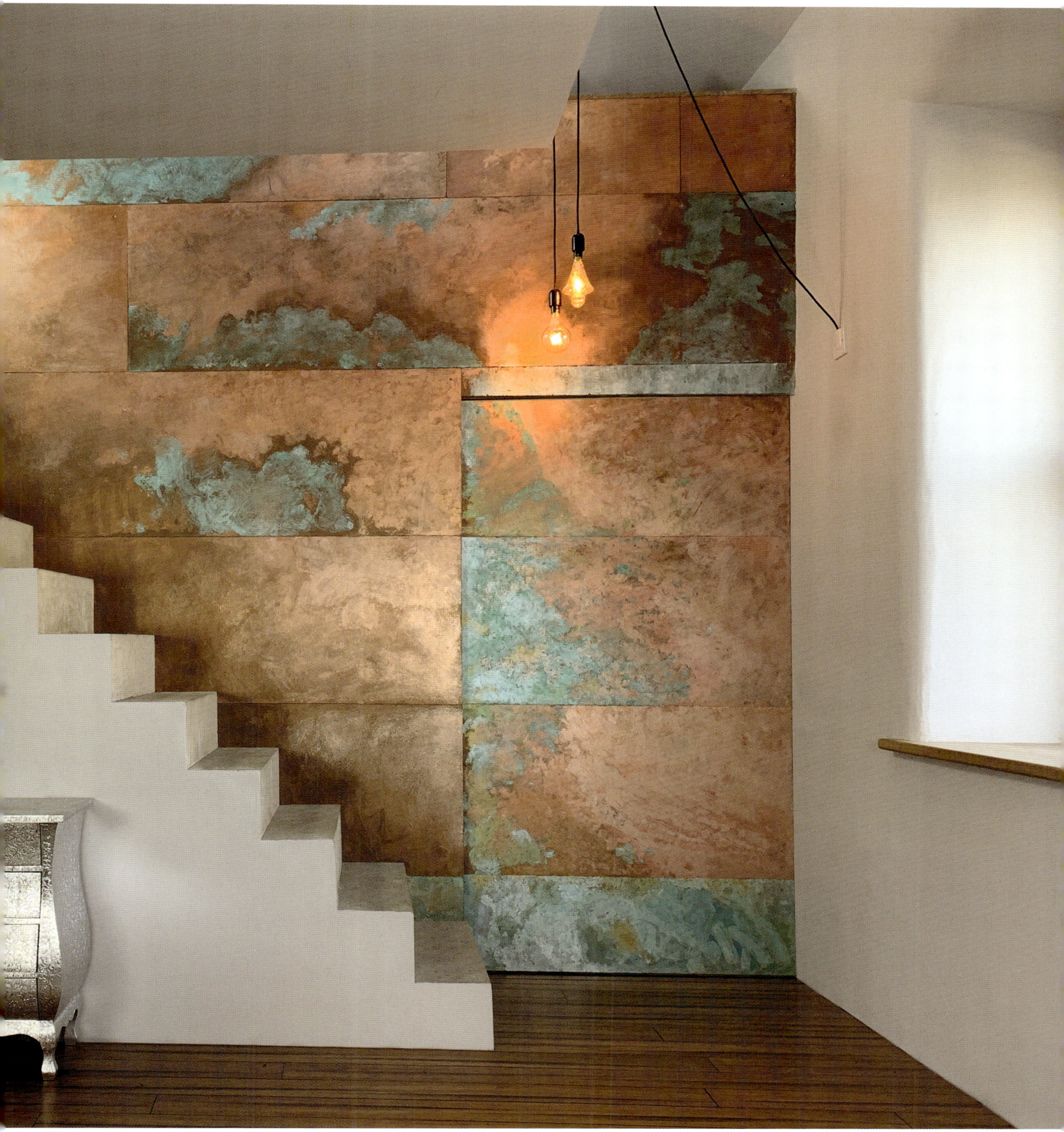

STEP-BY-STEP INSTRUCTIONS

YOU WILL NEED

For the colored mixes

- *Around a liter of acrylic wax*
- *4 empty glass jars or tins—they must be sealable*
- *A selection of mica powders—see steps 1 and 2*

To apply the wax

- *A coarse paintbrush, silicone kitchen spatula, and a small square-tipped palette knife*

Also

- *Scissors for shaping the spatula*

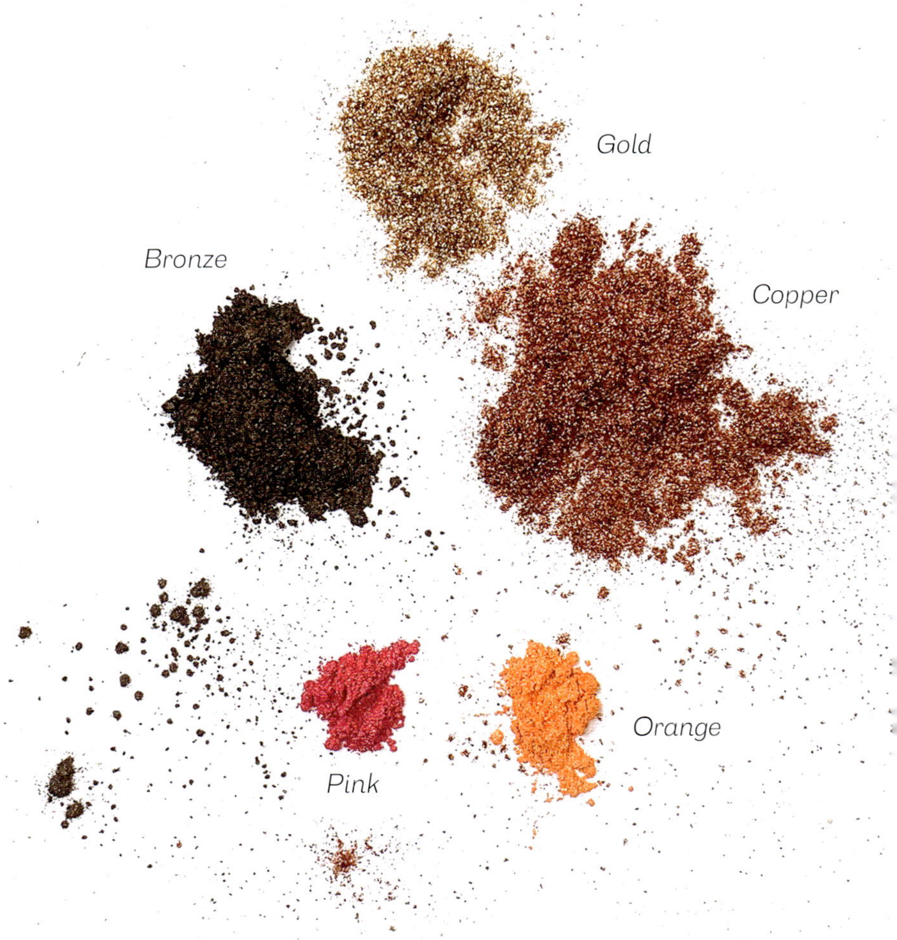

STEP 1

MIXING THREE TONES OF COPPER

This is base kit for producing the copper effect, and you need to make a mix for each tone. The essential pigments are bronze, copper, and gold. If your budget can run to it, adding a little orange and pink will give extra richness and variation, but they are optional. Mix enough powder into the acrylic wax so it's really densely pigmented—this will give it more body when you come to apply it.

Half-fill three of your empty containers with acrylic wax medium. Then use the space to add and mix pigment powder following the pictures below. Mix it until it's creamy. If you are using the optional pigments, they're added after these base colors are mixed. Do this by sprinkling small amounts on top. Look at the example of the verdigris mix to see what this looks like.

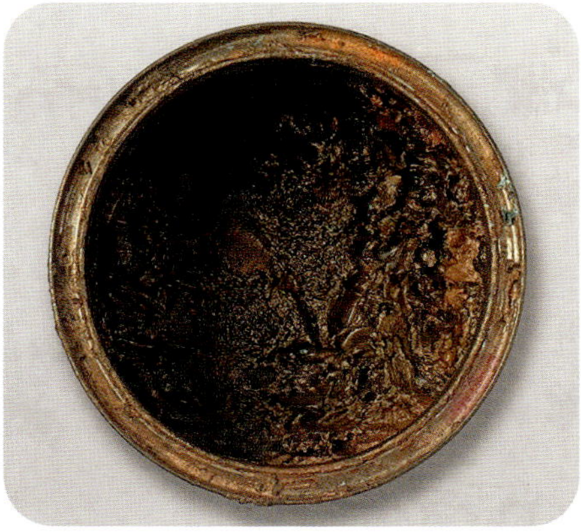

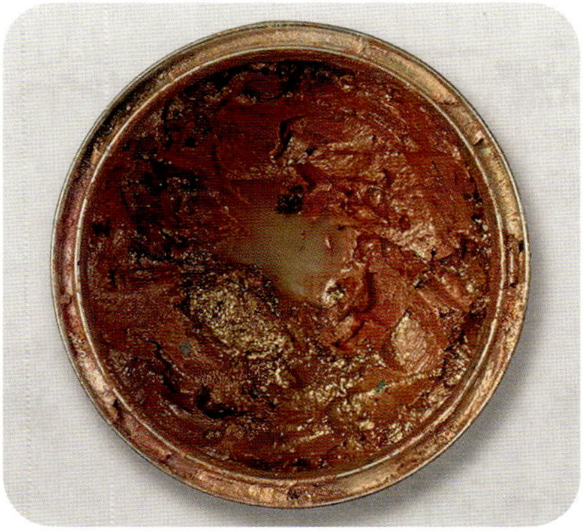

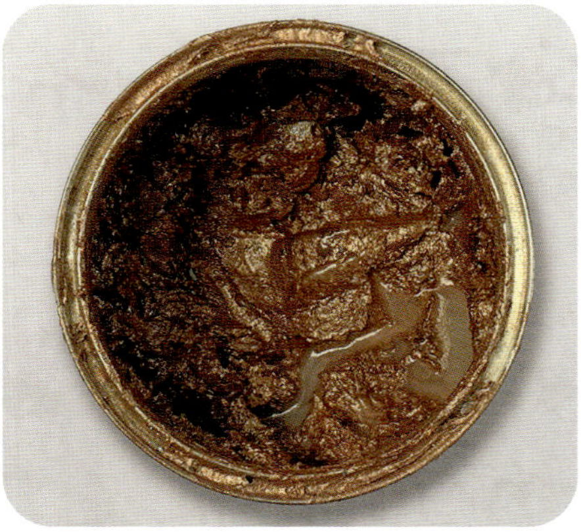

STEP 2

MIXING THE VERDIGRIS

If you are using a verdigris effect in your project, the essential pigments are turquoise and white. Adding a jade green will help with richness and depth of color.

Make your verdigris mix in your fourth jar or tin. When you've made your base mix, place some extra white pigment and some jade green (if you're using it) on top of the mix—like in the photograph. You will notice there's a green smear at bottom right, where a previous addition of powder has started to work into the base mix—this will add variation to the colors as they are applied.

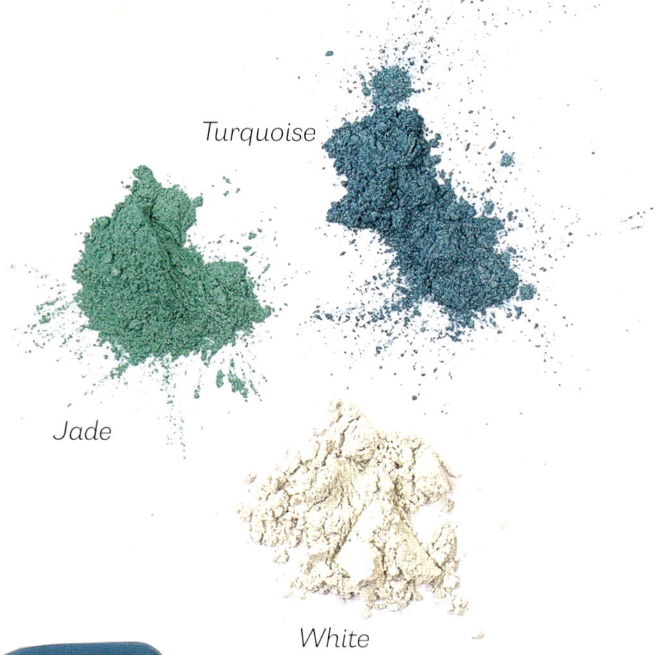

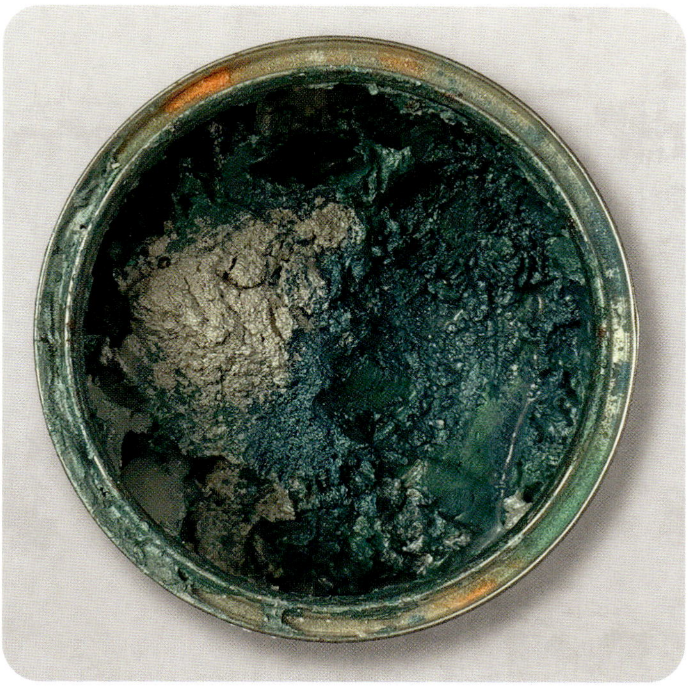

STEP 3

CUSTOMIZE YOUR SPATULA

Cutting out irregular bits into a silicone kitchen spatula will make a really useful tool for applying your mixes. Use sharp scissors.

The combed edges will replicate industrial scratches, and the straight ones will backfill into previous applications of wax or allow for fine, smeared layering of colors, all of which adds valuable textural effect.

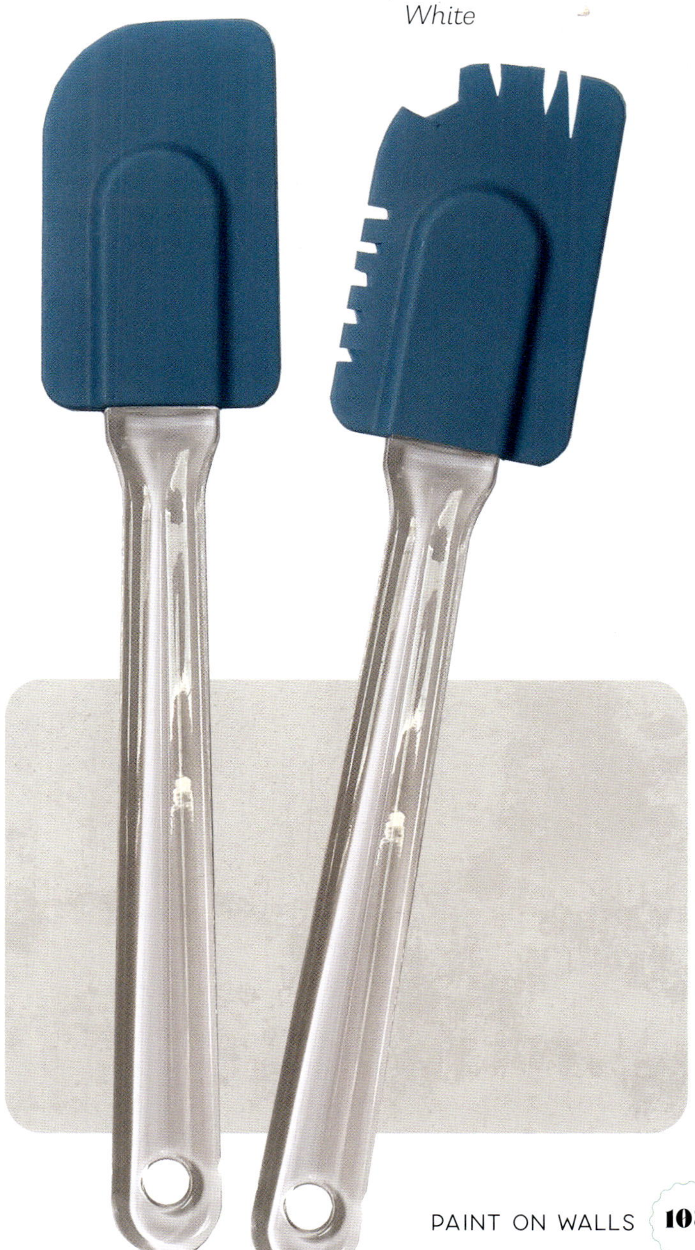

STEP 4

APPLY THE MIXES—TECHNIQUES AND EFFECTS

Using a variety of tools to apply the wax will give life and an authentic look to your mural.

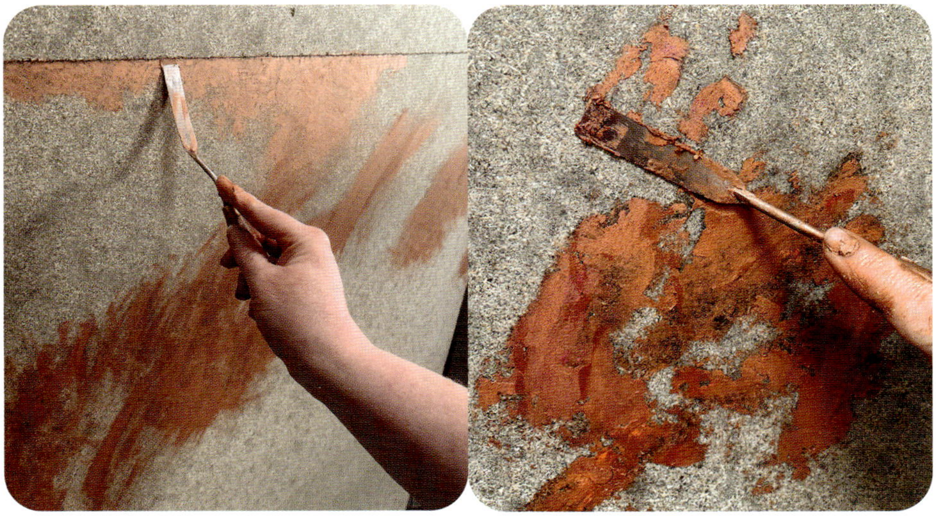

The small straight-edged and straight-tipped palette knife will give you sharp borders. It can also be used to crush and smear the mixes, then squish the paint between the blobs. This technique will spread the pigment in various directions that will catch the light differently from each other, resulting in authentic light effects as you pass by the finished piece.

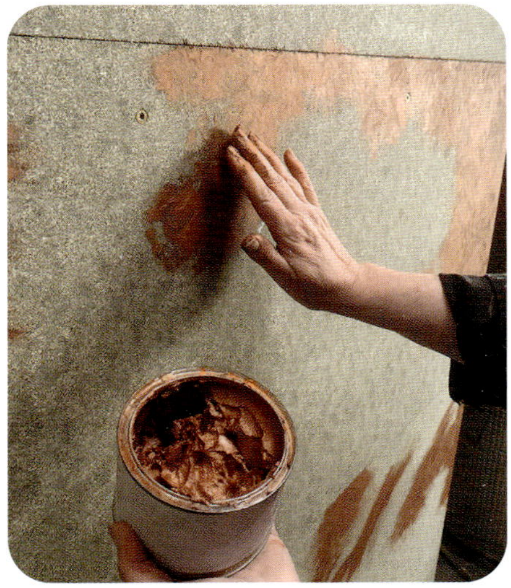

You can also use your fingertips to feather and make soft blends, or to tap the wax into small peaks.

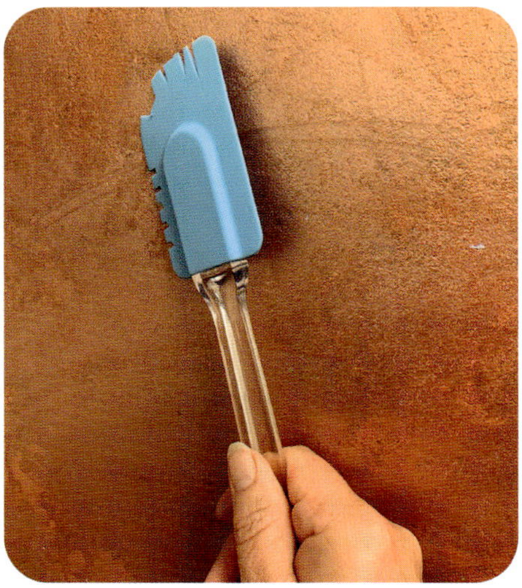

The spatula will prove to be one of your most useful tools. As well as adding random elements and enabling fine layering, it will encourage you to make larger, more gestural marks that will stop your work looking too pinched and controlled.

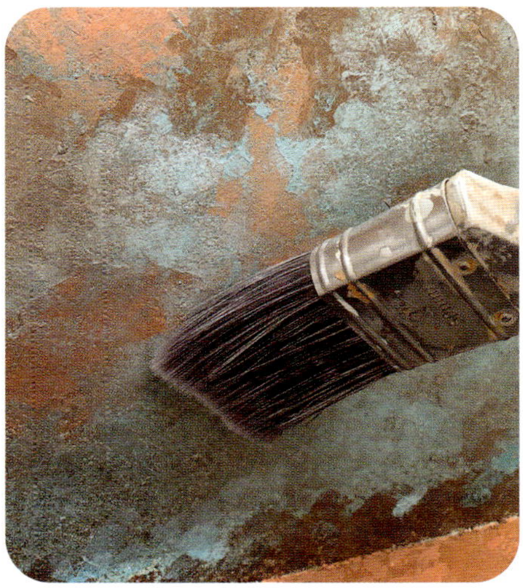

The large brush is handy for stippling and blending colors before the wax has dried. It's also great to try brushing raised areas of dry wax gently with an almost dry brush. This could be worked light over dark to imply verdigris, or dark over light for a dulling effect.

STEP 5

WORKING BACK INTO DRY WAX

A layer of wax will dry in a day or two. Working back into dried wax will enhance the copper effect and add depth. The finished result will be governed both by the techniques that the wax was applied with and by the colors used.

Using a variety of techniques—shown below—will prove interesting and satisfying to do, as well as give authenticity to the finished result.

TIP

Remember not to leave your containers of wax open, since acrylic wax will dry out in under an hour, especially in hot weather.

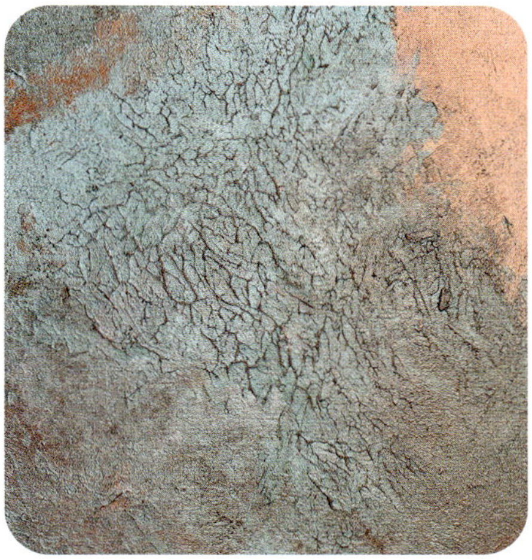

A base of copper and then verdigris applied with fingertips to make soft peaks. When dry, dark copper mix is lightly brushed on with large brush.

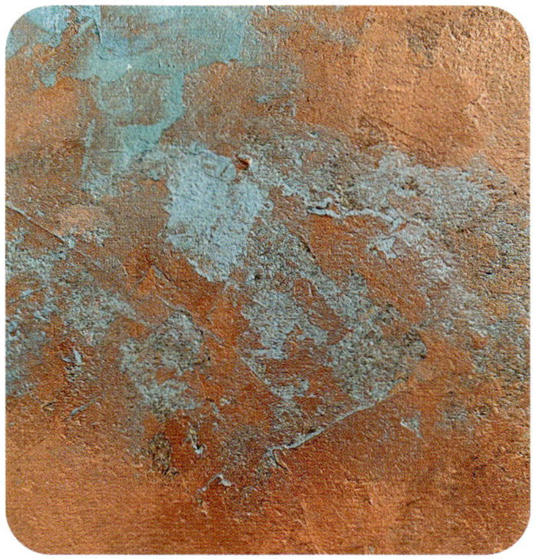

Copper layer applied with palette knife to give thick, sharp edges. When dry, the gaps are filled with verdigris, using the spatula.

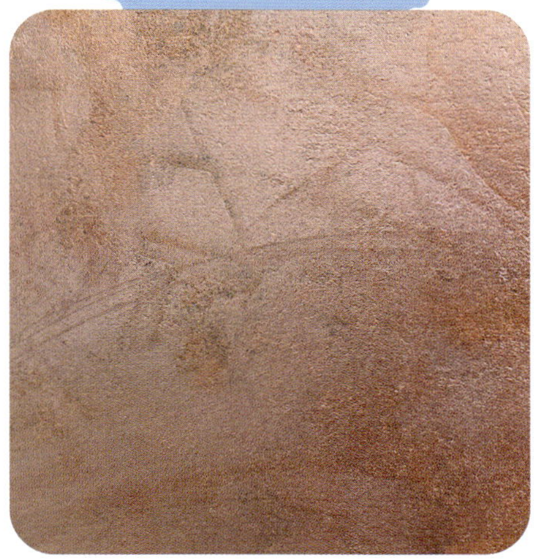

Soft, thin layering of copper mixes working from dark to light by using the spatula.

VARIATIONS

Don't be restrained by just thinking of this as a faux finish effect. This technique can be used as an abstract finish that is beautiful in its own right.

In this experimental sample we've worked into the texture of OSB (oriented stranded board), a.k.a. Stirling board.

First, a magenta mix was applied over the board. Then a second pass consisting of jade powder and holographic glitter was pushed down and worked right into the gaps in the board. A final orange mix was applied. On the left side, it was rubbed all over and buffed off. On the right, it was just buffed onto the raised surfaces.

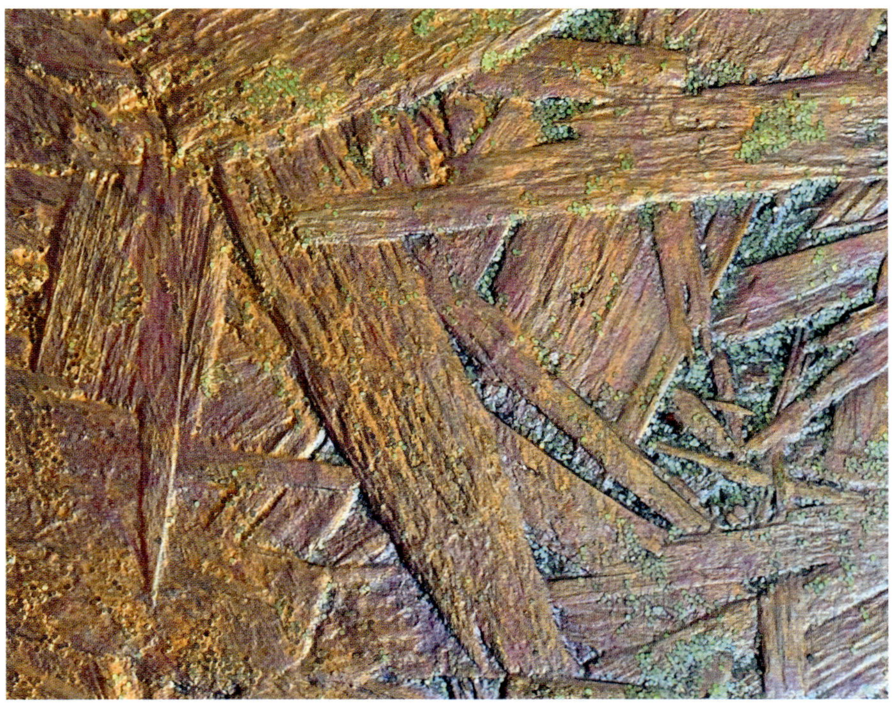

GHOST SIGN

Ghost signs are often found high on the sides of old buildings, left alone and neglected in remote areas that are difficult to reach and update. They could have remained, exposed to the elements, for over a hundred years—the weathering affecting them differently depending on whether they are on brick or mortar. Sometimes they have been rendered over with other signs, then that render falls away to reveal them.

These signs became popular in the eighteenth century after the traditional hanging signs were considered too dangerous because they could fall on passersby. So as a design format, they are a historical bridge between antique hanging signs and modern billboards. Keep looking up, when you wander around old towns and cities, to try to spot them.

Study them and you'll find the story of their paint. Has it stuck fast to tough solvent-based paints or soaked through soft lime render to appear in fainter layers? Which colors have worn faster than others? Replicating these parts of the story will add authenticity to your design. The annotations on page 111 will guide you in this. It's also possible to create this project on board and then fix it to the wall—then you can take it with you should you move!

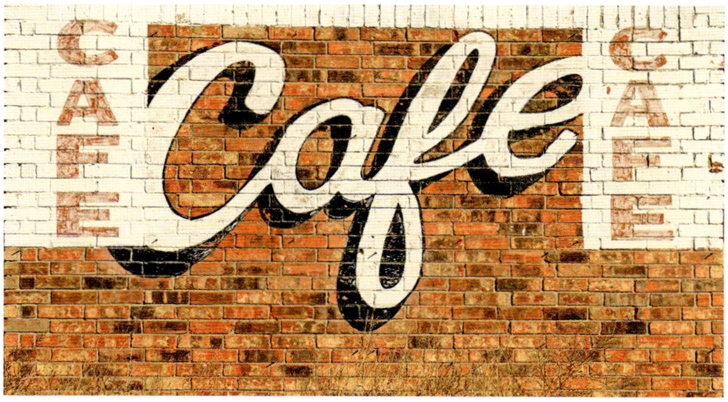

This beautiful sign can be seen along Route 66 in Texas. Note how the red paint has worn more than the other colors.

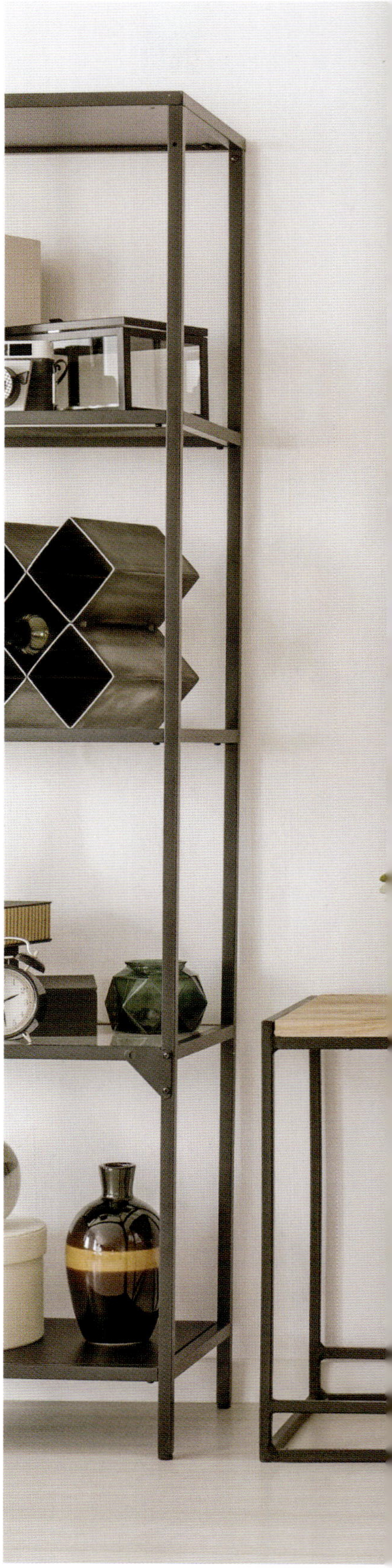

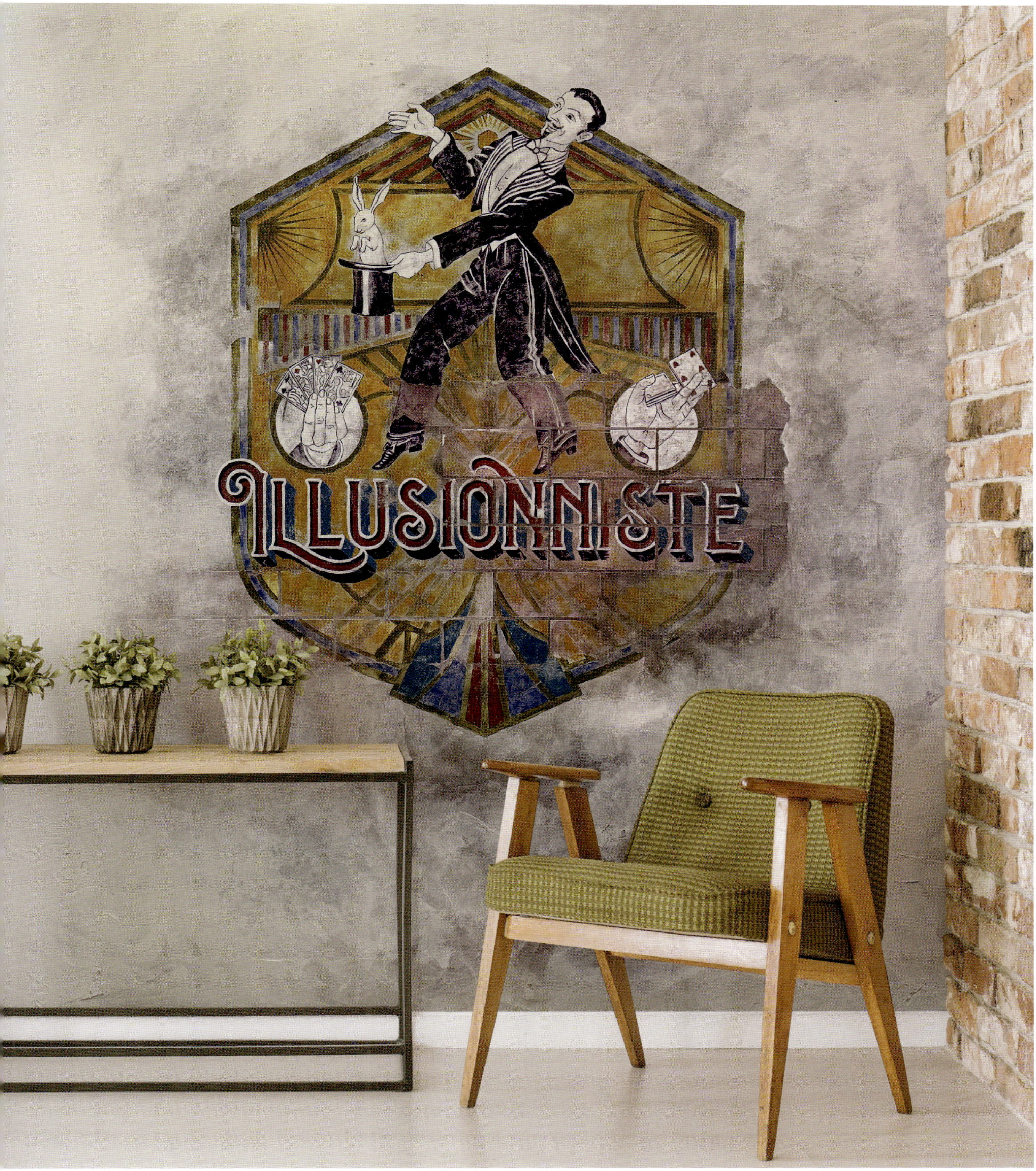
ILLUSIONNISTE

STEP-BY-STEP INSTRUCTIONS

YOU WILL NEED

To prepare the wall

- *2 mm foam tape*
- *Large tub of acrylic gesso primer*
- *Silicone spatula*
- *Spirit level and pencil*

To transfer the design

- *Ballpoint pen*
- *Magic tape (i.e., tape that appears opaque but is invisible when applied)*
- *Printer and graphite transfer paper*

To paint the design

- *Acrylic paint—see the picture for color guidance*
- *Empty half-pint containers*
- *Household sponge*
- *Selection of brushes. We used square-ended and stencil brushes*

Acrylic Paint Colors

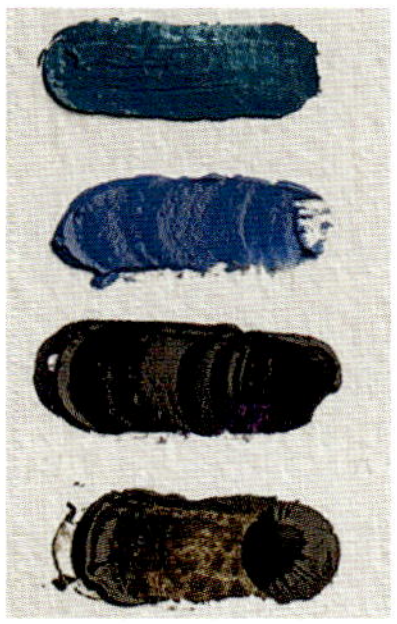

Cobalt turquoise

Cerulean blue

Dioxazine purple

Raw umber

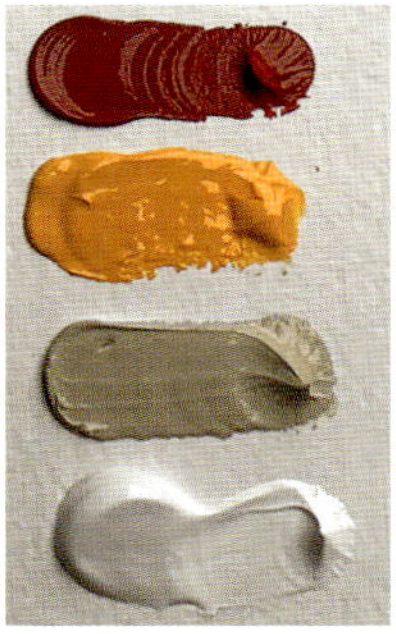

Crimson red

Deep cadmium yellow

Buff titanium

Titanium white

STEP 1

ADDING TEXTURE TO THE WALL

We started with a roughly plastered wall, but if you're faced with a smooth wall, it would be good to add some texture first with gesso. Give the pot a good stir and swoop some gesso about with the spatula. Let it start to stiffen, then work into it with a dry brush. If you have a delightfully rough wall already, go straight to step 2.

STEP 2

START THE BRICK TEXTURE

Some bricks poking through adds a lovely authentic feel, and they're really easy to do.

Decide where you'd like them and draw a horizontal line with the spirit level. Run the foam tape along the line. Keep adding horizontal lines at a convenient distance—these are two thicknesses of the spirit level.

When you have a few rows, make vertical divides—these are the width of an A4 sheet—8.25 x 11.75 in. (21 x 29.7 cm).

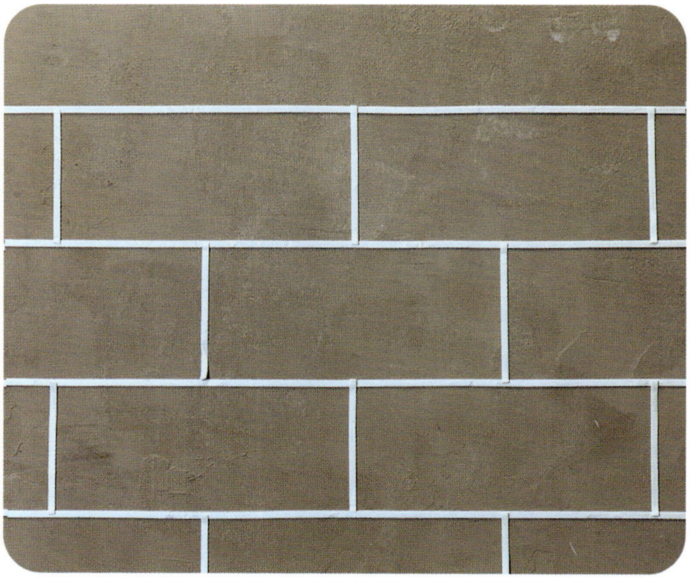

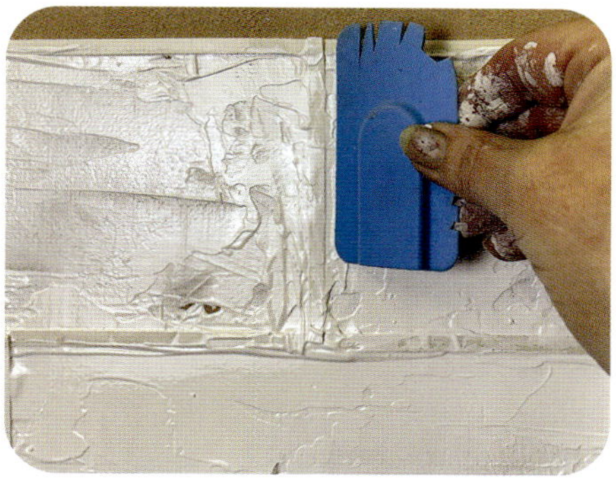

STEP 3

FILL THE BRICK TEXTURE

This bit is really fun! Using the spatula, fill between the foam tape with gesso to make slightly raised "bricks." Really play with the gesso, dragging it in layers and building it up to the tape. When the gesso has become dull looking, the tape can be removed.

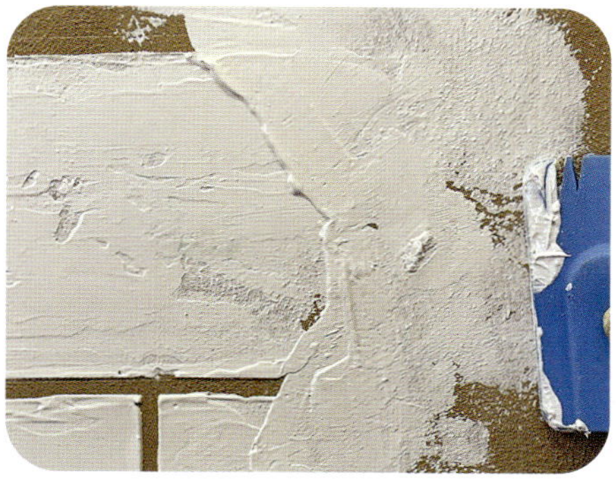

STEP 4

TEXTURE OVER THE BRICKS

Bricks are usually under a layer of render, so we are going to add some extra realism by adding gesso at the edges of the bricks to look like render that's broken away.

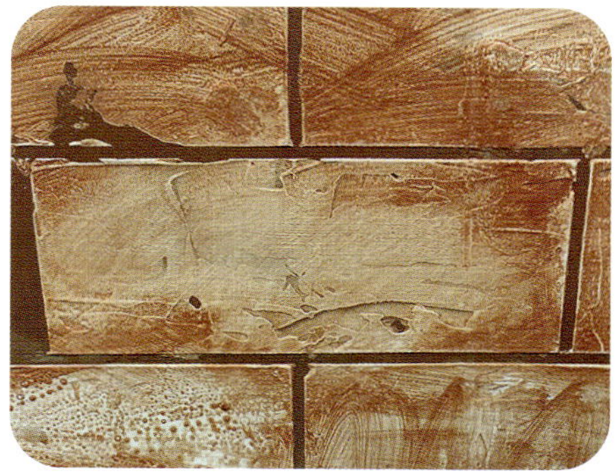

STEP 5

START TO TONE

In one of the empty containers, mix a brick color, using crimson red, cadmium yellow, and raw umber. Dilute with quite a lot of water. Don't worry about making it an even consistency—paint it thickly in places with the stencil brush, and as a runny wash in others. Wipe it lightly as it starts to dry to add more texture.

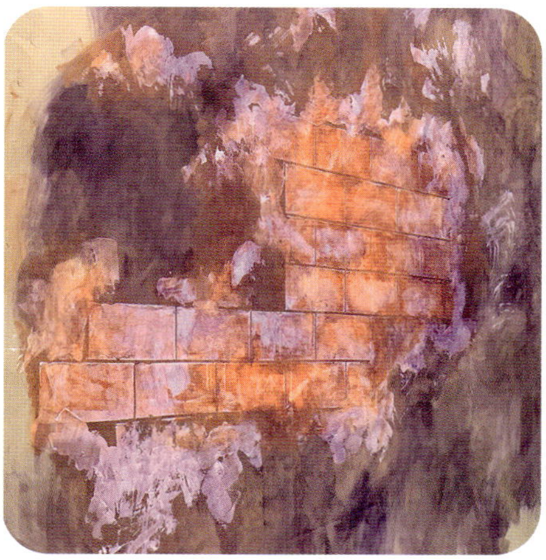

STEP 6

ADD A UNIFYING TONE

Next we are going to wash the whole wall with dioxazine purple with a bit of raw umber added to it.

This will do two things: put some dark color in all the recessed areas and unify the whole wall.

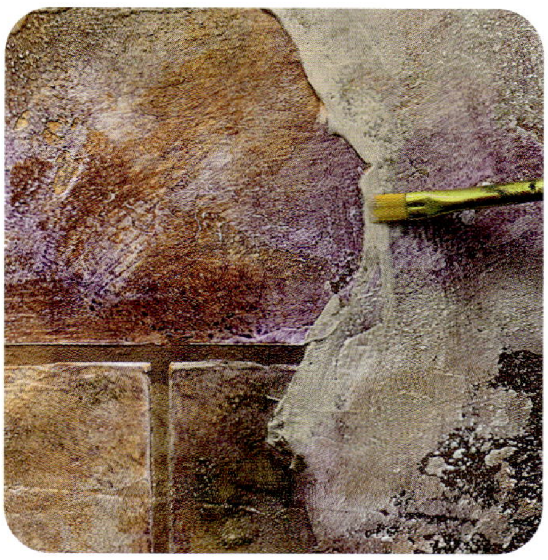

STEP 7

WORK IN SHADOW AND HIGHLIGHT DETAIL

Concentrating on just the brick area, with a square-tipped brush add buff titanium highlights to the edges of the "render." Add raw umber shadow washes to the areas between the bricks and anywhere else where the purple needs toning down a bit.

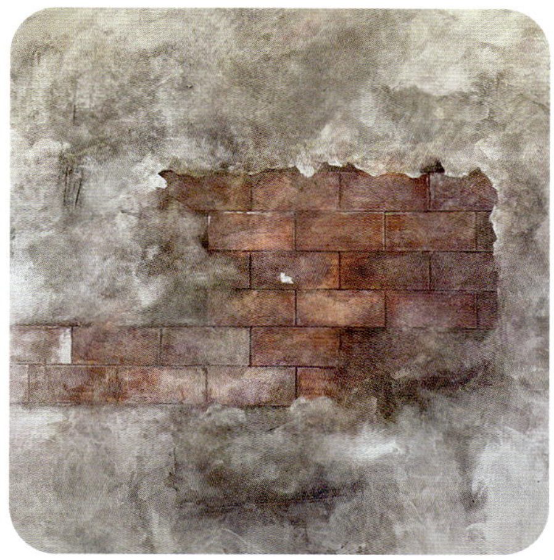

STEP 8

ADD A PALE WASH OVER EVERYTHING

Build up several washes of buff titanium mixed with titanium white. Away from the brick areas, the effect should be soft, cloudy mottles. We are now ready to start the design!

STEP 9

ASSEMBLE AND POSITION THE TEMPLATE

Print out all the parts of the template at the scale you have decided to make your design. Using some of the magic tape, stick together the first row and tack it to the painted wall.

Keep adding rows until the template is complete. It can make it easier to work with if you trim away any excess.

NOTE: Before starting to trace the design onto the wall, do make sure it's properly straight. Run a spirit level between the top and bottom points and check that the vertical is true.

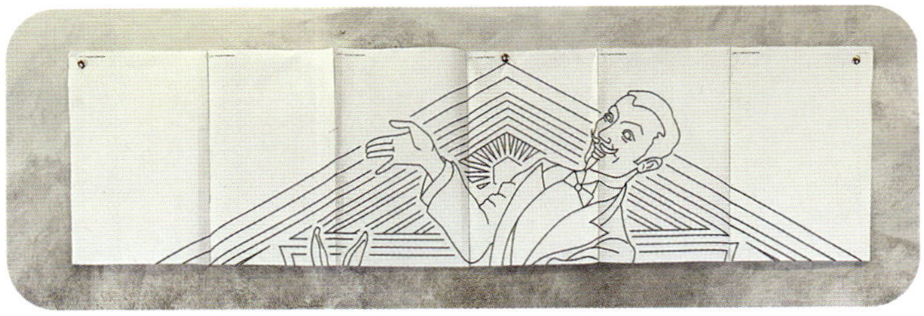

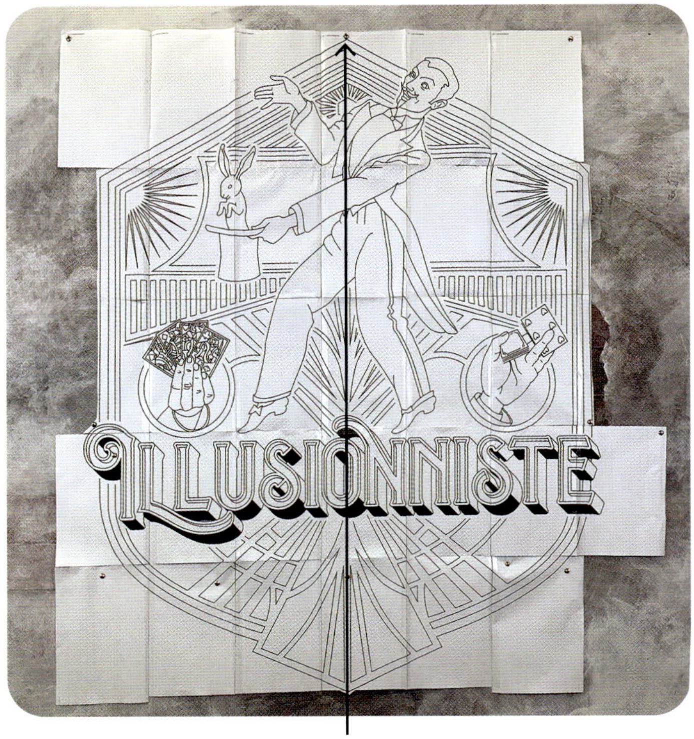

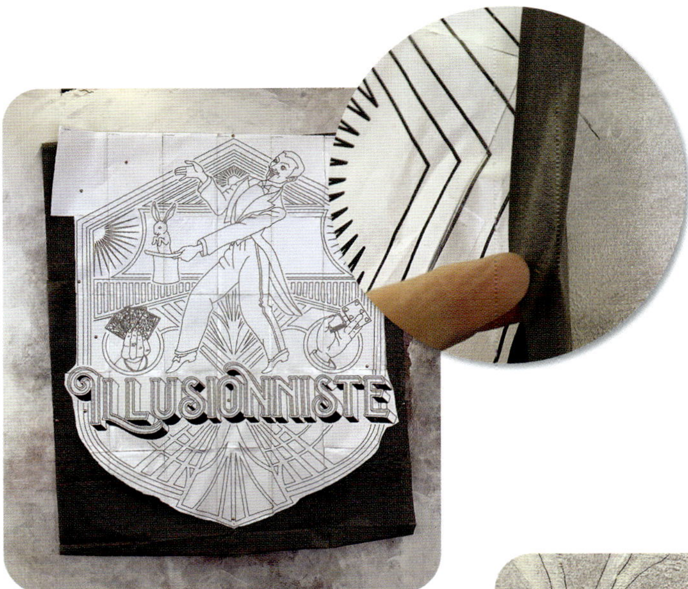

STEP 10

TRACE ONTO THE WALL

Tack the graphite paper between the template and the wall, then draw over the black lines with the pen. Just after you've started, check that you're using enough pressure to transfer the design, and peel back the template carefully—sometimes you have to scribble quite hard over them to get them to transfer.

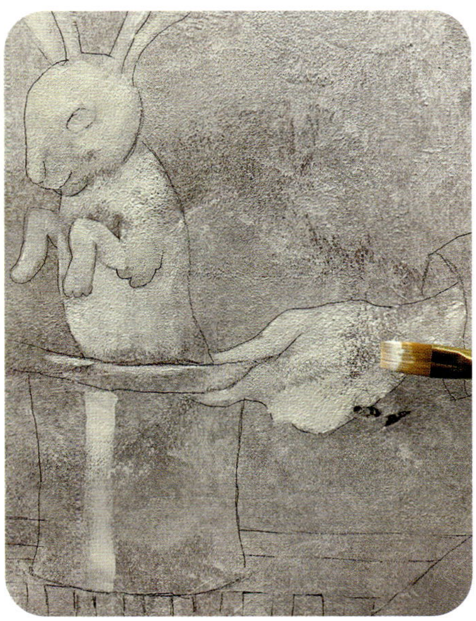

STEP 11

PAINT THE GHOST SIGN

At last the time has come to start to paint the sign. The attractive thing about ghost signs is the variety of textures in the fading paint. Let the texture and tones you built up earlier do the hard work.

Look at how the various textures and effects were achieved on the next page. Do bear in mind that this was how the paint worked in this example—yours will be different. So keep an open mind and have fun responding to the wall that you have.

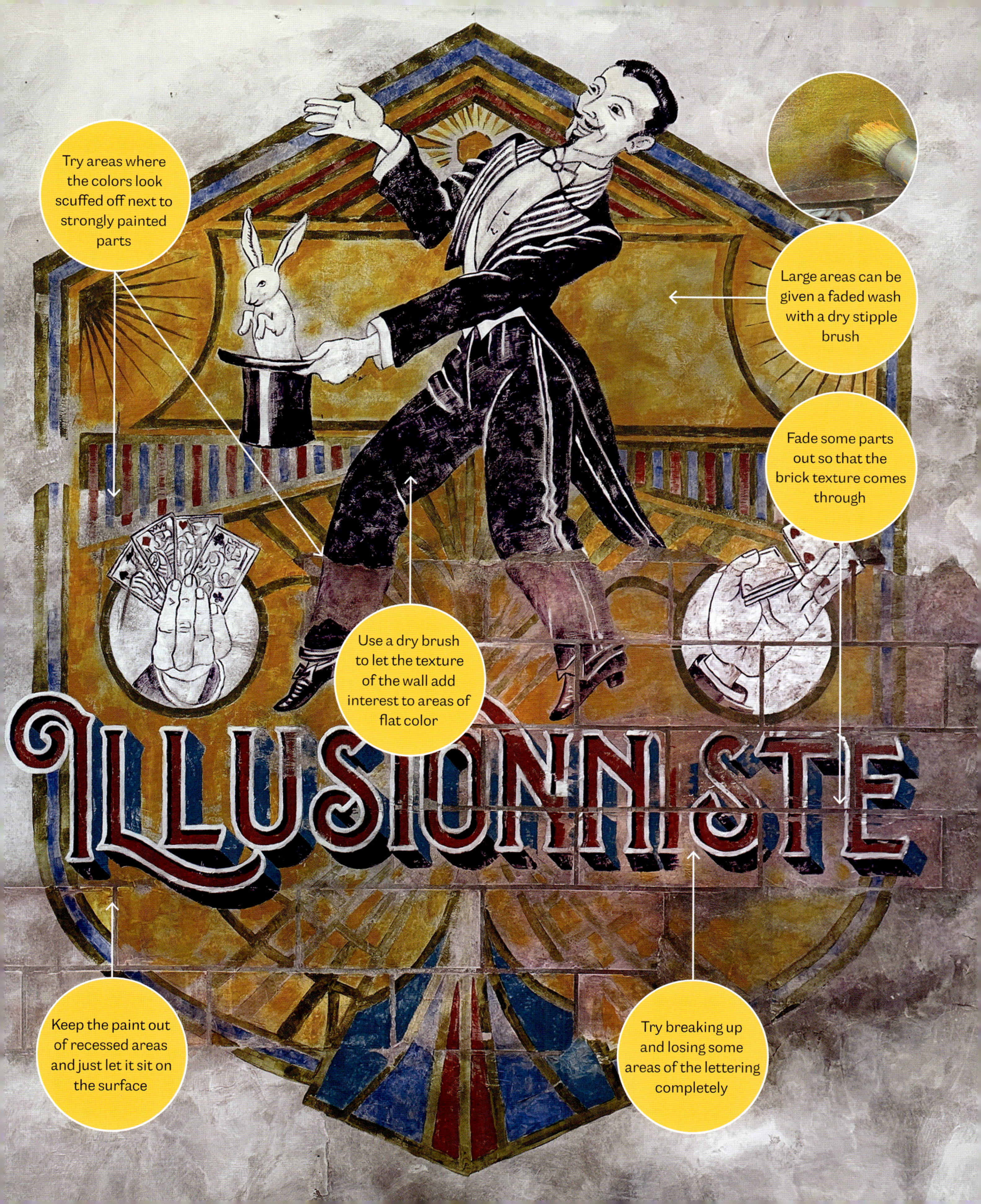
Try areas where the colors look scuffed off next to strongly painted parts
Large areas can be given a faded wash with a dry stipple brush
Fade some parts out so that the brick texture comes through
Use a dry brush to let the texture of the wall add interest to areas of flat color
ILLUSIONNISTE
Keep the paint out of recessed areas and just let it sit on the surface
Try breaking up and losing some areas of the lettering completely

ENLARGE BY 560 PERCENT = FINISHED SIZE OF 54 IN. (137 CM) TALL

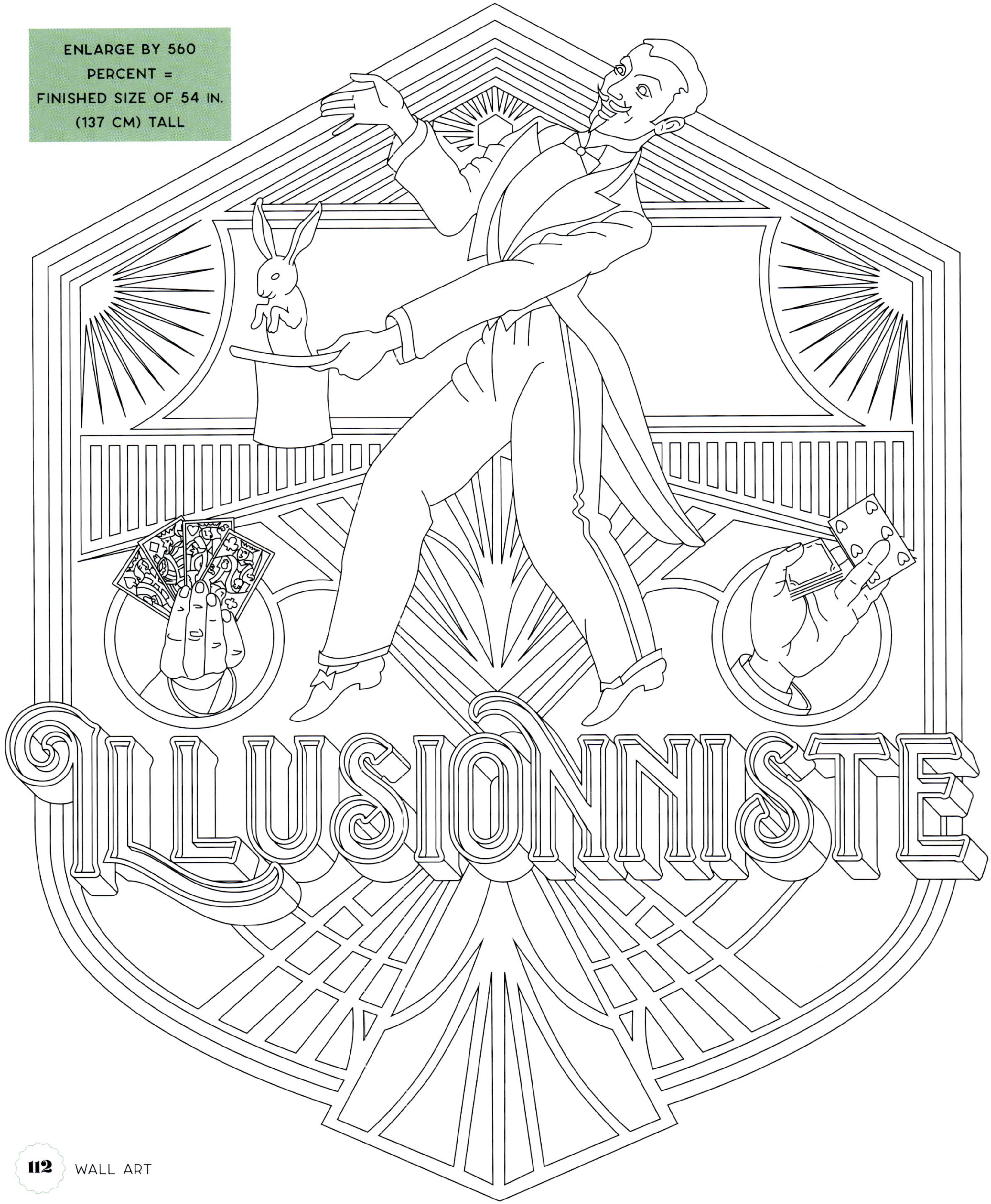

Cadmium yellow (deep) and raw umber

Buff titanium and cadmium yellow (deep)

Cerulean blue

Crimson red

Dioxazine purple

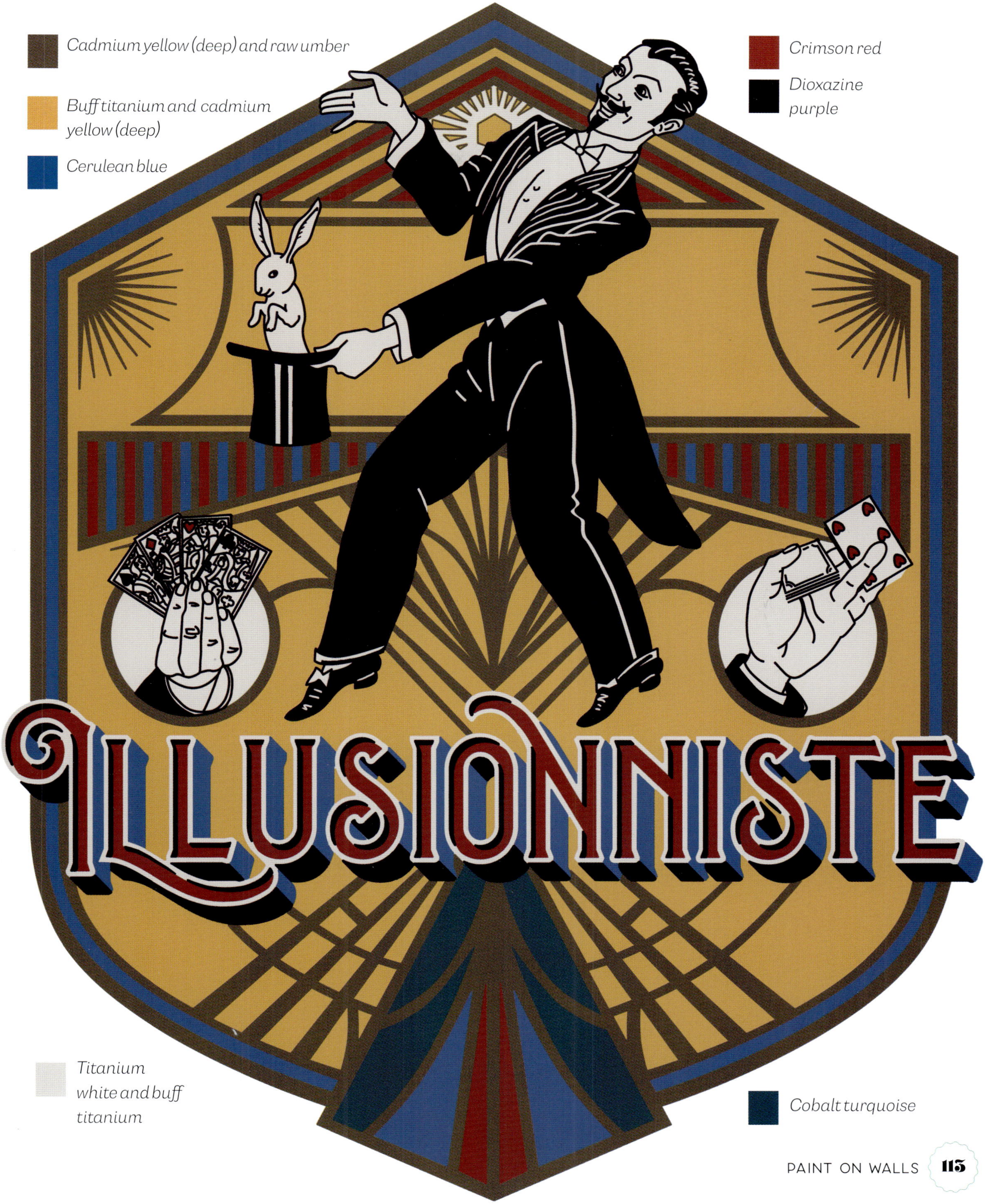

Titanium white and buff titanium

Cobalt turquoise

INDIAN FOLK ART MURAL

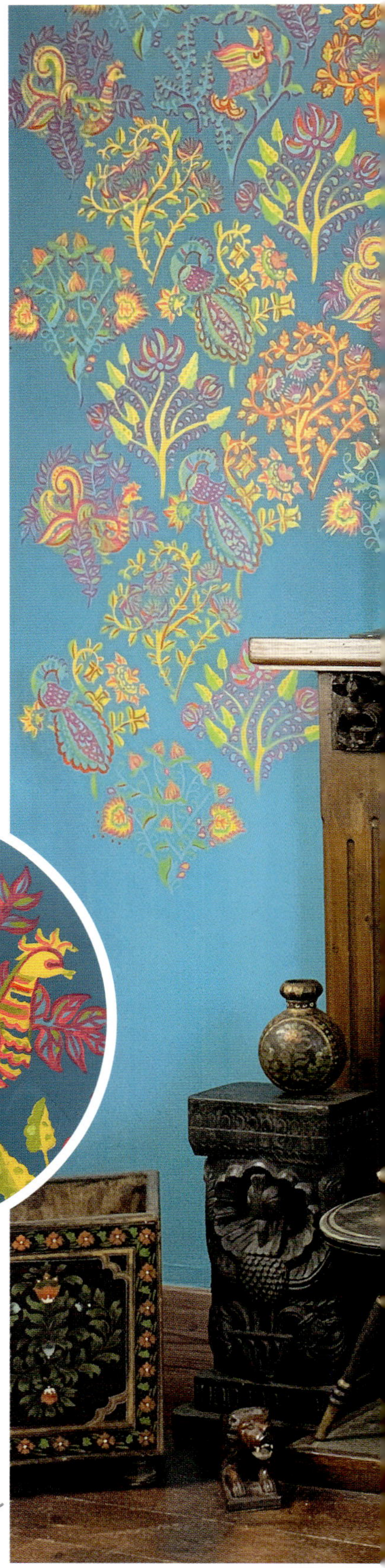

My mother bought a house in which the previous owner had made a fireplace assembled from Indian carvings. We thought a mural inspired by the birds in the fireplace and furniture would look lovely on the wall it was built into.

The forms found in Indian folk art are beautiful, but it's quite daunting to just go ahead and start painting on a wall using the confident strokes found in folk art. So we've designed this technique to help. First, the background shapes are stenciled onto the wall. This is a quick and easy process, and you could choose some nice colors and stop the mural right there—there's not even a need to cut out and use all six variations of our design.

For the detailed painted version, the stenciled work acts as a guide for the painting. To make it easy and give a nice hand-painted look, the painting part involves either outlining or coloring-in the stenciled work, plus some added dots here and there. We've used all the designs and covered a large area, but you could use them just as a border, building up the number of rows as many as you please.

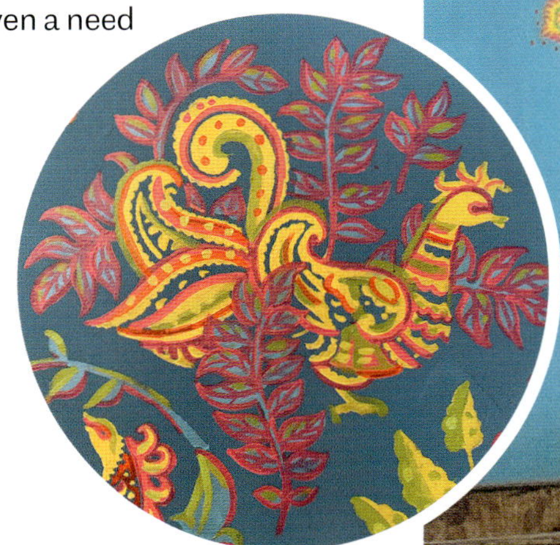

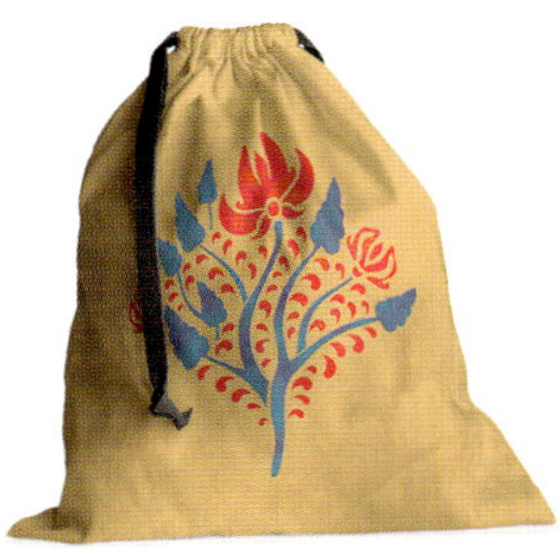

Try using fabric paint with the stencils. They can be used to decorate cushions or curtains, either to match your wall or as a contrast. Here we've used just the stencil process in a new, colorful way on a fabric bag.

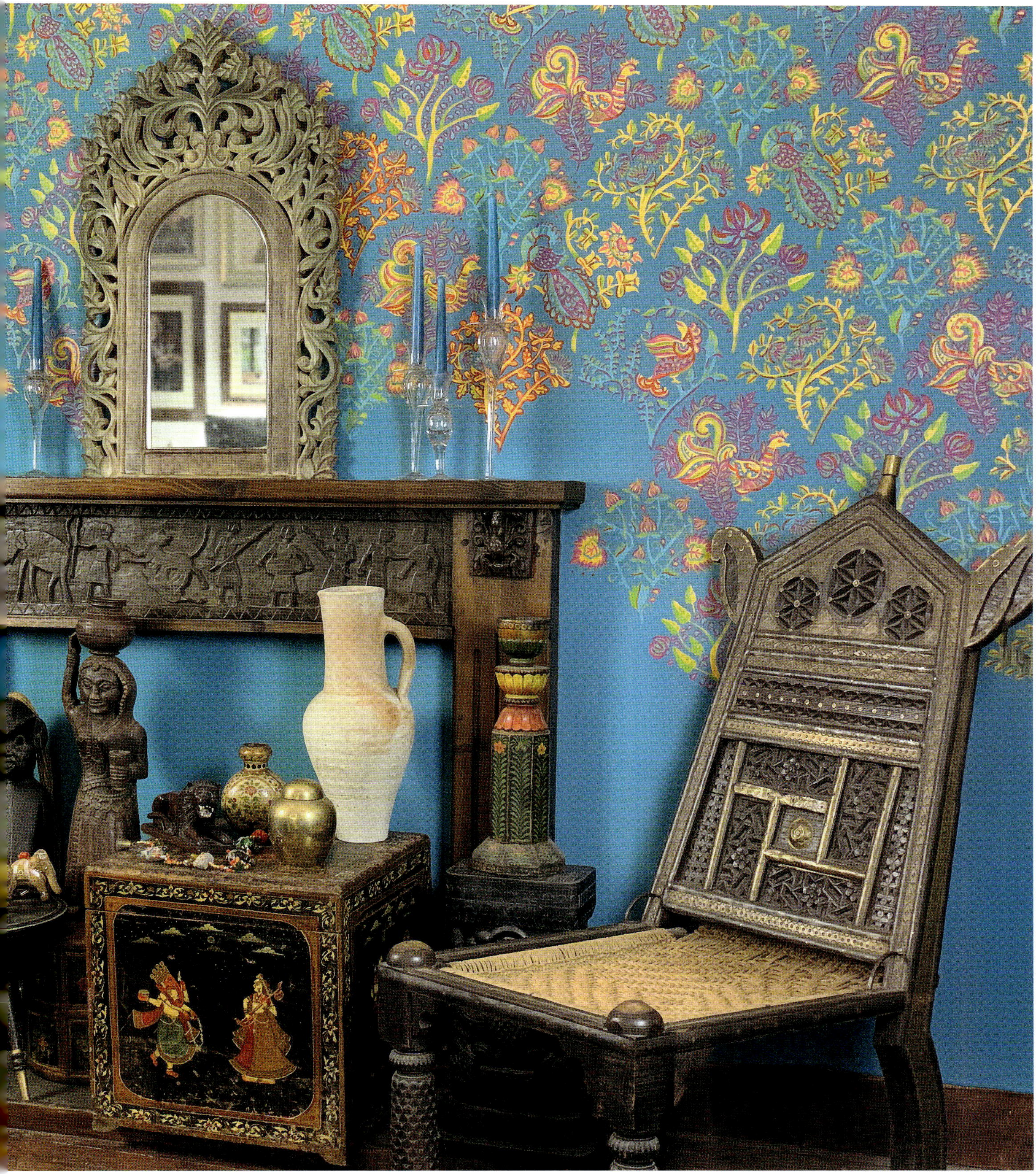

STEP-BY-STEP INSTRUCTIONS

YOU WILL NEED

To make the stencils

- *6 sheets of polyester stencil medium 12 x 12 in. (30 x 30 cm)*
- *Either craft knife and mat OR cutting machine*

To prepare the wall

- *3 ft. (91 cm) spirit level*
- *Pencil*

To paint the stencils

- *Acrylic paint*
- *Spray glue—MUST be of the repositional type*
- *No. 2 stencil brush*
- *No. 4 round painting brush*

Wall color

Deep turquoise

Stencil colors

Sky blue

Cadmium yellow

Painting colors

Magenta

Cadmium red

Olive green

Lime green

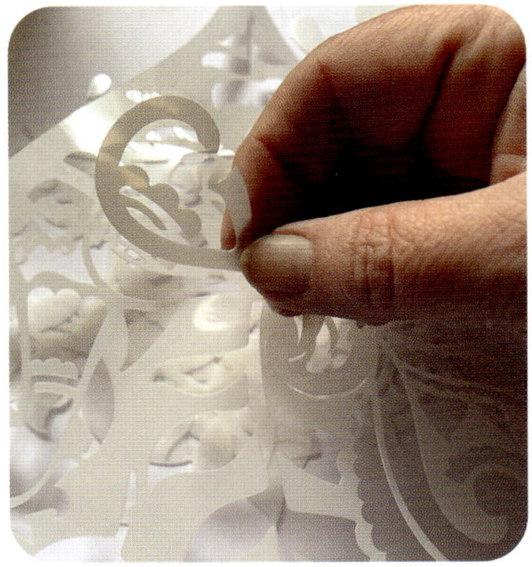

STEP 1

CUT THE SIX TEMPLATES

Either scan and enlarge the printed templates by 125 percent or import the SVGs. Cut them out and weed.

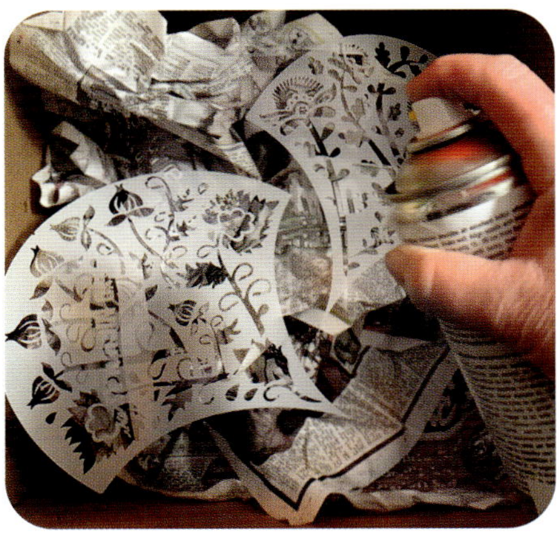

STEP 2

SPRAY GLUE

Use an old cardboard box and crumpled paper as a spray booth. In a well-ventilated area, spray the reverse of each template with the spray glue. Remember to let the spray glue to go "off" (i.e., dry a little) for some time before putting it on the wall, to make sure it's repositionable.

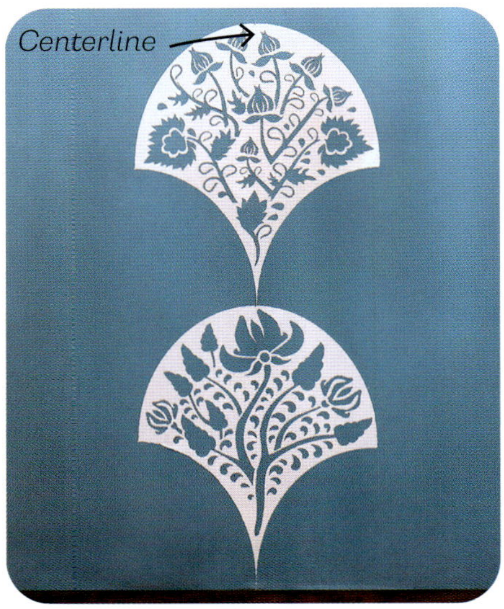

STEP 3

MARK YOUR CENTERLINE

Mark where the center of your design will be—I've made mine the center of the mantelpiece. Using the spirit level, draw a vertical line on the wall at this point with the pencil and align two of the templates on it.

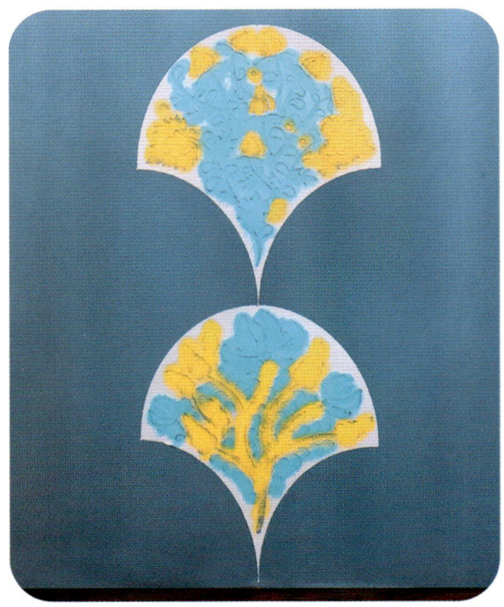

STEP 4

STIPPLE THE TWO BASE COLORS

Use the painting guides on pages 118 to 121, if you are following our example exactly. Stipple the two base colors through the templates onto the wall.

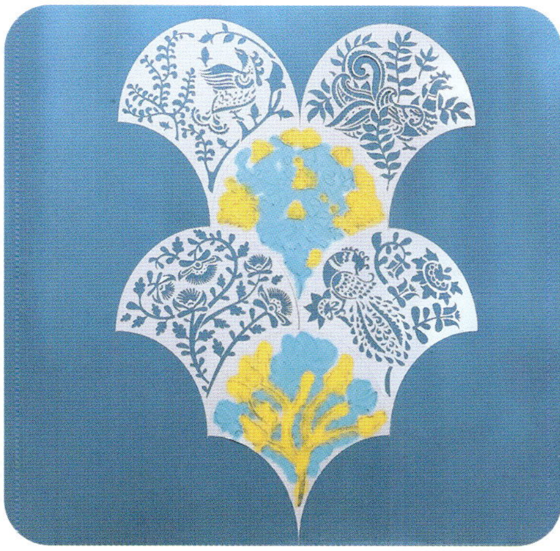

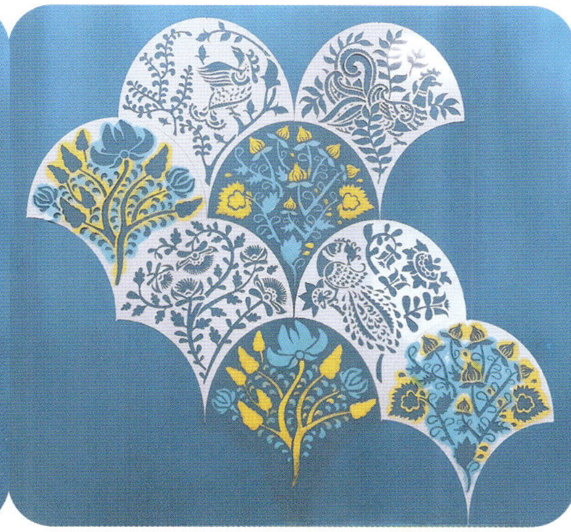

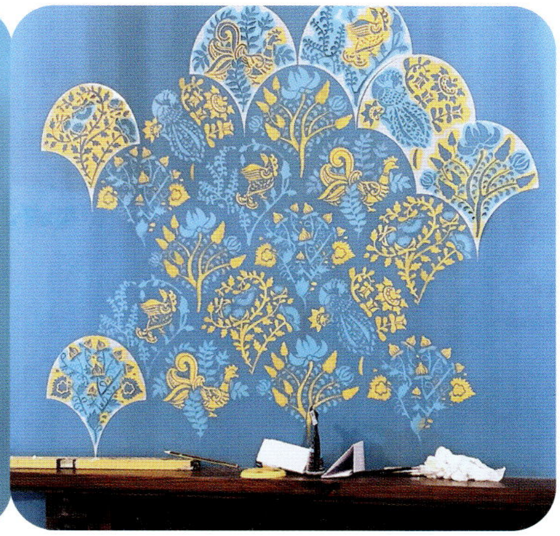

STEP 5

TILE THE TEMPLATES

Place the four remaining templates around the first two you have stippled, then move the first two to the outside. Continue to do this as you go. The only thing to remember is not to place the same design next to itself—with six different templates, this is easy to achieve.

NOTE: Don't leave a template that's been filled in in place overnight. The paint on the wall will bond to the paint on the template and may pull some paint off the wall when the template is lifted. Always leave your work with templates that are still "to do" in position. That is, it's fine to walk away from the templates in the picture in the middle, but not the ones on the left.

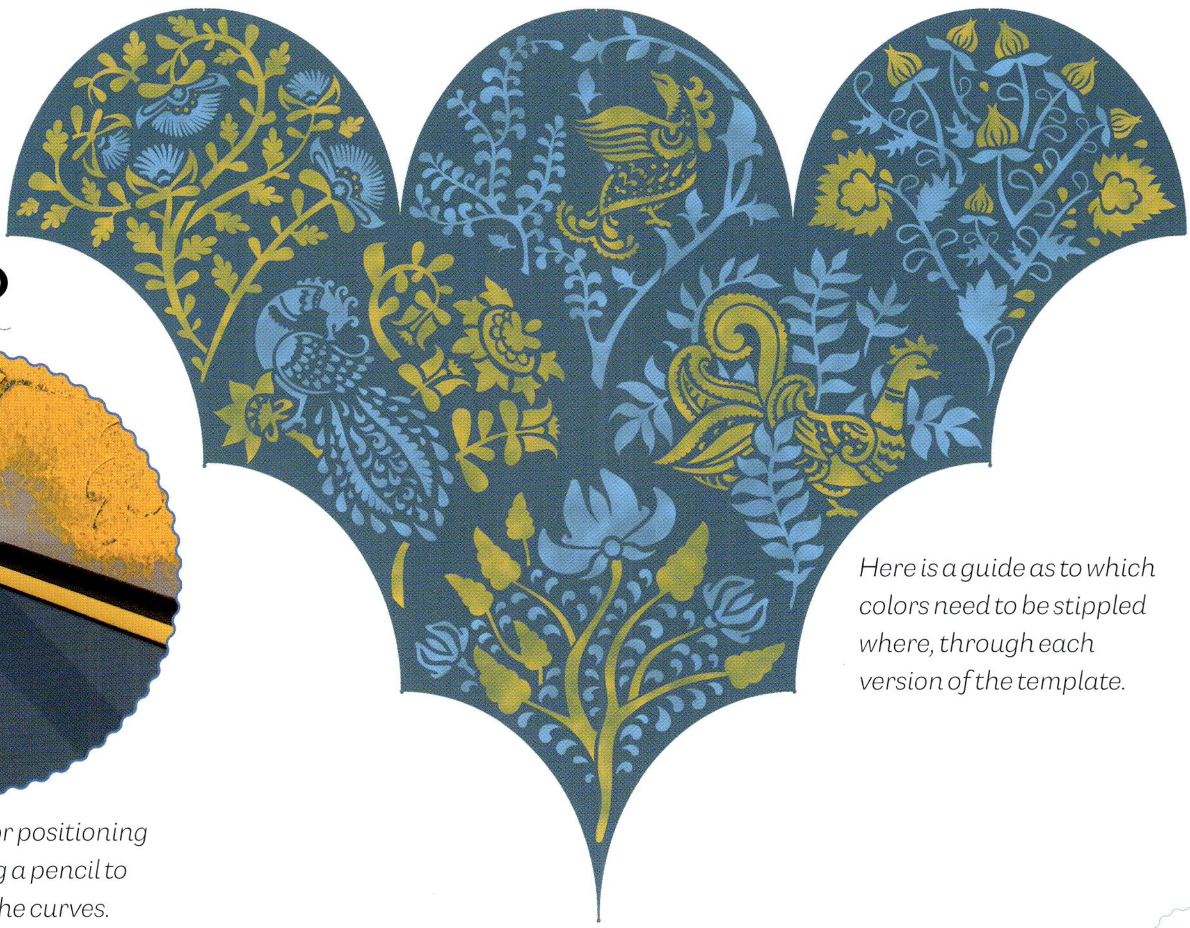

Here is a guide as to which colors need to be stippled where, through each version of the template.

TIP

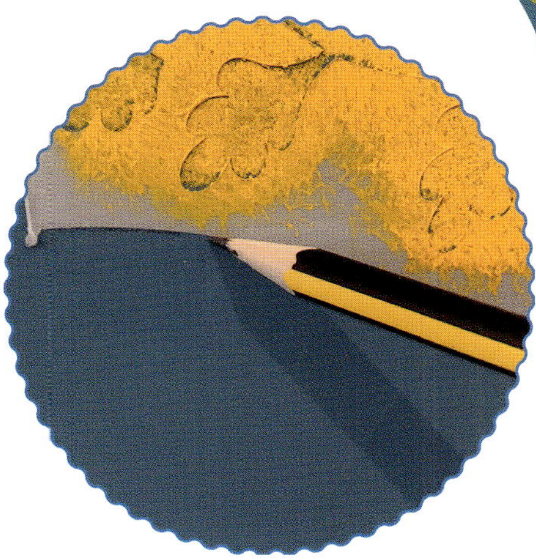

Additional guides for positioning can be made using a pencil to mark points on the curves.

STEP 6

PAINT THE OTHER COLORS

Next we're going to paint on the other colors with the no. 4 round brush. This will cover up the stenciled edges to really give that hand-painted, folk art look. It will also expand the area of each design so that they flow into each other more. A detailed painting plan for each design follows.

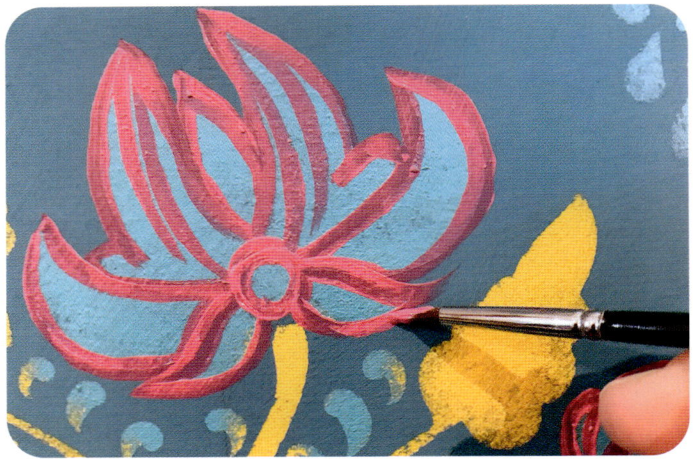

PAINTING PLANS

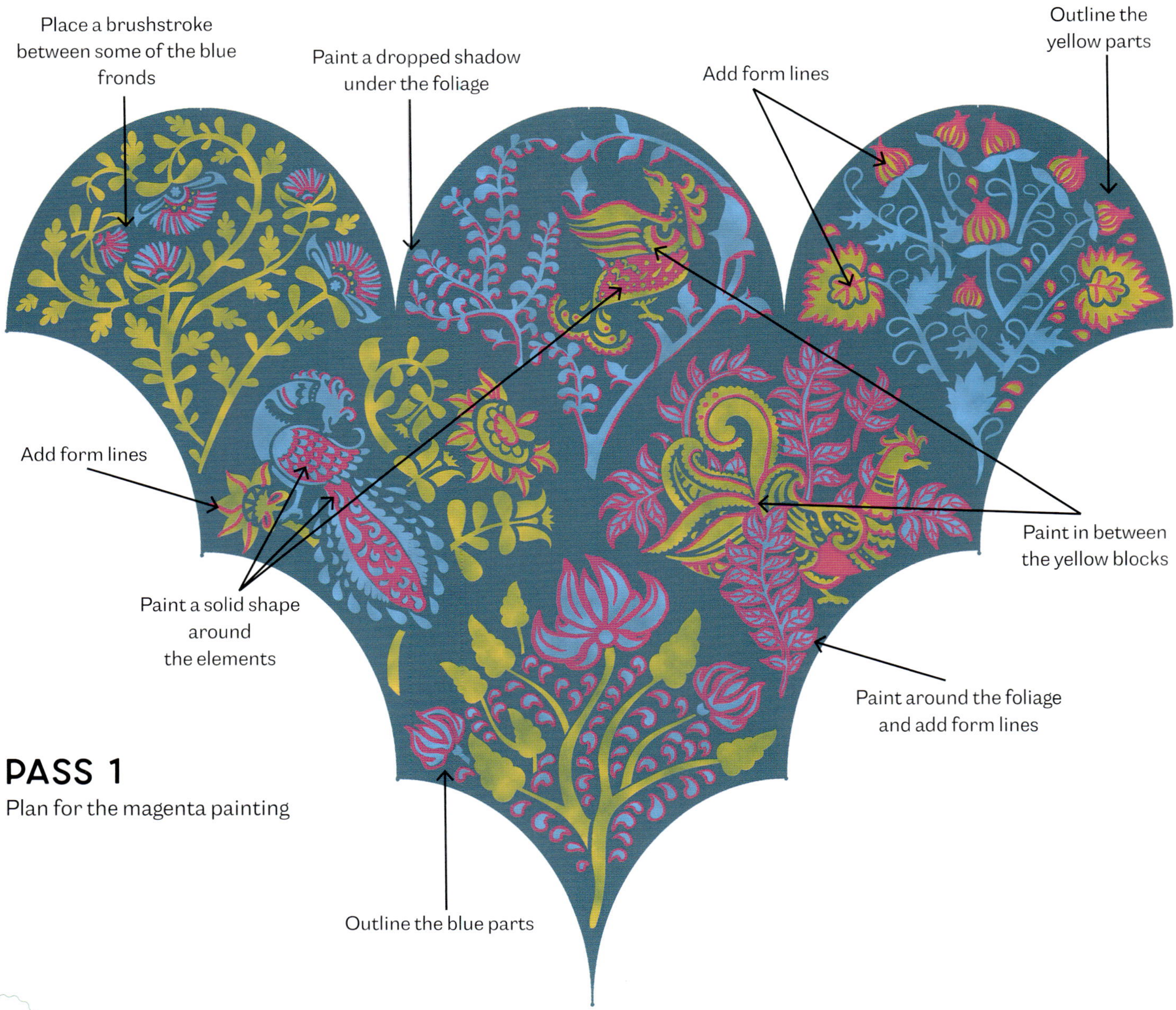

PASS 1

Plan for the magenta painting

PASS 2

Olive-green painting. This olive-green pass is important since it adds a tonal variation to both the yellow and the blue foliage. It also links parts of the stencil that had to have bridges to hold it together but broke up the design. Using the color to bridge and extend up over the edges of the stenciling helps achieve the hand-painted rather than a regular stenciled look.

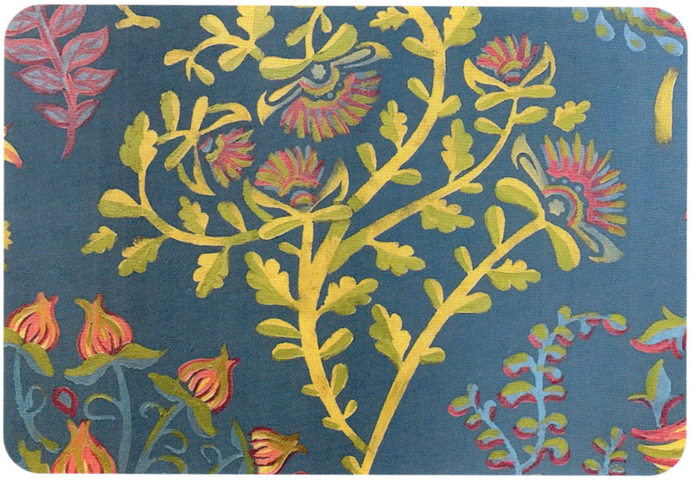

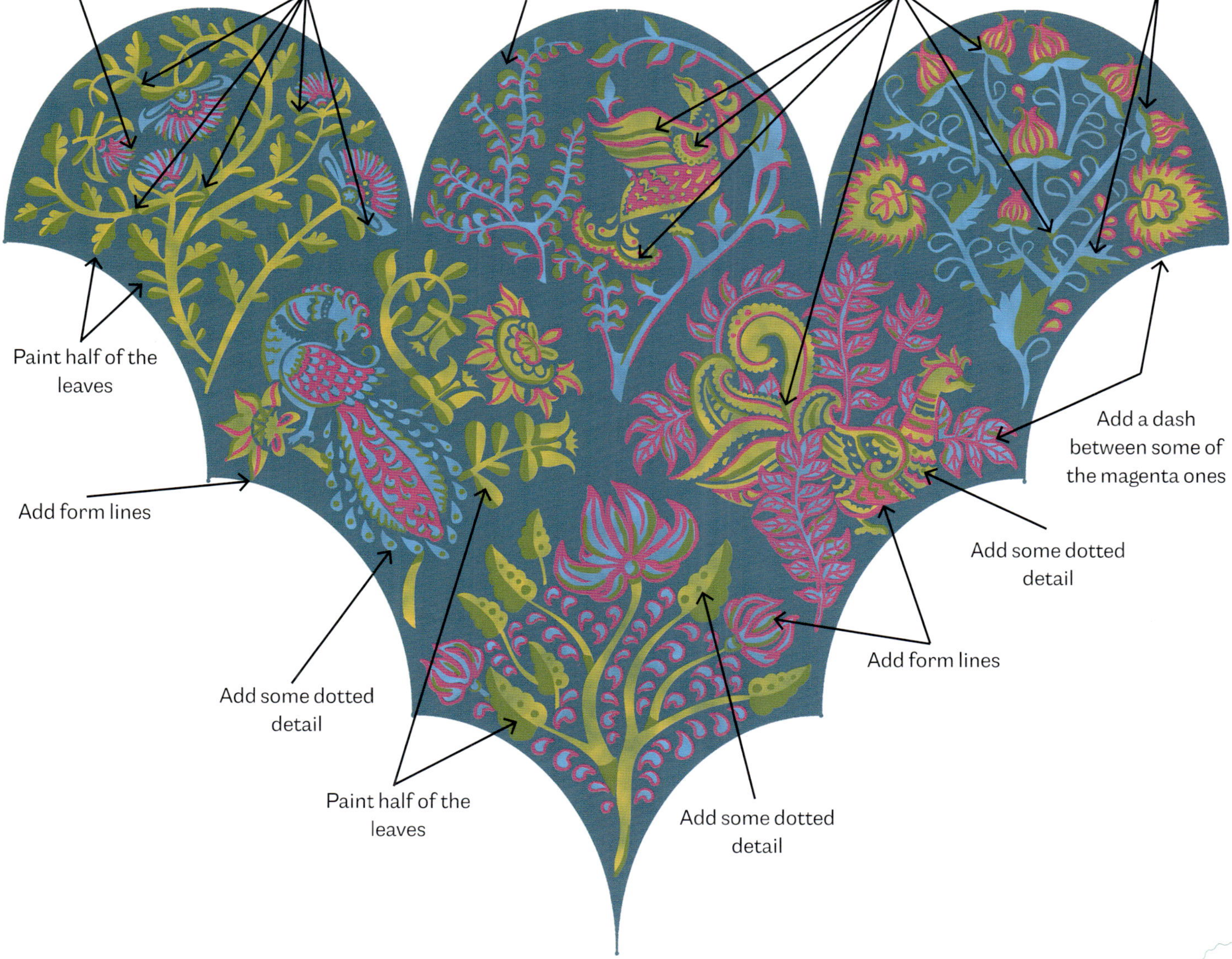

PASS 3

Cadmium red painting. The red paint contributes to the warm rich coloring in a similar way to the earlier magenta pass. Because they are so close in hue and saturation, having both colors gives a richness to the work, especially when seen from a distance.

The amount of each color used will diminish from the red pass. We're really just folding in richness at this stage with some light outline work, before balancing with some highlights next.

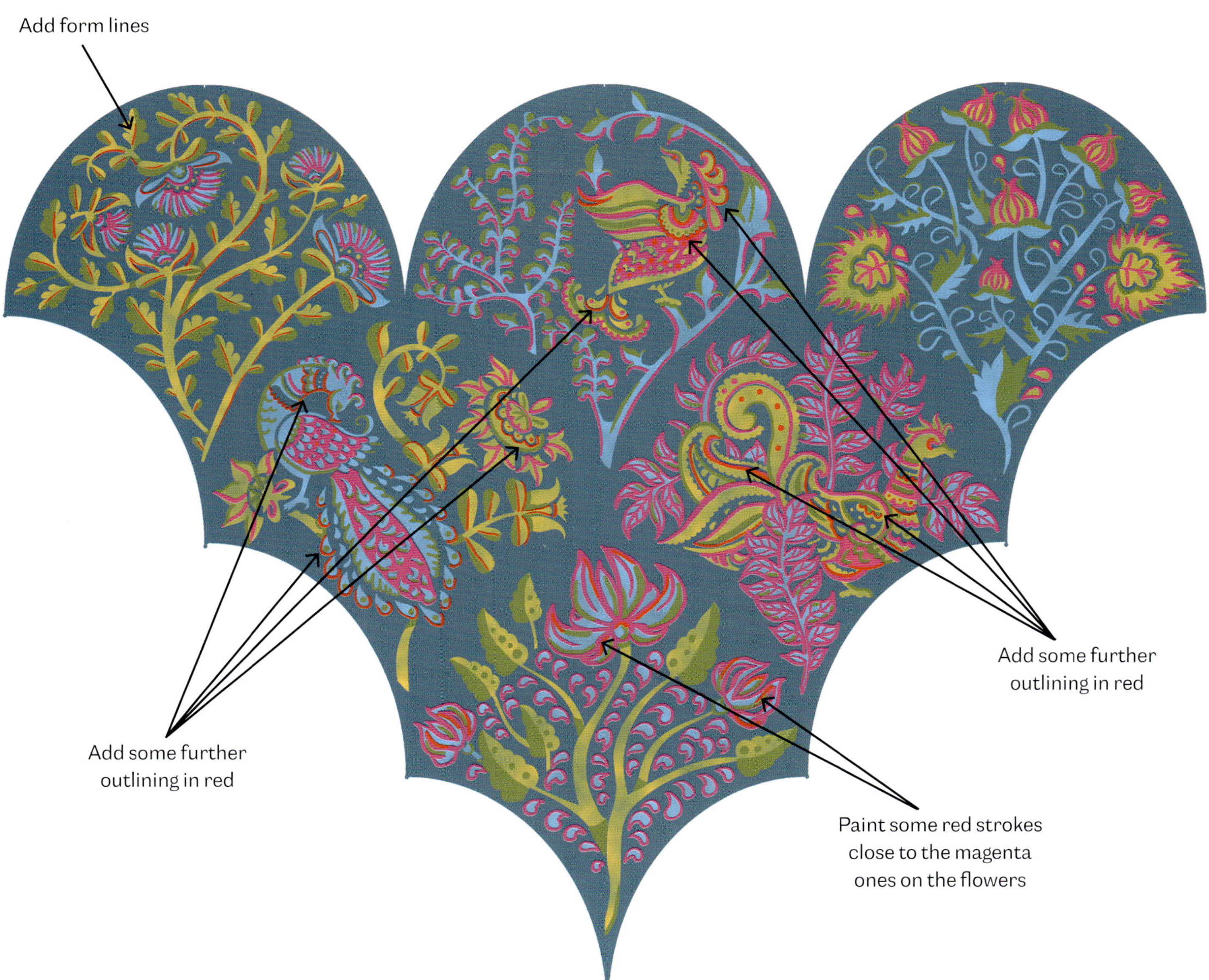

PASS 4

Lime-green highlights. In the same way that the magenta and red work together, the next stage is to add in a lime green that will pair with the cadmium yellow used in the stencil process.

These are the "twinkle in the eyes" of the design. Place some dots on top of the paintwork that have similar values to a color used in stenciling—thus tying the front and the back of the work together.

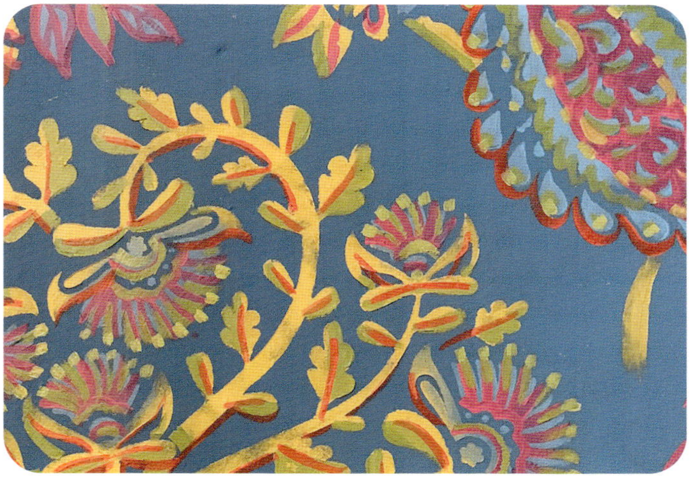

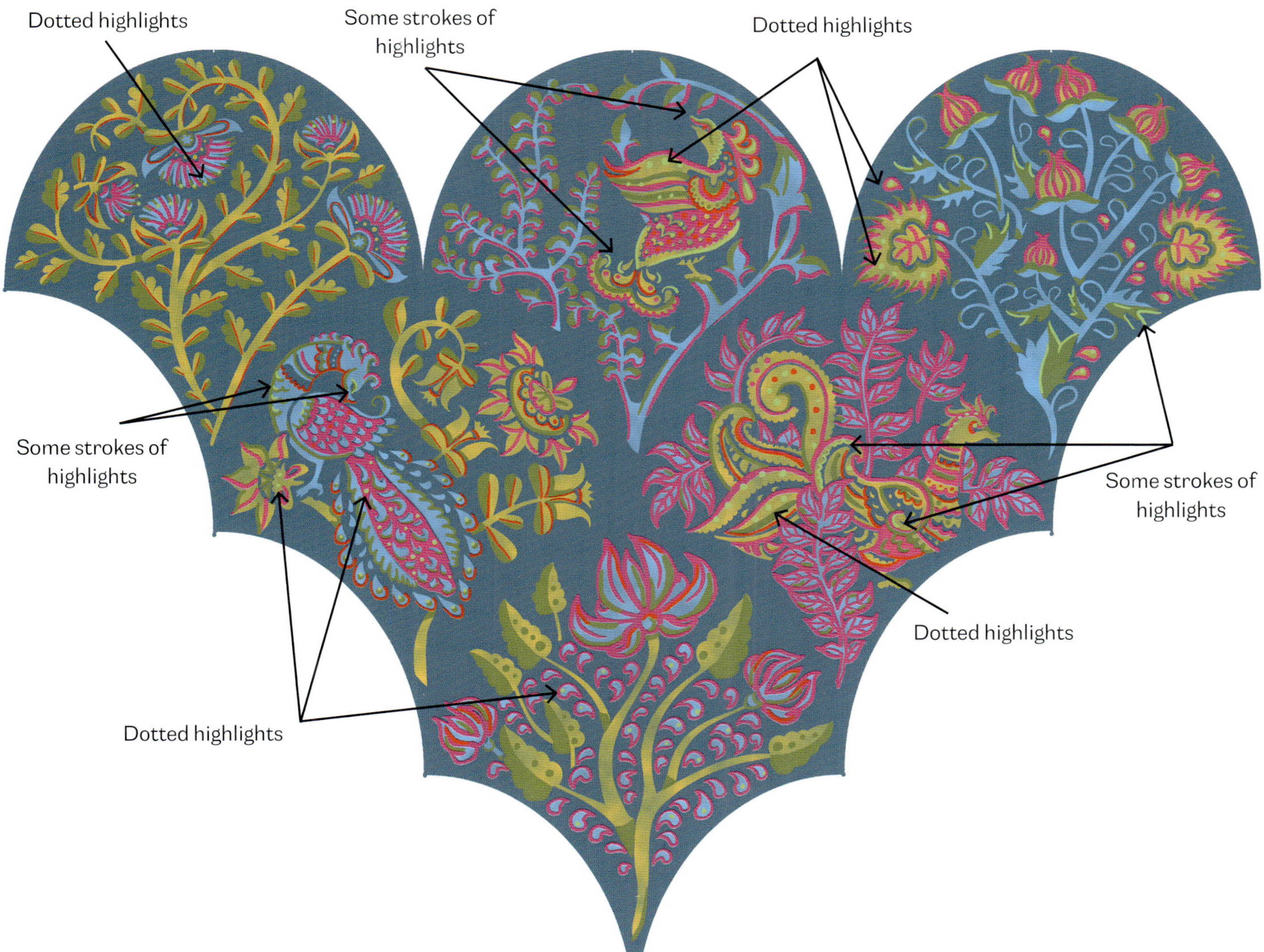

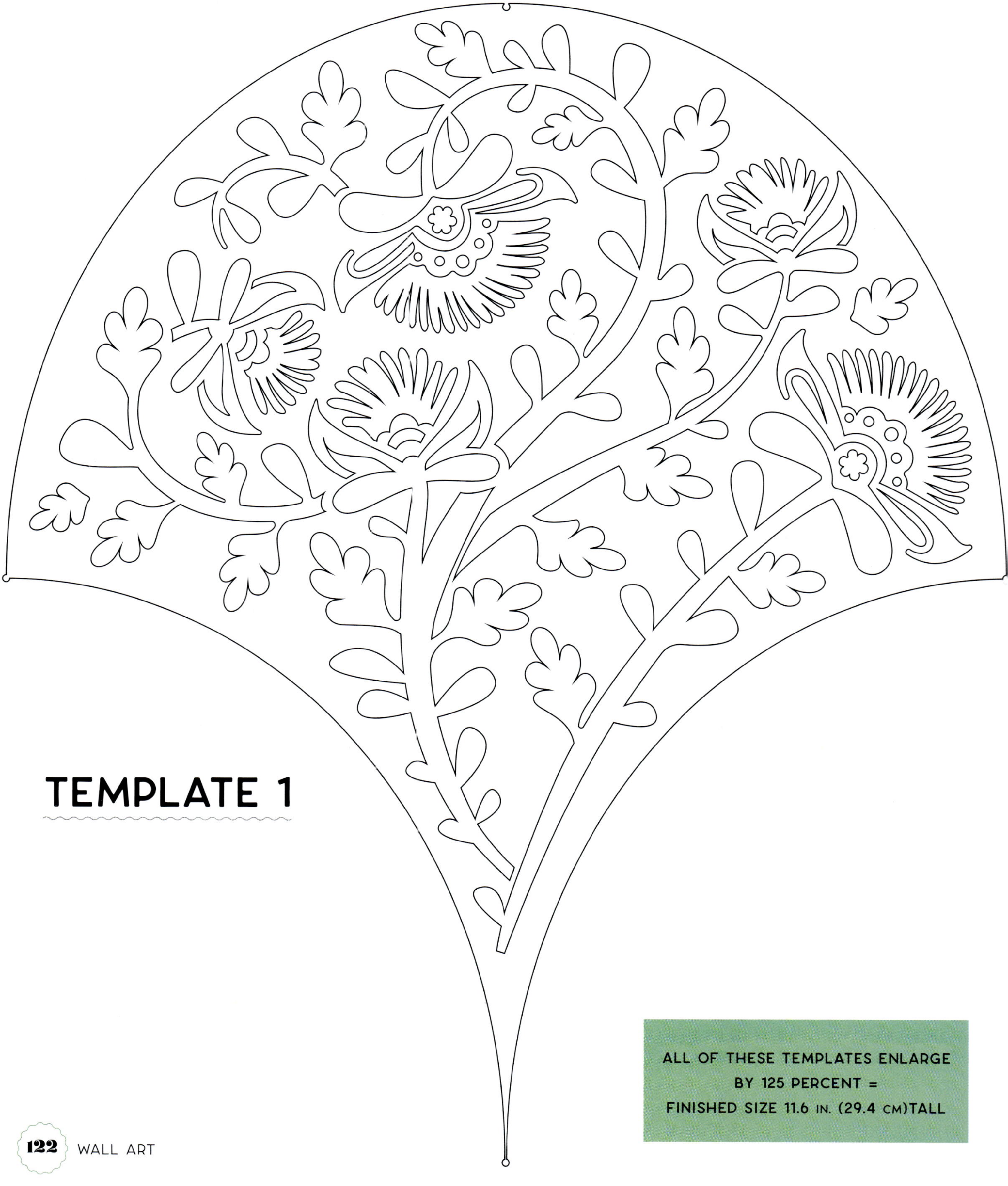

TEMPLATE 1

ALL OF THESE TEMPLATES ENLARGE BY 125 PERCENT = FINISHED SIZE 11.6 IN. (29.4 CM)TALL

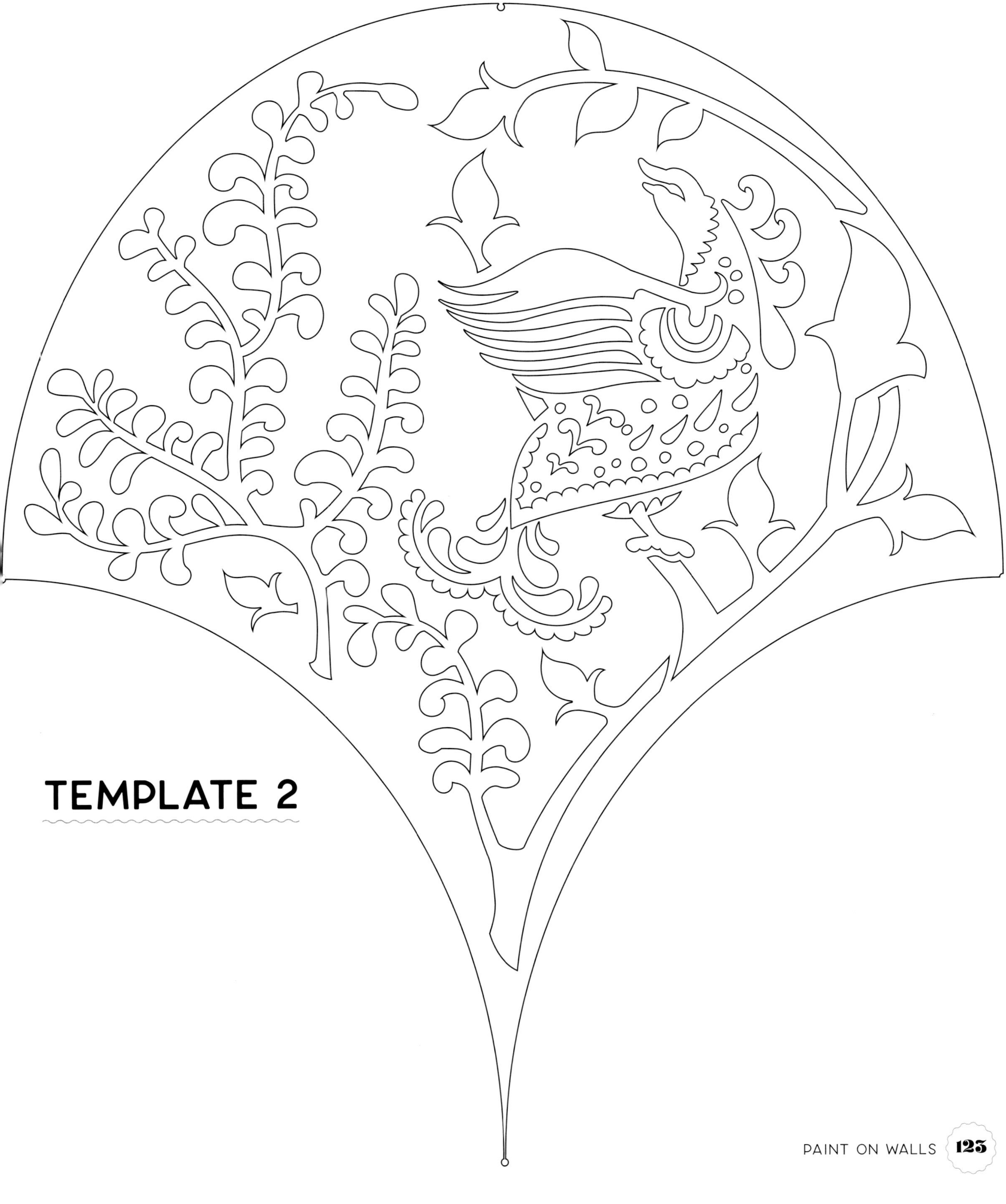

TEMPLATE 2

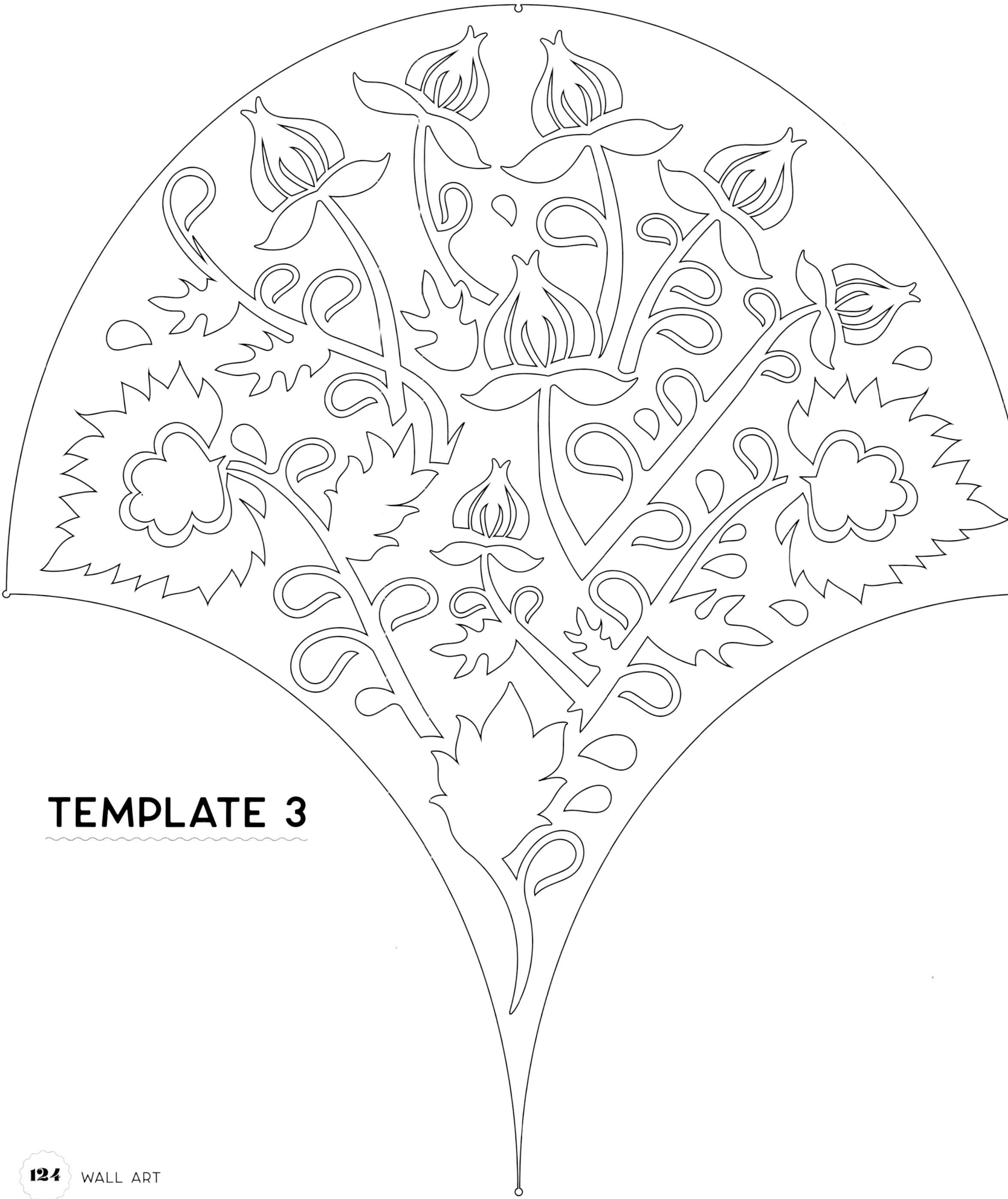

TEMPLATE 3

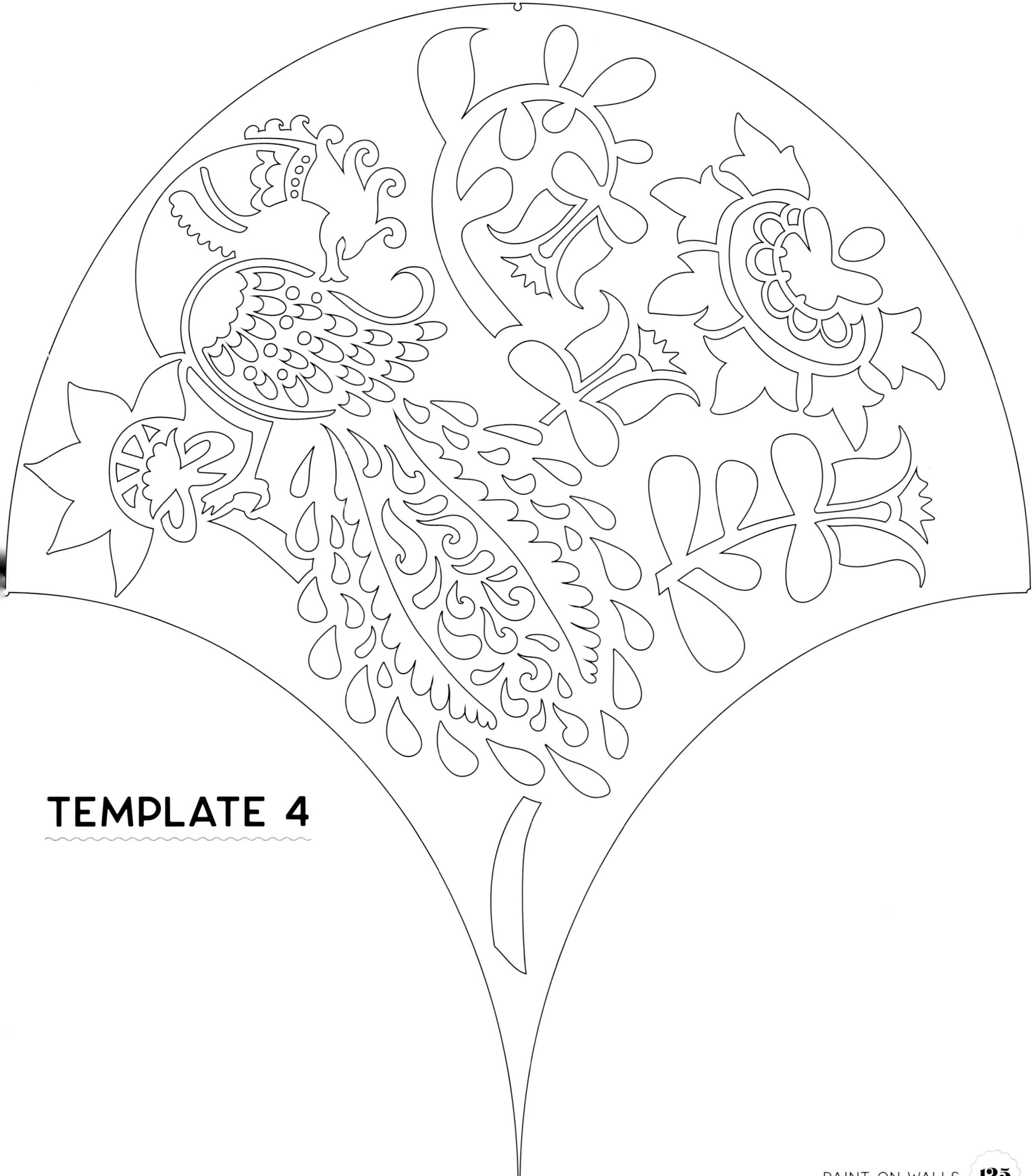

TEMPLATE 4

TEMPLATE 5

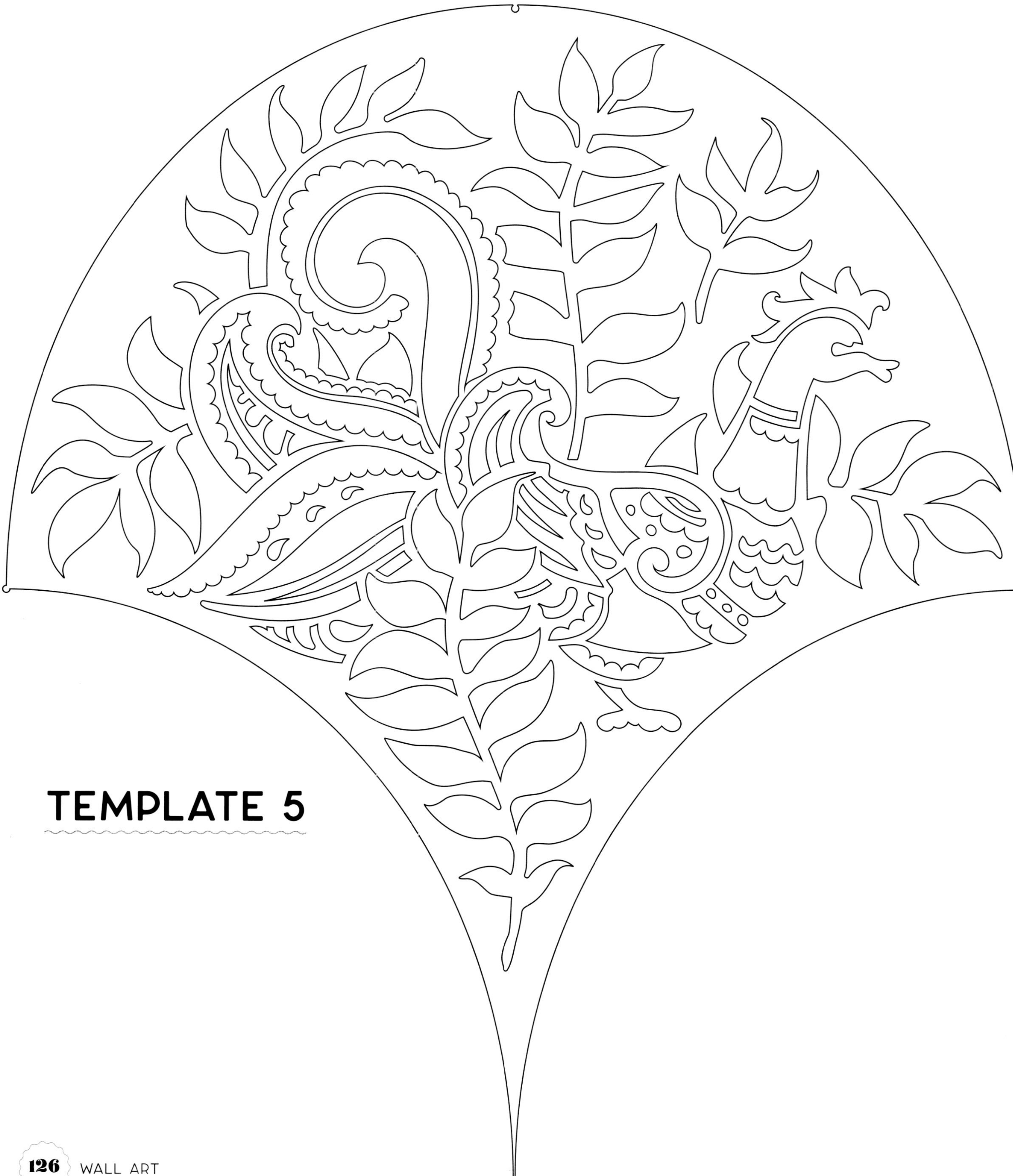

TEMPLATE 6

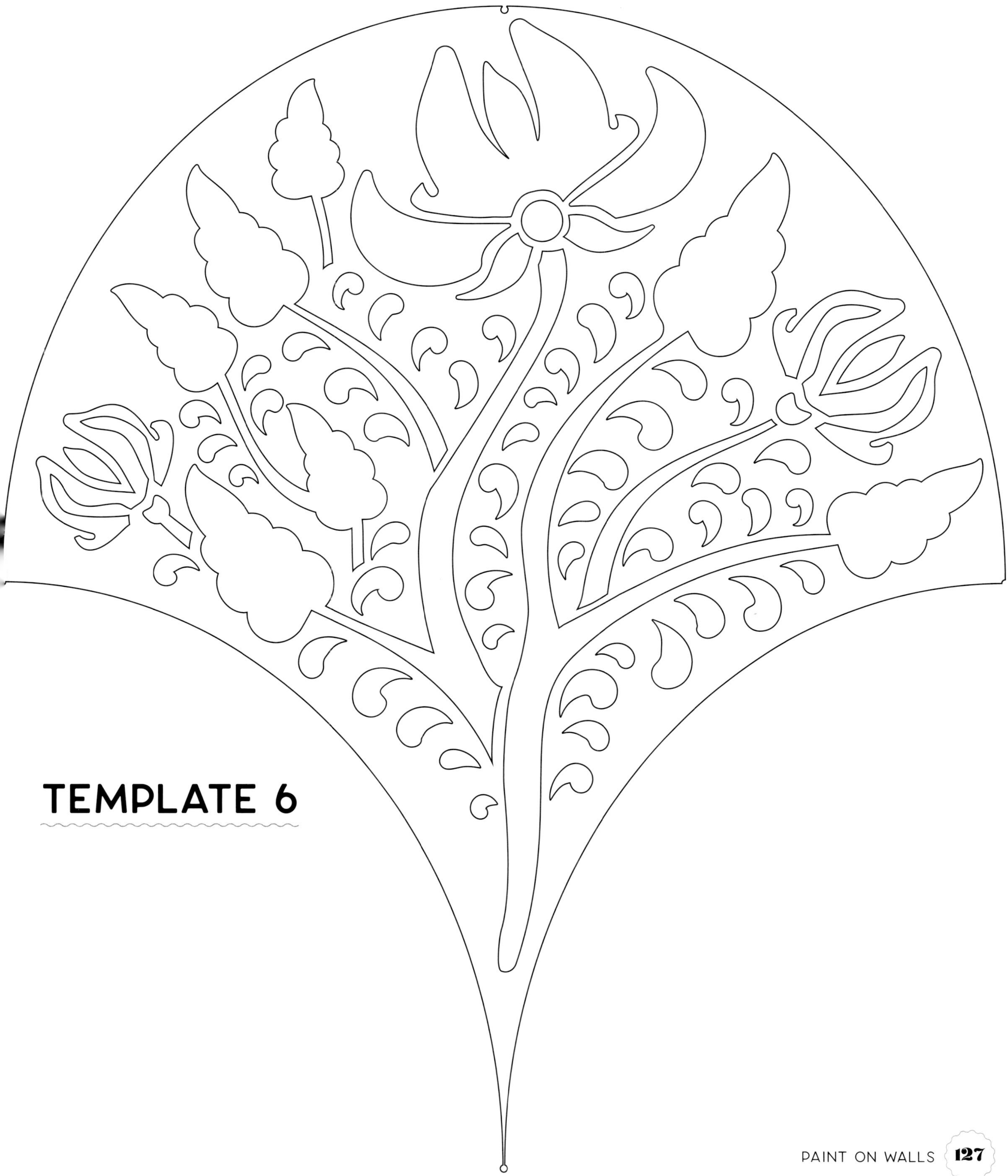

ACKNOWLEDGMENTS & CREDITS

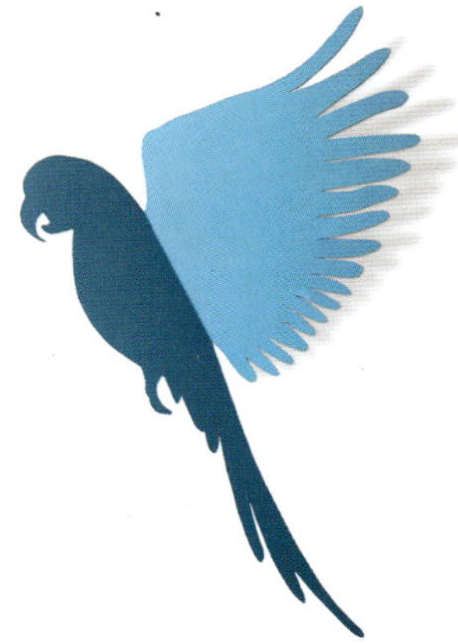

The authors would like to dedicate this book to our parents, who taught and inspired us both. For Clare—Mike, who made me believe I could build anything, and Pat, who let me play and draw endlessly. For Patricia—in memory of Sylvia, who always enjoyed drawing on the walls, and George, with his fearless DIY. Also to our amazing partners in crime, Kevin Beale and James Wall.

We would like to thank the following people; without them, this book would not have been possible, Jo Bryant at BlueRed Press, who has encouraged and let us make this wonderful book. To our Facebook friends who, when we asked questions about various types of paints, helped out, and to all those who lent their walls to us!

PICTURE CREDITS

The publishers would like to thank the following sources for their kind permission to reproduce the pictures in the book.

KEY: l = left, r = right, t= top, b=bottom, m=middle

ADOBE STOCK PHOTOS: 12b, 15, 21, 28, 77
ALEX MOCKUPS: 60, 86, 100
DESIGN CUTS: 6l, 10m, 19br, 23bm, 38, 44, 48bm, 51, 65br, 70, 84, 93, 95b, 96t, 96b, 114
FREEPIK: 9, 25bl, 81m
SHUTTERSTOCK: TFoxFoto 100

Every effort has been made to acknowledge the pictures correctly; apologies for any unintentional errors or omissions, which will be corrected in future editions of this book.

GO, HAVE FUN, AND CREATE!

SHOW US WHAT YOU HAVE DONE BY TAGGING US USING
#SCHIFFERPUBLISHING #WALLARTWITHPATSYANDCLARE

WE WOULD **LOVE** TO SEE WHAT YOU DO ON YOUR WALLS, AND IT'S GREAT TO **SHARE** WITH OTHER MAKERS

FOR OTHER BOOK IDEAS, FOLLOW SCHIFFER PUBLISHING ON **INSTAGRAM, TWITTER & FACEBOOK**